THE TANGIER ARCHIVE

THE GREAT WAR PHOTOGRAPHS OF CAPTAIN GIVORD

This edition first published by Uniform Press an imprint of
Unicorn Publishing Group

Unicorn Publishing Group
101 Wardour Street
London W1F 0UG

First edition, June 2014
by Casa de la Imagen, Logroño, Spain

www.unicornpress.org

A catalogue record for this book is available from
the British Library

ISBN 978-1-910500-156

Printed and bound in Spain

Acknowledgements:
Carlos Castuera, Elise Comarteau, Hervè Faure, Forum 14-18,
Andrés García de la Riva, Gorka Lejarcegui, Teo Martínez,
Javier Muro, Gala Pagniez, Ricardo Romanos, Bernardo Sánchez.

Every effort has been made to provide an accurate translation from the original slides and subsequent research. The publishers would be pleased to hear from anyone who identifies inaccuracies in the text.

THE TANGIER ARCHIVE

THE GREAT WAR PHOTOGRAPHS OF CAPTAIN GIVORD

EDITED BY CARLOS TRASPADERNE

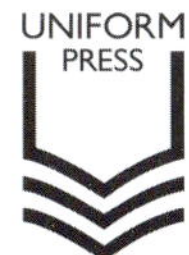

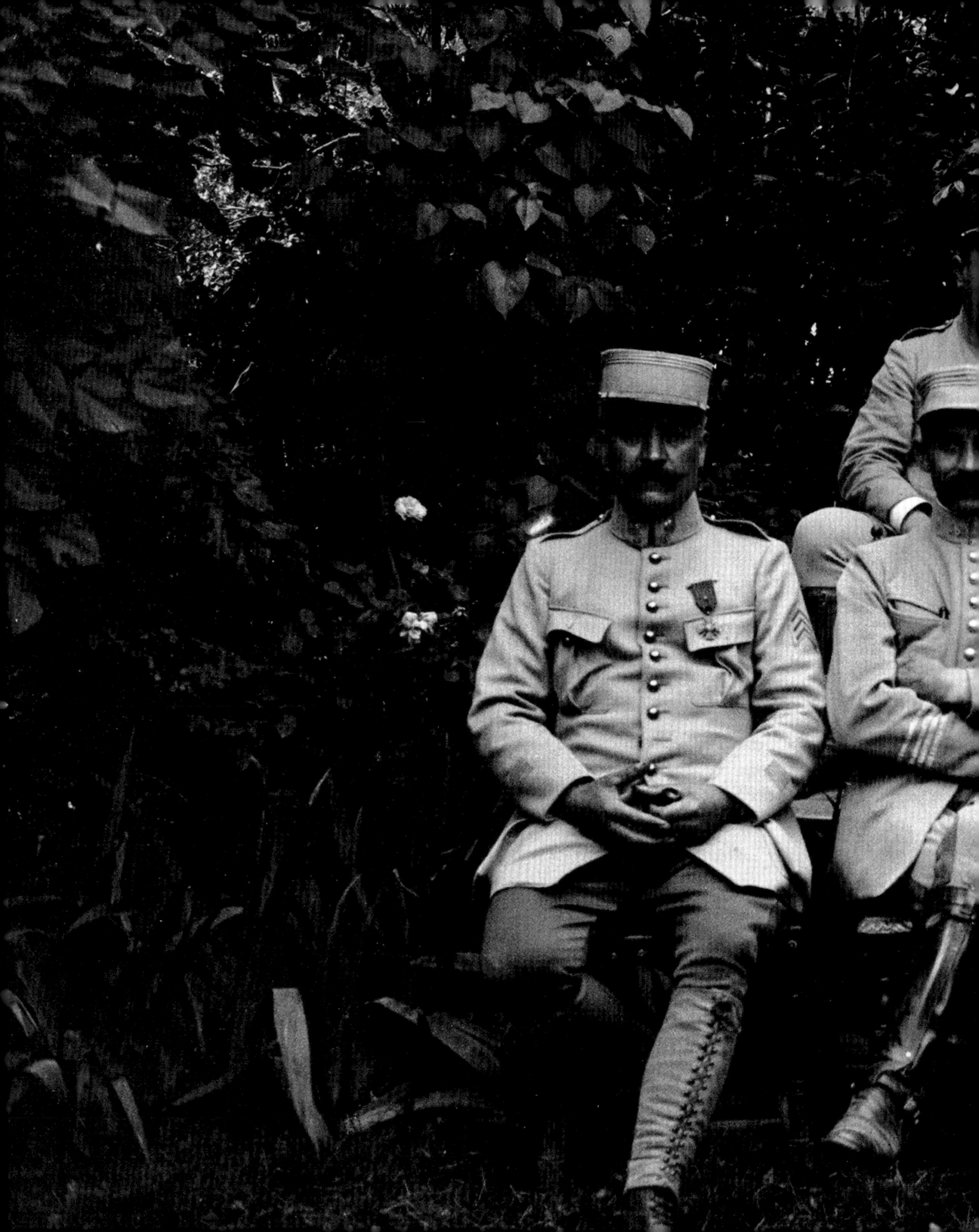

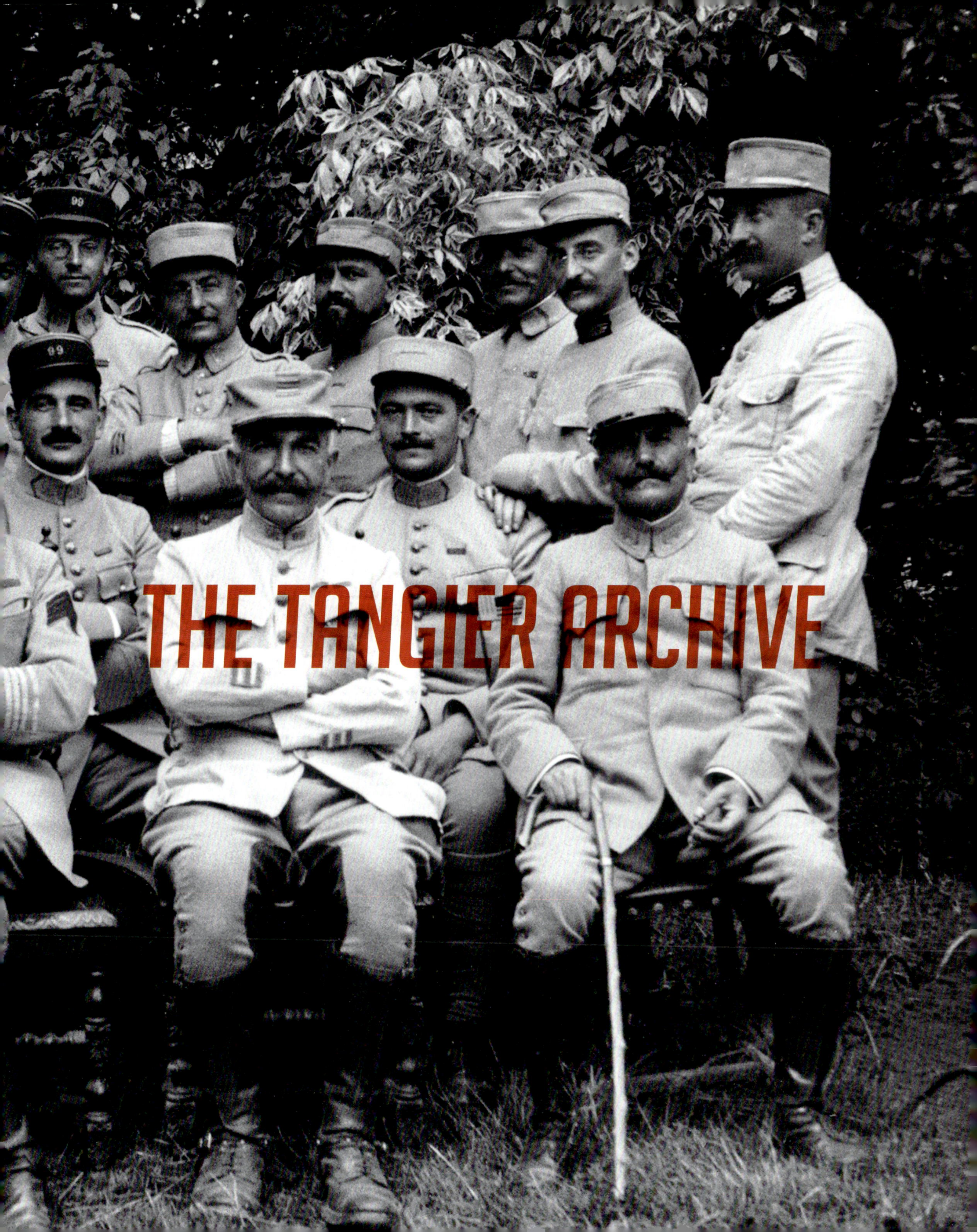
THE TANGIER ARCHIVE

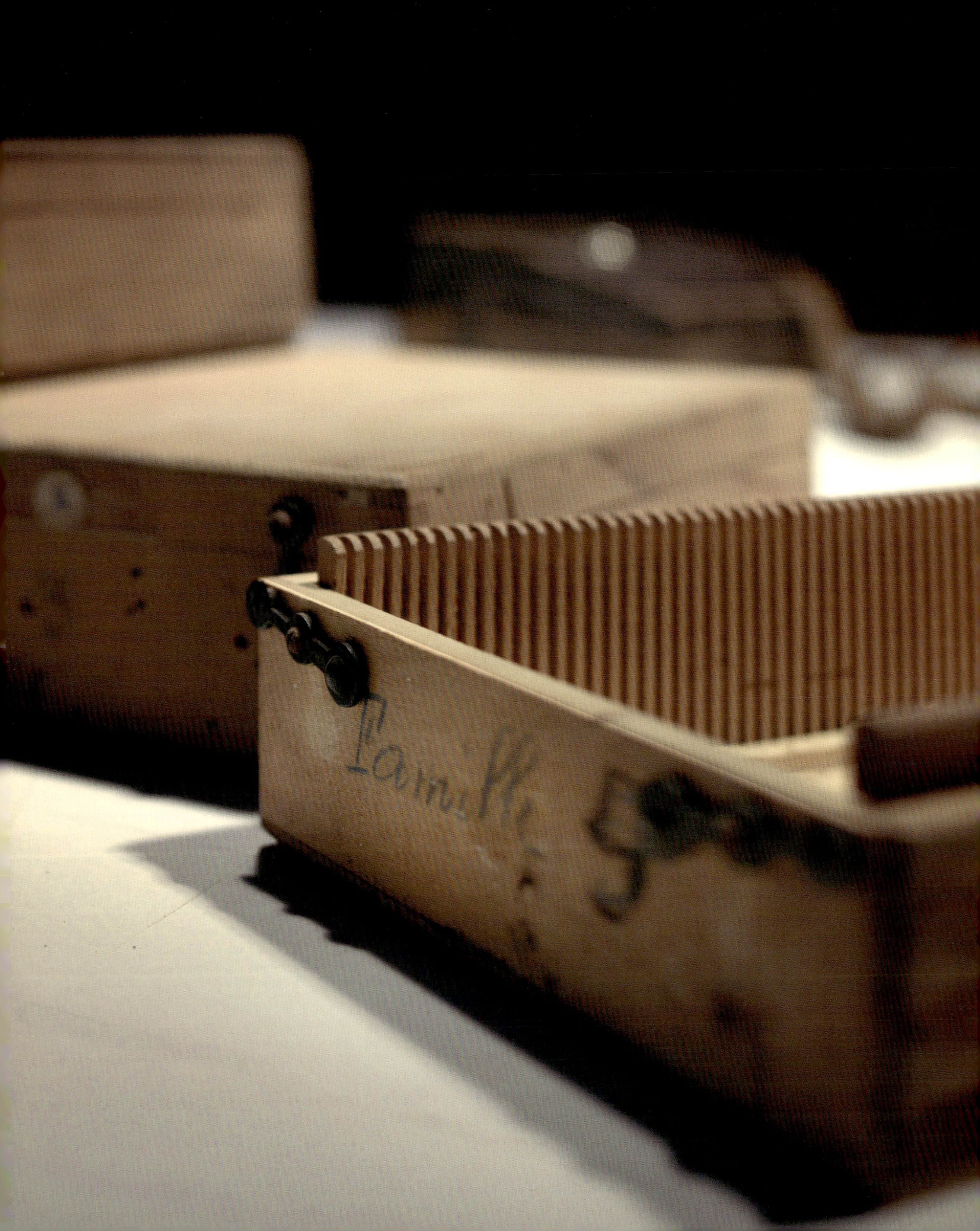

A CHANCE DISCOVERY / In 1999, Pablo San Juan, a Spanish photo-journalist then working on a story in Tangiers, (second only in the Western imagination to Casablanca as a place of mystery, intrigue and espionage,) made an extraordinary discovery. On a rare day off he was trawling the souk, as photographers often do, on the lookout for old photographs, cameras and other photo-related objects. One of the stallholders, curious about what he was seeking, beckoned him to follow, guiding him to the shop of an antiques dealer some distance from the market. There, he was shown a collection of ten small, wormholed, wooden boxes, each containing an assortment of glass-plate negatives. Gently extracting the plates one by one and examining them against the light, San Juan was astonished to discover each one imprinted with an adjacent pair of apparently identical negatives. Taken on a specially designed camera with a pair of side-by-side lenses, when printed and observed through a complimentary twin-lens viewer, the images (which are actually not identical but slightly offset), would coincide to give the impression of a stereoscopic – or in modern parlance: 3D – image.

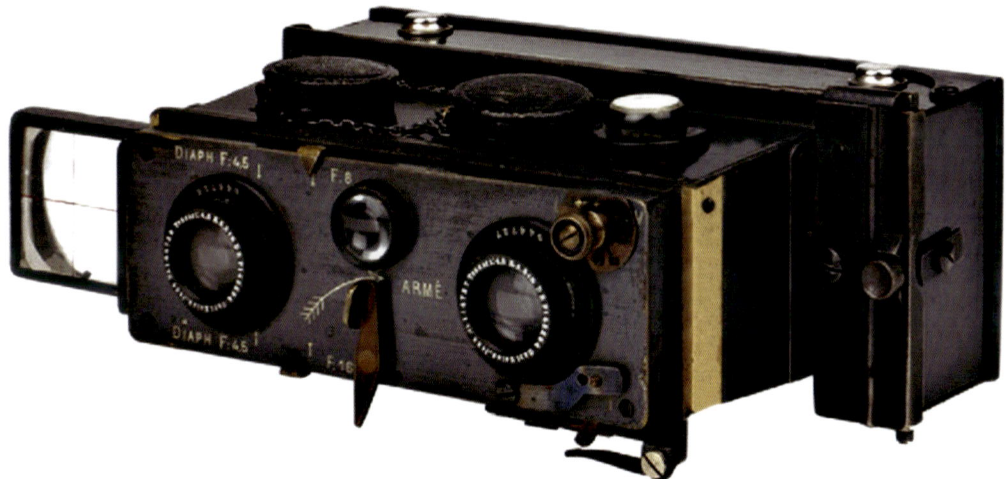

A RICHARD VERASCOPE STEREOSCOPIC CAMERA

What San Juan saw filled him with excitement. The first plate, randomly selected, revealed a primitive tank surrounded by soldiers, all wearing the famous *Adrian*[1] helmet. The next

1 The characteristic French metal helmet was introduced 21 May 1915. It takes its name from August-Louis Adrian, the Quartermaster General who adopted it. The Adrian continued in use until the end of the Second World War.

was an early biplane on an airfield. Others followed, all of military subjects, all clearly relating to the Great War. He asked the antiques dealer if the photographer was known, or if there were any clues to his identity. *Inconnu*, (unknown) came the reply.

Realising that the negatives would need skilled conservation work, San Juan decided to contact his colleague Jesús Rocandio, director of the Casa de la Imagen (House of the Image) in Logroño, Spain, and an expert in early photography. Rocandio gave an unhesitating response to the account of the discovery: the collection was unquestionably of historical importance; the negatives had to be saved. After brief negotiations with the antiques dealer, San Juan returned to Spain with the archive; but before arriving at Logroño he was overcome by a strange, unidentified toxin. Suffering from dizziness and a fever, he was bed-ridden for several days.

Finally arriving at the Casa de la Imagen, the plates were identified as the culprit. Both skin and respiratory tract had become irritated on coming into contact with the negatives. The unknown conditions in which they were kept had caused the organic elements in the coating of the plates and in their housing – that is, the chemicals and the wood, to produce a perfect habitat for parasites. As a result the archive had created its own little war zone.

ASSESSING THE TANGIERS ARCHIVE / Once decontaminated and made safe, the archivists at Logroño set about assessing and cataloguing the collection. The negatives were contained in ten unvarnished wooden boxes, each eighteen centimetres in length, twelve centimetres in breadth and five centimetres deep, with lids secured by metal clasps. Vertical wooden slats, interposed between the fifty plates slotted into each box, prevented them from coming into damaging contact with one another. Each box was also provided with a card, printed with numbered spaces for recording in briefest detail, date, location and subject matter directly opposite the corresponding negative. The reverse of the cards was imprinted with the legend, *Classeur Vèrascopique* (Verascope filing system). The camera used by the unknown photographer was a Verascope, manufactured by the French firm of Jules Richard.

This rudimentary but efficient means of classification was disregarded by the photographer, who left the numbered cards blank. Instead, he created his own system. Using small stickers, he numbered the boxes from zero to nine, and divided the archive into three main sections by subject: from box zero to four they were identified as GE; numbers five and six as *Montagne*;

and seven to nine as *Famille*. These generic labellings were written in pencil on the fronts of the boxes, giving easy access to each section, though not to each individual negative. Thus the indications are that our unknown photographer was an amateur; a professional would surely have numbered each negative separately for ease of subsequent access. The meanings of *Montagne* (Mountain) and *Famille* (Family) are clear, but the significance of the initials GE is more obscure but likely to represent *La Guerre Européenne*. As we shall see, these first five boxes, the GE boxes, contain the section of the archive relating to the Great War.

The full extent of the archive amounted to 478 negative stereoscopic pairs. Of this total, 254 plates covered the span of the war from about its midpoint through to its conclusion on 11 November 1918, whilst the lesser collection of 224 plates covered a period of seventeen years post-war. Could it have been that the 1916 photographs, commencing with box zero, were the first that our unknown photographer took? Perhaps so, though it is equally possible that he employed a conventional, not stereoscopic camera earlier on, and restarted at zero when he acquired his Verascope. If so, his earlier negatives are yet to be discovered. The case for this explanation is made by the work itself – it is far from appearing to be that of a novice. Ultimately, though, the reasons why the archive does not cover the events of the first part of the war are a matter for speculation; yet one might well be tempted to suppose that it was his experiences at the front and the sights that he encountered, that compelled him to take up photography, determined to reflect the war as he experienced it, in its many varied and dreadful aspects.

To some degree this is reflected in the idiosyncratic method of identification he adopted for his negatives. The format of the plates is 45x107mm, composed of a pair of 40x45 mm images separated by a strip of clear glass. Our photographer inscribed his data in ink on this strip. All the plates are dated and the location usually but not always given; but in addition he often records his impressions, which range from the descriptive to the ironic, and the monosyllabic to the exhaustive. The chemical fading of the ink used for these annotations made palaeographic work of interpreting them, and further difficulties were created by the author's fondness for using acronyms. Nevertheless, with time, patience and digital techniques they were transcribed, providing significant documentation of what would otherwise have been a collection of unidentifiable if dramatic images, and locating them in a historical context which makes sense of them.

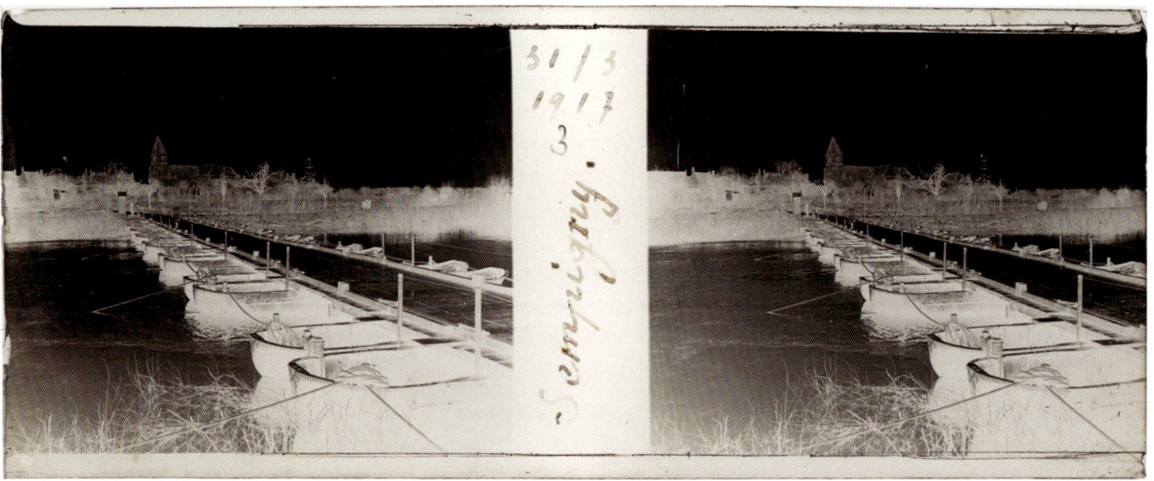

Once digitised, the negatives were reversed to produce positives, blown up to screen size, and examined for detail. Now, a thumbnail sketch of the anonymous photographer and his activities began to emerge. The overwhelming proportion of the images related to the French view of the war along the Western Front, a line of trenches that meandered through Northern France and Belgium, from the Vosges Mountains to the English Channel. Our man travels throughout the French regions that suffered most heavily in the conflict: Aisne, Marne, Oise, Somme and the Pas-de-Calais, alternating between the sites of the battles that took place during the time spanned by his photographs: Verdun and the Somme in 1916; Chemin des Dames in 1917; the German offensives and Allied counter offensives of 1918. Though his military function is undefined, he is clearly of the officer class, yet seen to be equally at ease in the company of his brother officers and other ranks.

The archive's subject matter covers almost every facet of the war on the Western Front. Hardly a detail escapes its scan of the trenches, tanks, artillery and aircraft; the marches and parades, the devastation and the dead. All are played out under the photographer's ubiquitous gaze. Each nationality that served on the Western Front is represented, from the kilted Scots digging trenches, and the despondent German prisoners burying the battlefield's dead, to the Annamite workers from the Indochinese colonies – forced labour behind the lines. But it is the British and French troops, being in the majority, that are naturally those most frequently depicted. The photographer records whatever he deems interesting or curious – a railway sleeper blown onto the roof of a house; the enemy's observation posts; the wreck of an aircraft; officers at leisure on a beach. Nothing is staged, but he takes every advantage of situations as they present themselves. By comparison, the official photography of the Great War was largely sanitised by the censors. In *The Camera Man, His Adventures in Many Fields,*[2] the author reports: *A large proportion of the pictures made in the European War are not intended for public exhibition. A rigid censorship is exercised over all photographic work by the governments.* Official and accredited news agency photographers equally, were burdened by relatively cumbersome cameras not designed for ease of use in a war zone – Collins goes on to cite the Graflex, a hand-held plate camera – and the Auto Graflex, a single-lens reflex, both, for preference, using heavy 5x4-inch glass-plate negatives, a significant factor, as smaller format cameras by then available could not produce negatives with sufficiently high definition to allow for blowing up to newspaper dimensions. In his autobiography Paul Martin, a pioneer of live action photography, provides confirmation: *The idea of taking a [small] square from a negative and enlarging it to 24 by 20 was unkown then.*[3] Here our man, not shooting his pictures for press publication, is at a distinct advantage. His Verascope is not much larger than a modern SLR, and it is fast in operation. Combined with his instinct for composition and his keen eye for detail it produces exceptional results.

A further characteristic that emerges across the span of the archive, besides the photographer's technical command of his medium, is the aesthetic qualities of his work. He has a rare visual acuity and an instinctive grasp of what the greatest of the photojournalists would later call, 'The Decisive Moment'.

On 19 May 1917 an agency photographer takes a picture of a shell-battered church in the town of Ribécourt (see page 14). It provides an adequate but mundane record, one of many such shots of buildings that are amongst the war's victims. But the photograph is opportune – perhaps being a church it is considered symbolic – and it is widely circulated in the newspapers.

---

2 Francis A. Collins, The Camera Man, The Century Co., New York, 1916
3 Paul Martin, Victorian Snapshots, Country Life, London, 1939

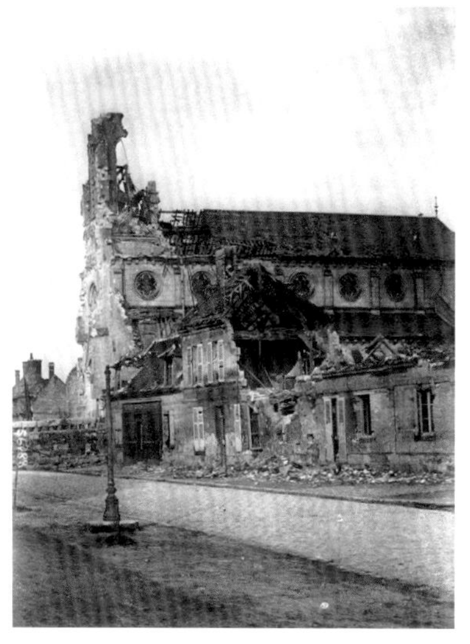

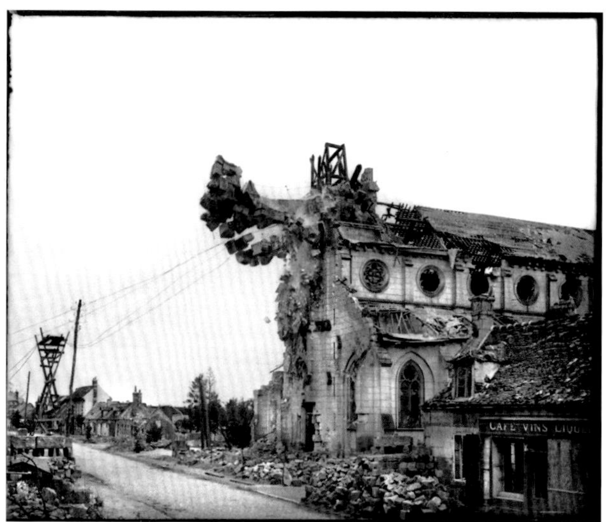

Our own photographer is in Ribécourt the same day and makes an exposure which at first sight looks as if it might be of the next Boche shell hitting the church. But a close examination of his photograph, [**ABOVE RIGHT, PHOT. 109**] tells a very different story. His selected viewpoint is carefully chosen. It is more elevated than the press photographer's was; he is perhaps on the back of an army wagon or at a first floor window; and it is further to the left and closer to the church, revealing that the stone wall at the front of the church has been demolished at some point between the taking of the two photographs. Some of the rubble is still lying where it has fallen, but a good deal of it – reusable for barricades – is now stacked outside the single-storey building immediately adjacent to the church. The camera position now reveals further detail. The shutters, closed in the press photo, have been pulled back, and we can see the sign above the frontage: it is a cafe and bar. In its present condition the church is clearly going to be a danger to local inhabitants. The explanation for the demolition of the bell tower is not that it has been hit again by the Boche, but that the French commander himself has called down the bombardment to demolish the hazard, and to eliminate a possible reference point for enemy artillery. Our photographer, prewarned, has time to establish his point of view and set up his apparatus in readiness. The result is an extraordinary split-second image in which one can all but feel the shock of the shell burst and the collapse of the edifice. It speaks to our photographer's skill, that he is at once able to create a stereoscopic photograph that will make full use of the three-dimensional dynamics of the medium, characterised by successive planes of visual interest advancing towards the camera's point of view, but that will also survive the transition to a single impactful image on the page of a book – something he achieves with consistency throughout the archive.

THE THIRD DIMENSION/ On 1 June 1838, the eminent scientist Sir Charles Wheatstone, presented a paper to the Royal Society on his new invention: the stereoscope, a device demonstrating his explanation of binocular vision, a phenomenon which had been under investigation for centuries. (Leonardo da Vinci grappled unsuccessfully with the problem in the early sixteenth century). Wheatstone's device employed a pair of mirrors, angled at 45 degrees to each of two drawings of the same subject, reflecting them back towards the eyes of the observer. The drawings were of the same subject, but crucially, varied to the extent that would be the case if seen separately by each one of a pair of human eyes. What appeared to the viewer using both eyes at once, produced an illusion of a three dimensional object.

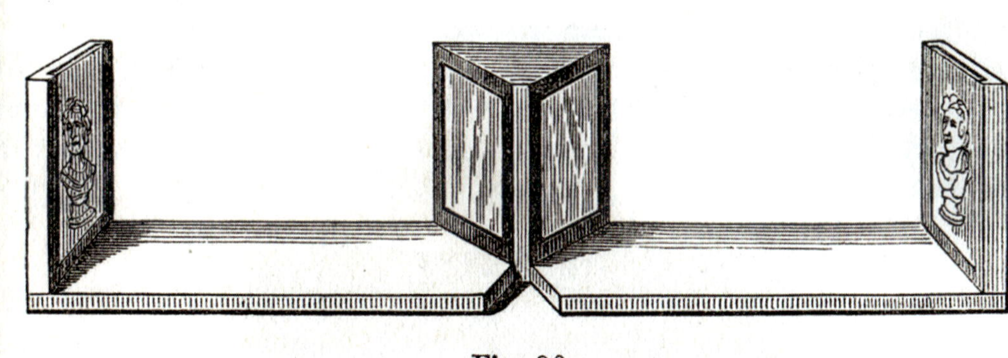

Robert Hunt, *A Manual of Photography*, 2nd edn., 1857

Wheatstone's invention had no practical application at the time, for it was not until seven months later, in January 1839, that L.J.M. Daguerre in France, and William Henry Fox Talbot in England, announced the invention of their separate and unrelated systems of photography. Wheatstone and Talbot corresponded briefly on possible improvements to the stereoscope, but both their inventions were as yet at too primitive a stage of development to consider any possibility of reciprocity between them. The breakthrough came in 1849 with the design by Sir David Brewster (already famous for his invention of another optical device – the kaleidoscope) for a lenticular stereoscope, that is, one incorporating a pair of lenses to focus the viewer's eyes on the images in such a way as to make them appear to be superimposed upon one another. This dictated that, to obtain the best result, the images in future be of a fixed format, whereby the central focus (or, interocular separation) would be equal to the average distance between the centre points of a pair of human eyes – about 65mm. This in turn dictated the overall width of each image at 60 to 65mm, with the height, controlled by that of the casing, at about 75mm. These dimensions would become an industry standard.

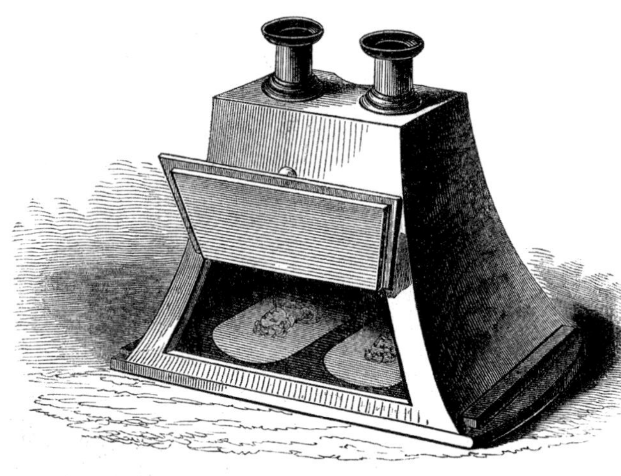

Fig. 97.

Robert Hunt, *A Manual of Photography*, 2nd edn., 1857

Brewster showed his first model stereoscope at a meeting of the British Association for the Advancement of Science in 1849, when he proposed the use of pairs of photographs in place, as hitherto, of pairs of drawings. Unable to raise much enthusiasm from his fellow scientists, (photography then still being an extremely esoteric pastime with very few dedicatees,) Brewster decamped to France with his invention, where it was taken up by a manufacturing optician, Jules Dubosq, who saw in it the vision of a great commercial future. In 1851, examples of Dubosq's stereoscopes, complete with stereoscopic daguerreotypes (the daguerreotype being the French form of photography) were exhibited at the Great Exhibition, where they were much admired by Queen Victoria, and Dubosq capped his triumph by presenting her with a unique, elaborate model of his work. The royal imprimatur proved to be a watershed in the history of stereoscopic photography; Dubosq was thenceforth inundated with orders for the lenticular stereoscope, often elaborately decorated, without which no lady's drawing-room might any longer be considered complete.

At the time of the Great Exhibition there was as yet no binocular camera to match the stereoscope. Stereoscopic pairs were initially created by taking successive exposures on a single-lens camera mounted on a grooved base, which allowed it to be slid left or right across the necessary span of 65mm. This naturally made portraiture close to impossible, as the subject would be hard pressed to remain absolutely rigid for as long as it took to reposition the camera and reload it with a fresh slide to make the second exposure. The favourite subjects for the stereographer would be the obvious ones: still-life, topography and architecture. It was not until 1856 that Benjamin Dancer, a maker of scientific instruments, produced a binocular camera; other manufacturers followed suit. By 1858 the London Stereoscopic Company, one of the first and most enterprising in the field, was advertising a stock of over 100,000 photographs from across the world. [4]

Regardless of its exceptional beauty, the nature of the daguerreotype condemned it to a limited lifespan: it consisted of a photo-sensitive emulsion coated onto a polished copper plate. Each one was thus unique – unlike Talbot's negative/positive system, which allowed for the printing of multiple copies. The daguerreotype was, in addition, expensive to produce, and in practical terms of limited size. The stereoscopic daguerreotype proved to be that wondrous invention's final burst of glory. The future lay in printing on paper (which was then mounted on card for rigidity) from the negative. The cost of stereos – both the stereoscopic viewers and the cards – became more affordable and they would quickly become a standard form of family entertainment in all but the poorest homes, and it might be said, those with exacting Victorian moral standards. Human nature being what it is, it was not long before some photographers saw commerce in expanding the range of stereographic subject matter. In its issue of 28 November 1858, *The Photographic News*, under the title: 'Questionable subjects for Photography', complained that,

4 The London Stereoscopic Company continued in business until 1922. After the First World War there was a steep decline in interest in stereo cards, which were increasingly replaced by twentieth century forms of entertainment.

In a recent number of this journal we noticed a stereoscopic slide under the attractive title of the 'Skeletons Carouse', which was not only revolting as far as the desecration of human skeletons goes, but was positively disgusting as beheld in the stereoscope, which of course added much more to the ghastly effects of the whole picture. Worse was to follow. The editors of the journal had also come across, positively improper pictures.

Such impropriety aside, the phenomenon produced by the stereoscope is in fact illusory. In normal human vision the brain interprets the world from the point of view of the observer as receding on a continuous scale into the distance. The stereoscopic photograph employs the reverse effect. So far as possible the photographer will create points of focus in separate planes in depths in the image he is composing. The brain, from its own point of view, not recognising these as receding (as they are indeed not doing so, since on the viewing screen of the stereoscope they are all at the same distance from the eyes) will have no means of interpreting what is presented to it as a view in depth. Since the camera lens is literal, it will have created an image in which the separate planes, as they approach the lens, will appear progressively larger. Thus, contrary to common experience, where the image appears to gradually merge into the distance, it will appear to be looming at an alarming rate towards the viewer, producing the stereo's characteristically dramatic effect. A large part of our unknown photographer's genius lay in the skill with which he manipulated this phenomenon.

PHOTOGRAPHY FOR THE PEOPLE/ For almost half a century after its invention in 1839, photography was a consumer product, except for the wealthy few, or the professional. Employing equipment well beyond the purse of ordinary wage earners, it required a knowledge of chemistry, optics and other esoterica. In particular, plates had to be sensitised by self-prepared chemical solutions immediately prior to exposure, and developed after exposure, on site, before the emulsion dried out. The 1880s saw the beginnings of a revolution: the packaging of factory-made dry plates, which when exposed could be returned to the maker (or often, the local chemist's shop) for developing and printing. 1888 saw a further dramatic turn of events: the introduction of the first Kodak camera, which came ready loaded – in place of glass plates – with a one-hundred exposure roll of film. It placed photography into the hands of everyone. Almost overnight, the era of the amateur photographer had arrived, and with it a huge boost for stereoscopy. The 1895

British Journal of Photography Almanac incorporates an extraordinary 880 pages of advertising, amongst which are included sixteen stereoscopic cameras made by a variety of manufacturers. Several others were yet to follow in succeeding years, though Jules Richard's Verascope, which was for sale in France in 1893, was apparently not yet available in Britain. It was first reviewed in the *British Journal Almanac* of 1899, where it was also advertised by its importers, Newman & Guardia. The Verascope was unchallengeably superior to its rivals: more robust – it was constructed of oxidised brass, more compact, more portable, more ergonomical in design, and having a greater range of available options and accessories. In successive variously enhanced models, it remained in production until the late 1950s. For the aspiring photographer of the First World War it was the perfect tool.

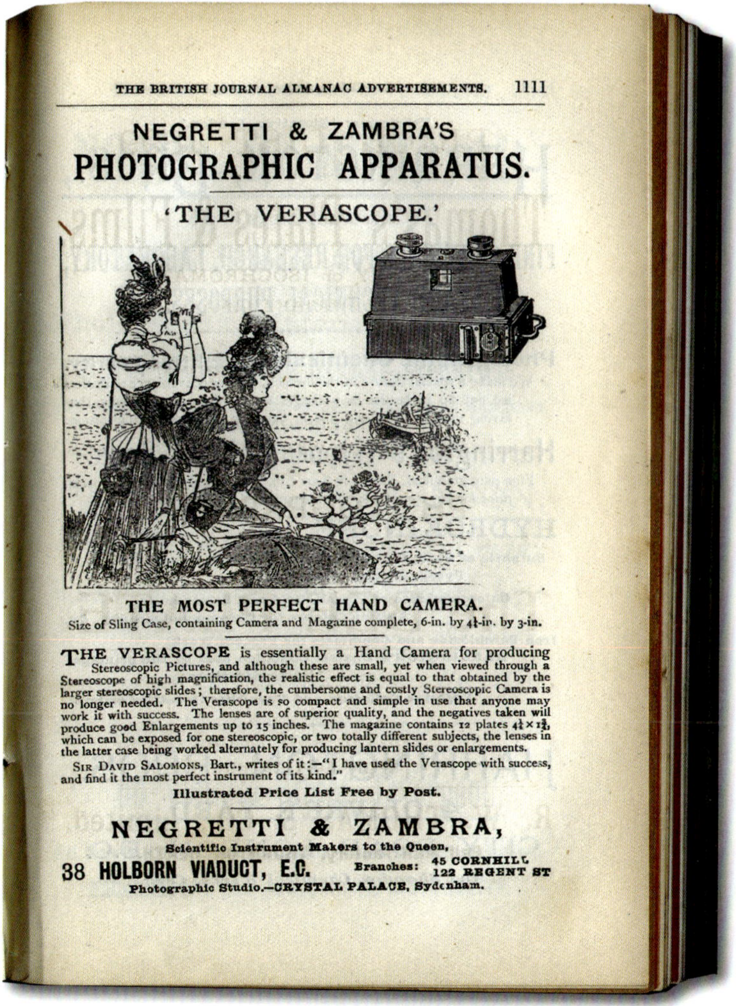

THE BRITISH JOURNAL ALMANAC ADVERTISEMENTS. 1111

NEGRETTI & ZAMBRA'S

PHOTOGRAPHIC APPARATUS.

'THE VERASCOPE.'

THE MOST PERFECT HAND CAMERA.

Size of Sling Case, containing Camera and Magazine complete, 6-in. by 4¼-in. by 3-in.

THE VERASCOPE is essentially a Hand Camera for producing Stereoscopic Pictures, and although these are small, yet when viewed through a Stereoscope of high magnification, the realistic effect is equal to that obtained by the larger stereoscopic slides; therefore, the cumbersome and costly Stereoscopic Camera is no longer needed. The Verascope is so compact and simple in use that anyone may work it with success. The lenses are of superior quality, and the negatives taken will produce good Enlargements up to 15 inches. The magazine contains 12 plates 4¼ × 1¾, which can be exposed for one stereoscopic, or two totally different subjects, the lenses in the latter case being worked alternately for producing lantern slides or enlargements.

Sir David Salomons, Bart., writes of it:—"I have used the Verascope with success, and find it the most perfect instrument of its kind."

Illustrated Price List Free by Post.

NEGRETTI & ZAMBRA,

Scientific Instrument Makers to the Queen,

38 HOLBORN VIADUCT, E.C. Branches: 45 CORNHILL, 122 REGENT ST

Photographic Studio.—CRYSTAL PALACE, Sydenham.

THE PHOTOGRAPHER REVEALED/ Once the plates had been digitised and fully annotated they were filed in chronological order. Two of them out of a group of five taken at the same location are dated 8/8-17 (8 August 1917). They depict a group of French army officers photographed at leisure on the banks of a river; a break away from the conflict, a memento for the years to follow, an ordinary kind of subject. Both are dated, while but only the second adds identifying detail: Groupe Givord Monchy-Humières (the Givord Unit [at] Monchy-Humières). It is a village in the Picardy region of northern France.

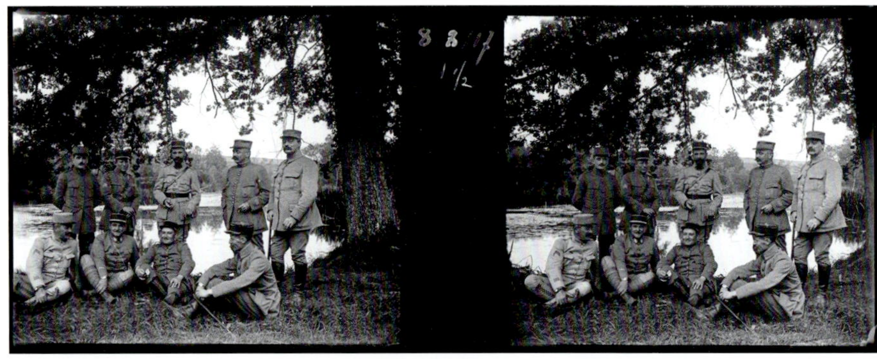

PHOT. 147: 8/8-17
(08/08/1917)

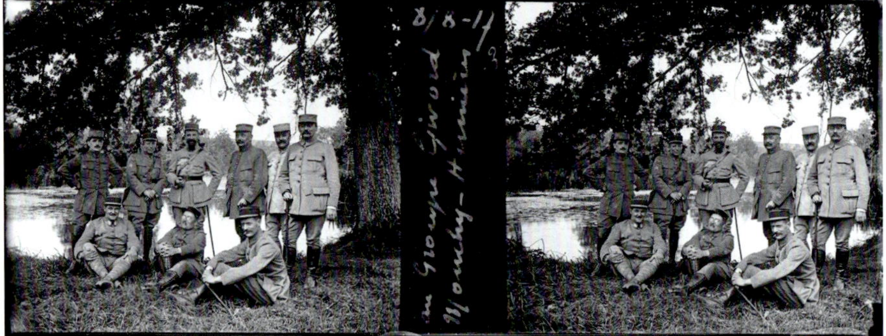

PHOT. 149: 8/8-17
Groupe au Givord Monchy-Humières
(08/08/1917 *Groupe Givord at Monchy-Humières*)

The two photographs **[PHOT. 147 AND 149]** are practically identical: a frontal shot of the group with the river in the background. The first of the photographs shows five men standing and four squatting on the grass in front of them. The second photograph shows six standing and three squatting. The second man from the right, now standing, was previously the one seated on the extreme left in the first shot. Unless we suppose that the person taking the photographs never appeared in shot (though it is unlikely he would want to be left out) the explanation is surely that the officer who moved to the back was the photographer. His magazine holds ten plates, and he would have had to feed the next one into position, ready for exposure. He would then have set and tripped a self-timer on the shutter, allowing him some seconds to move quickly to the back row, judging it faster than finding a space at the front.

Now that we know him from his appearance, we discover him in other photographs. In that summer of 1917 he shows up as a mature man, alert, in good shape, with the heavy moustache that most of his fellow officers wear, and hair going silvery-grey at the temples. He has been at the front for at least two years, as indicated by the three chevrons on his left sleeve. The first would have been awarded after a year of service, with additional ones for each further six-month period. And he has been awarded the military medal, the *Croix de Guerre.* [5] The insignia on his cap, or *képi*, having three bands of braid, identifies him as a captain in the French army, though his uniform does not help identify the branch of the army in which he served. The annotations on the second of the negatives, however, contain further clues: *Groupe* and *Givord*. In the French army, the *groupes* (units) take their title from the officer in command. The unit, composed of three or four squads, was formed on 2 August 1914 as part of the *Train des équipages militaires* (military transport formation – which in the Great War included horses). It was charged with providing drivers for motorised vehicles, ranging from command vehicles to trucks. The *Revue des deux mondes*, a longstanding journal containing a miscellany of politics, the civil service and society, gives an account of the fighting at the village of Plèssis-de-Roye in March 1918, which confirms the existence of a *Groupe Givord* within the *Service Automobile.* [6]

5 The Croix de Guerre is a military medal created on 2 April 1915, destined to reward valour in combat, individual or collective. It is estimated that more than two million were awarded throughout the Great War.

6 *Revue des deux mondes*, 1 January, 1919, p.343.

La 77e division est encore sans équipages : elle a été amenée si vite ! Mais le groupe Givord, section automobile 434 T. M., sous les ordres du maréchal des logis Gassier (conducteurs : Potard, Bigot, Moussy, Turpin, Jaloux, Got, Queuille, Lamure), a été détaché en plein combat pour la ravitailler. Pendant dix-huit heures il roulera sans arrêt, portant ses ravitaillements jusqu'à proximité immédiate de l'ennemi, afin d'exécuter intégralement sa mission. — Chics types ! diront les fantassins. Et chacun sait que le fantassin n'admire pas volontiers les automobilistes. Mais dans cette bataille, il louera jusqu'aux aviateurs. Il est vrai que, riche de ses propres exploits, il pourra se montrer prodigue.

The 77th division was brought up so fast that it is still without supplies. But the Givord Unit, motorised division 434 T.M., under the orders of Sergeant Gassier (drivers: Potard, Bigot, Moussy, Turpin, Jaloux, Got, Queuille, Lamure) was dispatched in the middle of the fighting to fetch fresh supplies. For eighteen hours they drove non-stop, bringing the supplies right up close to enemy lines, in order to fulfil their mission to the ultimate degree. Great guys! the infantrymen called them. And everyone knows that the infantry don't readily express admiration for drivers. But in this battle they praise them as much as the aviators.

This confirms the existence of a *Groupe Givord* within the *Service Automobile*. Furthermore, several issues of the *Journal officiel* (the official gazette of the French Republic) confirm the service of a Pierre Antoine Henri Givord, sometimes simplified to PAH Givord. Having discovered a complete name and a division, his record in the *Service historique de la Défense* (SHD) – the French Ministry of Defence's records of military service, can be accessed. SHD entries confirm Givord's identity and his service record. The hitherto anonymous photographer and his work are finally rescued from oblivion.

CIVIL & MILITARY CAREER/ Pierre Antoine Henri Givord was born on 9 January 1872 in the 2e arrondissement of the city of Lyon. He was the first-born son of Jean Baptiste Givord (b.1831), a civil engineer, and Adelaïde Marie Joséphine Françoise Troccon (b.1844), who were married in 1866. At the time their son was born, Jean Baptiste was mayor of Marlieux, a small town of 600 inhabitants in the department of Ain, where he owned land. Their main residence, however, was at 1, Place Gensoul, in Lyon, which indicates the Givords were a family of substance. Some years later the family moved to a house in Rue de la Baleine, in the old medieval quarter.

In 1892, at the age of twenty, while studying law, Pierre Antoine Henri enrolled as an army volunteer for a period of three years. His file describes him as a young man, 1.72 metres in height, with brown hair and grey eyes. He was posted to the historic 99e *Régiment d'Infanterie,* then stationed in Lyon. The following year, Givord was promoted to corporal and was placed on the reserve list of his regiment, which was transferred to Gap, a city 200 kilometres to the south, in the Hautes-Alpes. As a reservist, Givord had the obligation of returning to his unit periodically for instructional exercises, which he was called to observe in four of the six years following. He was promoted to the rank of sergeant in 1895, and again to sub-lieutenant in 1899.

Rég. d'infanterie de Bourgoin. — M. Givord (Pierre-Antoine-Henri), sous-officier de réserve. [7]

In October that year he presented his doctoral thesis, under the title: *Les sociétés de secours mutuels et l'assurance obligatoire contre la maladie* (mutual aid societies and compulsory sickness insurance), a subject that might seem to indicate a commitment to humanist values. If so, they would shortly be put to the test. Having gained his Doctorate of Law, he was soon practising as a *clerc d'avoué* (attorney's clerk). In July 1900, Givord married Marie Louise Joséphine Besson. The newly-weds set up home in the exclusive Champvert district of Lyon, in a house that had belonged to the Givords since the 1860s. There they raised a family: two boys and a girl. Life was

7 *Journal de l'Ain*, 5 November 1871, p.3

kind to them and they were clearly deemed to be socially acceptable by '*Le Tout Lyon*', to whom they offered open house every Thursday – as listed in the *Annuaire des salons à l'usage des gens du monde* (The Annual of Salons for the use of Society People).

GIVORD (Pierre), [C.C.], et Mme, née BESSON, chemin des Massues à Champvert, Point-du-Jour. *Jeudi*

141

THE LONG ROAD TO WAR/ In 1870, in the wake of the disastrous defeat of the French in the Franco-Prussian war, the emperor, Napoleon III, was deposed and the French Third Republic proclaimed. At the Treaty of Versailles, which followed in 1871, Wilhelm I of Prussia was declared emperor of a newly united Germany; a war indemnity of five billion francs was levied against France; and her humiliation was made complete by Germany's successful annexation of Alsace and Lorraine. The desire for revenge would haunt the French collective subconscious for years to come.

For the army and for French society at large, these were years of tension, marked by the dispute at the heart of the *affaire Dreyfus*. The case, in which Alfred Dreyfus, a Jewish captain in the French army, was accused – without evidence – of espionage for the Germans, divided France between his supporters, or *dreyfusards*, and opponents, *antidreyfusards*. Its long judicial journey, which began in 1894, saw the defendant sentenced by court martial to loss of his army rank, public degradation by having his insignia cut from his uniform and his sword broken, followed by a life sentence in penal servitude. The case shocked many, with its exposure of widespread anti-semitism and chauvinism, as Émile Zola wrote in *J'accuse*, which he addressed to the president, Felix Faure. It was published as an open letter on the front page of the newspaper *L'Aurore* on 13 January 1898, accusing the government of institutionalised anti-semitism and the illegal jailing of Dreyfus. The affair must have been deeply troubling to Givord, because of his double role as lawyer and soldier. Apart from any juridical interest he may have had, it revealed a military class that was exclusive, influential, reactionary, institutionally racist, of dubious competence, and which closed ranks to avoid having to listen to public reproach. The reopening of the case under public pressure would eventually end with the reinstatement of Dreyfus, a broken man, in 1906. The army remained unapologetic.

In the wake of the political agitation generated by the Dreyfus case, French nationalist sentiment intensified, compounded by the increasing friction with Germany over the future of Morocco, the focus of French colonial ambition in North Africa. In 1905, a crisis was provoked by a visit to Tangiers by Kaiser Wilhelm II, when, in the face of the French, he issued a proclamation guaranteeing Moroccan independence. At a joint conference held in Algeciras the following year, a fragile compromise was reached over the relative spheres of influence of France, Spain and Germany. However, in the long run it served only to heighten tensions between the *Entente Cordiale*, formed by France, the United Kingdom and Russia, and the opposing the Triple Alliance of Germany, Austria-Hungary and Italy.

1911 saw the onset of a second Moroccan crisis, when the French sent troops to support the Sultan of Morocco's appeal for help in quelling a tribal uprising. Ever wary of France's ambitions in North Africa, Germany responded by sending a naval cruiser, Panther, to the port of Agadir, in a direct challenge to the French. Eventually, confronted by the combined powers of the *Entente Cordiale*, and unsupported by its own allies (possibly because the Panther was ordered to Agadir by a secretary of state, not by the governent), Germany was forced into a humiliating climbdown. By now it was clear to all parties that a full confrontation was fast becoming inevitable. The spark that finally ignited the conflagration was the assassination of the heir to the Austro-Hungarian throne, the Archduke Franz Ferdinand, in Sarajevo, on 28 June 1914, by Gavrilo Princip, a Bosnian-Serb nationalist and a supporter of pan-Slavic independence. Exactly a month later, Austria responded by declaring war on Serbia, sending its troops across the border on 28 July. The action was supported unconditionally by its ally, Germany. Russia, in support of the Slav nationalists, responded in turn by mobilising its troops, to which Germany reacted by declaring war on Russia. On 2 August, France too passed the order for full mobilisation, with Britain following suit the following day by declaring war on Germany. As of 4 August 1914, the world was at war.

Some years previously, after thirteen years of service, Givord had transferred to the *Armeé Territoriale*, assigned to the 109e *Régiment d'Infanterie Territoriale* (or RIT) in Vienne, close to Lyon, with the rank of second-lieutenant.[8] The territorial army was the last phase of military service for the French, where they would remain until they were forty-five. Jokingly called the *pépères* (grandads), their responsibility was to defend rear-guard actions in a hypothetical conflict. Confronted with the reality of the Great War, this mission would rapidly evolve.

The territorials were amongst those who were immediately mobilised. Givord was ordered to join his unit, the 11th Company, Third Battalion, 109e RIT. At the start of the war the batallion numbered 14 officers, 666 other ranks, 7 horses and 9 mules.[9] Initially the unit remained in the reserve to defend the Lyon region, not departing for the front until October. By then, the French setback that took place in August had been halted, with a victory in the decisive battle of the Marne, which took place 5-12 September 1914. The *109e RIT* deployed in the North of France, in the Champagne region, between Reims and Verdun. What followed was a succession of attempts by each of the belligerents to envelop the opposing force, taking them both northwards towards the sea, before coming to a halt in October in a stand-off that would last for more than three years. The territorial regiments did not occupy front line positions except those relatively quiet, and they participated only indirectly in combat. The missions undertaken by the *pépères* included the defence of forts and arms dumps, guarding prisoners, train lines, roads and trenches, building accommodation and providing transport for staff, ammunition and provisions.

21 February 1916 saw the onset of the most brutal battle of the war for the French army: the Battle of Verdun, in which 300,000 would die. On 1 April Lieutenant Givord received orders reallocating him to the motorised unit of the *4e Armeé*. But despite the huge cost in human lives and material resources of the three hundred day battle, it seems that Givord and his transport unit were not called upon, for between March and May he was still in Marne, more than a hundred kilometres from the scenes of devastation.

8 *Journal officiel de la République française*, 21 November 1905, n.316, p.6760.

9 *JMO (Journal de marches et operations) 109e Régiment d'Infanterie Territoriale.*

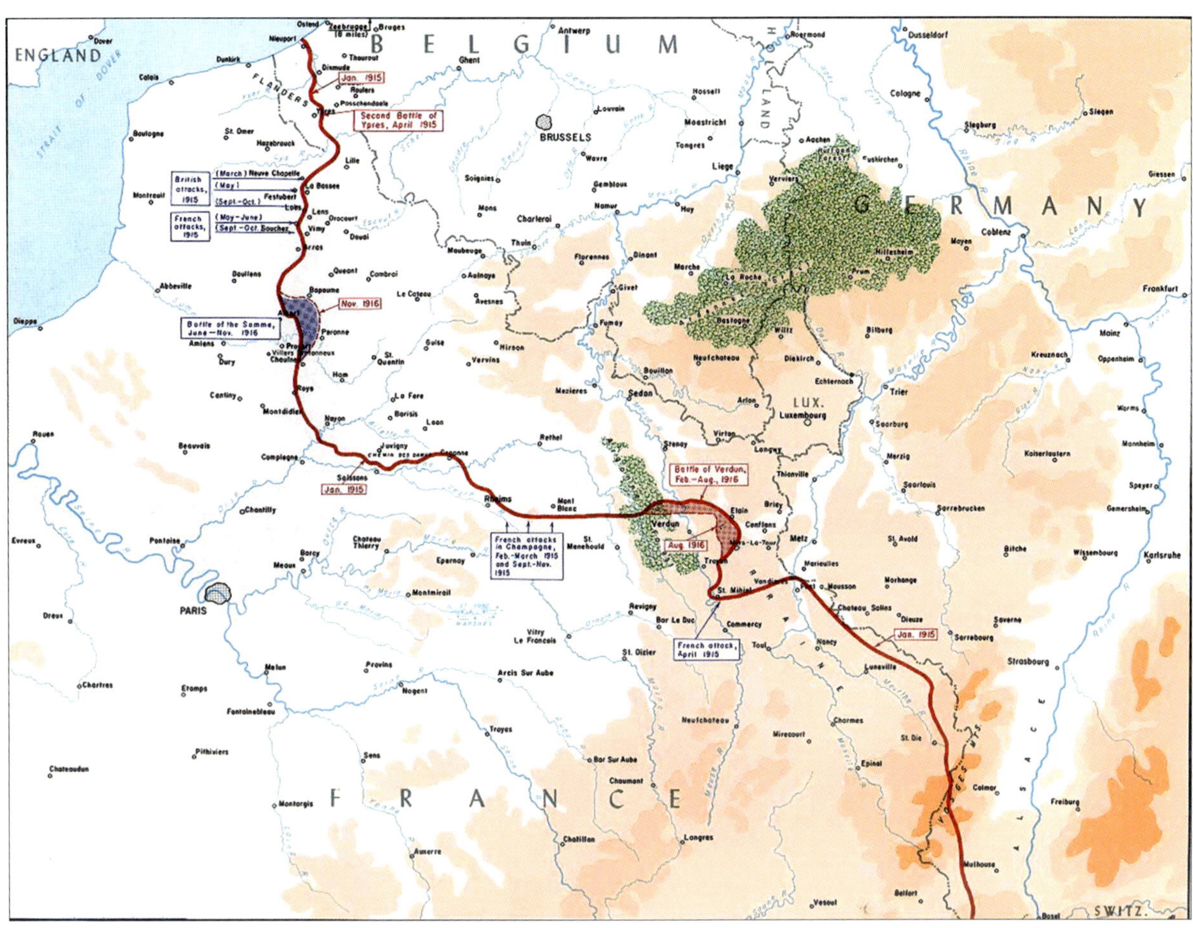

The Western Front: the red line follows the route of from the Vosges Mountains, through Northern France and Belgium, to the English Channel

Records show that in July 1916 Givord received a field commission, being promoted to captain within the motorised unit of the 8e *Escadron du Train* (the 8th Squadron, Military Supplies Formation),[10] and confirmed in rank shortly after. This rank qualified him to command a group of *transport de materiel:* the *Groupe Givord.*

10 *Journal official de la République française*, 3 August 1916, n. 209, p.6958

M. Givord (P.-A.-H.), lieutenant au 8e escadron du train, affecté au service automobile. — Maintenu.

Each *groupe* of the *Service Automobile* derived its name from its commanding officer. He would command four units, each being provided with twenty vehicles, forty-five men and one junior officer.[11] It was a year later, in August 1917, that the photographs of Captain Givord on the banks of the river were taken (by himself, using the self-timer) in the company of the officers of two of the units (see p.20). Immediately afterwards *Le Capitaine* enjoyed a rare two week leave permit. He used it to take a holiday with his family.

Givord began using his stereoscopic camera for the first time on 8 February 1916, when he took a shot of the shelled church of Souain, in the department of Marne **[PHOT. 1]**. From here on and for the duration of the war, *The Tangier Archive* guides us through Givord's personal odyssey on an almost daily basis, despite the fact that he sometimes failed to note the precise locations of some of his photographs.

Shooting more than a hundred photographs between February and August 1917, the escalation of his photographic activities coincided with the German retreat to the Hindenburg Line, where they entrenched themselves in new, impregnable bunkers. It was a skilled defensive manoeuver in which they relinquished territory in order to shorten their front to forty kilometres. What the French subsequently discovered in the newly vacated area between Arras and Soissons left them horror-struck. The Germans had put their doctrine of 'scorched earth' into practice with the utmost brutality, blowing up houses, burning down farms, mining monuments, pulling up trees and poisoning wells. Cities such as Ham, Noyon, Roye and Nesle were reduced to rubble. Givord, sent to that barren terrain and appalled by what he saw, dedicated himself to recording it systematically, a personal testimony to the consequences of war.

---

11 *Historique du 8e Escadron du Train: guerre de 1914-1918*. Print. J. Belvet, Dijon 1920. A summary of the intervention of these units in the war: *La Voie Sacrée. Le poumon de Verdun (Direction de la mémoire, du patrimoine et des archives).*

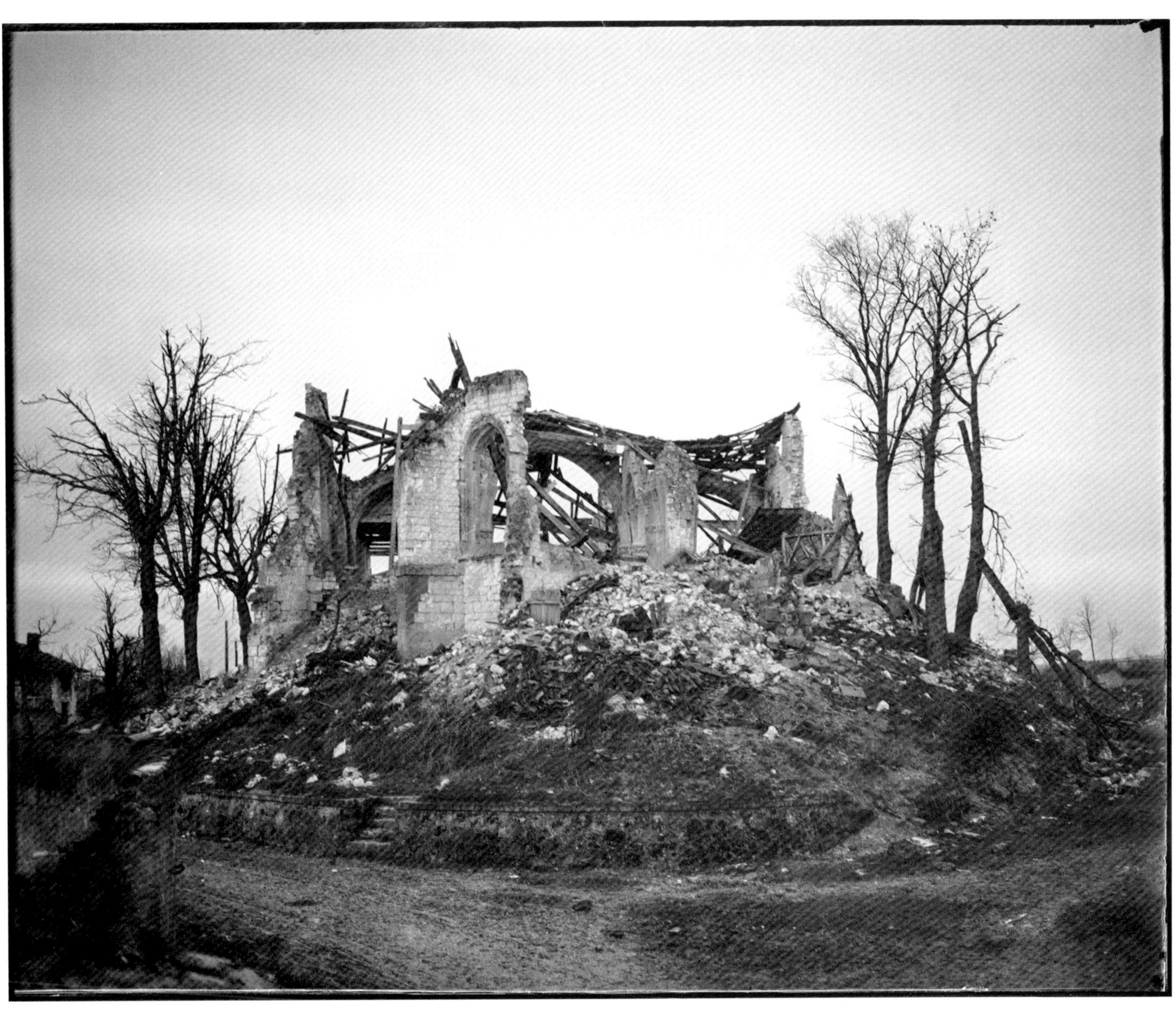

PHOT. 1. 08/02/1916 *Ruins of Souain church*

After the stabilisation of the Western Front in 1914, the town of Souain (department of Marne) remained dangerously close to the combat zone.

In the meantime, on the other side of the front, to the west of Soissons, General Nivelle mounted a futile assault on the near impregnable ridge along the plateau of Chemin des Dames. It cost the French army dear; between April and May, the French took 187,000 casualties there. Assault followed upon assault until the troops were close to rebellion. The situation finally came to a head in the summer, when some of the men mutinied, refusing to return to the front. In the face of this disaster Nivelle was removed from his post and his place was taken by Marshall Petain. Petain meted out a token measure of punishment, so to speak, (twenty-eight men who had turned their weapons on their officers were executed) but he also brought in improvements in rations, medical attention and home leave, which served to relieve the tension. On 23 October 1917, the French returned to the offensive. In a well planned manoeuvre they attacked the ridge of Laffaux, to the west of Chemin des Dames. The operation, preceded by six days of heavey bombardment, was a success, being brought to a conclusion in two days with a sustained advance of three kilometres. It was at this point that we find Givord on the field of battle, taking pictures of German prisoners forced to clear the corpses from the combat area close to Moulin de Laffaux. The prisoners were no more than a fraction of perhaps 20,000 captured. Thanks to this success the French recovered their optimism, but they decided to wait until their new American allies were fully deployed before renewing their offensive.[12] Givord's first regiment, the 99e, took part in the action at Chemin des Dames, and we find him, in a tranquil moment, enjoying a reunion with them – which of course he photographs.

Right: 07/07/1917
General Staff of the 99e Régiment d'Infanterie

[PHOT. 133]
Givord (extreme left) poses with his old regimental comrades. Among them, his Commander, Lieutenant-Colonel Borne (centre), his deputy, the Chef d'escadron, Nativelle (between Givord and Borne),the band leader, July (rear, with arms crossed), and two military doctors(on the right, with dark lapel badges)

12 America joined the war in April 1917, but its forces were not yet fully deployed when the Laffaux offensive took place.

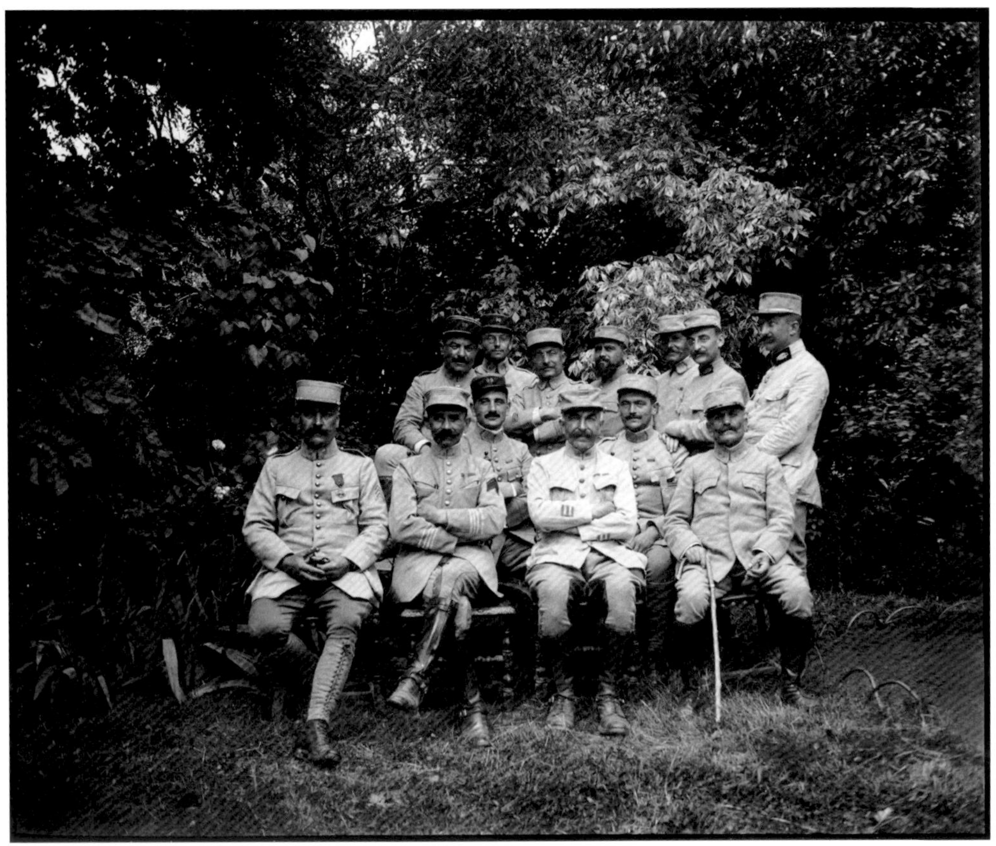

In November the same year, in the immediate aftermath of the Bolshevik Revolution, it became ever more likely that Russia would seek a separate peace with Germany, leaving the Alliance high and dry, and allowing the Germans to concentrate their offensive on the Western Front. On the orders of the *3e Armeé*, the *Groupe Givord* was transferred to the *Groupement Heilman*, formed by the amalgamation of six groups. Captain Givord himself was destined for Combles, in Picardy, in anticipation of the coming storm. The storm broke on 21 March 1918, when sixty divisions of the German army achieved a spectacular advance between Arras and Oise River that put full stop to the short-lived French advance. The Allies went into headlong retreat, as photographed by Givord, bogged down in the chaos of the roads. On 24 March his own *Groupe* was hastily reassigned to the *3e Armeé*.

Between 5 and 15 April, while the Germans were advancing, threatening Paris, Captain Givord directed the daring evacuation of substantial quantities of much needed medical supplies and equipment from the hospital in Ressons-sur-Matz, while under enemy fire, an act of heroism noted on his war record. A month later Givord received a leave permit that allowed him to return home in time to attend his son Leon's first communion. Returning to service, Givord spent May and June on the north coast, close to Dunkerque, possibly on military exercises. He spent some time photographing the locality and enjoyed leisure time on the beach with his artillery colleagues. In July he was reassigned to the front line as part of the 20th squadron of the Military Supplies Formation. [13]

By then the German offensive was over and the Allies had begun a counterattack. From 18 to 21 July, Givord and his *Groupe* were charged with the dangerous mission of resupplying ammunition to the front lines. By August, the German line was in tatters and the morale of their troops at a low ebb. Once again, Givord turned his camera on the destruction around him. The footprints of battle were a devastating sight as the Allies penetrated deeper into the enemy positions. In September Givord was designated deputy to Commander Lebel. Assigned to Belgium, in October Givord passed through Ypres en route to Hooglede, where he was caught by surprise by the announcement of the Armistice, to take effect at the Eleven Hour of the Eleventh Day of the Eleventh Month, 1918. *La Grande Guerre* had finally come to an end. It had claimed 37 million victims, the dead and the maimed, the soldiers and the civilians.

Nevertheless, the ceasefire did not mean official peace; for the time being the troops were kept on guard at their positions. It would not be until the end of the year that Captain Givord would be demobilised. In January 1919, while the detailed terms of the Treaty of Versailles were still under discussion, Givord was reassigned part of the *14e Escadron du Train*. The *14e* was, fortunately, already stationed in his home town of Lyon. On 11 November 1920, celebrating the second anniversary of the victory against the Germans, Pierre Antoine Henri Givord was officially designated a *Chevalier de la Legion d'Honneur*. [14]

---

13 *Journal official de la République française*, 12 July 1918, n. 188, p.6012.

14 *Journal official de la République française*, 11 November 1920, n. 308, p.18038. The *Legion d'Honneur* is the most important French distinction and is awarded to civilians or soldiers, nationals or foreigners, for extraordinary merit.

The following year Pierre Antoine Henri took his family to visit the battlefields of Verdun, where he familiarised his now grown-up children with the places that would be forever remembered in the collective memory of the French people, such as Fort Vaux. A further anecdote from that year reveals how Givord himself sensed the historical importance of the times through which he had lived as a protagonist. He organised an excursion with his children to Noyon, where four years earlier he had photographed the aftermath of the destruction of the nearby *château* of Mont Renaud **[PHOT. 236]**. Although the castle was devastated, he had his children pose in the very same place where before there had been no trace of humanity. It could be interpreted as a small family victory.

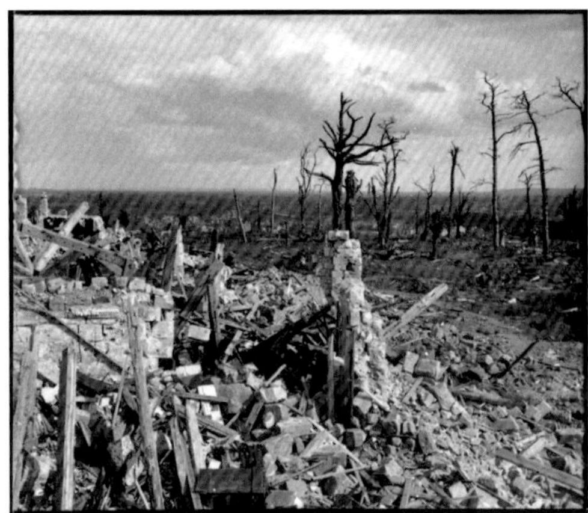

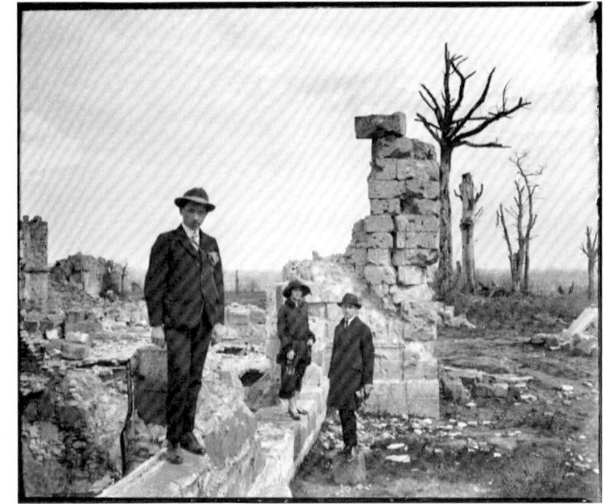

Left: **[PHOT. 236]**. 7-1918 Restes du château au Mont Renaud (07/1918 *remains of the Château at Mont Renaud*)
Right: Avril 1922 Voyage à Noyon (*April 1922 Trip to Noyon*)

In 1922, after spending thirty of his fifty years in the army, the old *Capitaine* asked to be allowed to continue serving on the controlling board of the *Armeé Territoriale*. His request was granted. Finally, in 1928, he was promoted to the rank of *chef d'escadron* – a rank equivalent to Commander.[15] On 8 January 1933, the day before he turned sixty-one, he reached military retirement age. So far as we know, his photographic life – at least the stereoscopic one – ended a couple of years later.

15 *Journal official de la République française,* May 10 1928, n. 111, p.5220.

After demobilisation some months after the end of *La Grande Guerre*, Givord devoted much of his time to his two great hobbies: alpinism and tourism. Apart from extensive travels throughout his beloved France, he visited Algiers in 1921, Austria in 1922, Tunisia and Italy in 1923, Monaco in 1925, the desert regions of North Africa in 1932 and 1934, Italy again in 1935....In the 1930s, in addition to his voyages and indulging in the pleasures of family life, Monsieur Givord dedicated himself to editing his war diaries, adding his collection to the *Association des Anciens Etudiants en Droit* of Lyon University. [16]

Pierre Antoine Henri Givord died on 1 January 1960 in the city of Lyon. He was about to turn eighty-eight.

GIVORD: THE ENIGMAS/ Captain Givord's exploration of stereoscopic photography spans almost twenty years. The crucial period for the purposes of this study covers part of the Great War, from approaching its mid-point to its final days. Yet of the beginnings of his stereoscopic photography and of its mysterious ending, we seem to know virtually nothing. And yet... perhaps a consideration of the photographs themselves might provide some useful insights.

It would be easy to believe that the perfect framing of the earliest dated photograph – of the ruins of the church at Souain, 8 February 1916, might have been accidental, were it not for it being followed by a further fifty shots in the same year, for the most part demonstrating an equal grasp of the medium. Are we to believe that Givord acquired his skill with the Verascope without having had any prior experience of photography, and that against the din of battle? It seems unlikely.

We have already seen how the introduction of dry-plate and roll film photography created a revolution that, by the outbreak of the First World War, was some twenty-five years old. By then, the popular snap camera had become at the very least a part of most families' annual holiday. Yet the 880 pages of photo-related advertisements in the *British Journal Almanac* of 1895 (cited

16 *Annuarie de l'Université de Lyon: livret de l'étudiant. Année scolaire* 1946-1947. Print. A. Rey, Lyon 1946.

earlier) were clearly not aimed at people simply wanting a keepsake, a souvenir of an outing to the seaside; they served a new constituency – that of the serious amateur. It seems more than likely that Givord was one of their number. If he did not at first take a camera with him onto the field of battle, it might perhaps have been because he had yet to discover the Verascope, and with it a sense of mission, a visual equivalent of the many war diaries kept by men of all ranks, and their letters home.

For this visual-minded diarist there was no choice. The Verascope, a piece of precision engineering of the first order, was the most robust, portable, high-performance camera then available; one that could be handheld, as required; had an eye level viewfinder, the sharpest of lenses, and magazines that each loaded twelve glass plates, successively available at the push of a lever; a spare magazine could easily be slipped into the pocket of a field jacket, along with the camera itself; (or as alternatives – cut film magazines, or a roll film back). Fast in operation and unobtrusive, above all it did not call attention to itself. It would not attract the attention of the censors, nor appear to be hampering the mobility of the user to the detriment of his military duties. In fact, in many ways the Verascope anticipated the yet-to-be-invented Leica, which became the camera of choice for a later generation of photo-journalists.

Between early February and the end of September 1916, Givord used his camera to considerable effect, but then did not resume his photography until February 1917. The gap might perhaps point to the more urgent call of duty as an officer; but it might equally suggest that at the time he was not close to the action, and therefore the most dramatic subject matter. What is certain is that during the autumn and early winter months he had time and opportunity to assess his photographic work. It is even possible that given the difficulties of processing his exposed plates while on the move, he may have held back and processed them during this spell. Having time to reflect on what he had accomplished, he would have become aware that the images, though of a generally high standard (and certainly far more so than might be expected from a photographic novice), they were not uniformly successful as stereographs.

Thus, From February 1917, we observe a stereoscopic axiom at work in the compositions that

Givord seeks to construct, and a secondary principle where circumstances provide. In the first case, he looks for architecture – and more often than not discovers it in pairs of parallel lines that he can employ in framing the image. In real life the viewer naturally perceives the lines as receding gradually into the distance, according to the rule of single vanishing-point perspective. With the artificial perspective created by stereoscopy the rule reverses itself, the lines appearing to diverge as they approach threateningly *towards* the camera, therefore towards the viewer. Thus the wings of a biplane [PHOT. 56]; a street with the ruins of shelled houses [PHOT. 67]; a demolished bridge [PHOT. 72]; a river [PHOT. 78 AND 83]; a military dirt road – in the distance, an arms dump has exploded [PHOT. 107]; a horse-drawn convoy [PHOT. 119]; and so on. The most striking effect, Givord has discovered, is achieved where he stations himself at an oblique angle of between some thirty to forty-five degrees to the lines, so that they will be heading with rapidity out of the sides of the frame, just missing the viewer, as it were.

Givord's second stratagem is where possible to place a human figure in the foreground, creating depth in successive planes, and not incidentally, characterising the resulting image. Where he is able to do so he will combine both methods, the parallel lines and the foreground human interest (replaced occasionally by a material object). In fact, the characterisation of the soldiers, French, English or Scottish, the dead Boche and the indentured Orientals, is very much a part of his intention.

It is clear from Givord's success rate that he is enviably cool and clear-headed under pressure, choosing his viewpoint and setting up his shots with care, apparently unhurried, yet retaining a sense of spontaneity and animation where appropriate. These are some of the telltale signs of a master at work, and the results are the portrayal of the titanic, tragic, wasteful struggle that was the Great War, in close-up, as the telling experiences of a single individual – an officer in the French army.

Just as the Great War proved to be a turning point in the conduct of warfare, with the introduction of tanks, aircraft and poison gas, so it was equally a turning point in its depiction, brought about specifically by technological advances in two fields. The first of these was photography, [17] enabled

17 Including cinematography, though amateurs were barred from the front and even from behind the lines.

by advances in portable camera design, and the development of dry emulsions, as we have seen; the second was the introduction of halftone printing of photographs, which made it possible to reproduce them in daily newpapers; (the first newspaper to include photographs instead of, as previously, illustration from woodcuts or woodblock engravings, was the *Daily Mirror*, launched in 1903). It is, then, more than a little ironic that Captain Givord's extraordinary – even perhaps unparalleled opus, taken over two-and-a-half years of warfare, face to face with the action, depicting with the utmost skill and insight the daily lives and deaths of the combatants, should have remained unseen for a century after origination.

We know that Givord was in North Africa twice after the end of the war. The first occasion was in 1921, when he took a photograph of the new French Minister of the Navy, Gabriel Guist'hau, on his arrival at the port of Tangiers.

We have no record of why Givord, with no known connections to the French navy, attended the minister's arrival, nor indeed what was the significance of his presence in Tangiers at that date, except that it will have been involved with representing the interests of the *Armeé Territoriale.* His final visit to Tangiers was in 1934, the year before his last dated stereo negative, and it is around this visit that the mysterious question of the lost (or abandoned?) archive revolves.

What was it that could possibly have induced Givord to subject his entire, fragile collection of original negatives to the hazards and uncertainties of travel? If it was to show them to a person or persons unknown, why did he not not take a set of positives – safe because replicable – instead? As negatives the images would have made little sense even to another photographer, let alone to a person unfamiliar with photographic media. And why Tangiers? How other than by Givord's own hand could the negatives have come there? And once there, were they simply abandoned? This would truly be an idea beyond reason or comprehension. And if accidentally left behind when Givord travelled on, why were they never recovered?

To these, and other unformulated questions we have no answers. We know only that Givord's unique work resurfaced, intact, after seventy-five years in limbo. And for this we give thanks.

27/3
1917 2
Ercheu
Sucrerie

PHOT.

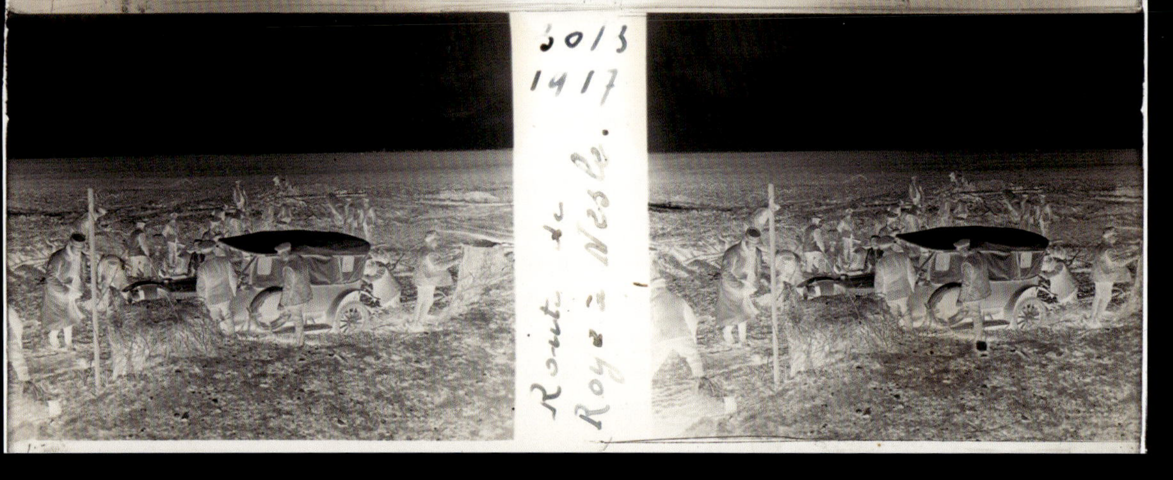

PHOT.

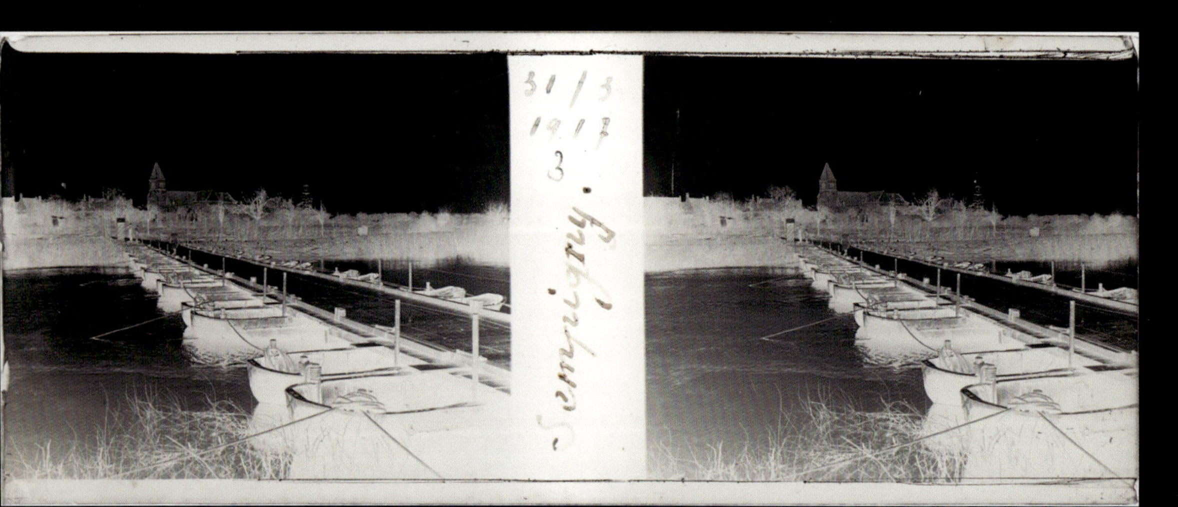

PHOT.

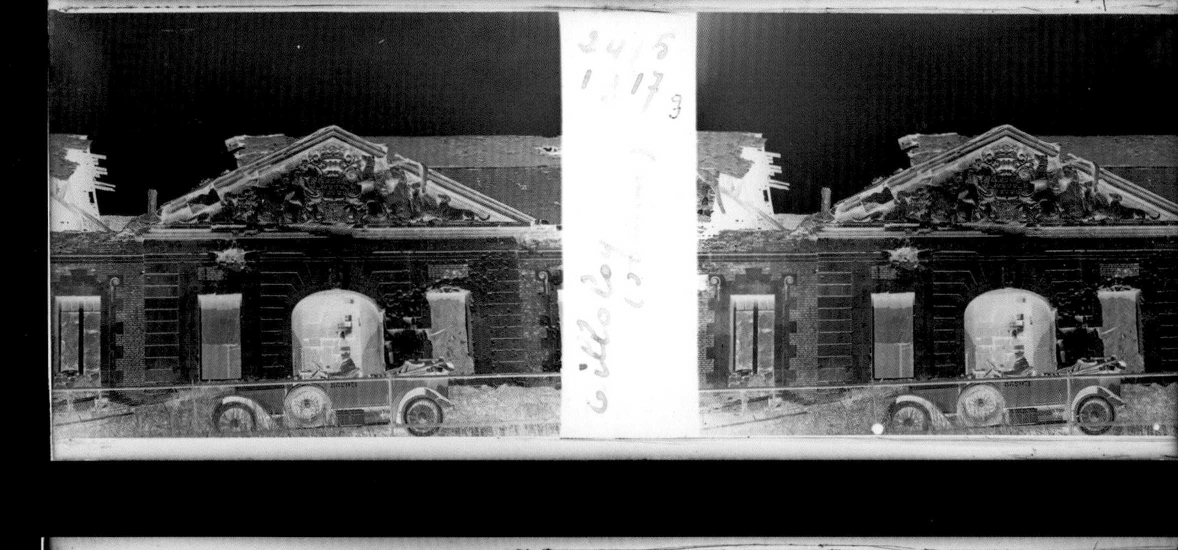

PHOT. 112

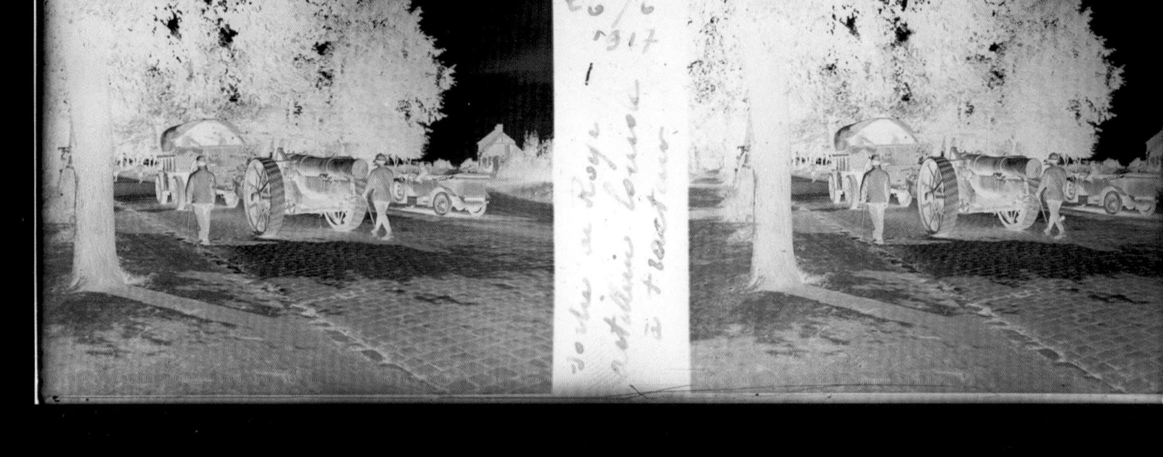

PHOT. 124

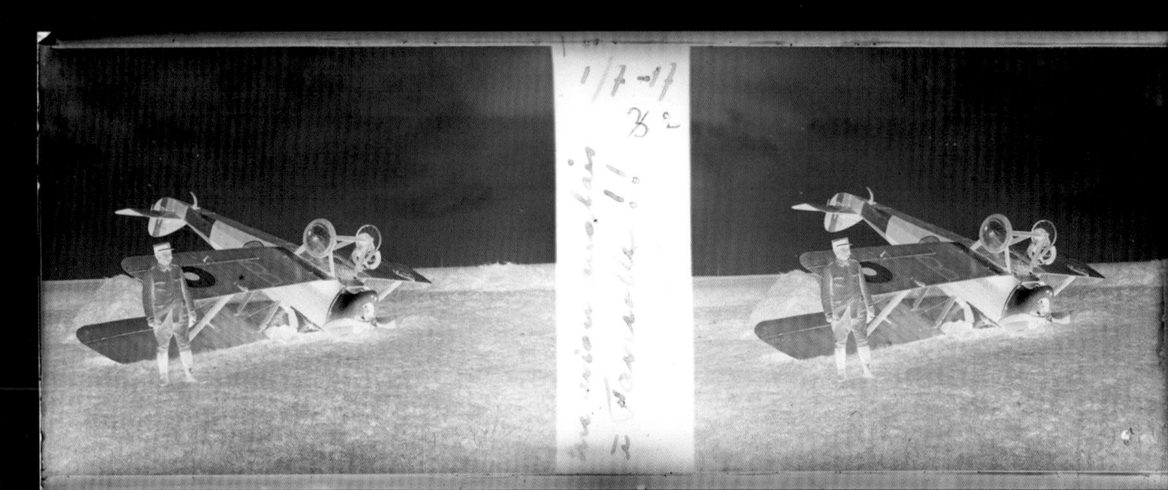

PHOT. 130

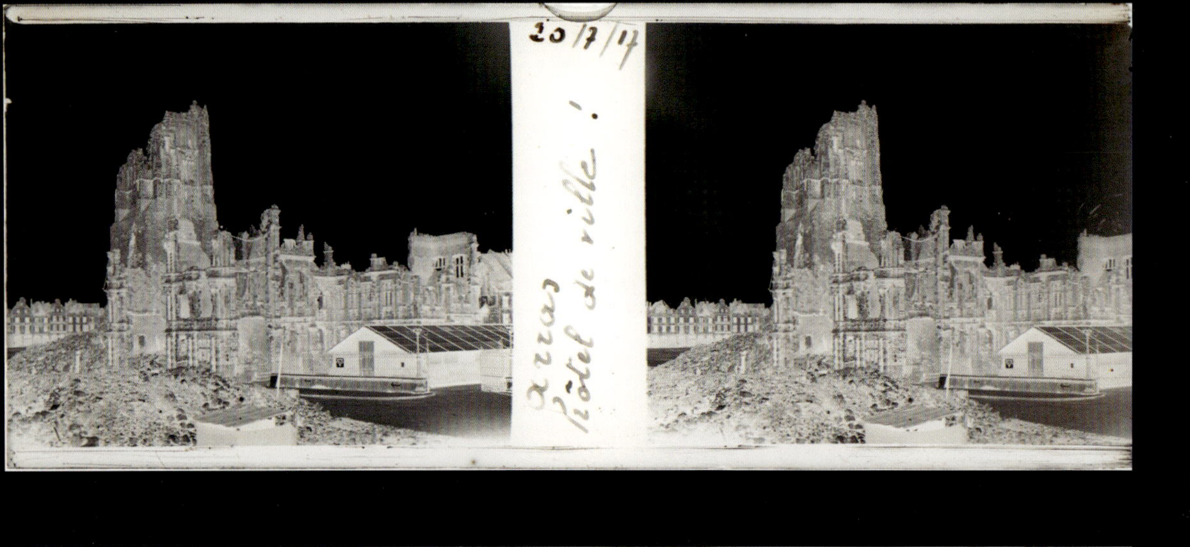

PHOT. 136

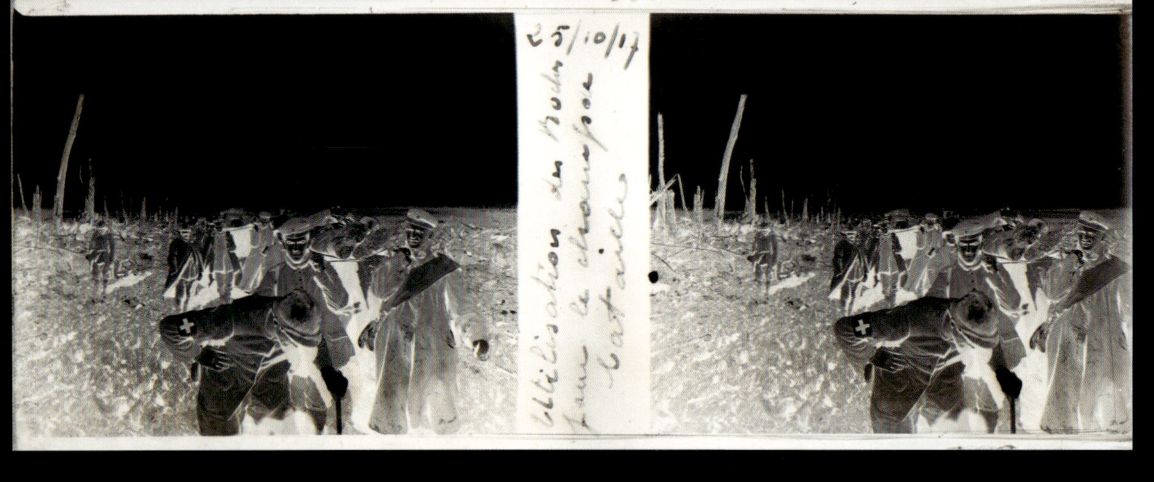

PHOT. 169

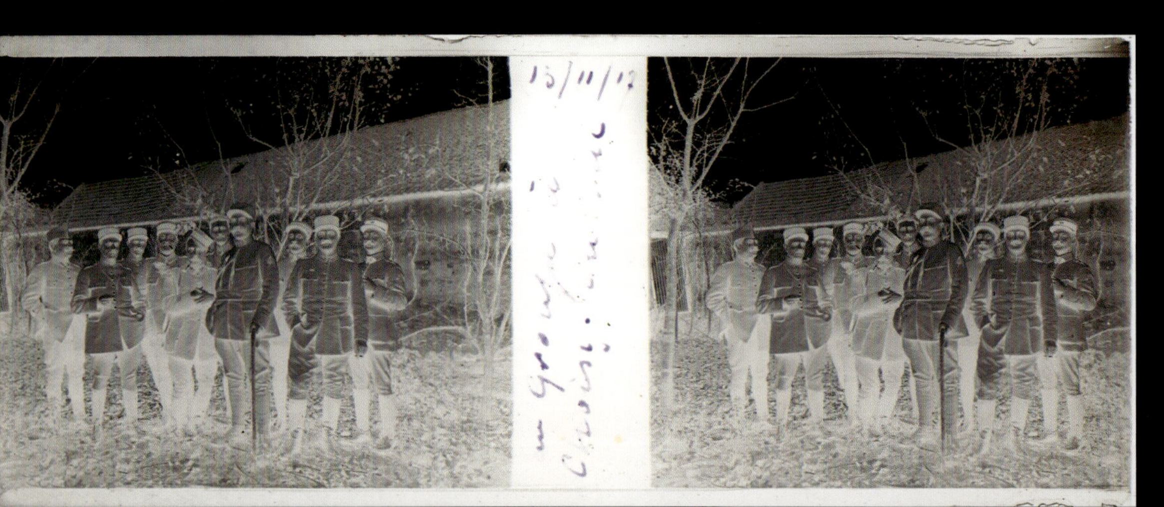

PHOT. 177

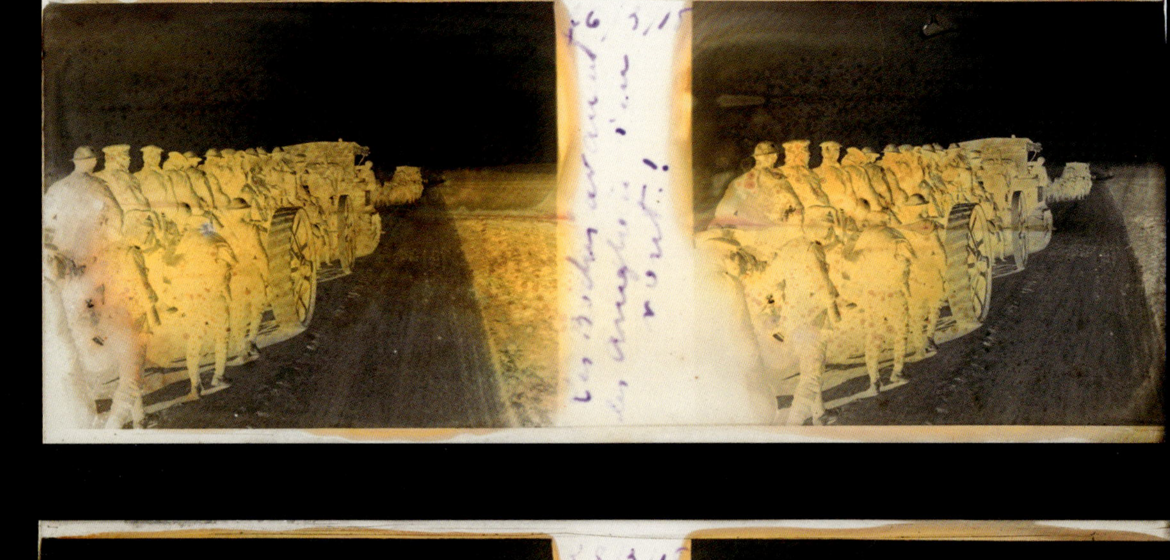

PHOT. 193

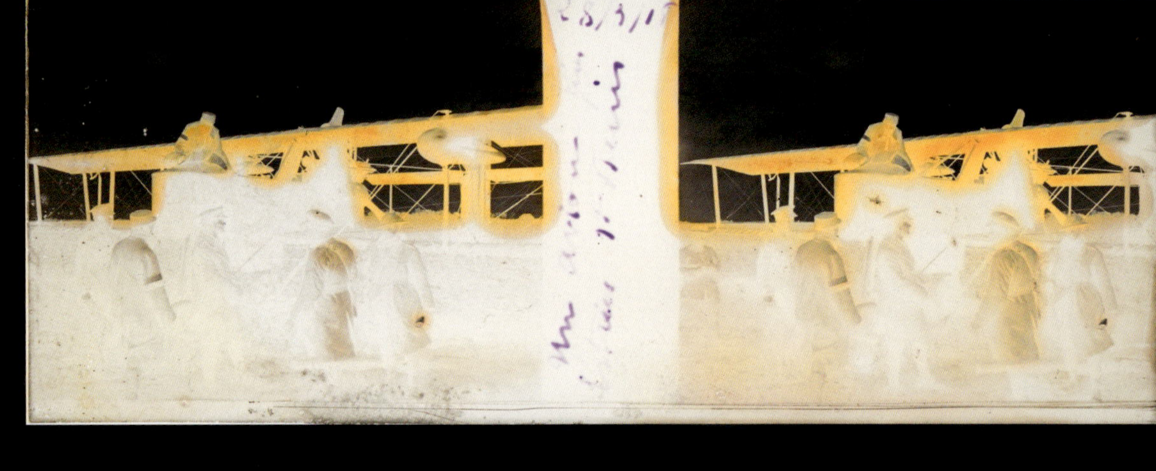

PHOT. 195

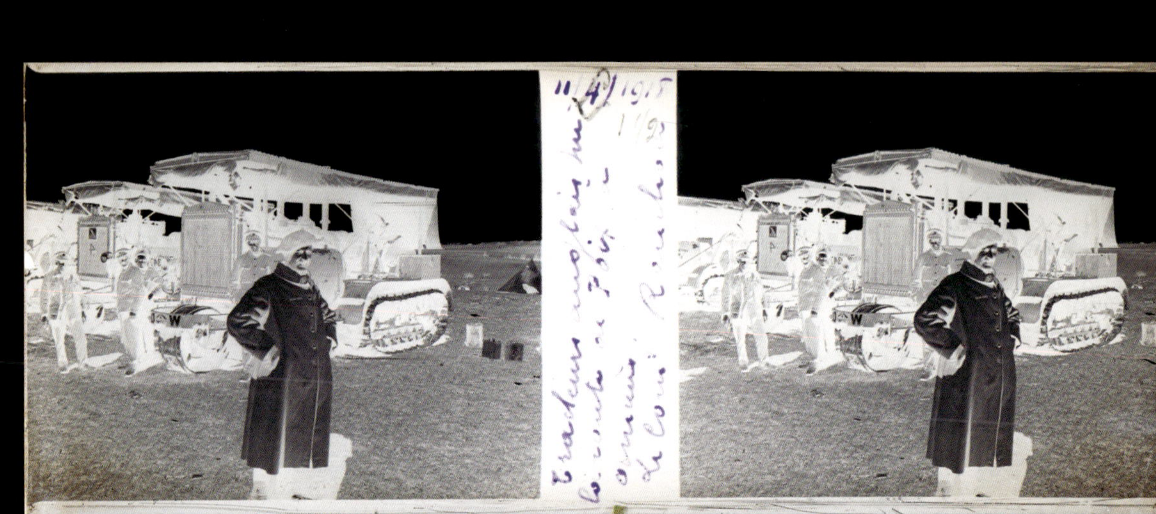

PHOT. 197

BIBLIOGRAPHY

150 years of photojournalism (Könemann 1995).

LIFE La fotografía (Salvat 1976).

BRUCE, *J.M. Bristol Fighter vol. 1* (Albatros Productions 1997).

BRUCE, *J.M. Bristol Fighter vol. 2* (Albatros Productions 1998)

BULL, S. *World War I Trench Warfare (1) 1916-18* (Osprey 2006).

BULL, S. *World War I Trench Warfare (2) 1916-18* (Osprey 2006).

CHAPPEL, M. *Scottish Units in the World Wars* (Osprey 1994).

CHAPPEL, M. *The British Army in World War I (1) The Western Front 1914-16* (Osprey 2003).

CHAPPEL, M. *The British Army in World War I (2) The Western Front 1916-18* (Osprey 2006).

CLARKE, D. *British Artillery 1914-19 .Heavy Artillery* (Osprey 2004).

CLARKE, D. *British Artillery 1914-19 .Field Army Artillery* (Osprey 2004).

DONNEL, C. *Fortifications of Verdun.1874-1917* (Osprey 2011).

FLETCHER, D. *British Mark I Tank 1916* (Osprey 2004).

FLETCHER, D. *British Mark IV Tank* (Osprey 2007).

FLETCHER, D. *Mark V Tank* (Osprey 2011).

FRANKS, N. *Nieuport Aces Of World War I* (Osprey 2000).

FRANKS, N. *Sopwith Pup Aces of World War I* (Osprey 2005).

GILBERT, M. *La Primera Guerra Mundial* (La Esfera de los Libros 2004).

GRAY, R. *Kaiserschlacht 1918. La ofensiva final alemana* (Ediciones del Prado 1994).

GRIFFITH, P. *Fortifications of the Western Front 1914-1918* (Osprey 2004).

GUDDMUNSON, B.I. *The British Army on the Western Front 1916* (Osprey 2007).

GUTTMAN, J. *Bristol F2 Fighter Aces of World War I* (Osprey 2007).

GUTTMAN, J. *SPA124 Lafayette Escadrille* (Osprey 2004).

HOLBORN, M. *The Great War* (Jonathan Cape e Imperial War Museum 2013).

HORSFALL, J y N. CAVE. *Cambrai. The Hindenburg Line* (Pen & Sword 1999).

HOLMES, R. *The First Wold War in photographs* (SevenOaks 2001).

LAVÉDRINE, B. *(Re)conocer y conservar fotografías antiguas* (CTHS 2007).

MCCLUSKEY, A. *Amiens 1918 The Black Day of the German Army* (Osprey 2008).

MACMILLIAN, M. *1914. De la paz a la guerra* (Turner 2013).

MARTIN, W. *Verdun 1916 'They shall not pass'* (Osprey 2001).

NEWHALL, B. *Historia de la fotografía* (Gustavo Gili 2002).

PLEGER, M. *British Tommy 1914-18* (Osprey 1996).

REED, P. *Combles. Somme* (Pen & Sword 2002).

REYNAUD, F., C. TAMBRUN y K. TIMBY. *Paris in 3D* (Paris Musées 2000).

ROGERS, L.A. *Bristol Fighter* (Albatros Productions 1987).

SÁNCHEZ DURÁ, N et al. *Ernst Jünger: guerra, técnica y fotografía*

(Universitat de València 2000).

SUMMER, I. *The French Army 1914-18* (Osprey 1995).

SUMMER, I. *French Poilu 1914-18* (Osprey 2009).

TAYLOR, A.J.P. *La guerra planeada. Así empezó la Primera Guerra Mundial* (Nauta 1970).

TUCHMAN, B. *Los cañones de agosto* (RBA 2006).

TURNER, A. *Messines 1917. The zenith of siege warfare* (Osprey 2010).

VERNEY, J.P. y J. TARDY. *¡Puta guerra!* (Norma 2010).

VERNEY, J.P. *The Great War in 3D* (Black Dog & Leventhal 2013).

WILLMOTT, H.P. *La Primera Guerra Mundial* (Inédita 2004).

ZALOGA, S.J. *El carro ligero Renault FT* (Osprey 2010).

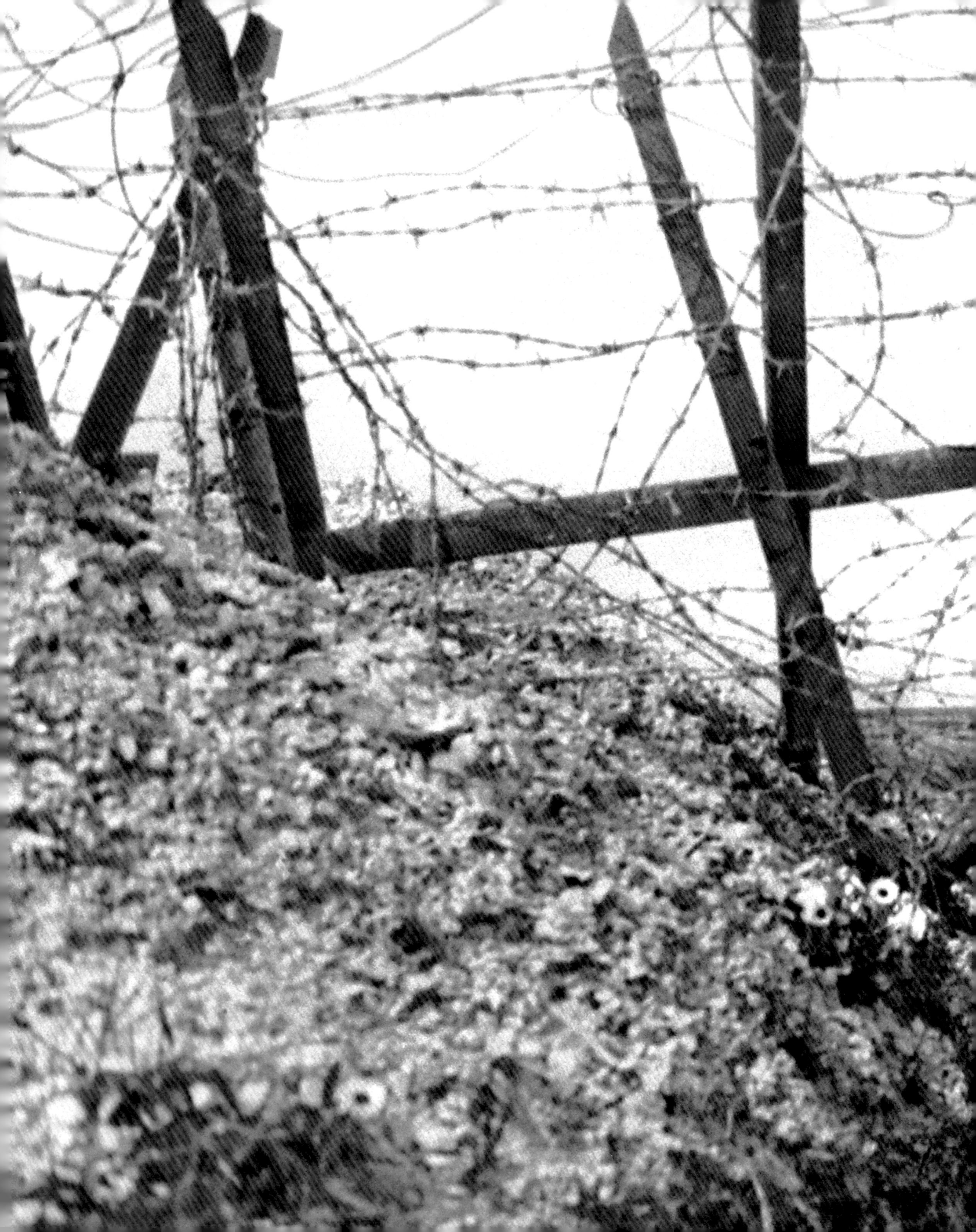

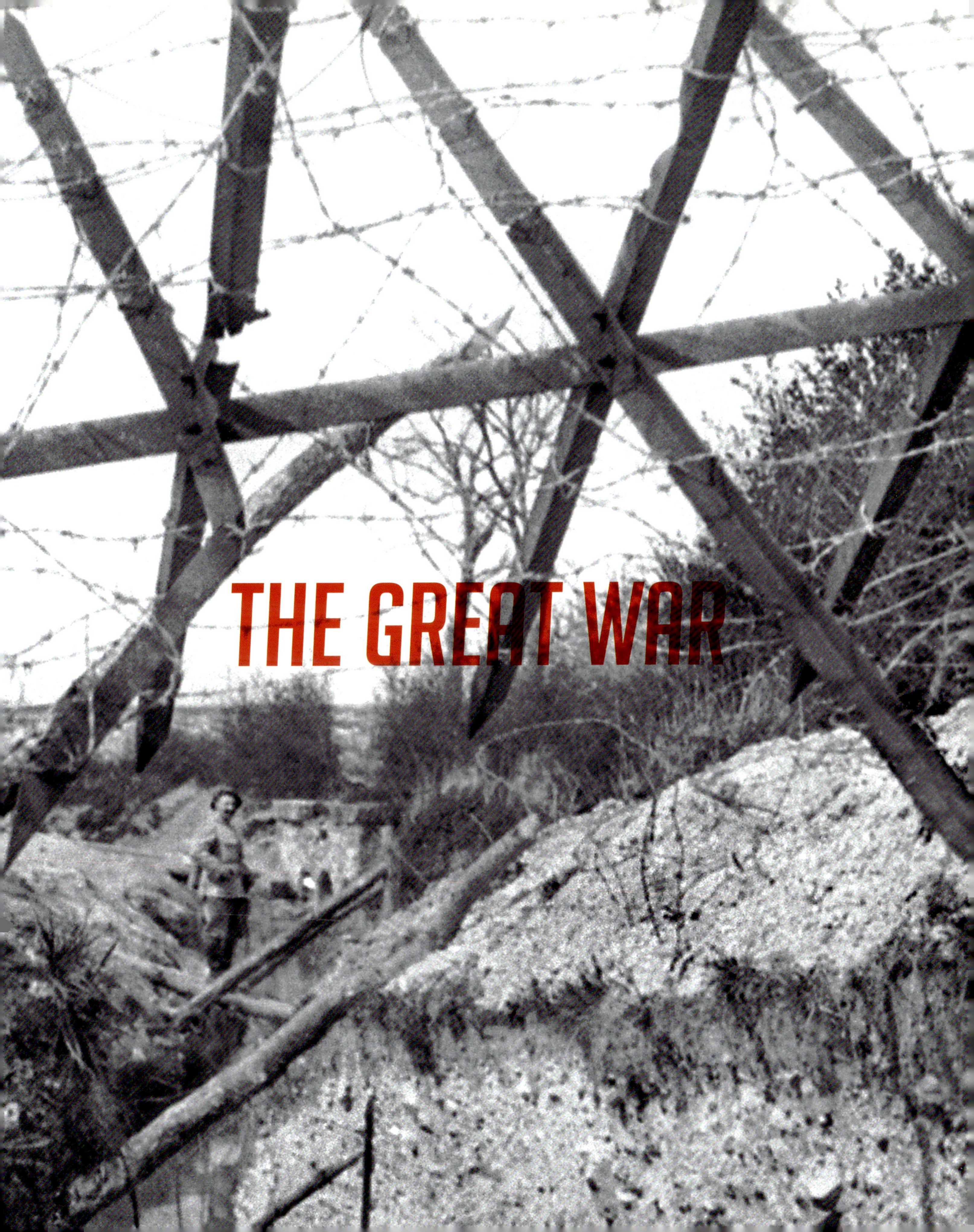
THE GREAT WAR

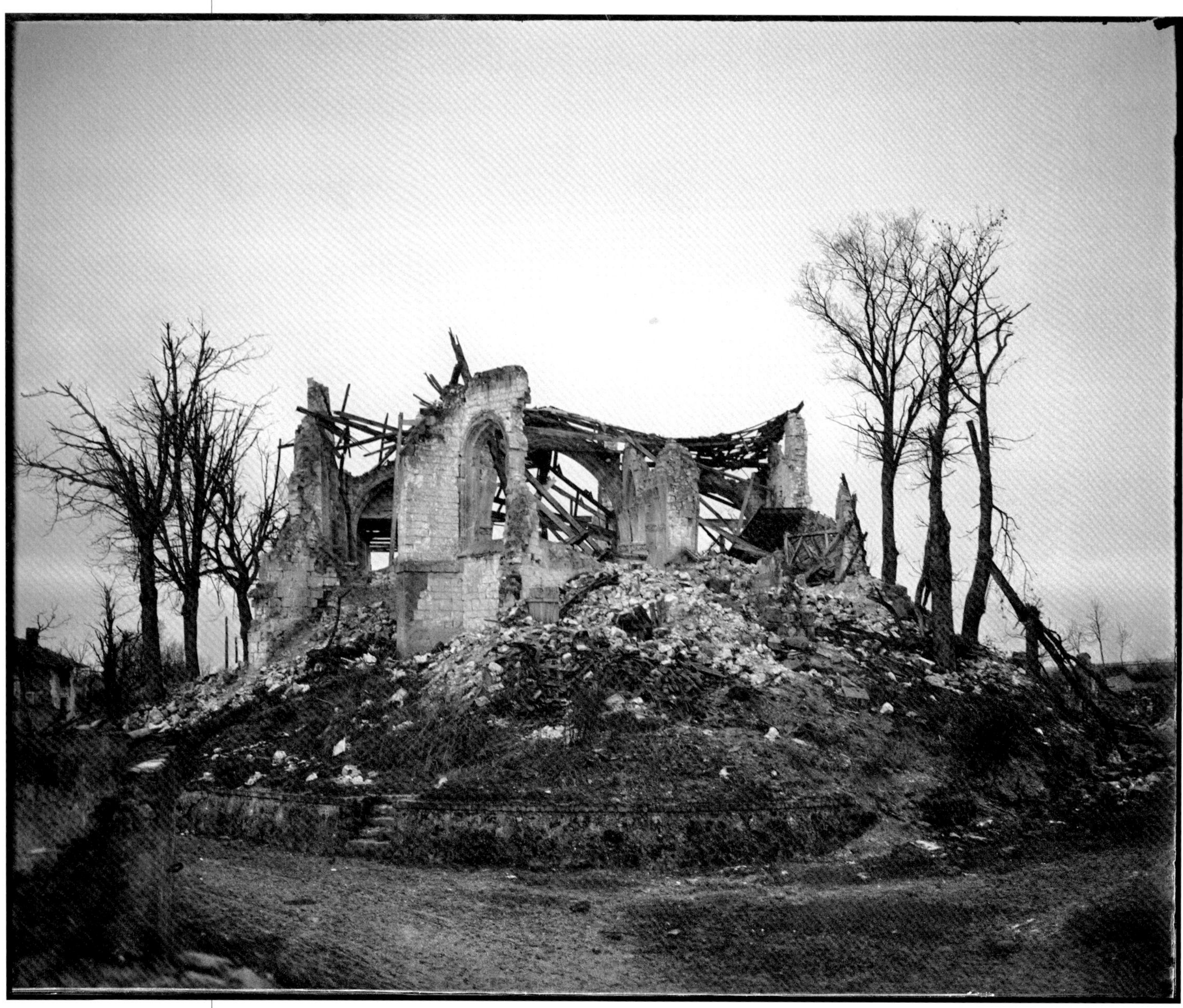

PHOT. 1
08/02/1916
Ruins of Souain Church

After the stabilisation of the Western Front in 1914, the town of Souain (department of Marne) remained dangerously close to the combat zone.

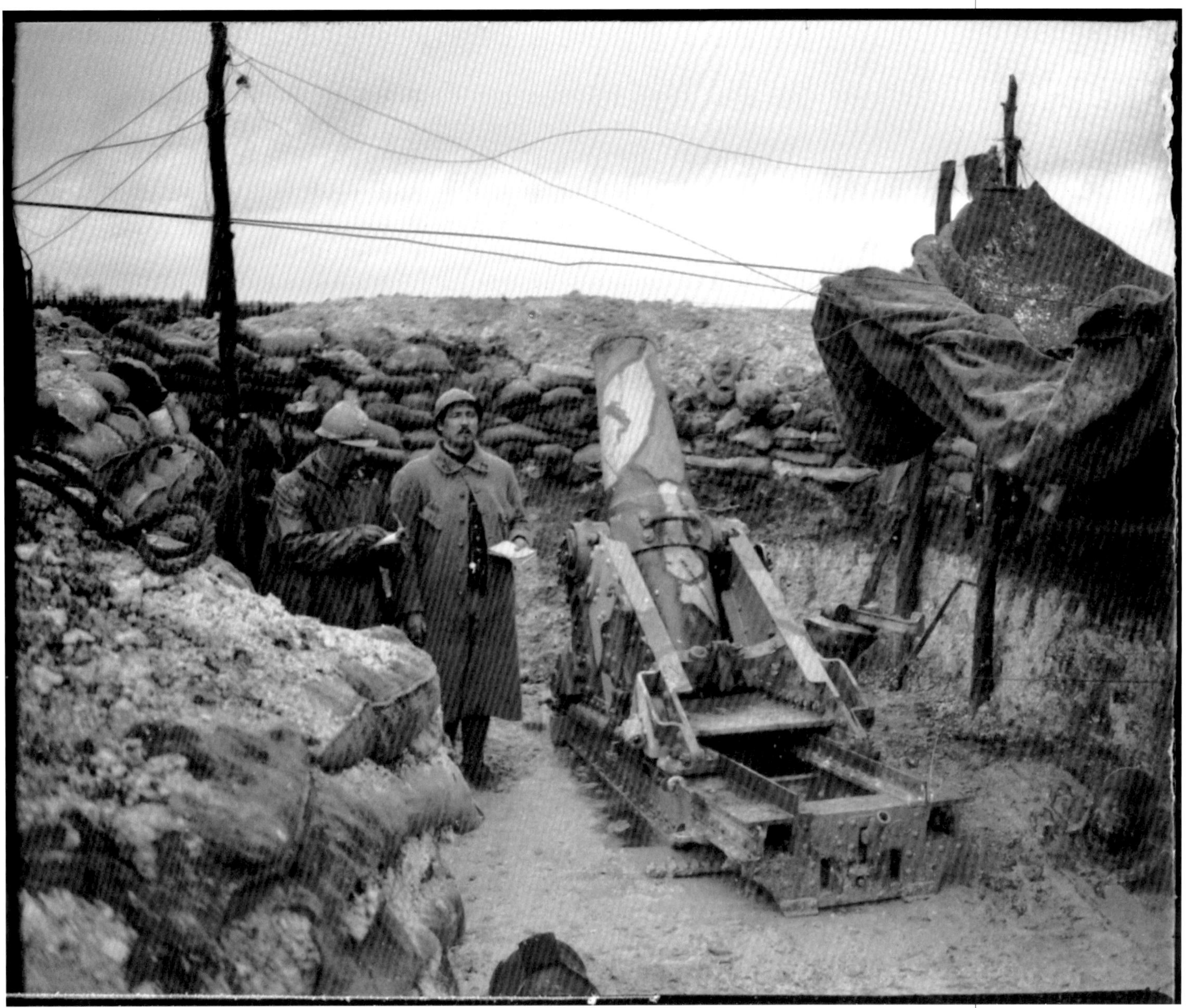

PHOT. 2
14/02/1916
220 mm mortar

This mortar model designed at the end of 19th century was outdated for the era, but it was one of the few heavy units that could be found in the French arsenal. The shells weighed 98 kg.

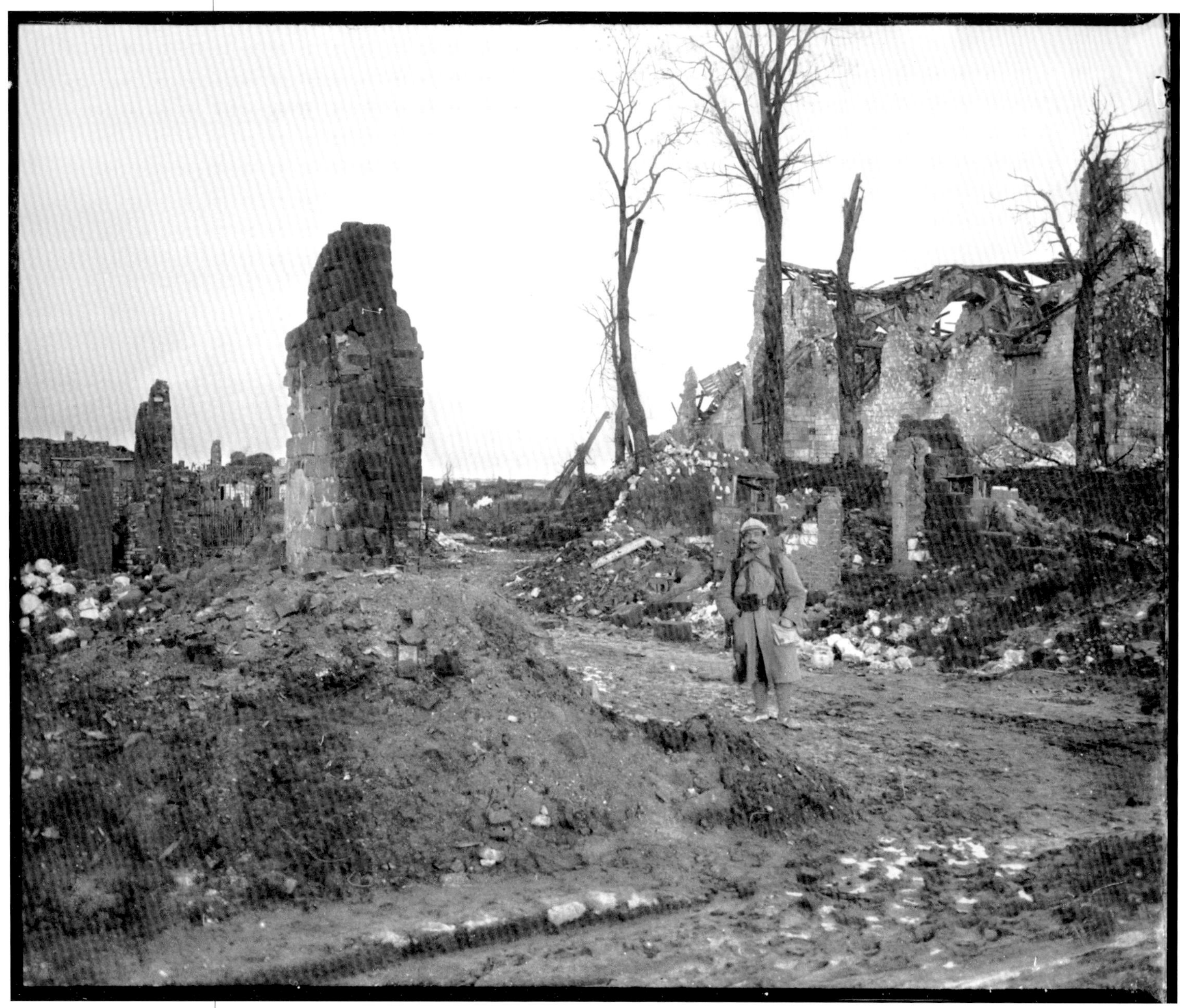

PHOT. 3
17/02/1916
Ruins of Souain

The town of 416 inhabitants was devastated during the second battle of Champagne, in September 1915. The French suffered 180,000 casualties taking three kilometres along a front of five kilometres.

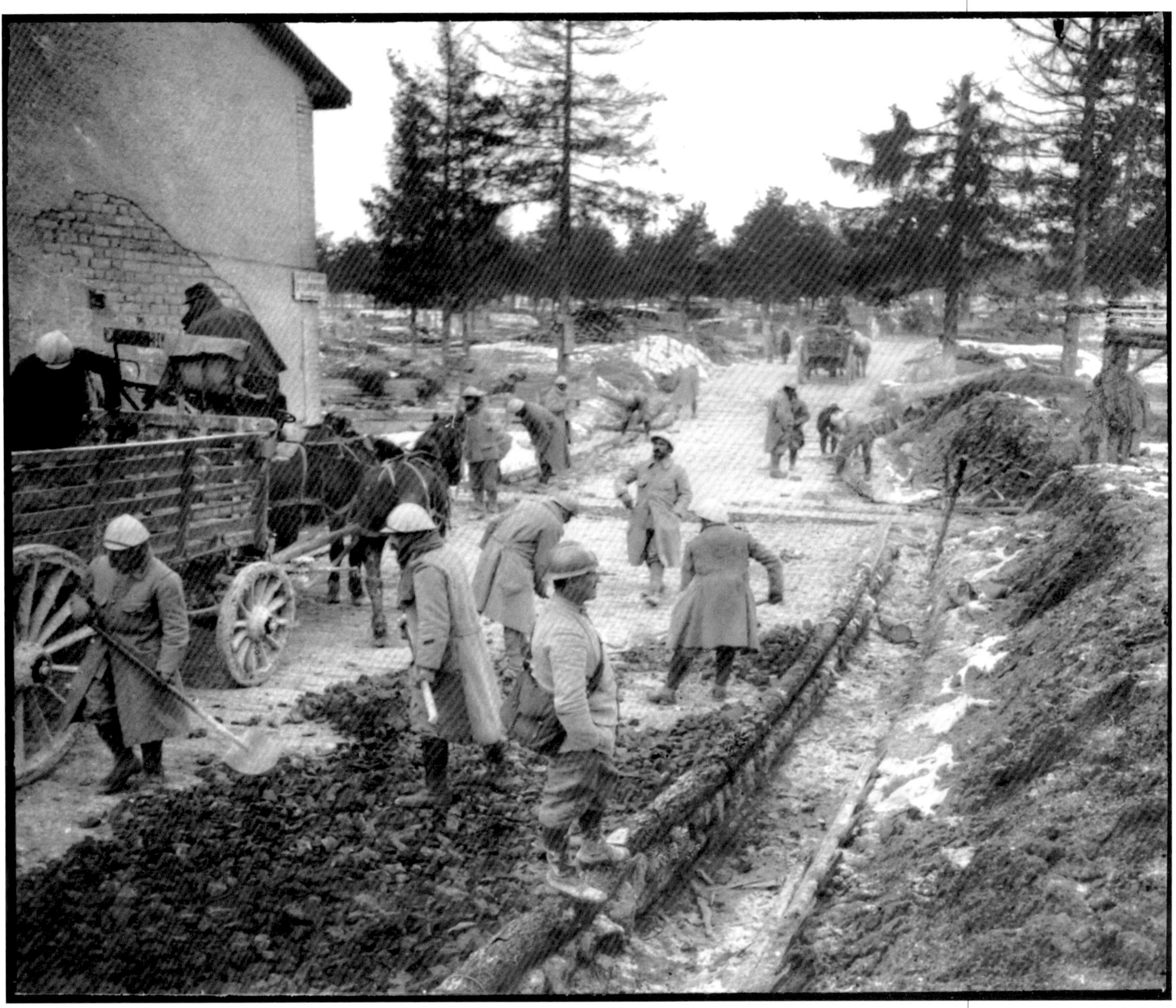

PHOT. 4
24/02/1916

One of the duties entrusted to territorial soldiers was road building. The earth was compacted with rubble to allow vehicles with tyres of solid rubber. This job was essential during the battle of Verdun, as only one road connected the city with the rear-guard at Bar-le-Duc. Through the road called *Voie Sacrée* (Sacred Road) a truck passed every fourteen seconds, hence they needed 8,500 men working continuously to maintain it.

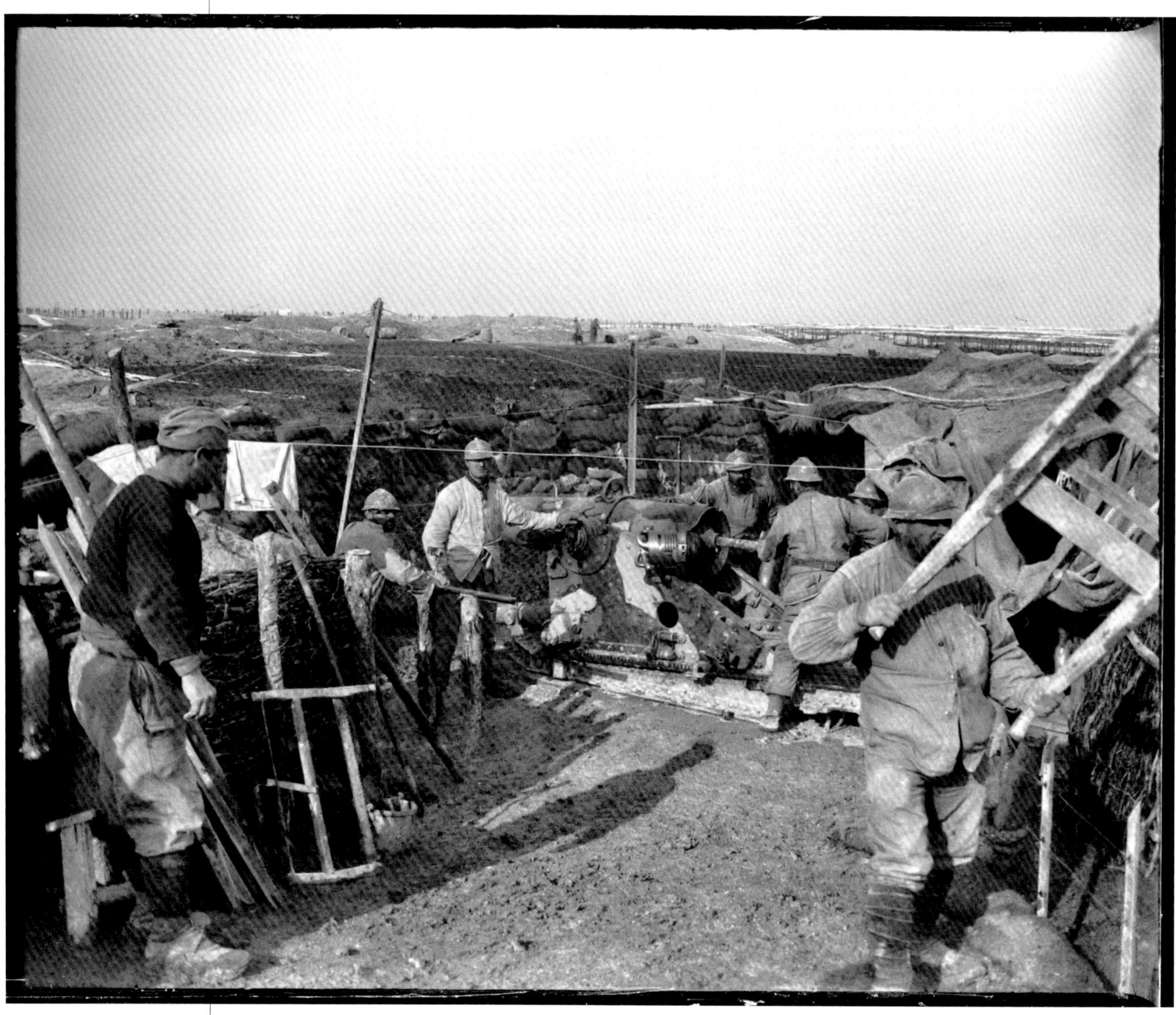

PHOT. 5
24/02/1916

A 220 mm cannon in action. The process of charge and shoot took about three minutes.

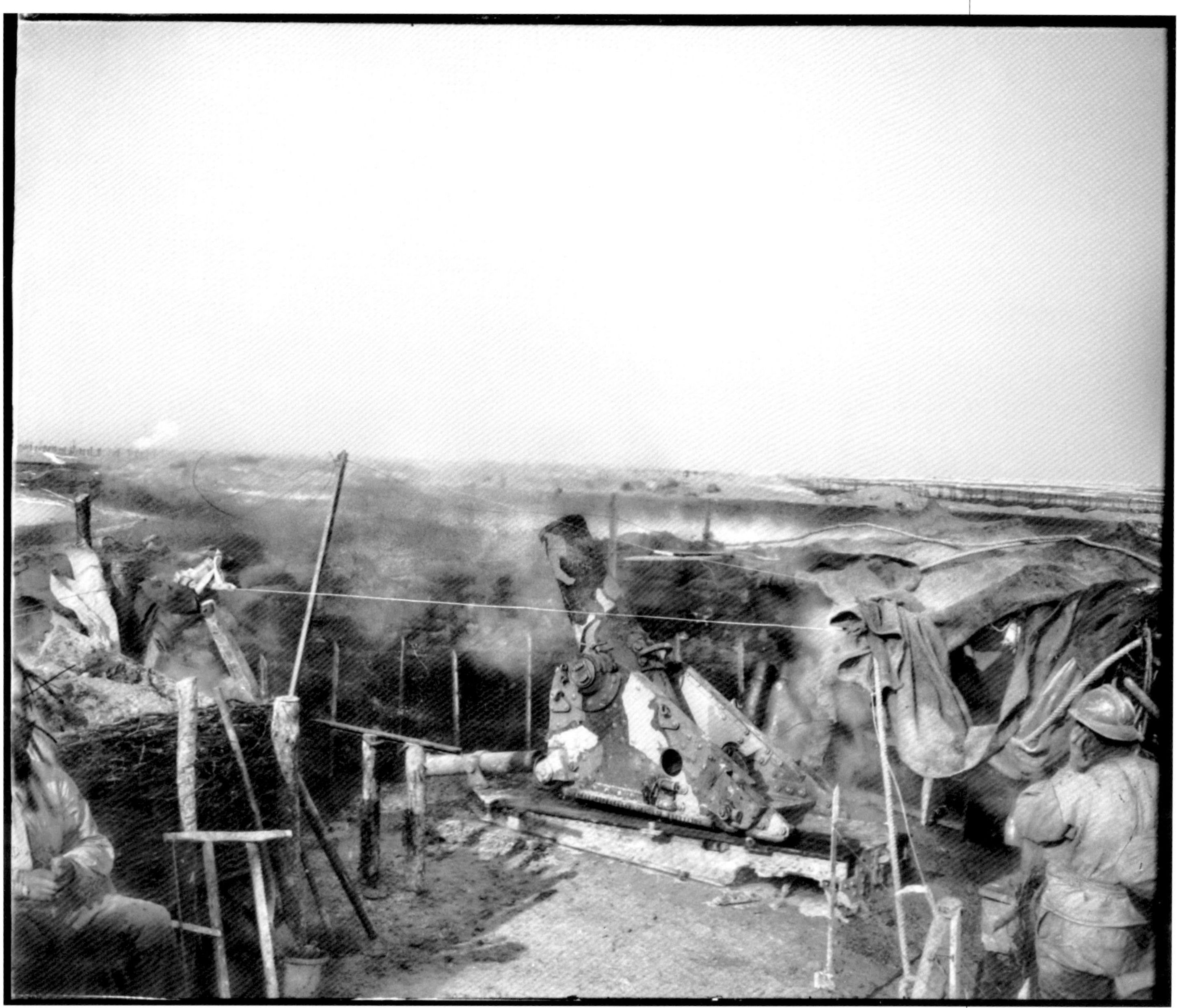

PHOT. 6
24/02/1916

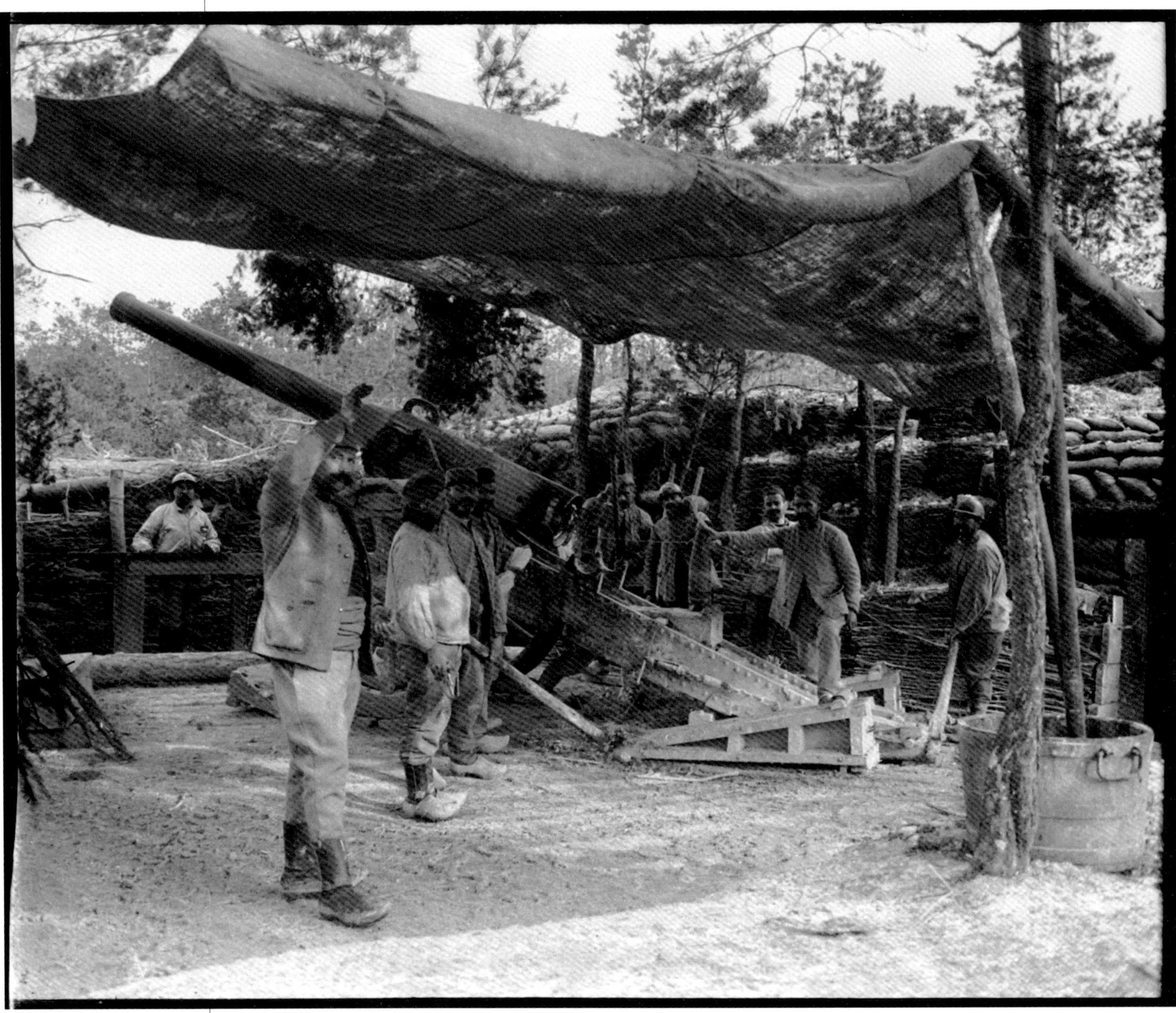

PHOT. 7
24/02/1916
155 mm 'Long' field gun

The De Bange 155 mm of 1877 was another old relic that the French hastily incorporated to the battle. It was so archaic that it did not have any recoil movement. They were progressively substituted from May 1916.

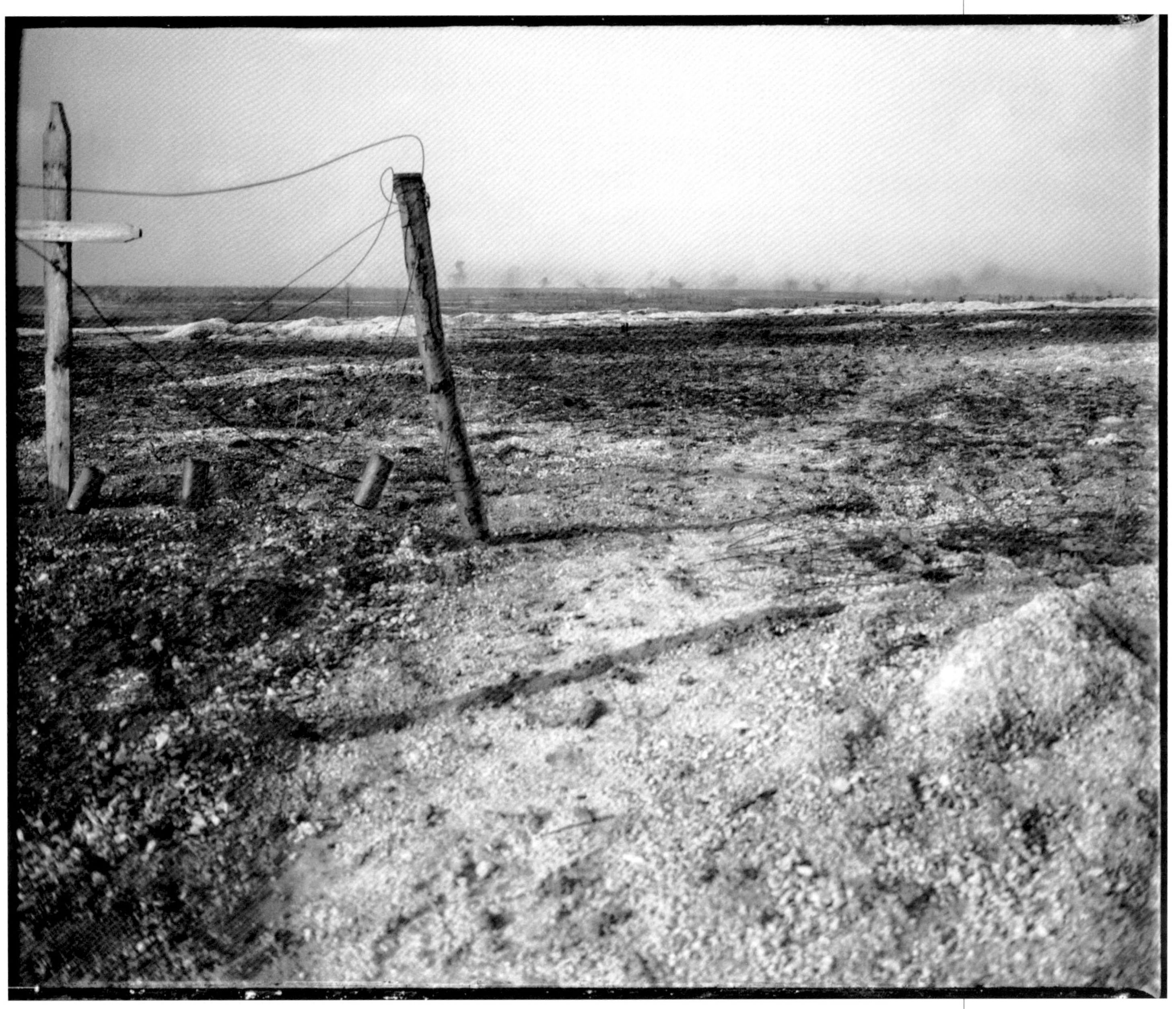

PHOT. 8
27/02/1916

Fire barrier in *No Man's land,* a term that was popularised by this war.

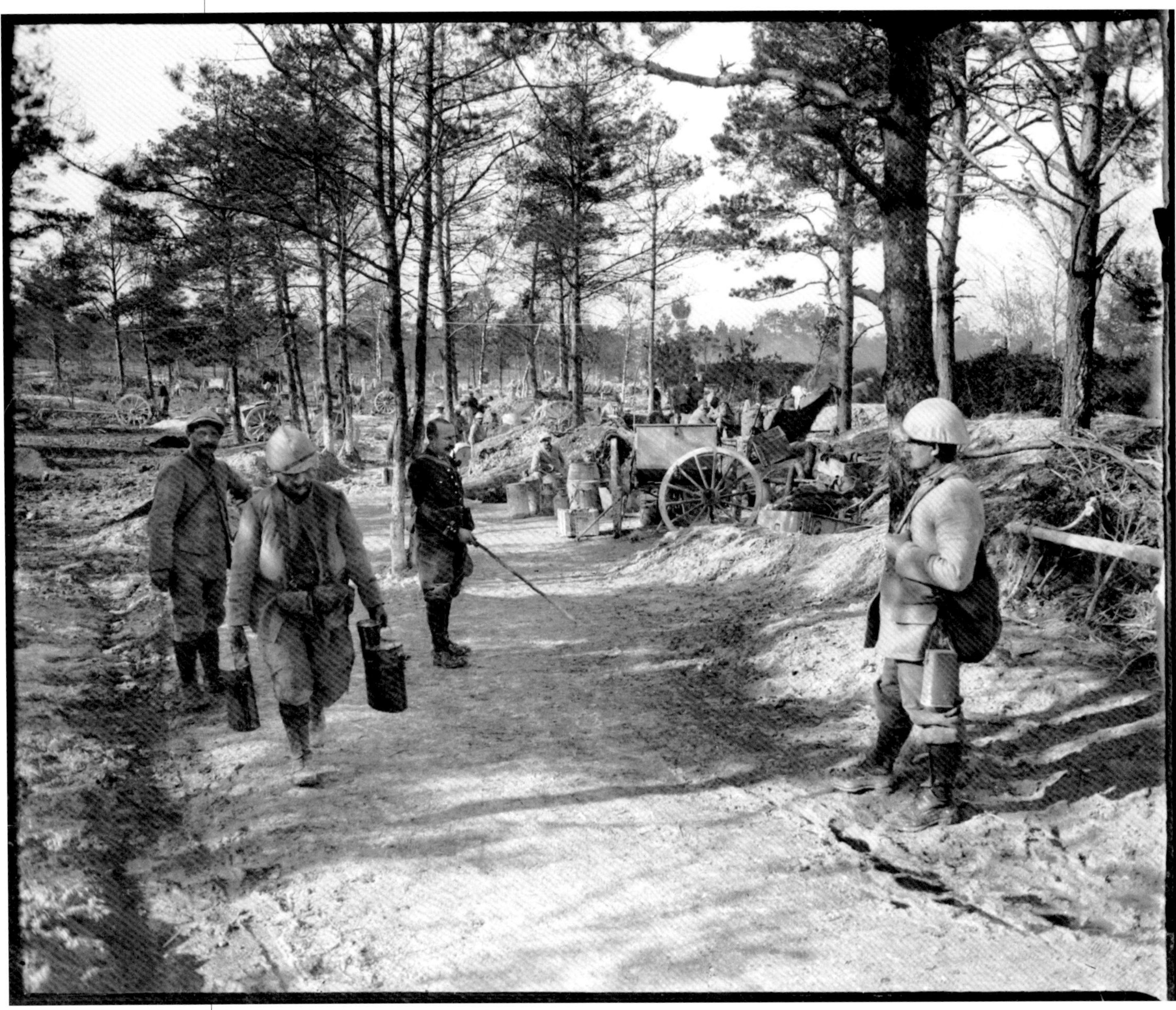

PHOT. 11
16/03/1916

Field kitchens in the rear-guard. The food arrived to the soldiers on the front line, in the best of cases, cold, and in the worst, never.

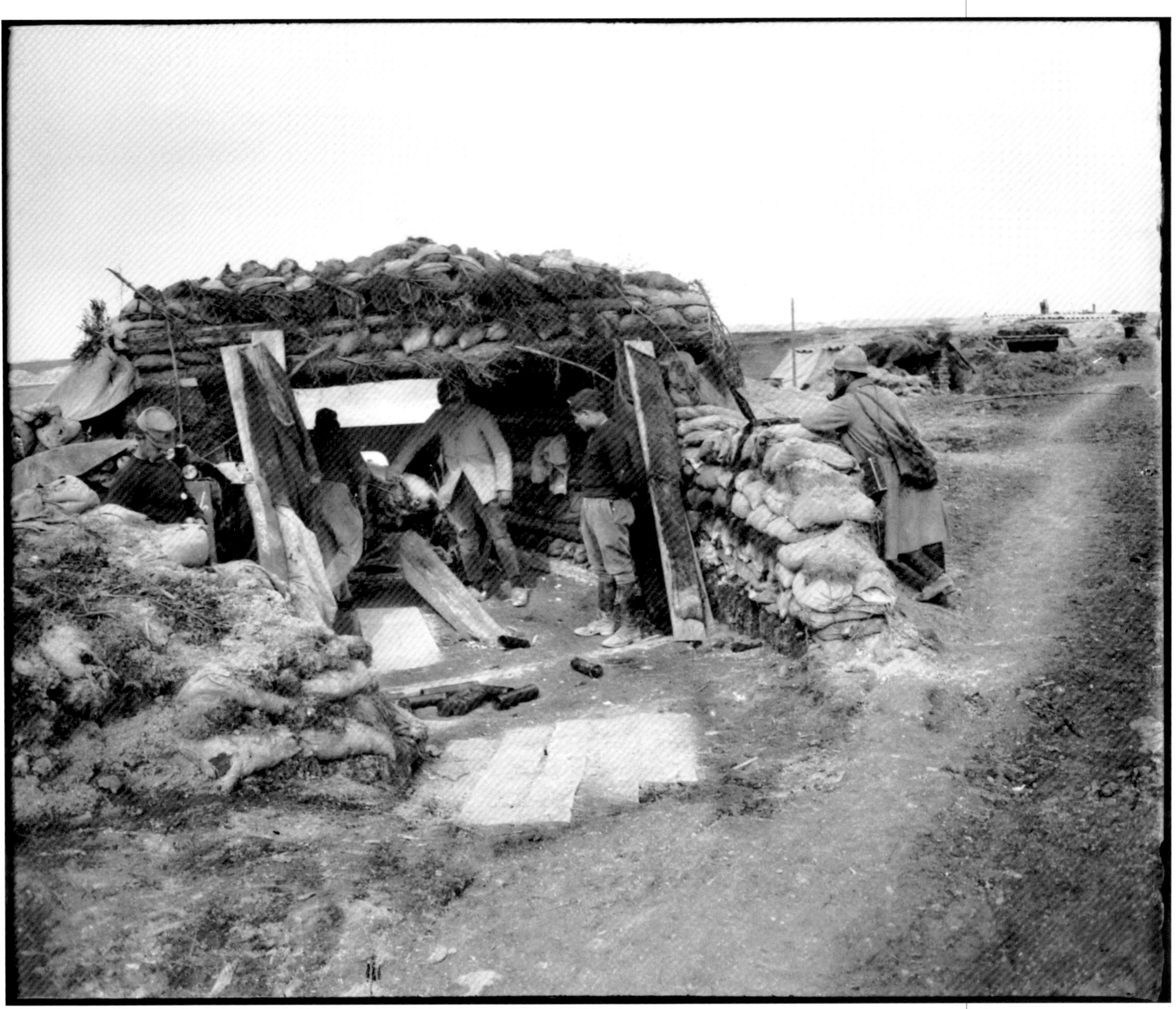

PHOT. 13
19/03/1916

The famous *soixante-quinze* of 75mm, pride of French engineering and base of its doctrine of *attaque à outrance* (attack at all costs), which was exposed as totally useless for this kind of war. An experienced gun crew was able to fire twenty rounds per minute.

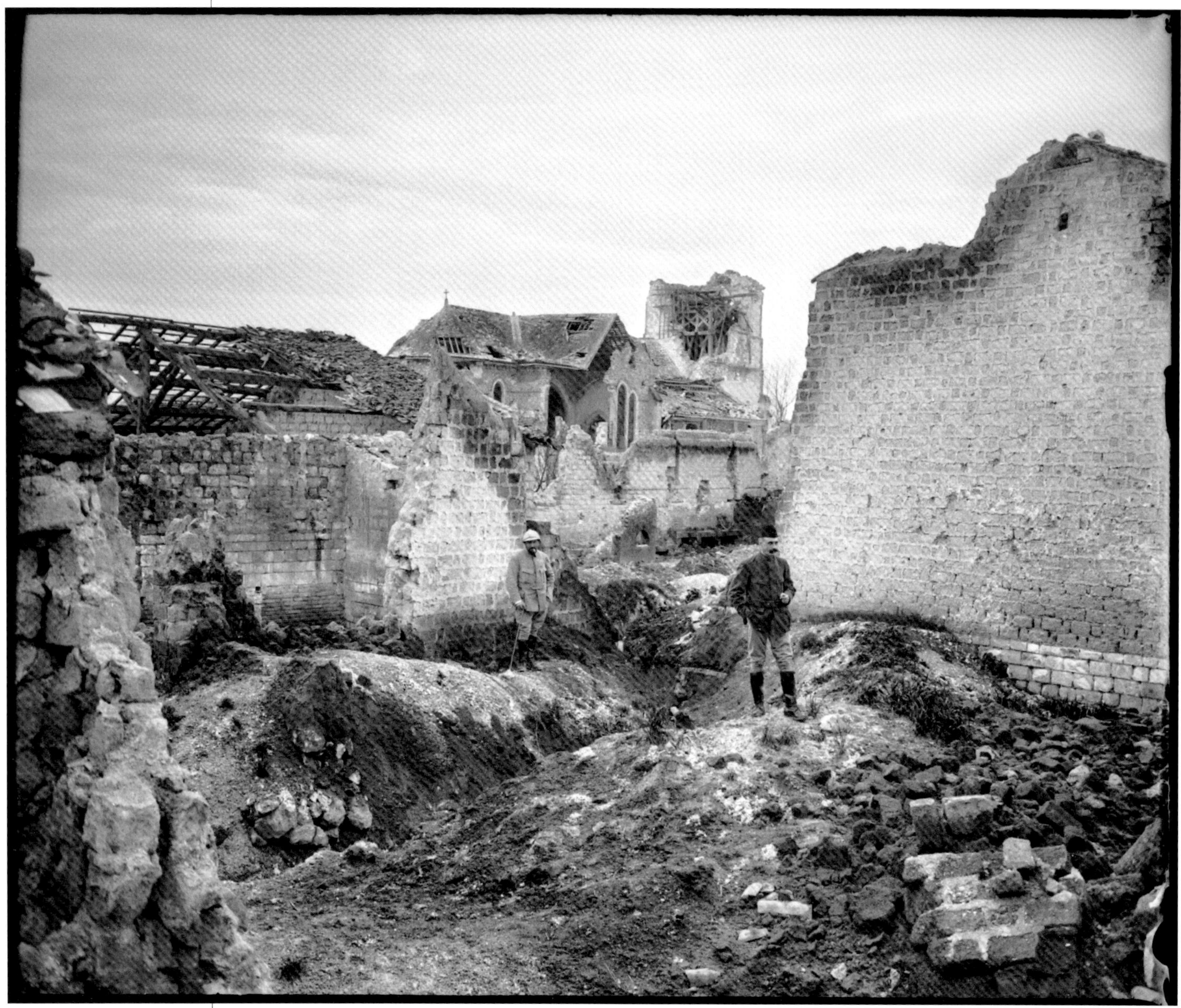

PHOT. 14
20/03/1916
Church of
Saint-Hilaire-le-Grand

This town barely six kilometres from Souain also knew the fury of artillery. Peytral could be the surname of one of the officers visiting the ruins.

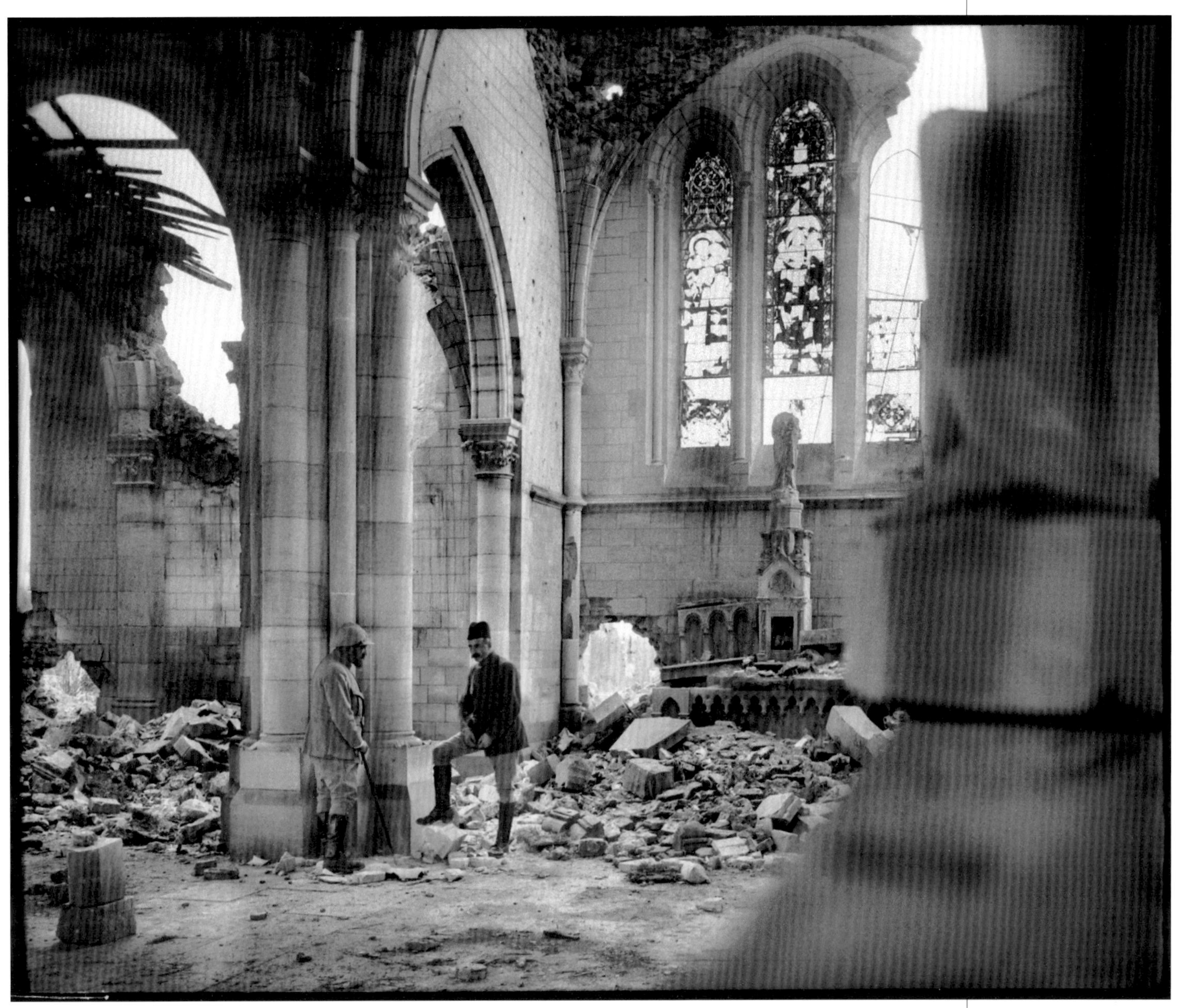

PHOT. 18
20/03/1916
Church of
Saint-Hilaire-le-Grand

The gothic church was reconstructed in 1925. By then the municipality barely numbered half of their 500 pre-war inhabitants.

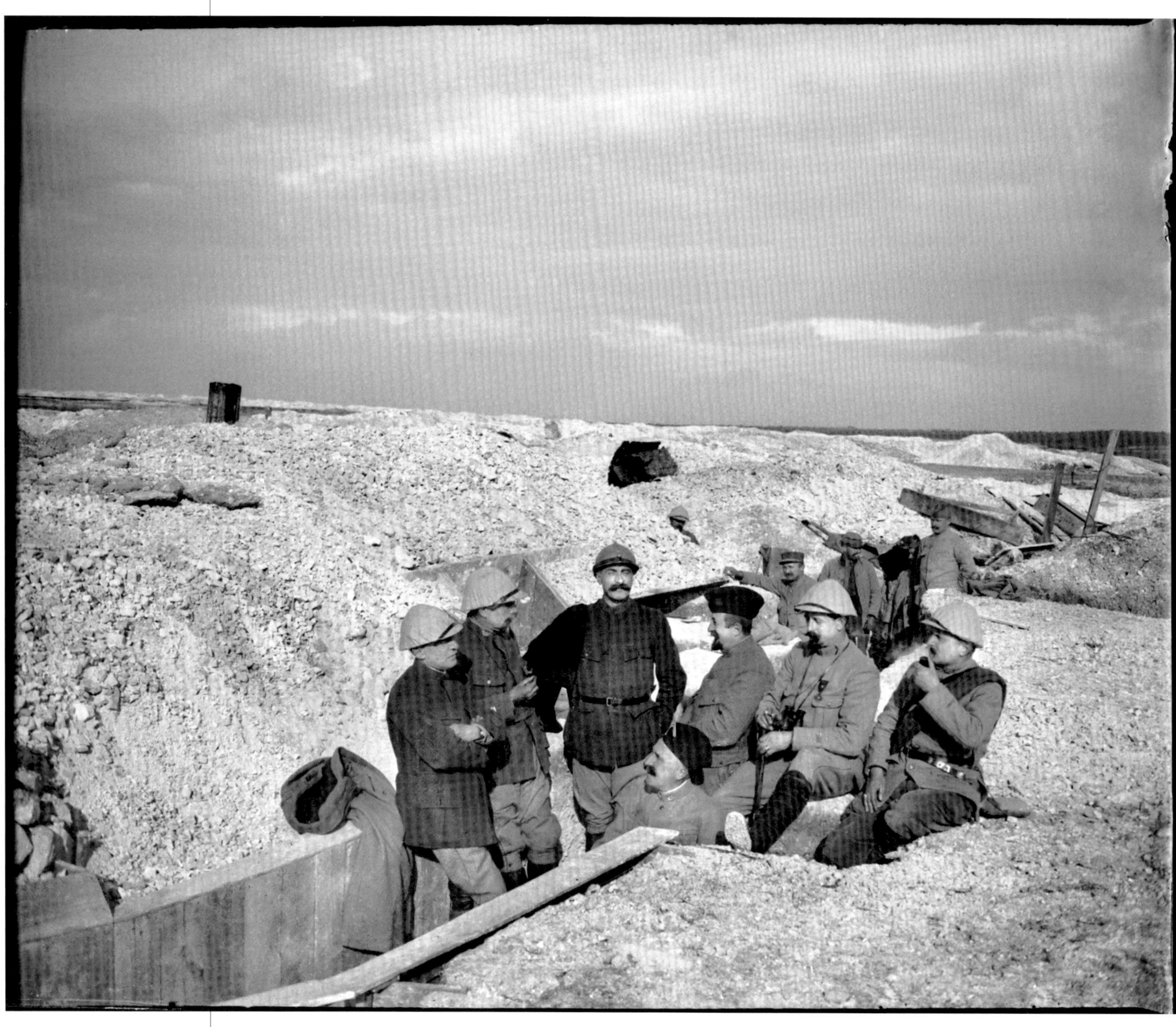

PHOT. 20
22/03/1916

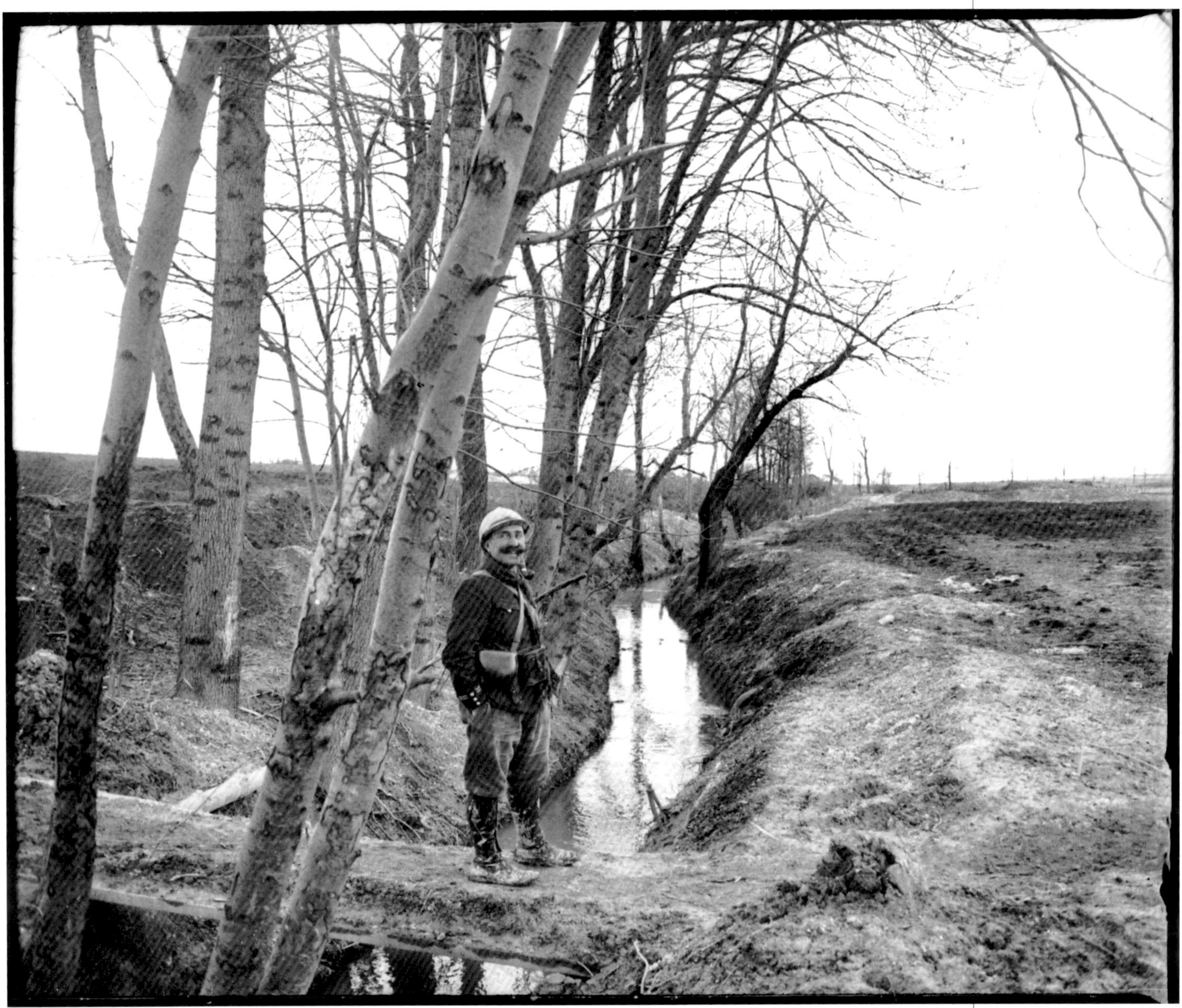

PHOT. 21
29/03/1916
The Ain

The Ain is a little river that runs between Souain and Saint-Hilaire-le-Gran. During the war it was the main stage for the first Champagne battles of 1914 and 1915. The smiling deputy with the pipe is a character that appears in many of the photographs of these months.

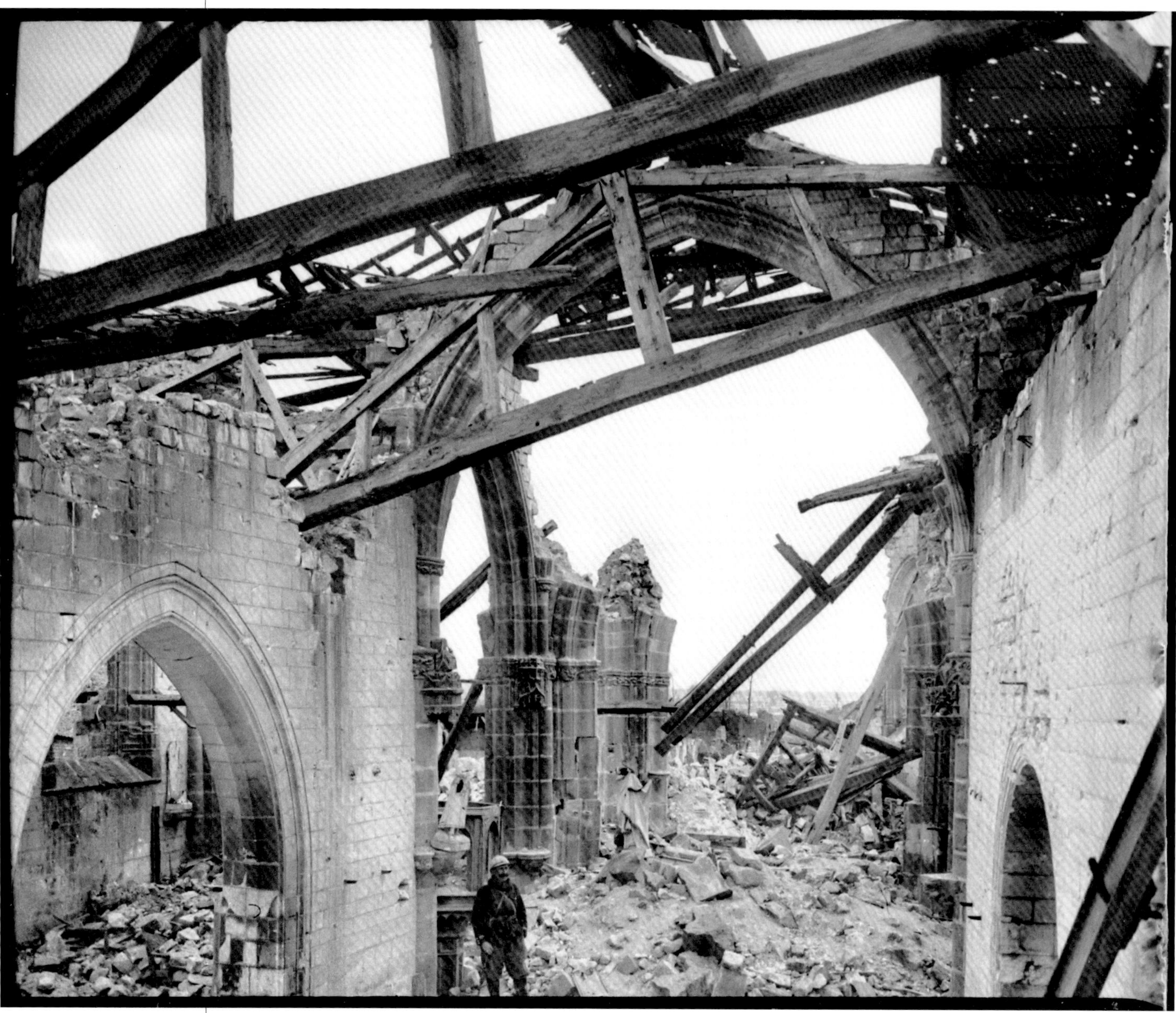

PHOT. 22
29/03/1916
Church of Souain

In this town one of the most shameful facts of French military history occurred. On March 10th 1915, the 21st company of the *336e Régiment d'Infanterie* rejected undertaking a suicidal bayonet attack, so the General in command, Réveihac, ordered the shelling of his own lines. Hs own artillery refused. Nonetheless he executed four corporals chosen randomly as an example.

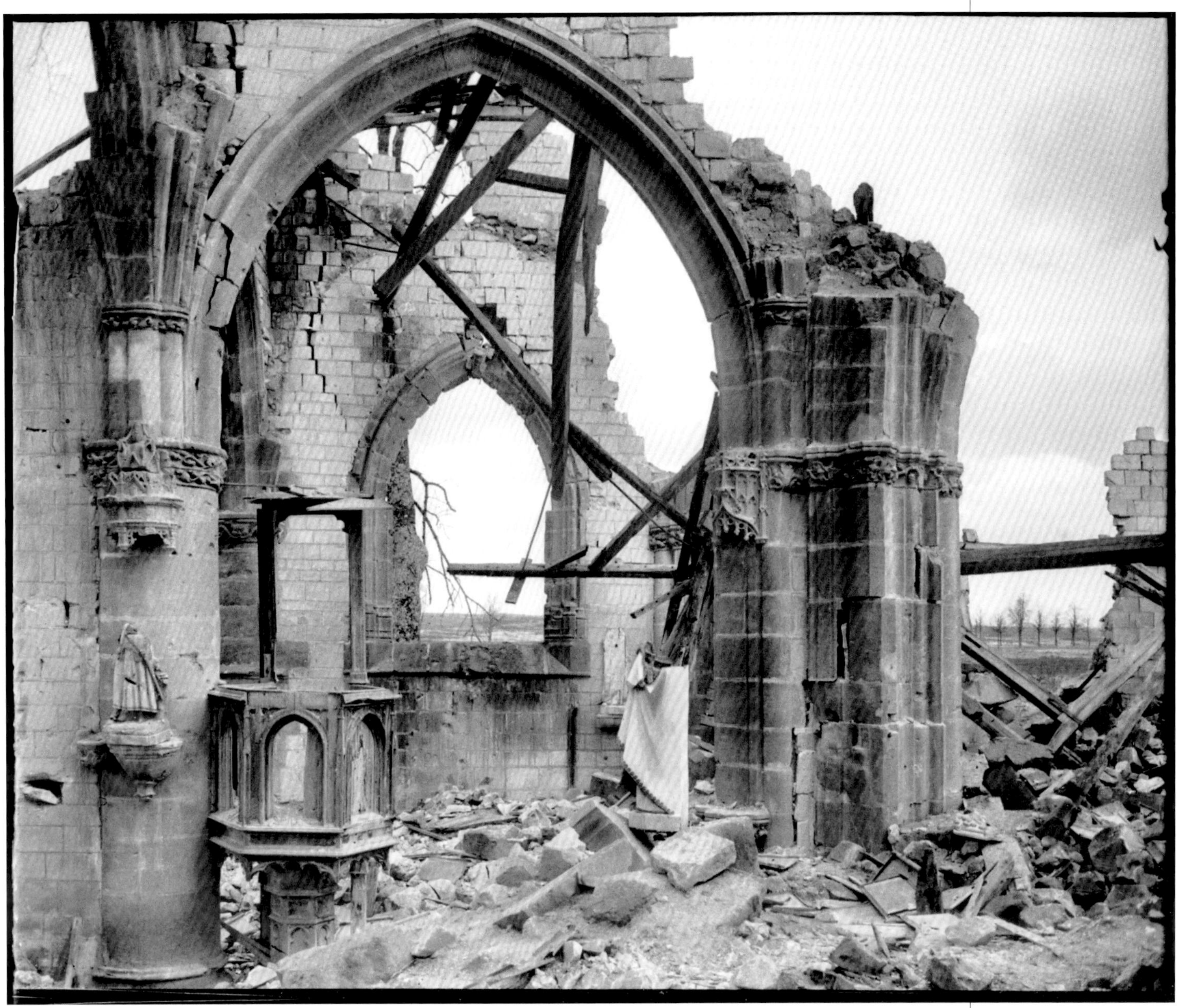

PHOT. 23
29/03/1916

Another perspective of the same church. The execution of the Souain Corporals Théophile Maupas, Louis Lefoulon, Louis Girard and Lucien Lechat, caused deep indignation in French society and served as inspiration for the novel and film *Paths of Glory*.

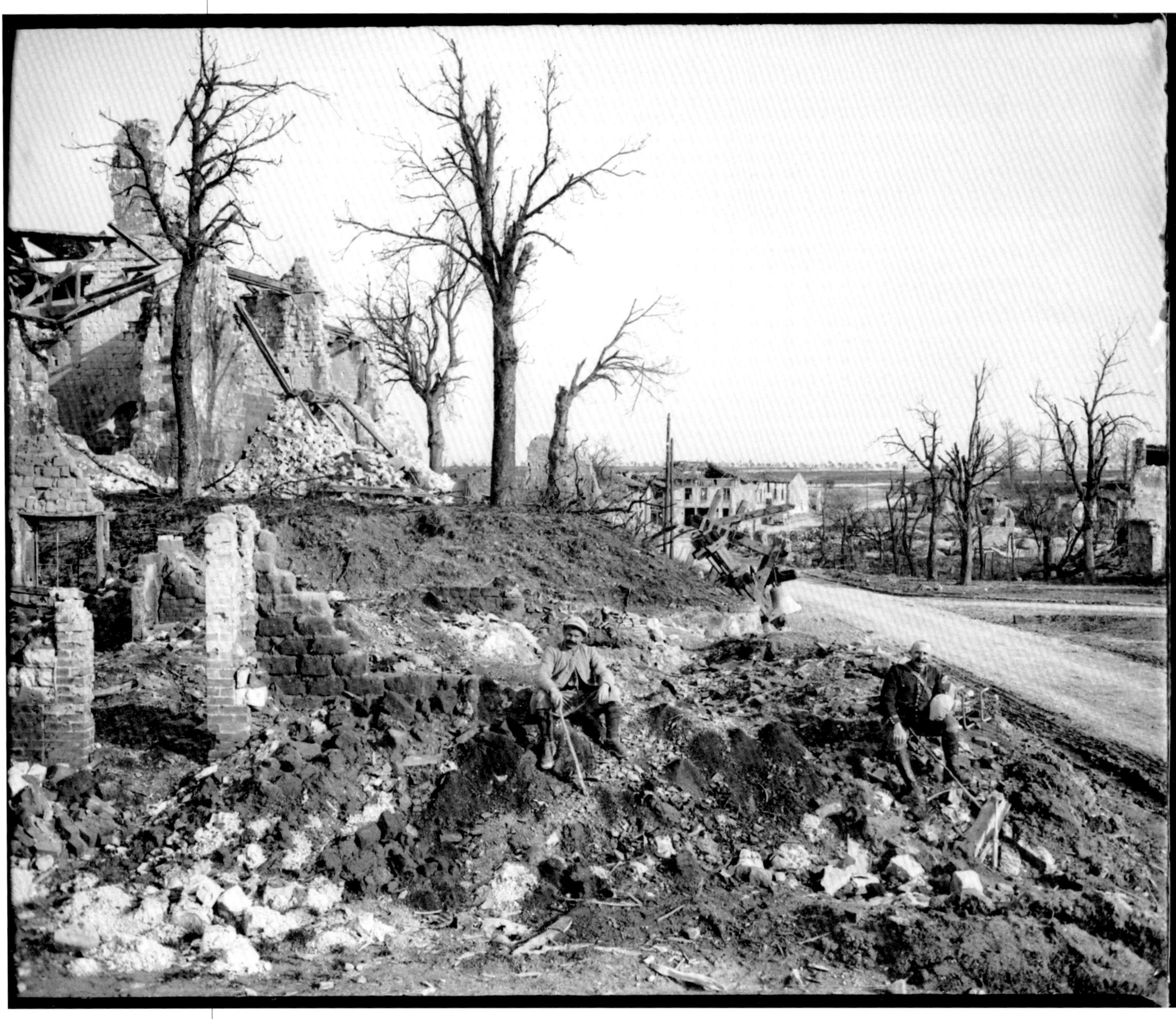

PHOT. 24
30/03/1916

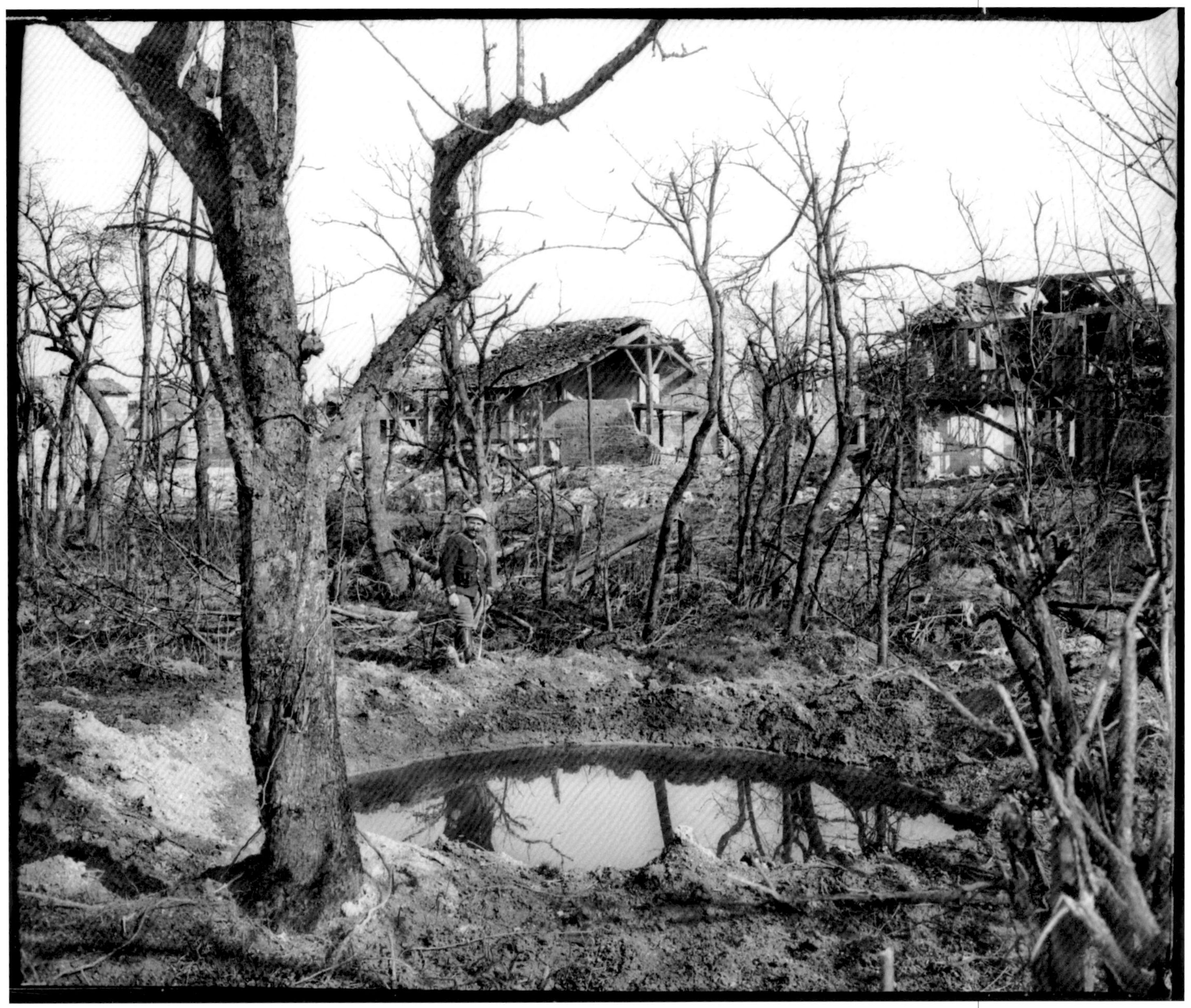

PHOT. 25
30/03/1916

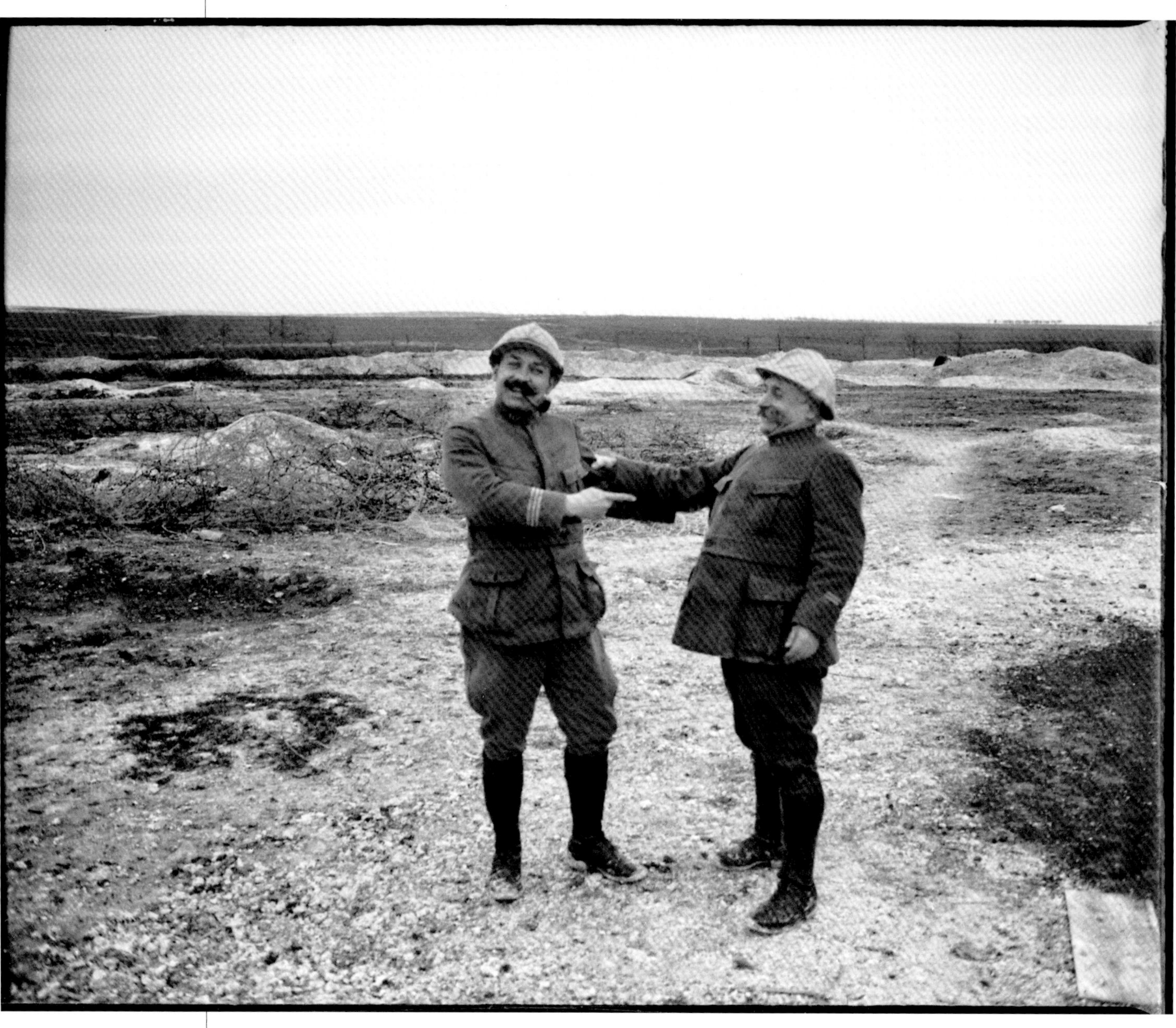

PHOT. 28
05/04/1916

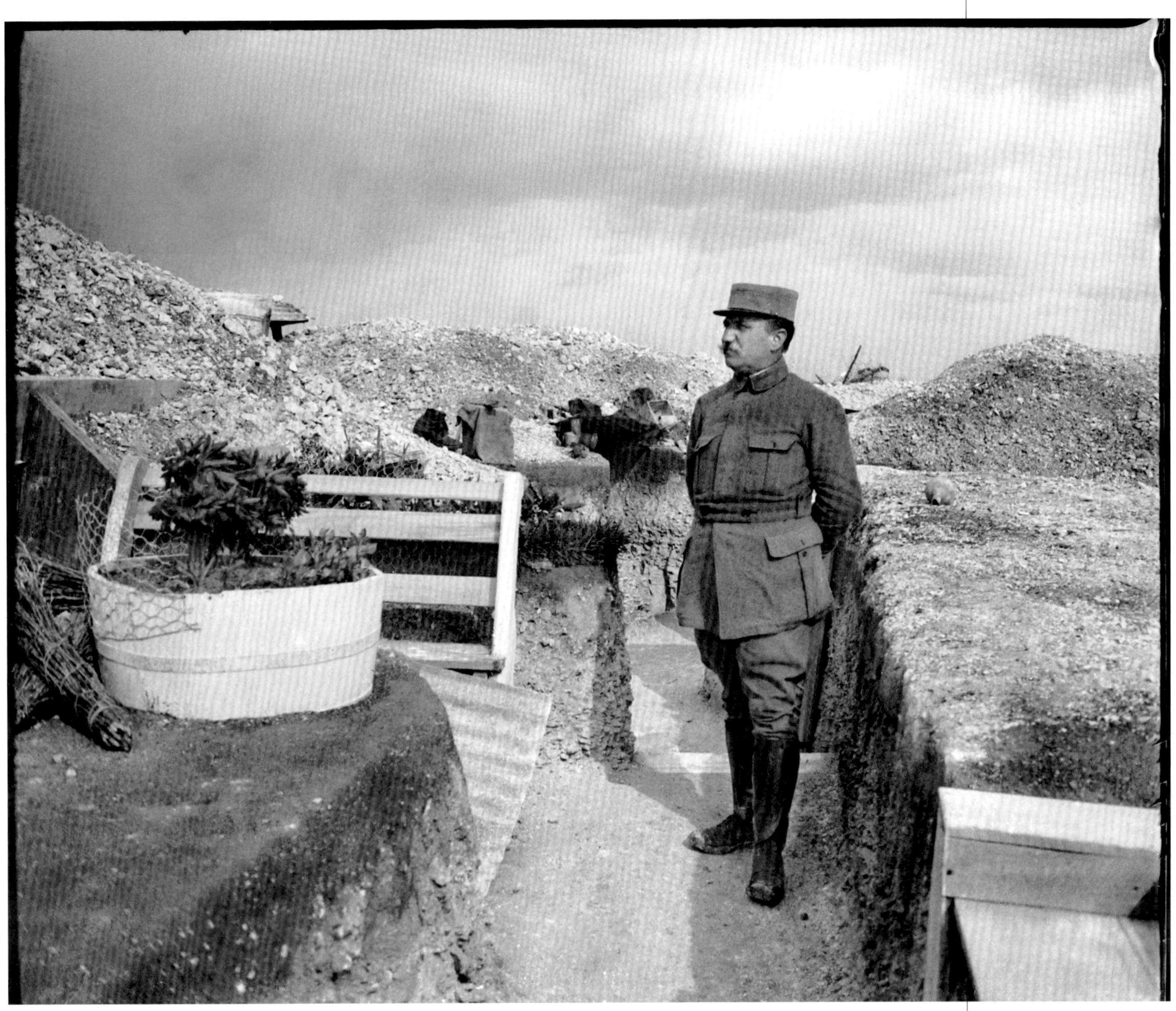

PHOT. 29
13/04/1916

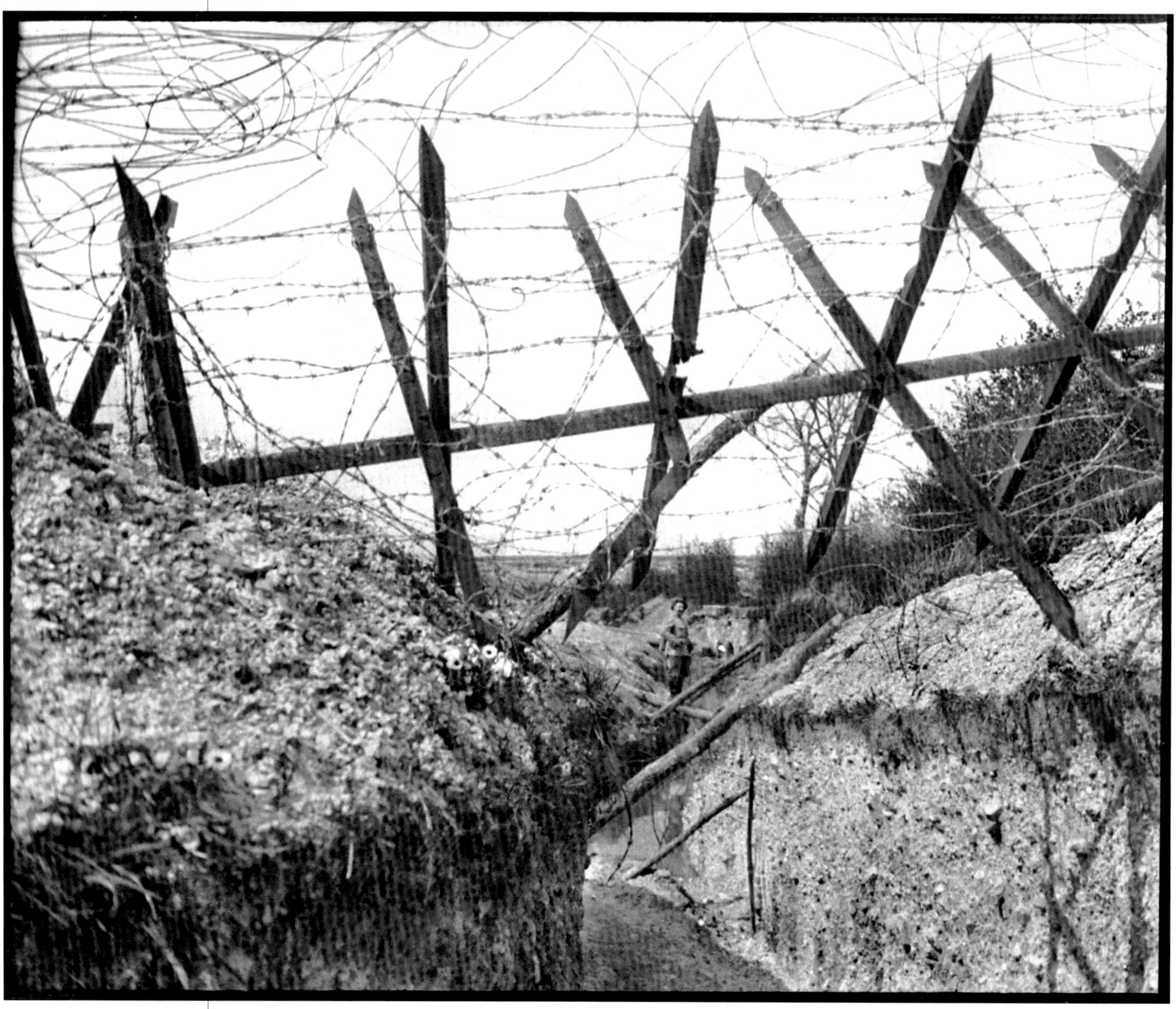

PHOT. 33
23/04/1916

The trench system was extended in several lines (first, support and reserve, usually) lengthening over the terrain for several kilometres.

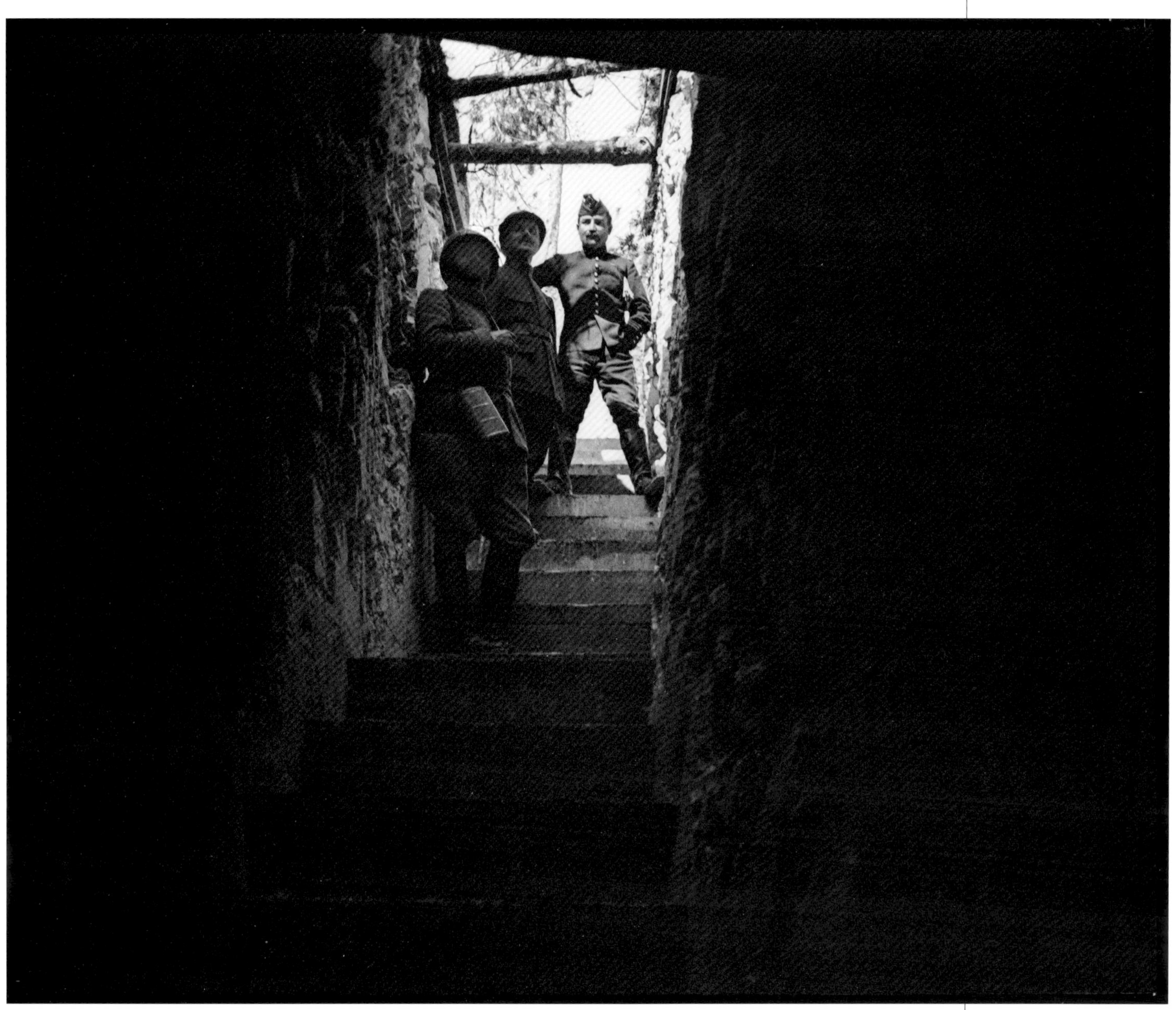

PHOT. 34
17/05/1916

This deep concrete shelter was an exception at the French lines. Its positions were famous for being the most uncomfortable and unhealthy.

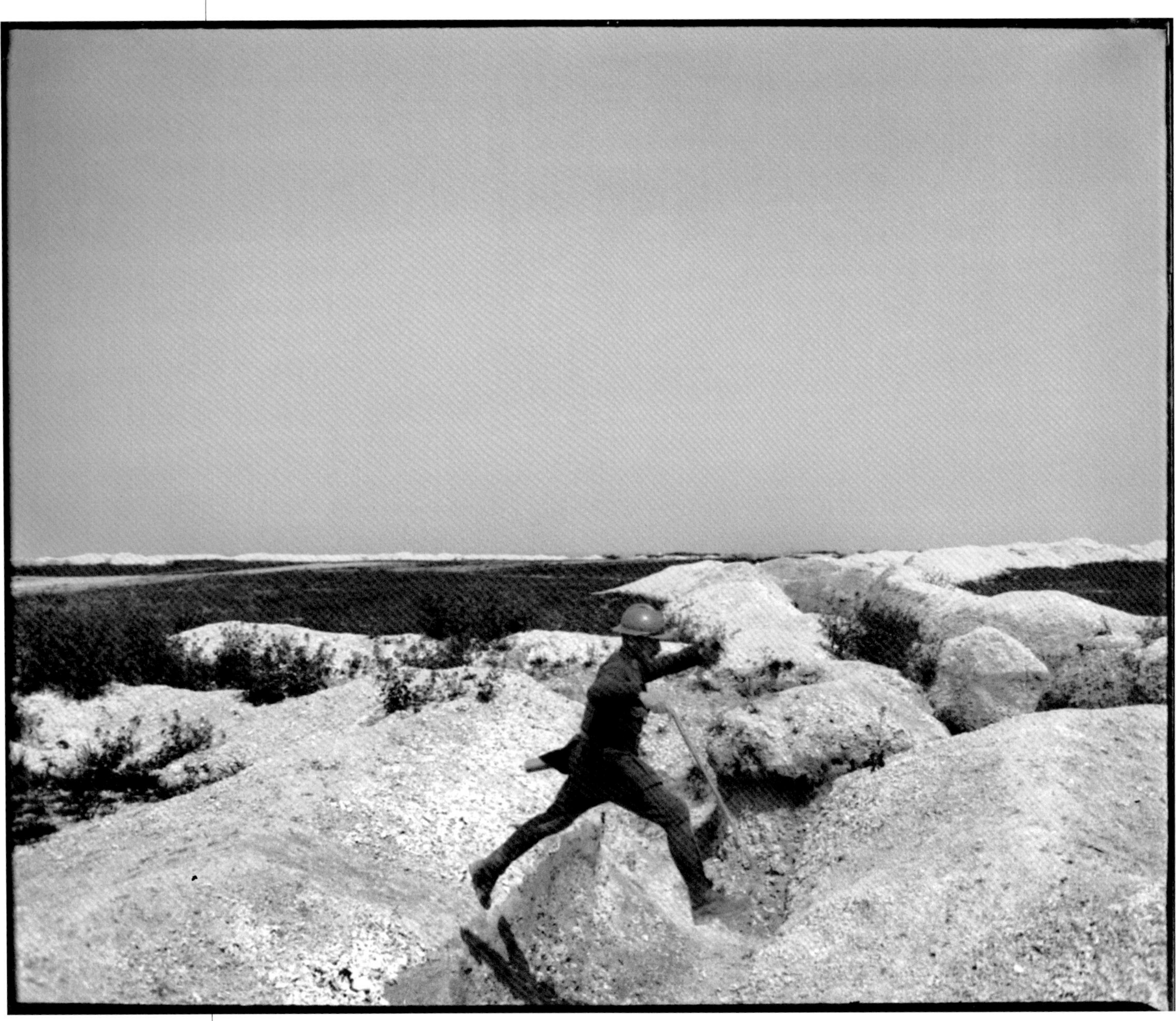

PHOT. 35
17/05/1916

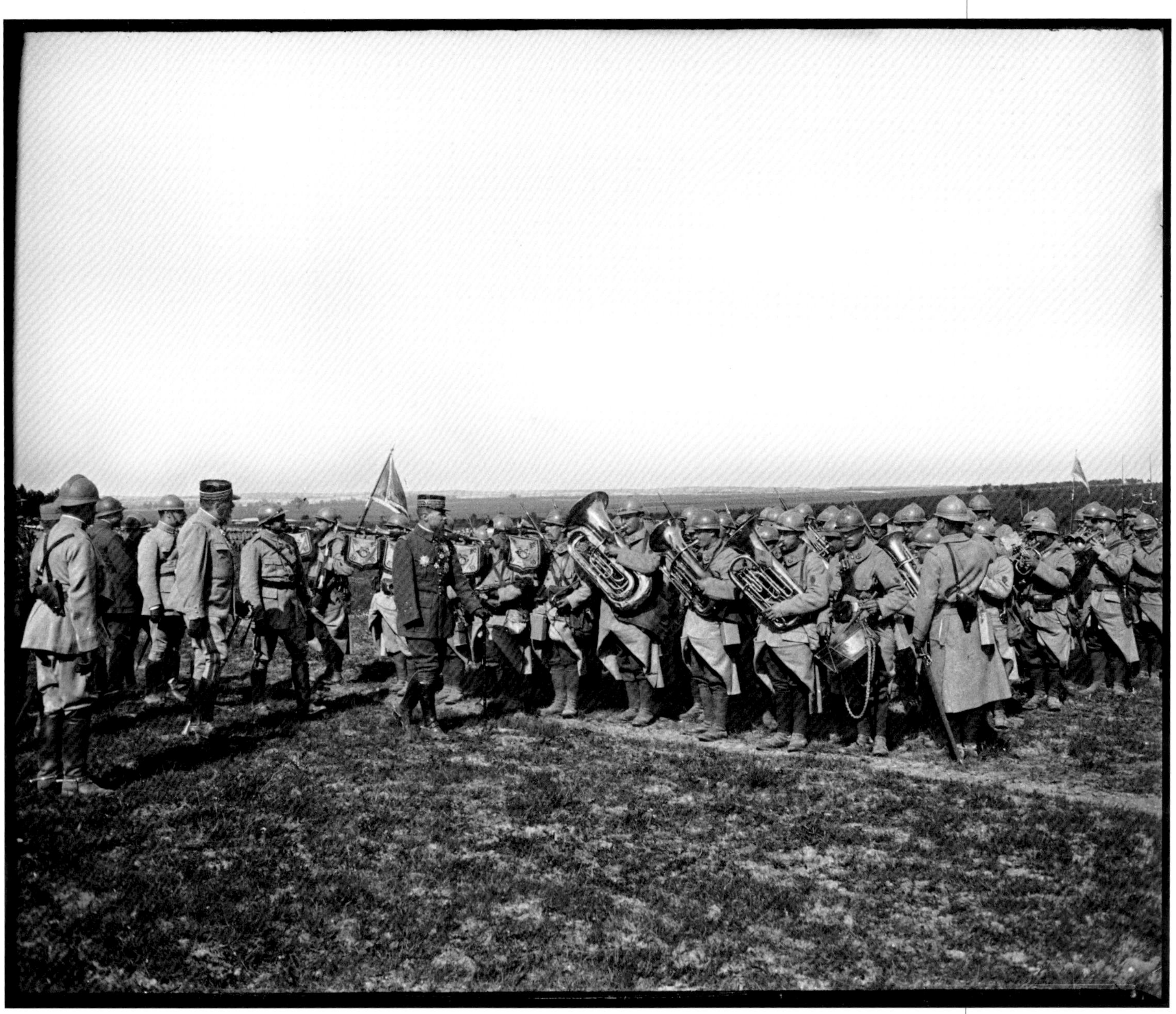

PHOT. 36
19/05/1916

The music band belongs to the *10e Bataillon de Chasseurs à Pied* (hunters by foot).

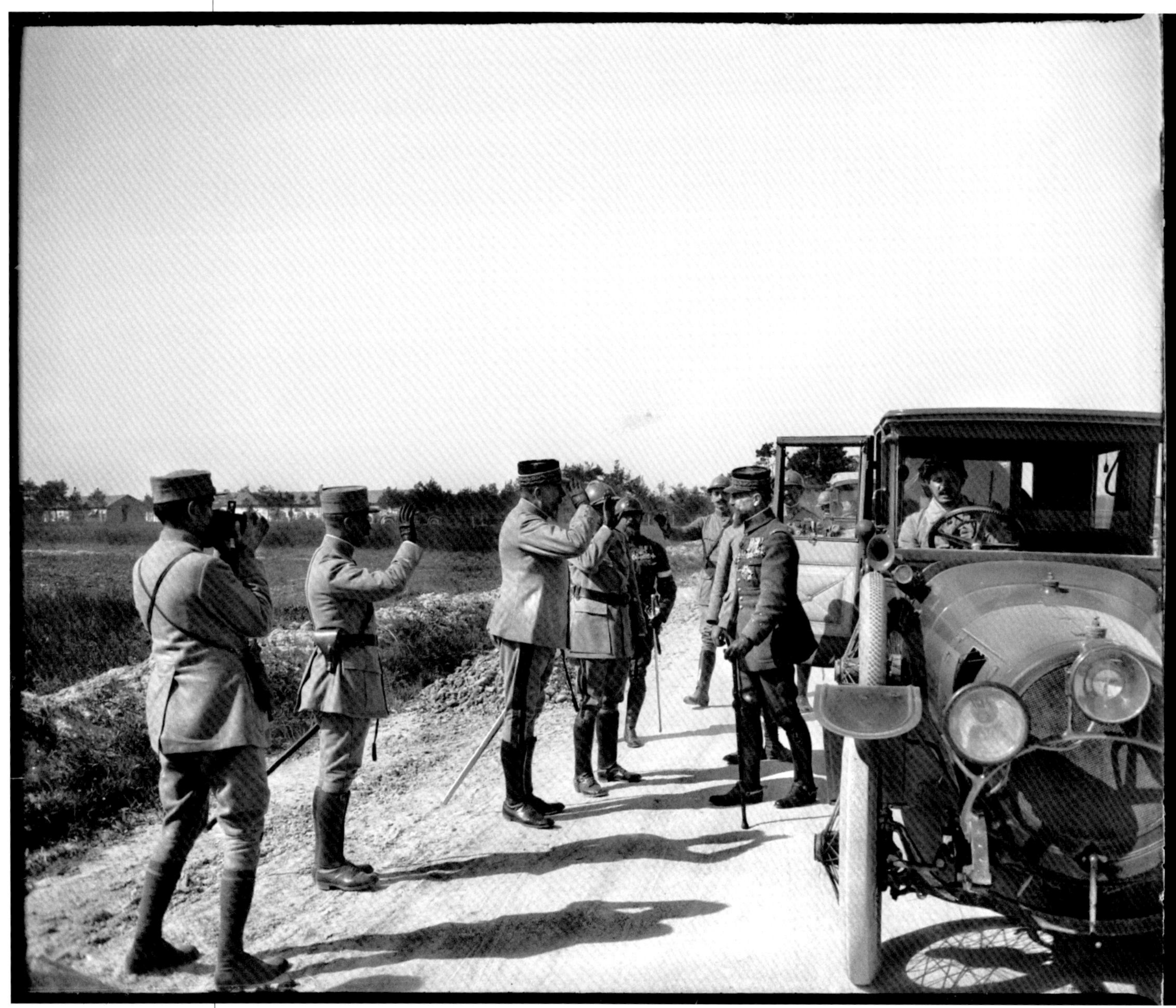

PHOT. 37
19/05/1916

General Paulinier salutes General Gouraud during his visit to the *6e* and *21e Corps d'Armée* on May 19th 1916. Marie-Jean-Auguste Paulinier (1861–1927) was by then Commander of the 6e. Givord's camera was very similar to the one used by the man on the left.

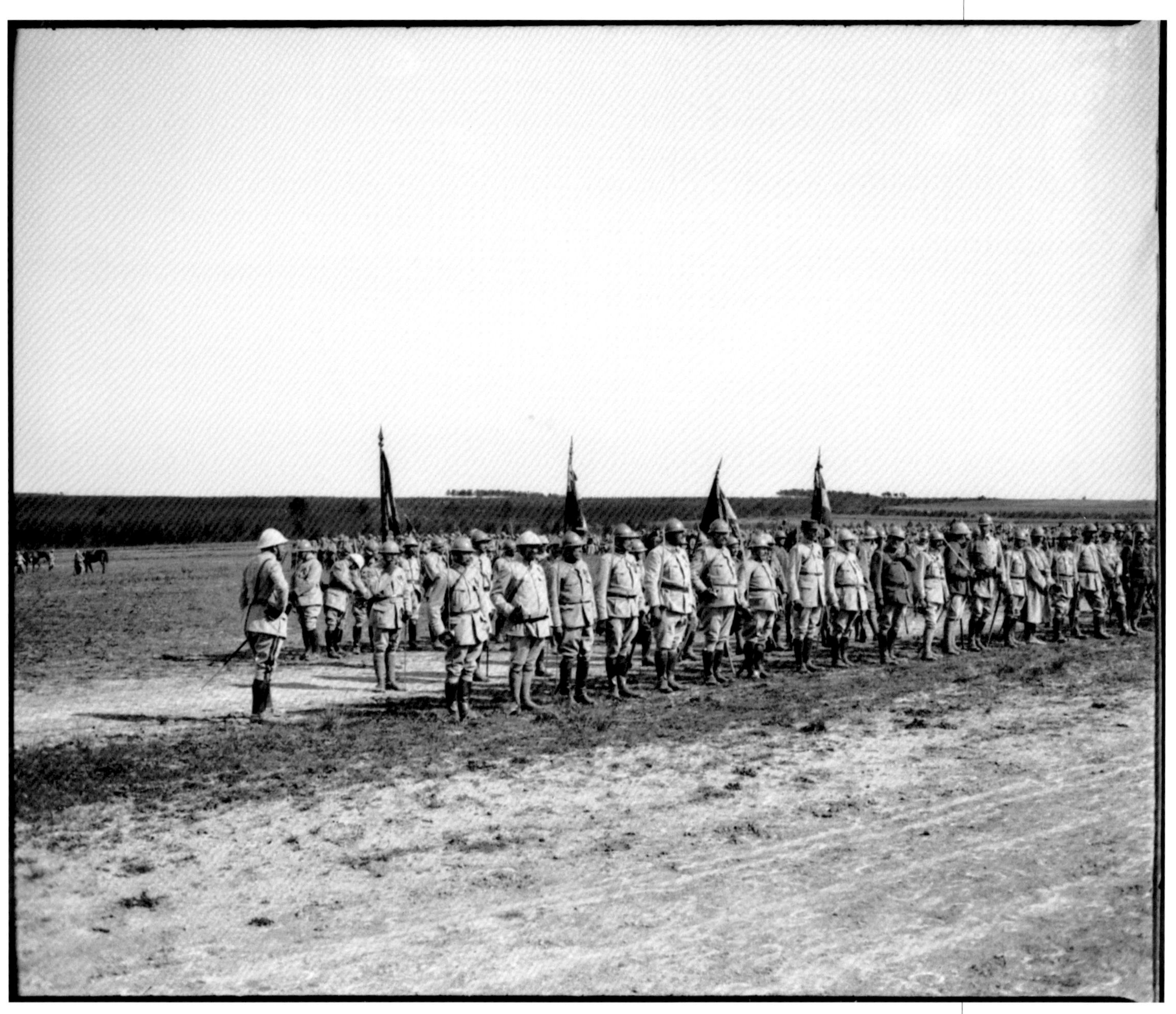

PHOT. 38
19/05/1916

Officers waiting General Gouraud's arrival. The parade was carried out two and a half kilometres south of Suippes station, very near to Souain.

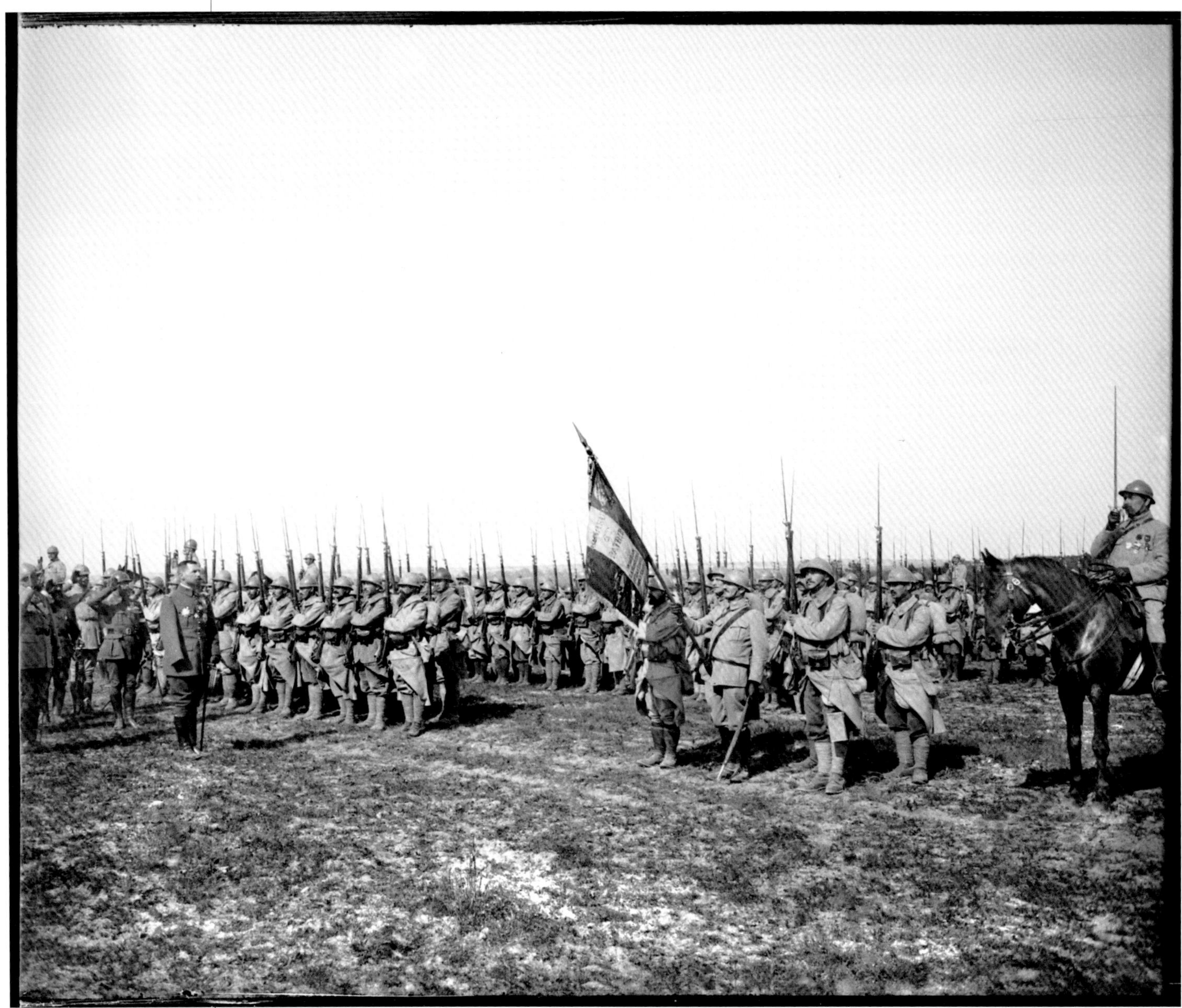

PHOT. 39

19/05/1916

Presentation of the flag to General Gouraud. Henri Joseph Eugène Gouraud (1867–1946) was a famous French General, a veteran of African campaigns, who commanded the *4e Armée* posted to Champagne. He lost his right arm the year before at Gallipoli.

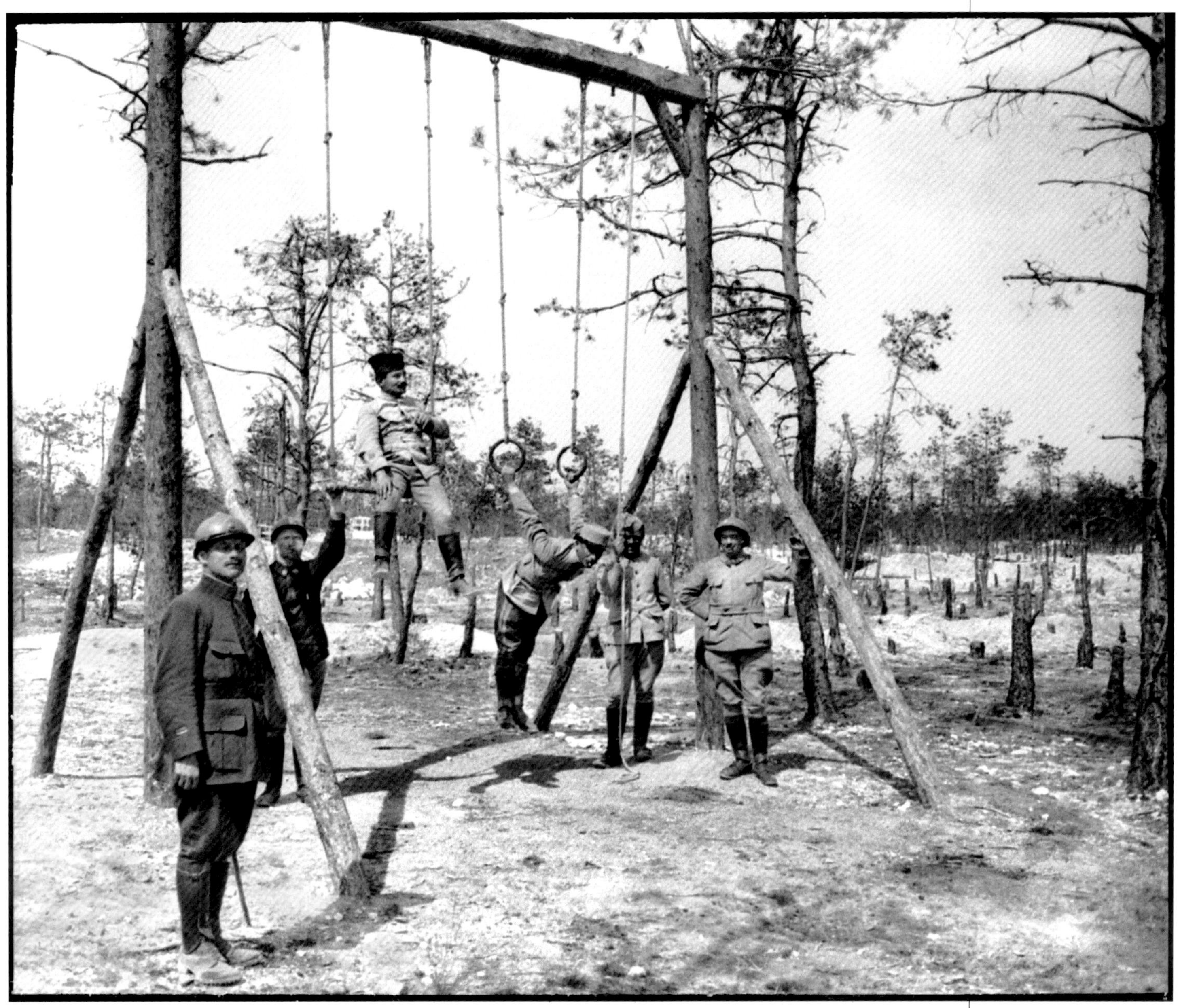

PHOT. 43
22/05/1916

The French soldier in 1914 had an attractive uniform which included a blue combat jacket with red trousers and military cap. This patriotic outfit which was highly visible revealed itself to be very dangerous in modern warfare, hence it was substituted with the *bleu horizon*. This strange option was a result of the determination in maintaining the tricolour essence with a mix of blue (60%), red (30%) and white (10%). After official approval it was discovered that the international production of red colourant was concentrated in Germany, resulting in combining blue and white. This mixture was not easy to imitate, but unfortunately the bad quality of colourants caused the uniform to discolour quickly, acquiring a similar tone to the mud of Artois and Champagne.

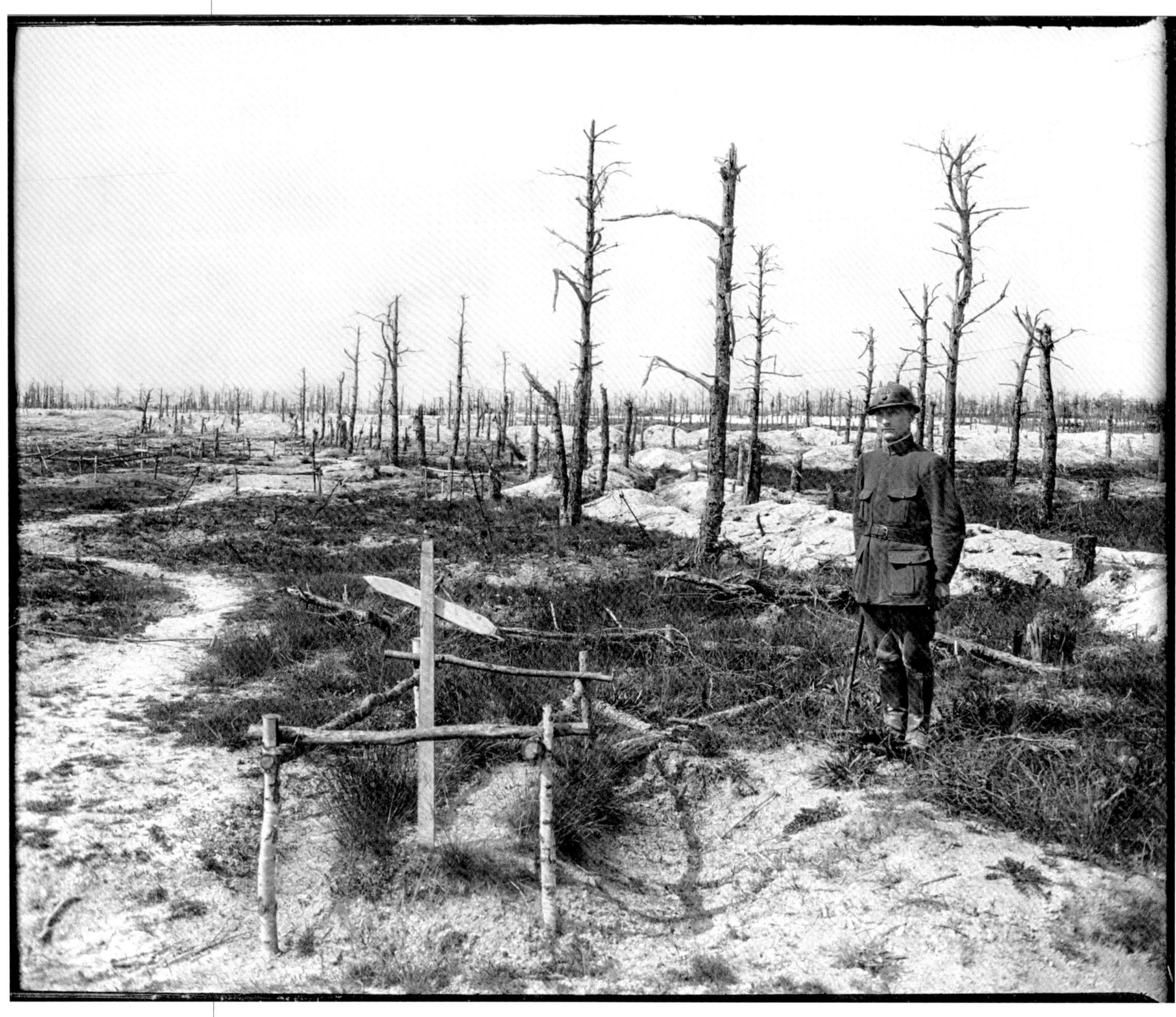

PHOT. 44
22/05/1916

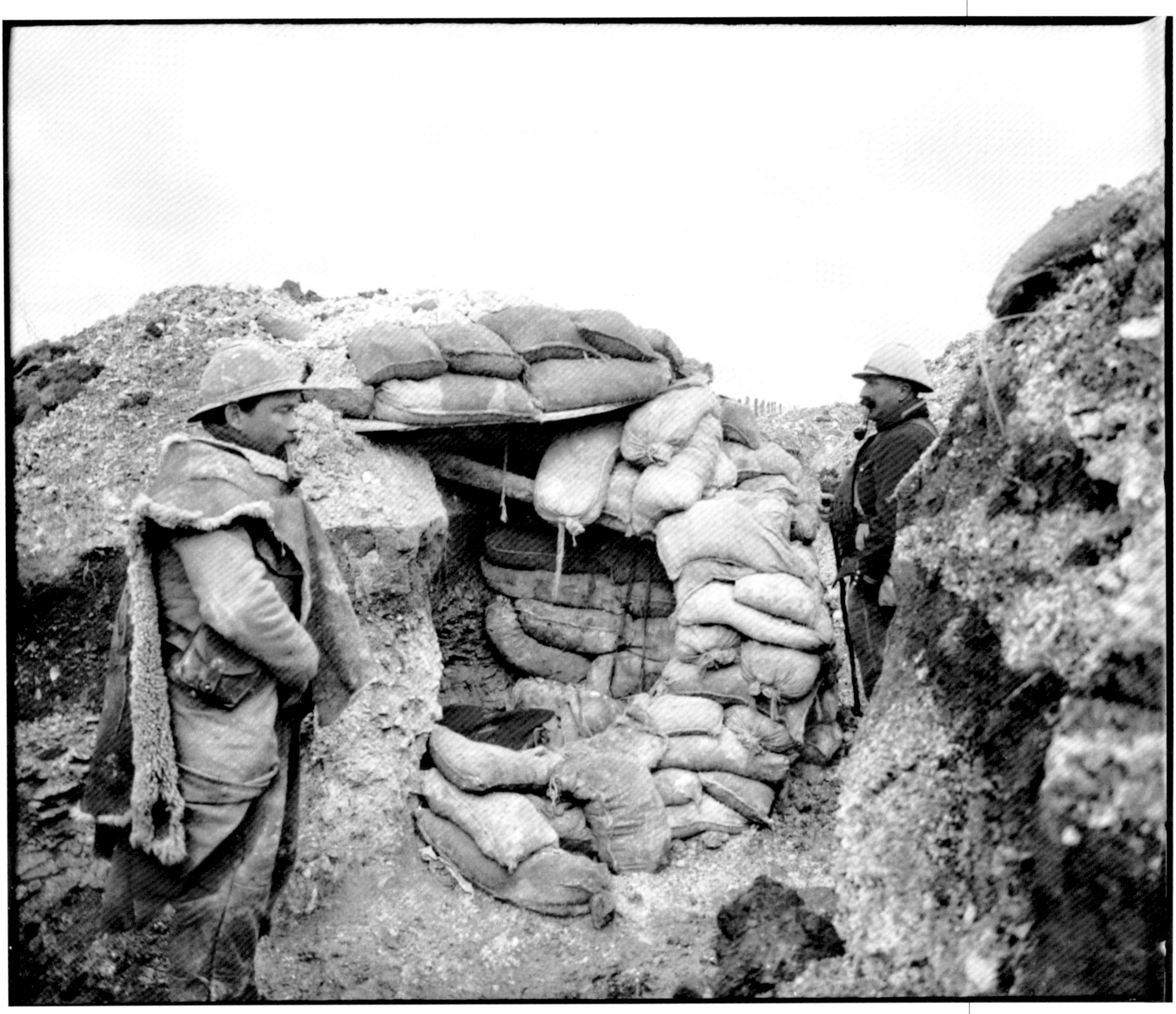

PHOT. 51
29/09/1916

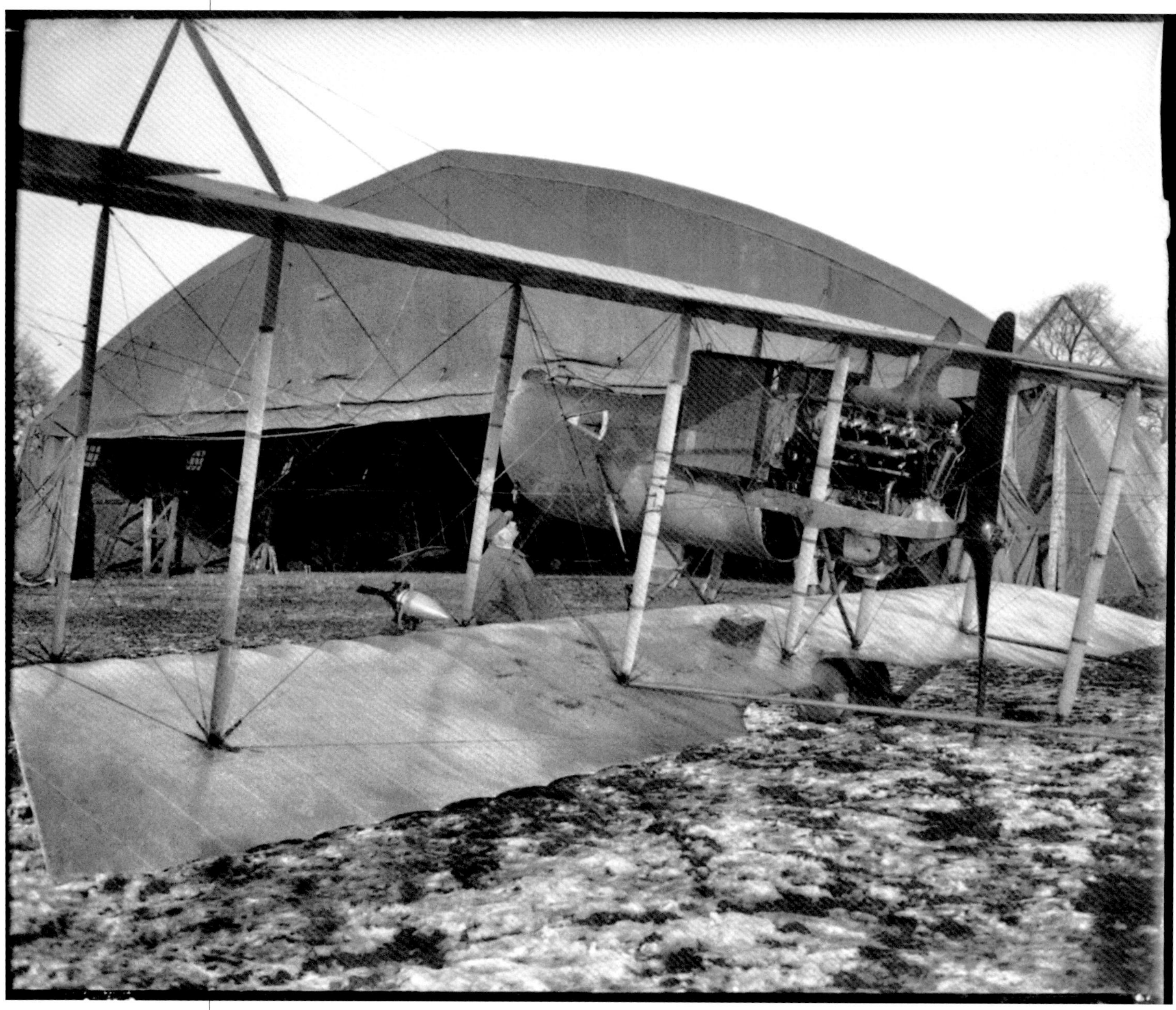

PHOT. 56

13/02/1917

In early 1917, Givord is posted between Amiens and Soissons. Here we see a Farman F40 for reconnaissance belonging to the *escadrille* F54 opposite to a hangar on the airfield of Montididier. Probably the most important mission undertaken by the aviation squadrons was reconnaissance, equipped with special cameras. In the last year of war, some French units produced up to 10,000 photographic plates per night.

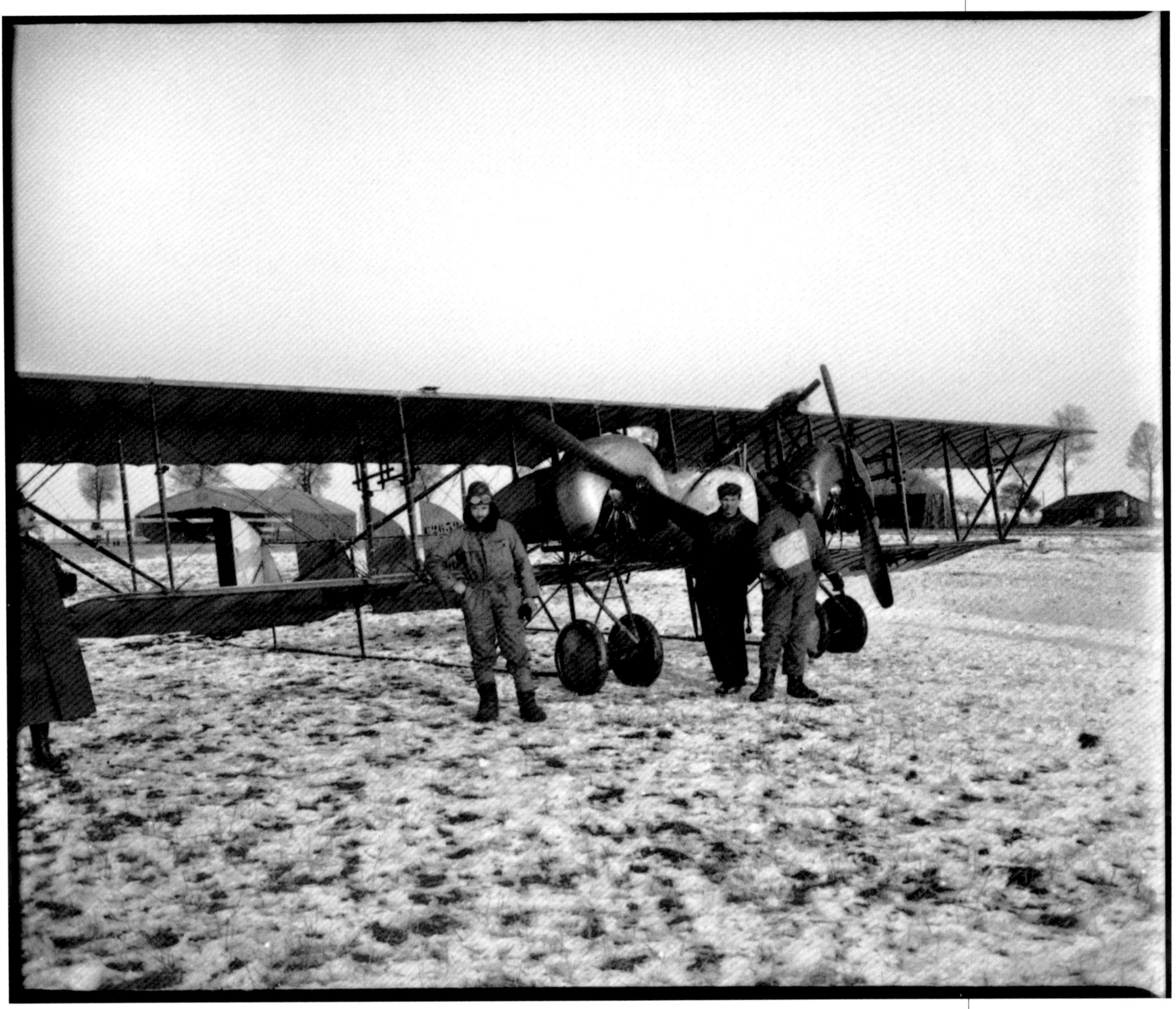

PHOT. 57
13/02/1917

Pilots with flight clothing on pose in front of a Caudron G.4 of the *escadrille C28 de la Aéronautique Militaire*. At that time the unit was posted to the *14e Corps d'armée* which was undertaking night bombing missions, hence it had used this aerodrome for the first time just two days before. This plane with the numbers 2639 joined the squadron on January 27th. At the back we can see the plane and the hangar from the last photograph.

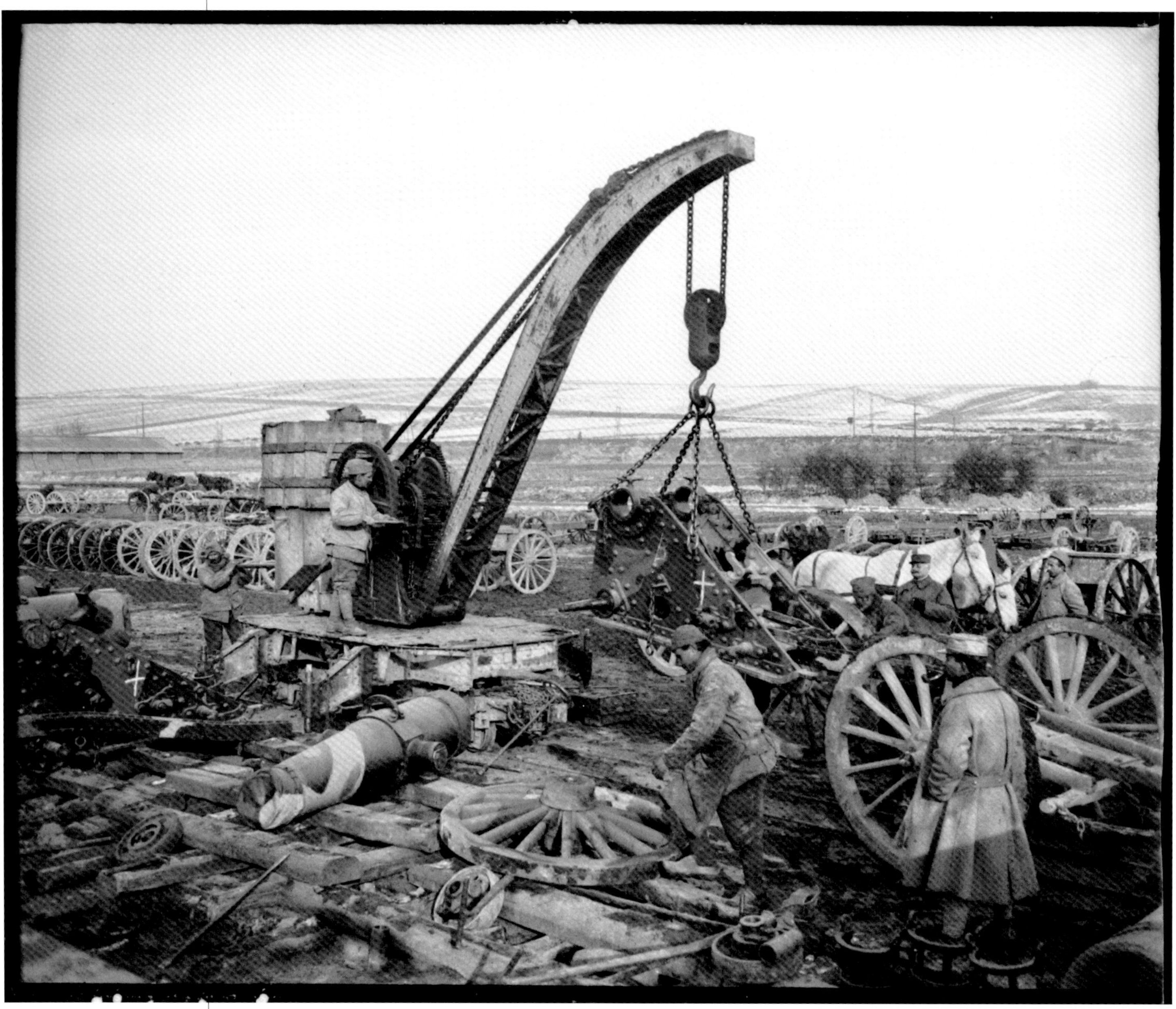

PHOT. 58
13/02/1917
Artillery deposit in Moreuil

The assembly and disassembly process to transport heavy artillery pieces was long and complicated. Each of the cannons weighed more than four tons.

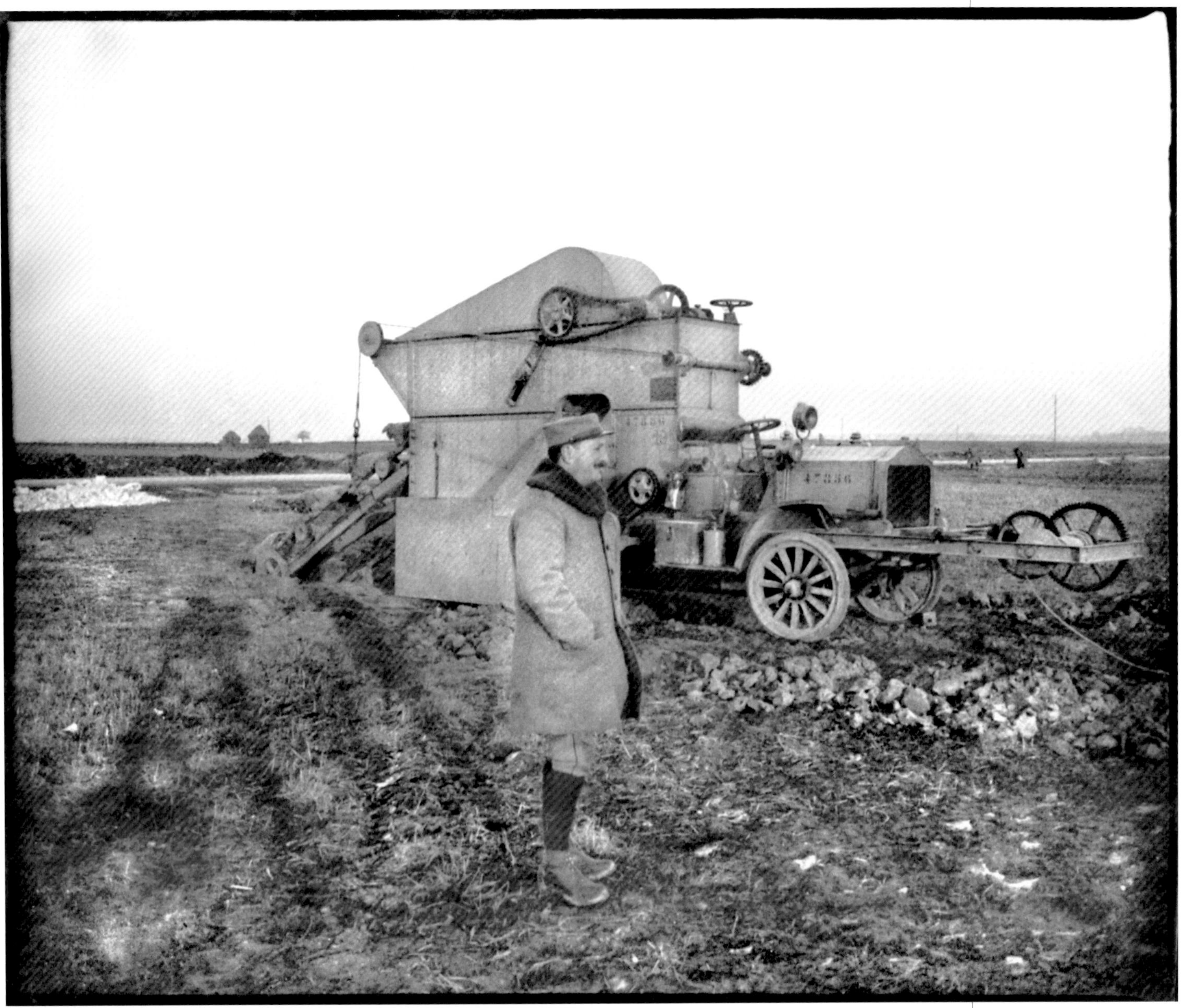

PHOT. 60
15/02/1917

Mechanisation arrived on the battlefield with equipment as strange as this *Mascard-Dessoliers* trench excavator.

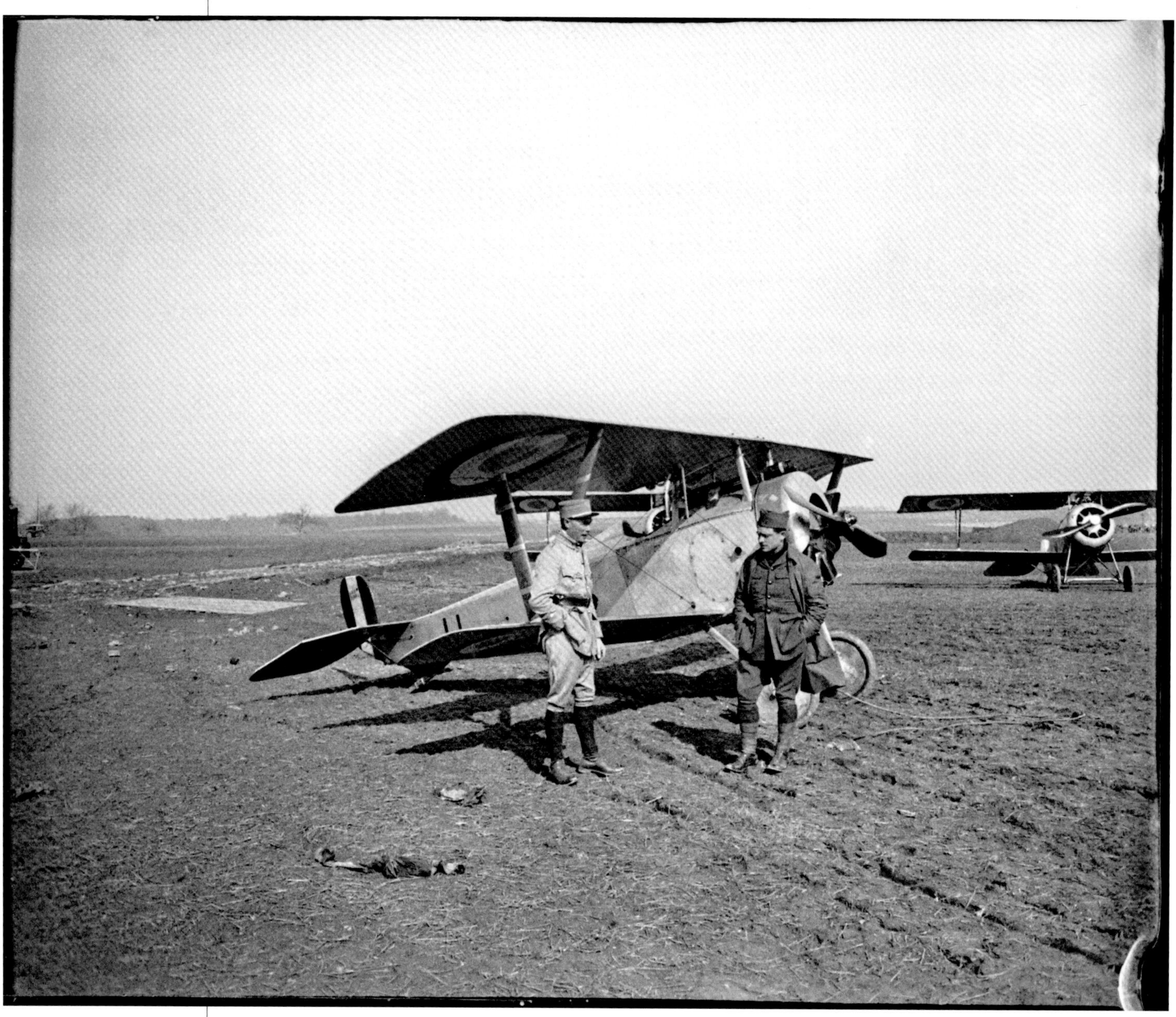

PHOT. 64
17/03/1917

These two pilots are members of one of the most famous hunting units of all times: the *Escadrille N124 Lafayette* of American volunteers. The one on the left is Lieutenant Alfred de Laage de Meux, executive officer of the unit who died on May 23rd of that year while he was testing the new Spad VII. The one on the right is the ace of the squad: Raoul Lufbery (1885-1918). This iconic pilot made his first kill over Verdun in the summer of 1916, achieving seventeen accredited victories before being downed in May 1918. Currently he is remembered at the *Lafayette Memorial du Parc de Garches* in Paris. The planes, stationed at the field of Ravenel-dans-la-Somme, are Nieuport 17s. The aircraft that is by the pilots, possibly has the number 1587, being received by the squad in September 1916. Behind the Lieutenant can be appreciated the famous Sioux profile, emblem of the unit. According to the *journal de marches de la escadrille*, on this day Lufbery flew between 13 and 15 hours on a patrol mission over Roye, Lassigny and Ribécourt, without locating any enemy aircraft. Other pilots did detect suspicious movements which corresponded with the German retreat to the Hindenburg line.

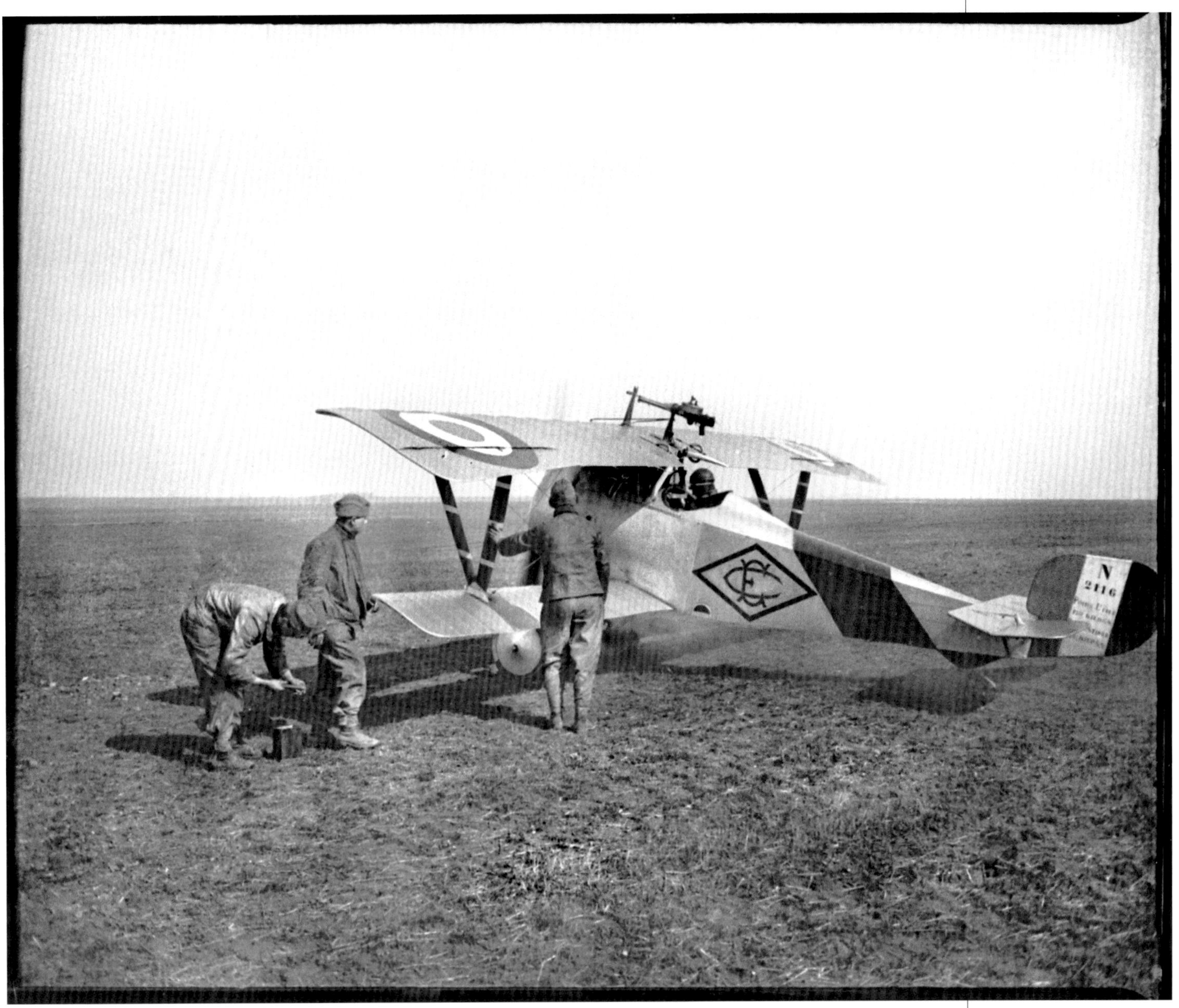

PHOT. 65

17/03/1917

A Nieuport 17 taking off from the field of Ravenel. The first series of this fast and agile plane had Lewis machine guns mounted on the wing, as shown in the photograph. Because of the initials on this device no. 2116 it belongs to Yves Chambaudoin d'Erceville, Commander of the *escadrille N15.*

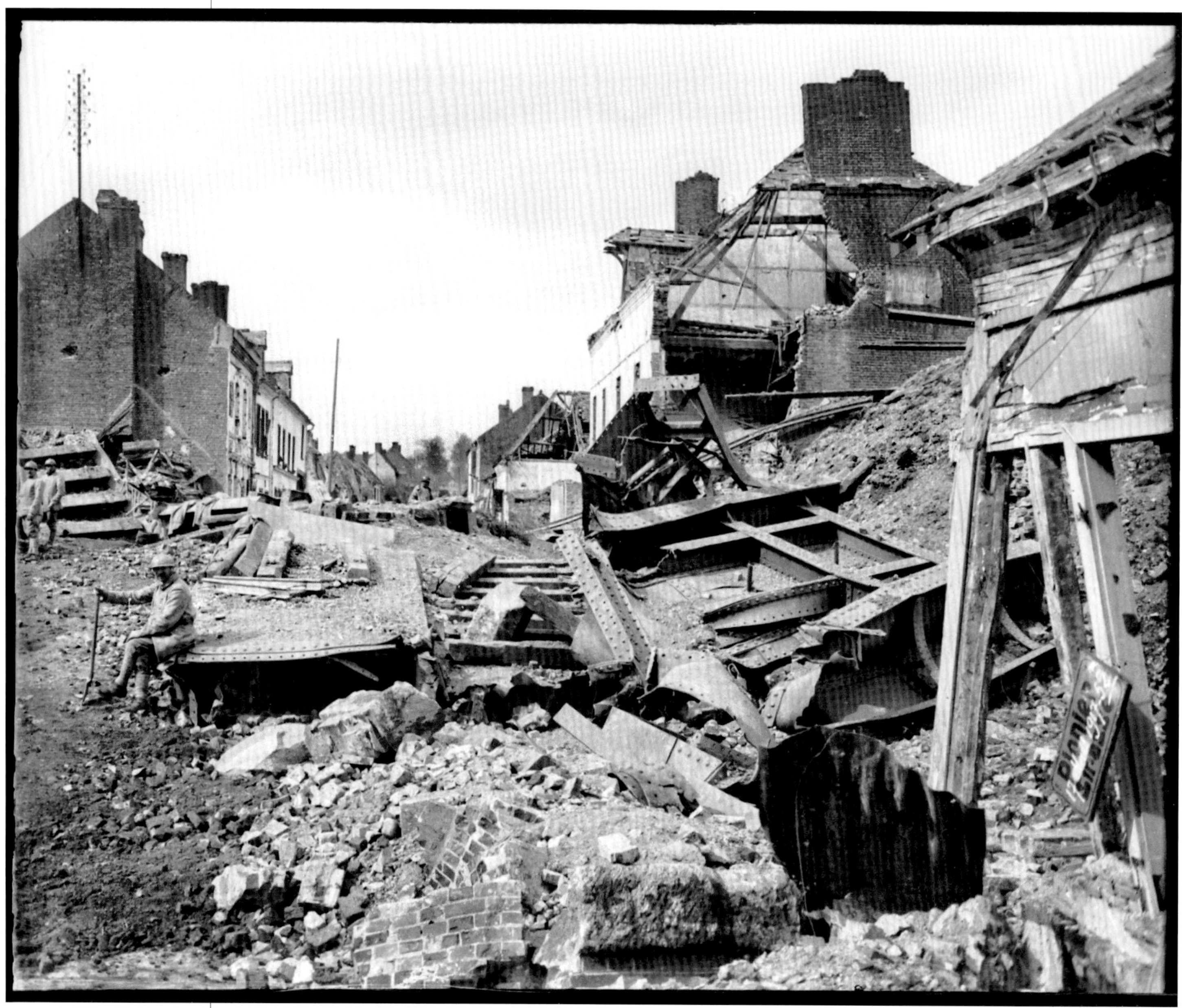

PHOT. 66
19/03/1917
Roye

With this photograph, Givord begins his series on the destruction left by the Germans in their retreat to the Hindenburg Line. Written in chalk on the sign on the right is the date of liberation by the French, the very same day.

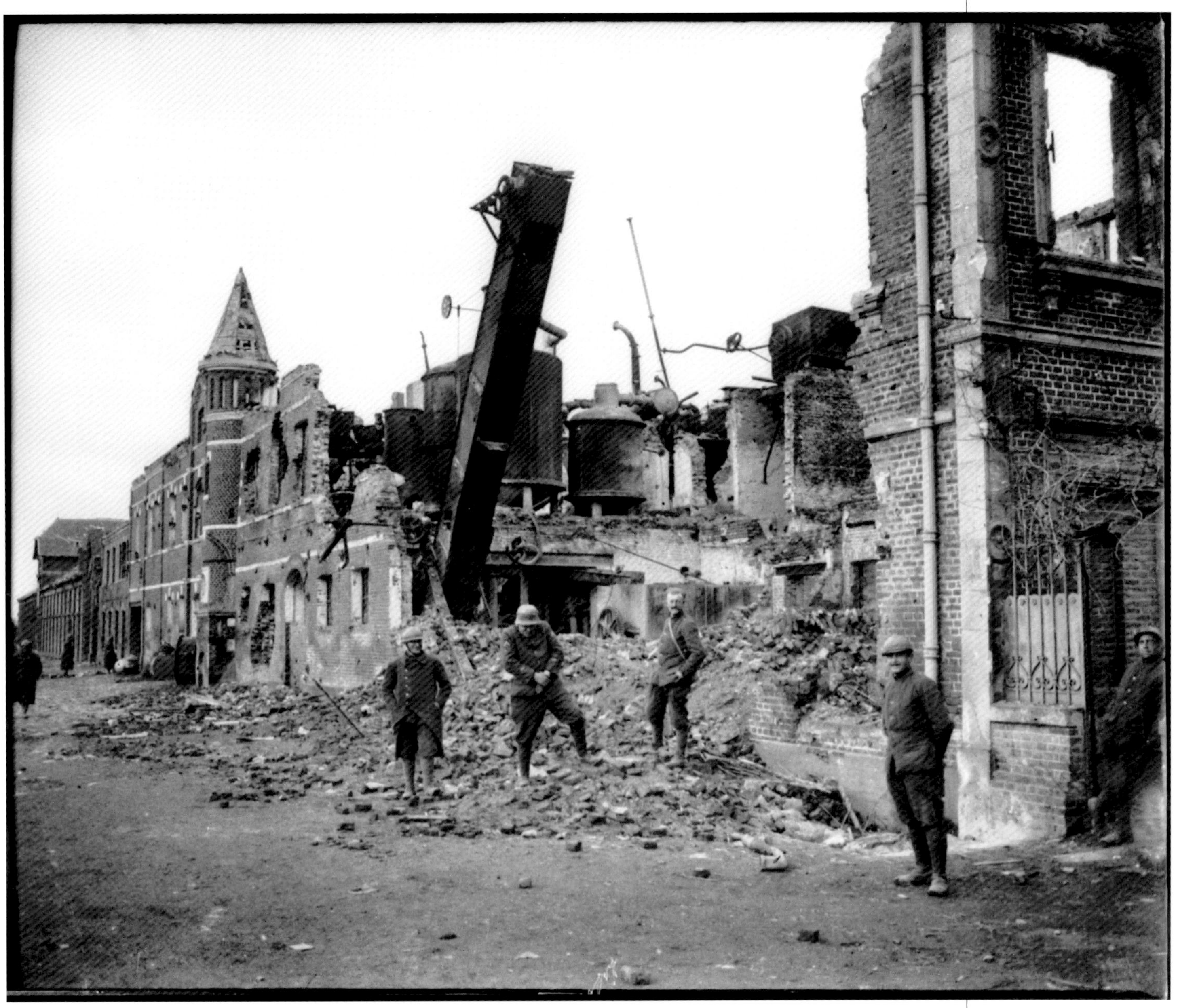

PHOT. 67
19/03/1917
Roye, a factory?

To answer M. Givord, it was a sugar factory. An agency photographer took a very similar view, although with less humour.

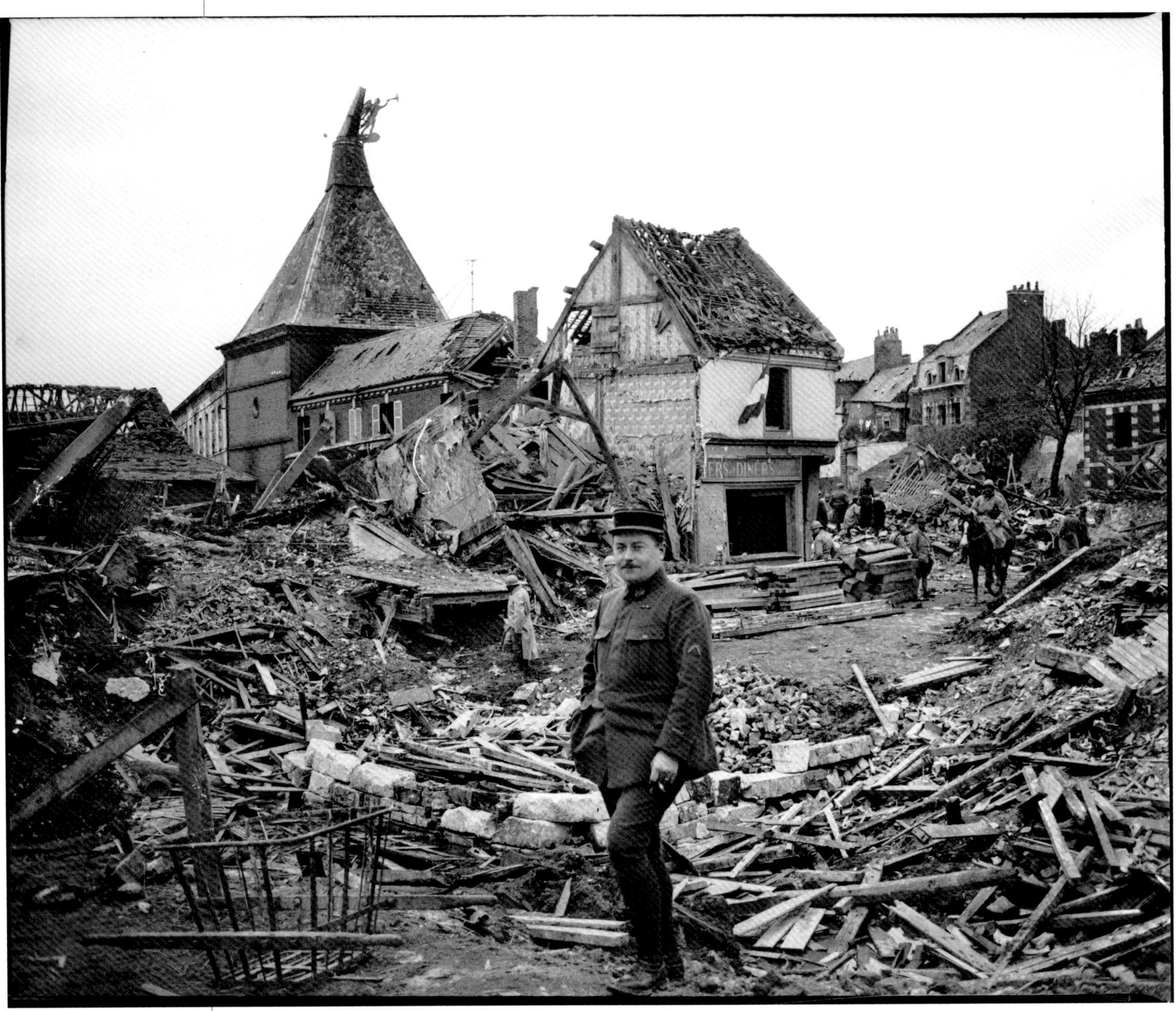

PHOT. 68
19/03/1917
Roye

The city of Roye was systematically pillaged (if it could be taken to Germany, it would have been) and devastated (if it could not be moved from its place, it was destroyed).

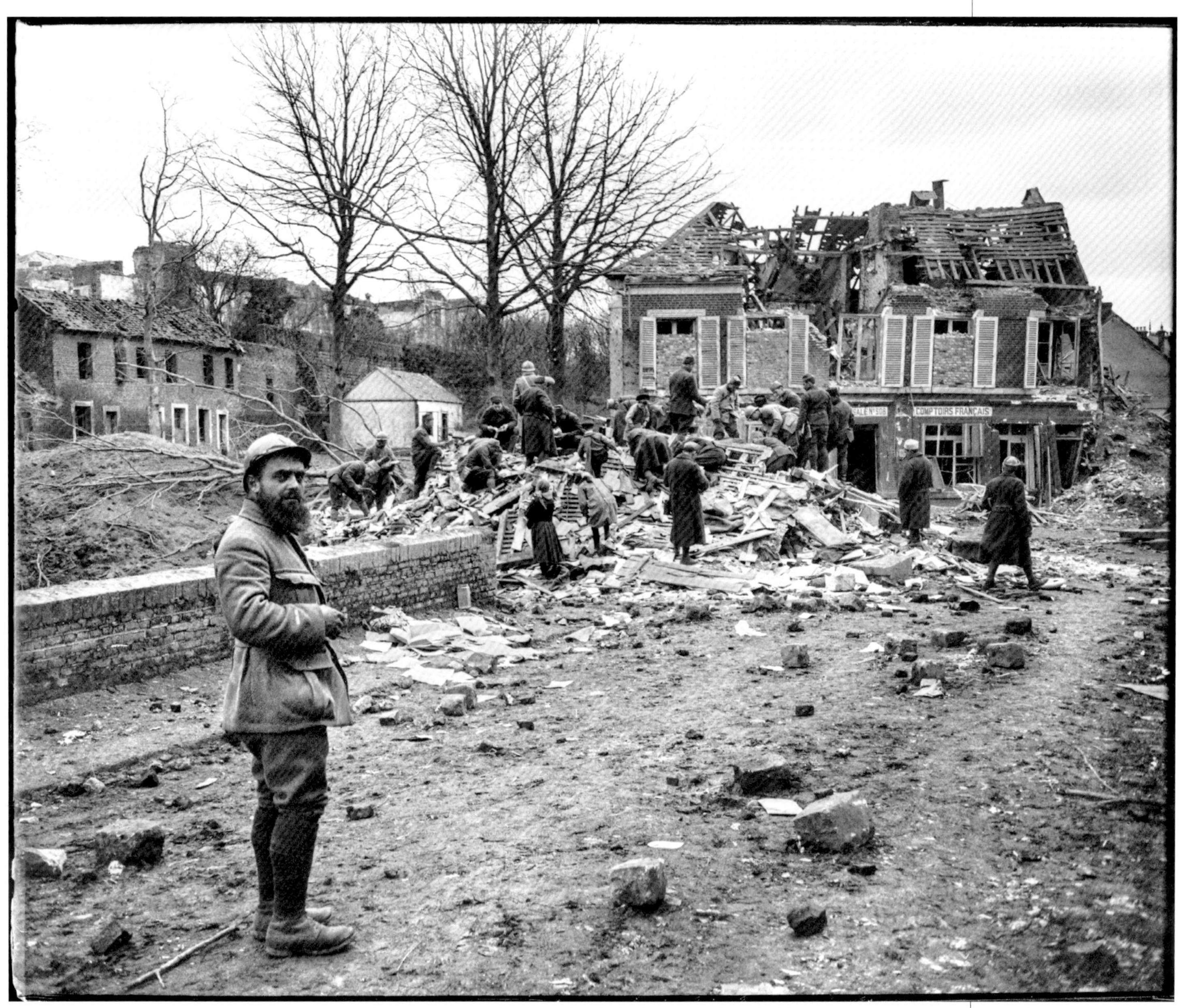

PHOT. 69
19/03/1917
Roye

The French private of the Great War passed to history with the nickname of *Poilu*, literally 'furry' but it can also be translated as tough guy. The proliferation of beards and moustaches in the unhygienic trenches were an origin for this nickname.

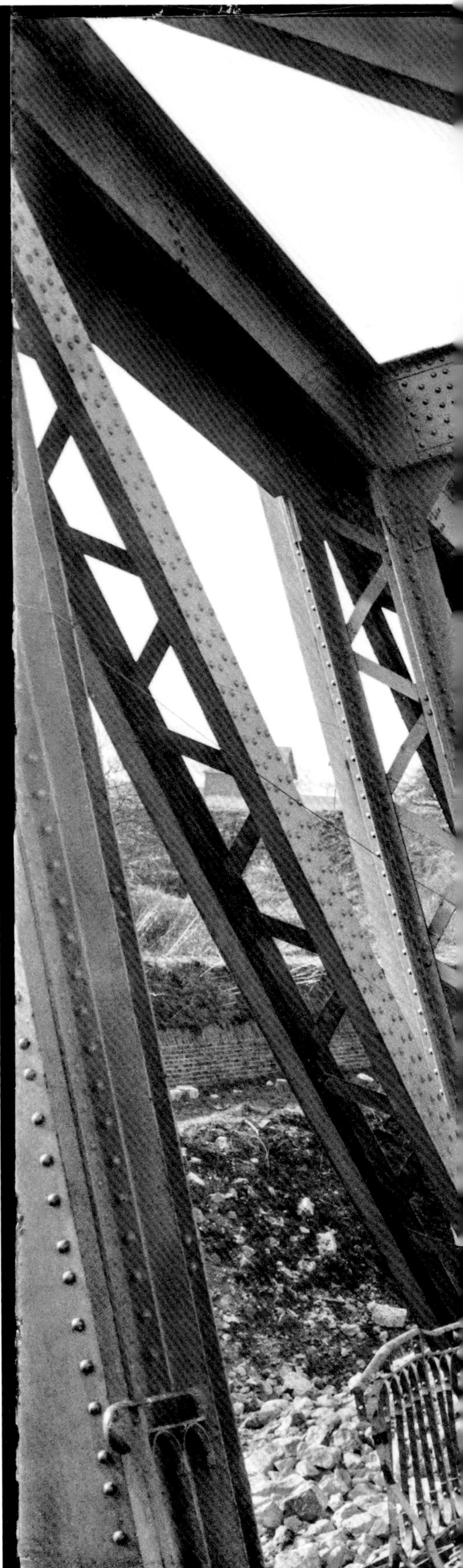

PHOT. 72
05/03/1917

Any paths of communication were a preferential target for the German sappers.

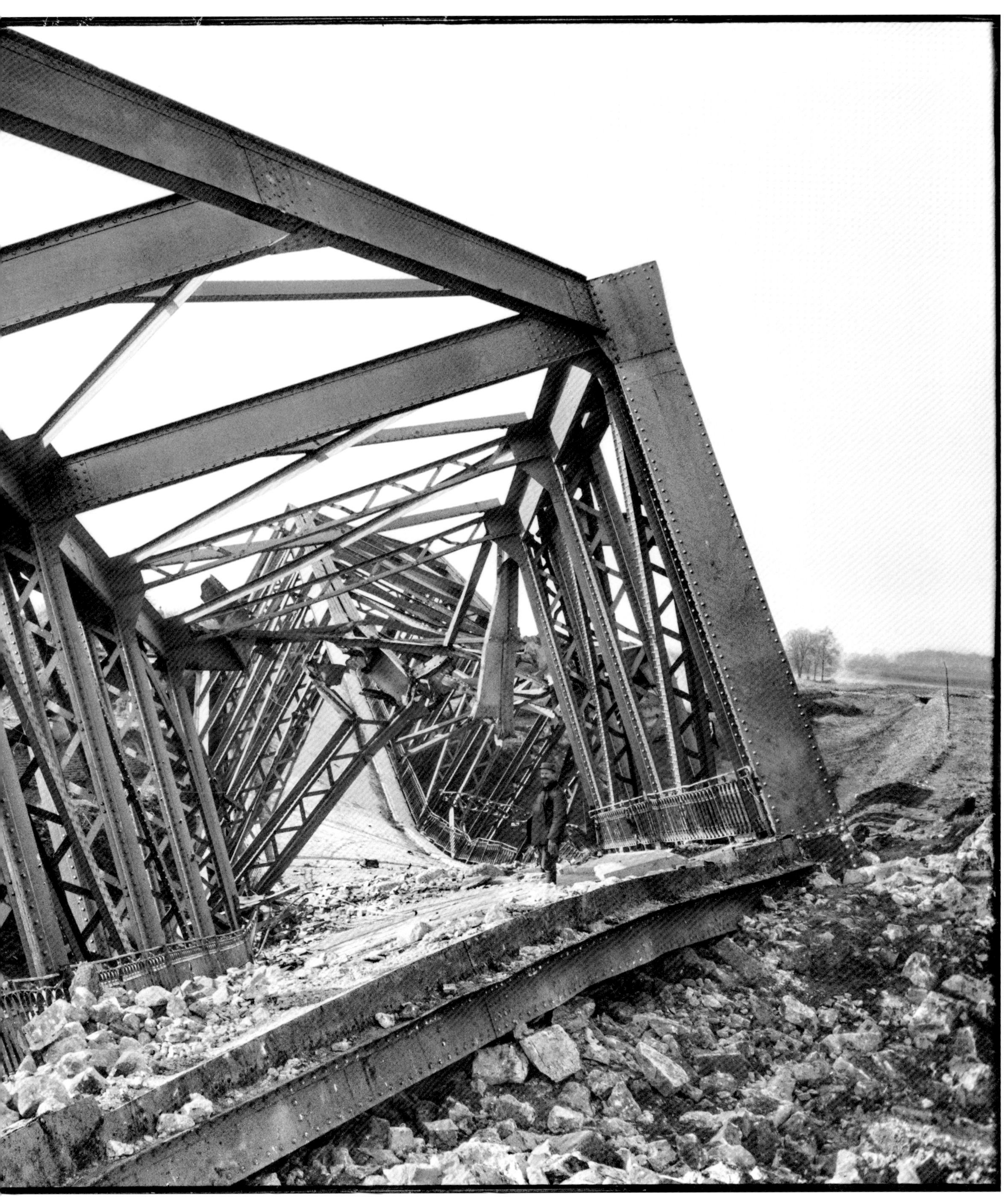

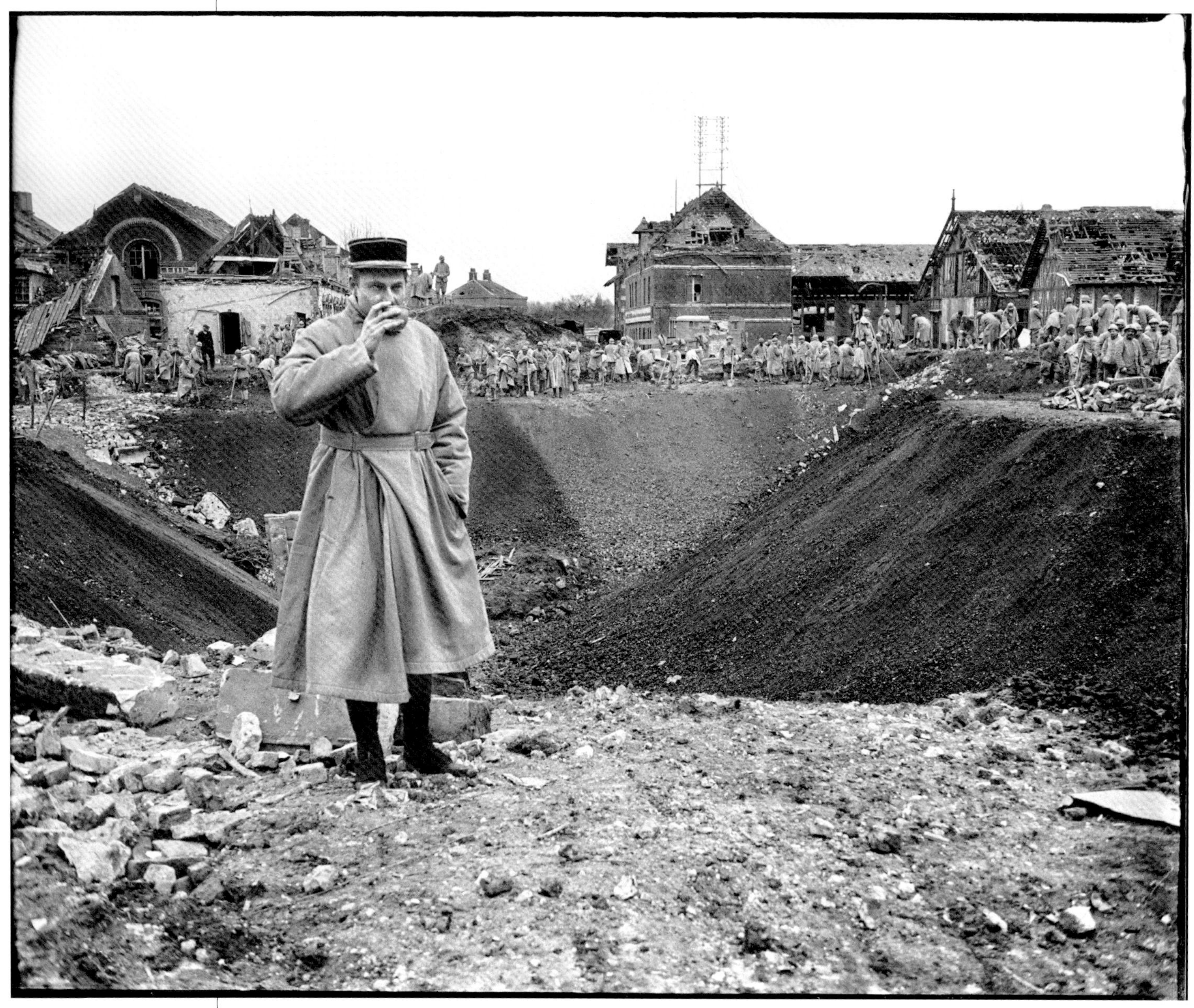

PHOT. 74
27/03/1917
Boche bottleneck at the entrance of Ham (...)

In their meticulously planned retreat, the Germans blew up strategic locations with tons of explosives to slow down the allied advance. The historical castle of Ham was dynamited to its foundations. Included on the illegible part of the annotation is the name of the officer in the foreground.

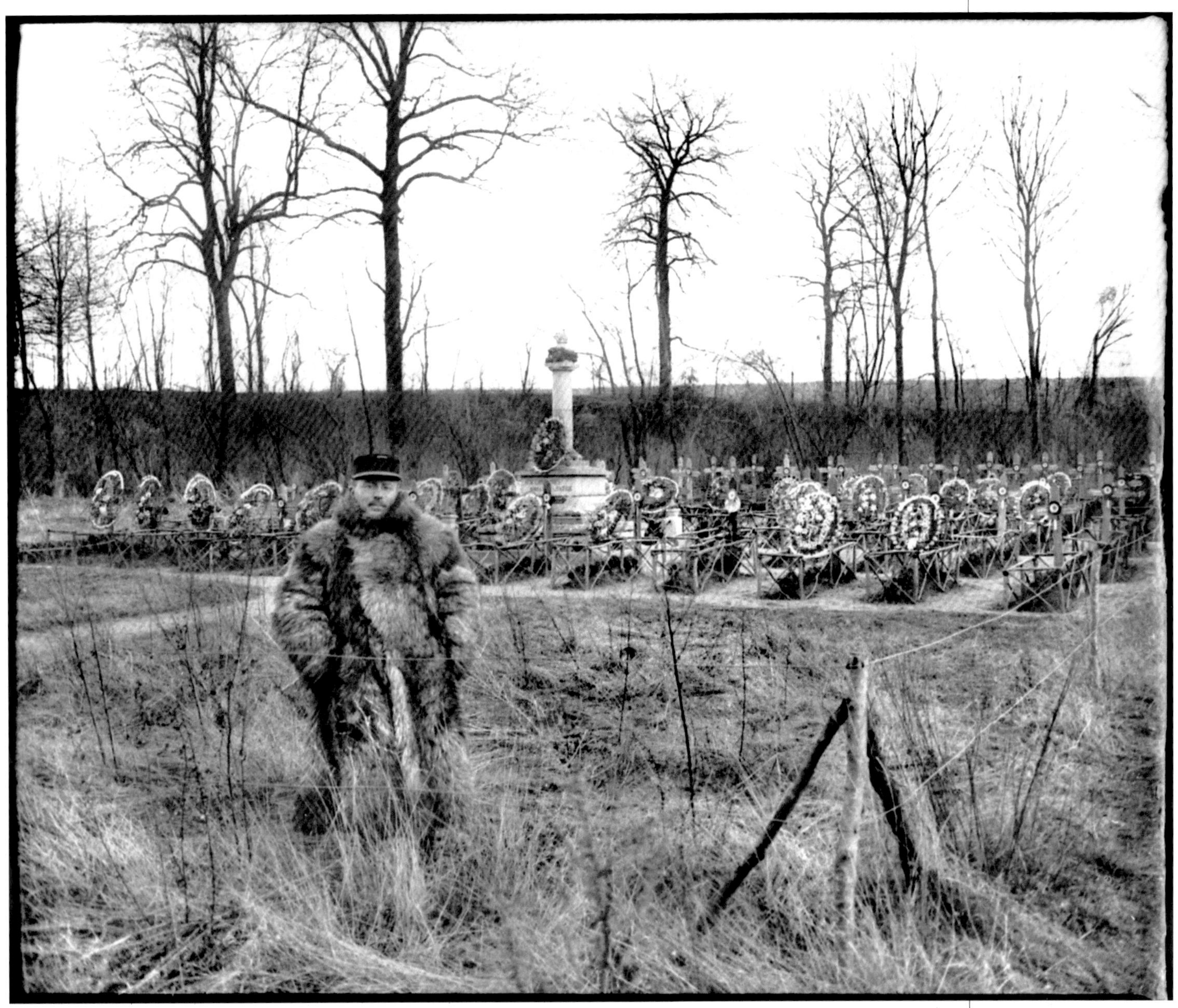

PHOT. 77
31/03/1917

The drivers of the vehicles were supplied with thick coats to protect them from the cold in the open cabins.

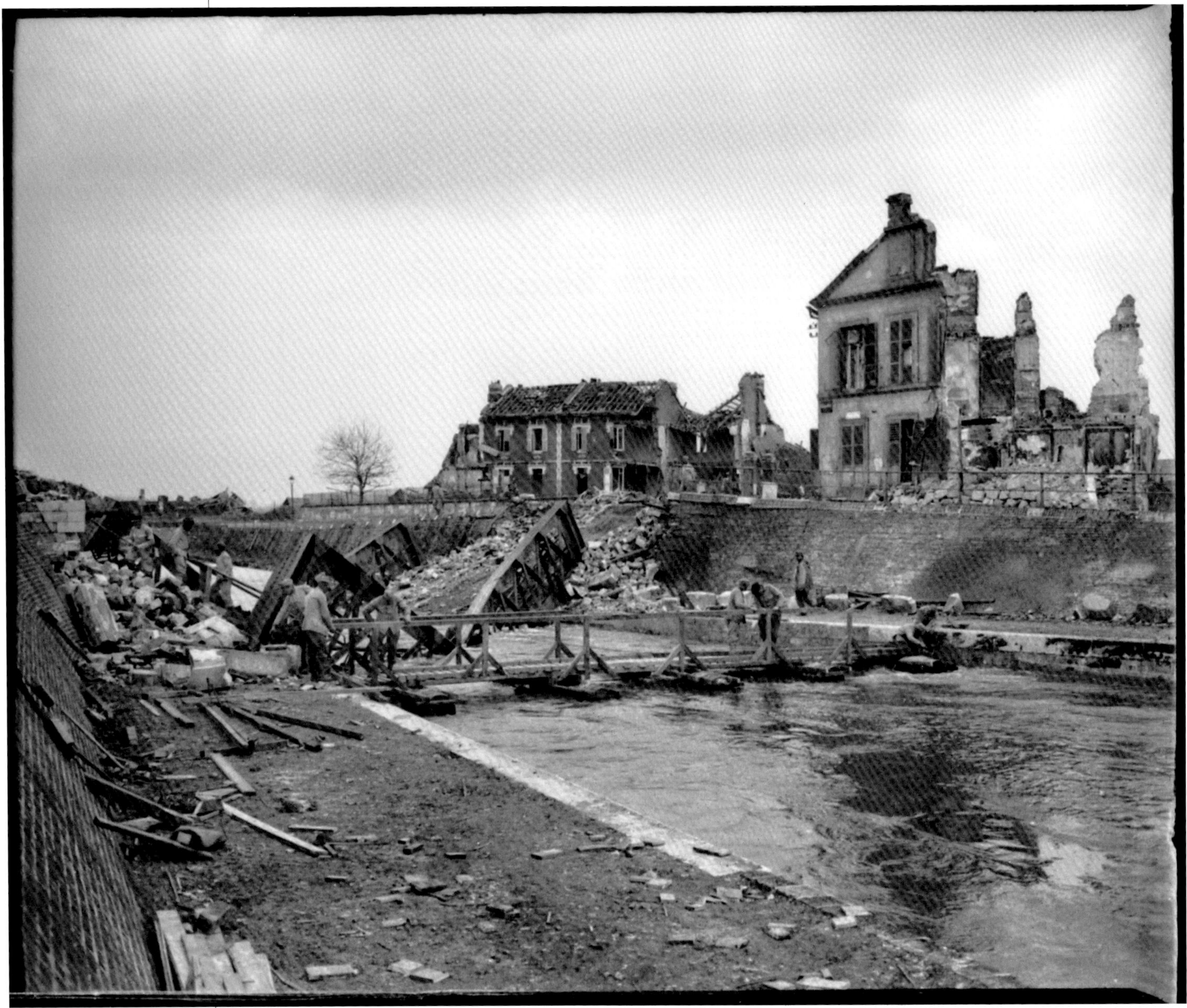

PHOT. 78
06/04/1917
Bridge over the canal at Chauny

A team of engineers builds an alternative to the bridge blown up by the Germans.

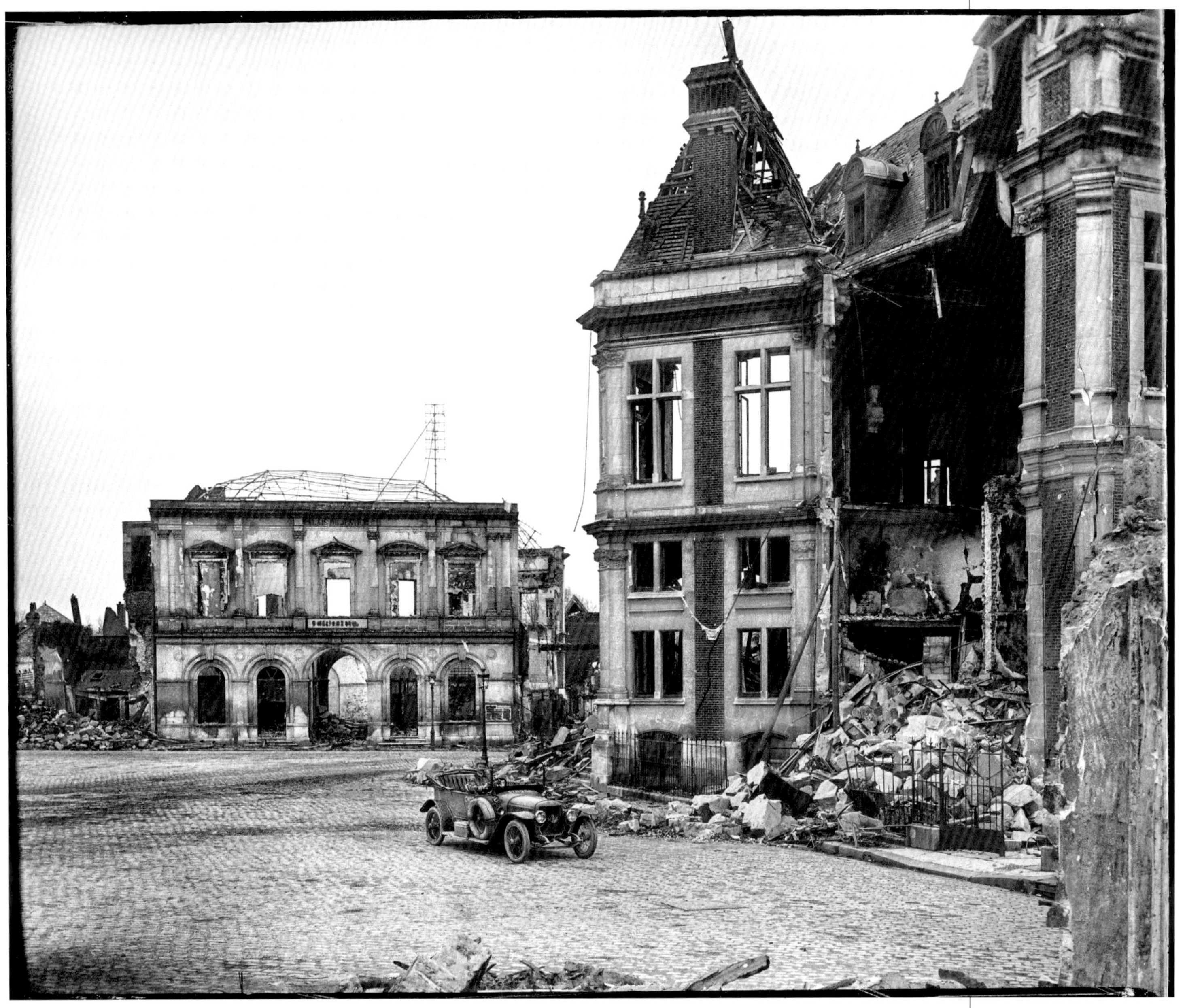

PHOT. 79
06/04/1917
Council and palace of justice of Chauny

For the first time, in this photograph we see the vehicle that Givord used on his trips. The Council's sign is written in German.

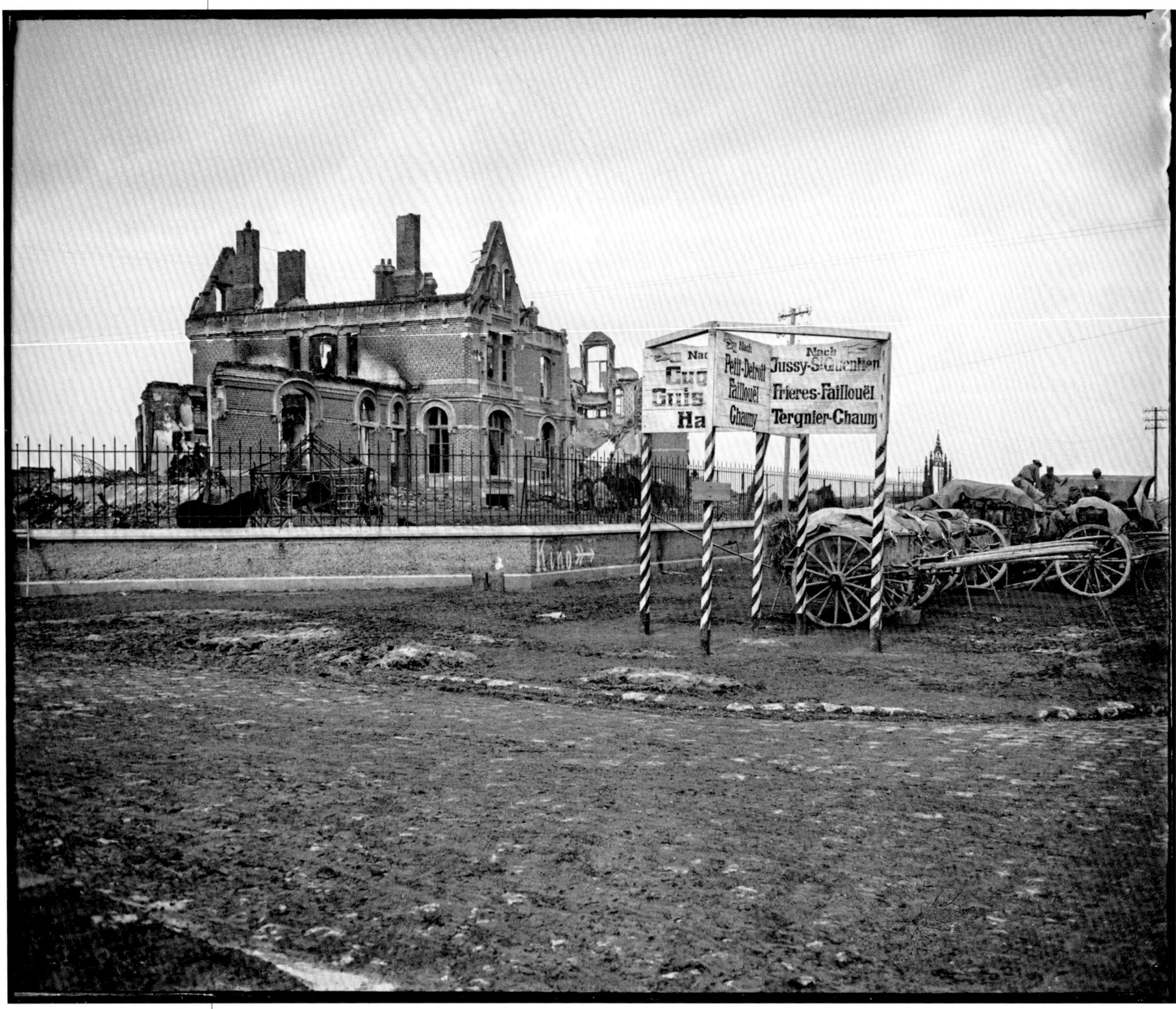

PHOT. 82
06/04/1917
The remains?

A German signpost at a crossroad of Flavy-le-Martel. Life in the rear-guard brought along with it luxuries such as the cinema that is indicated on the writing on the wall.

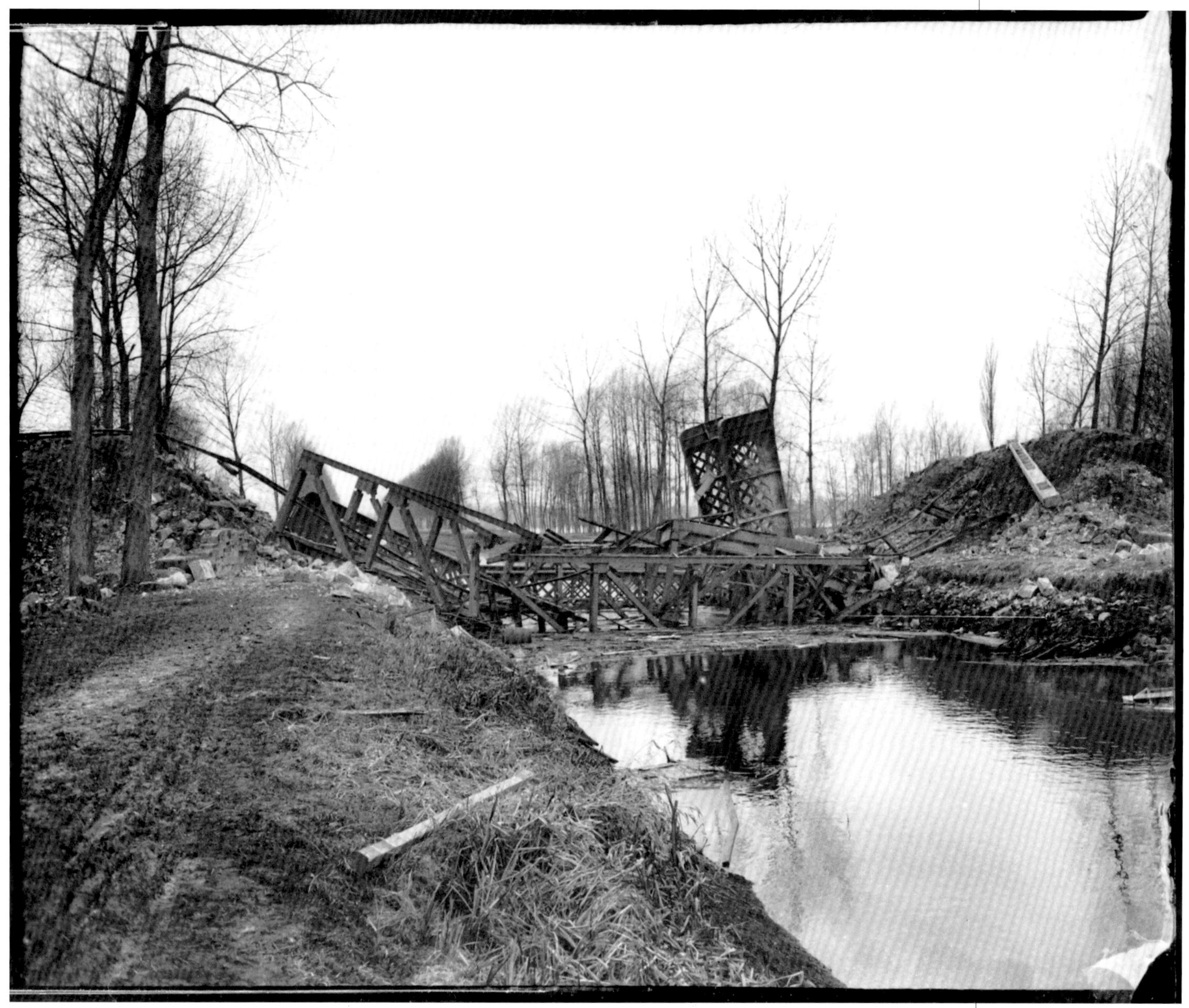

PHOT. 83
06/04/1917

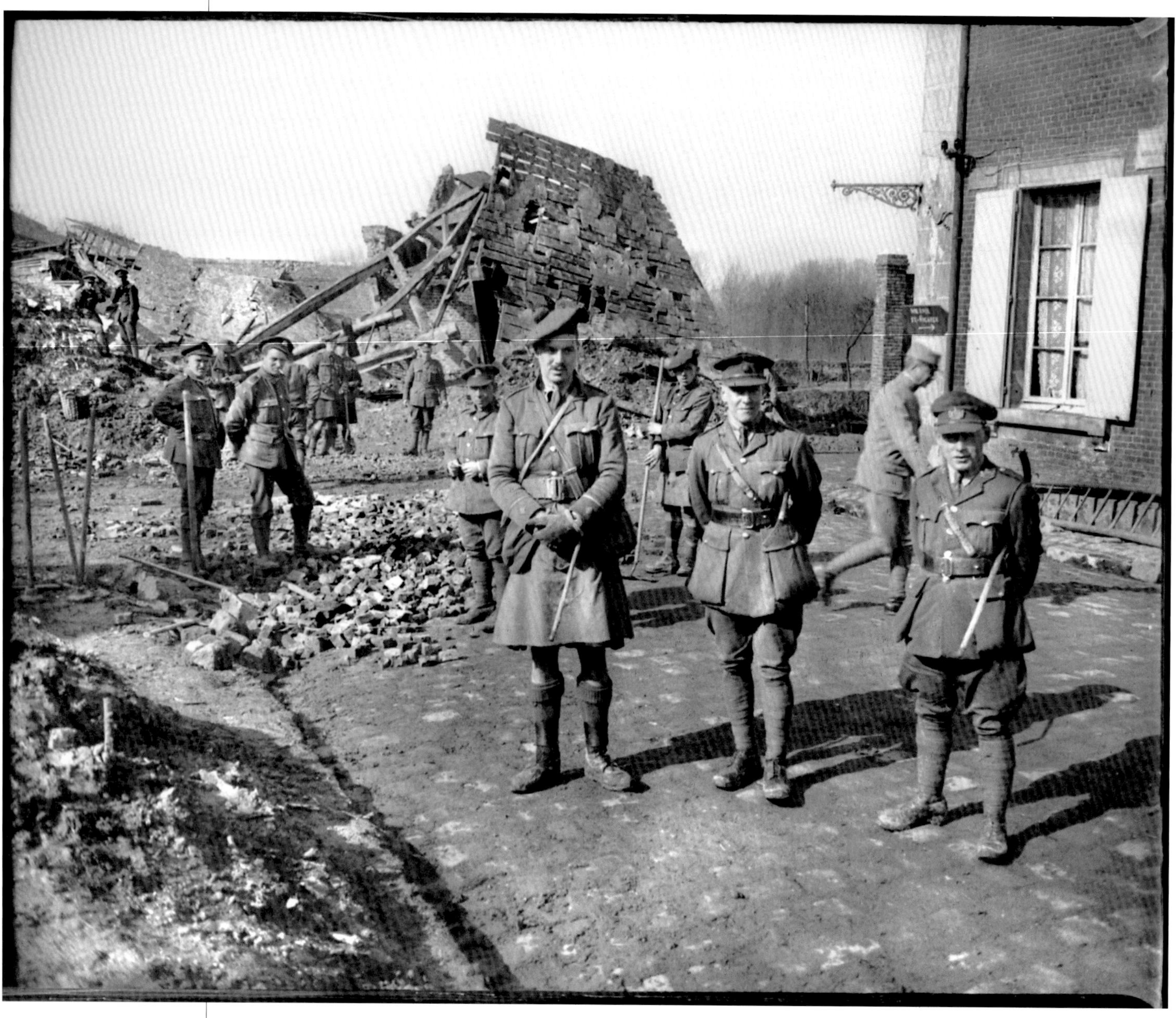

PHOT. 84
06/04/1917
English soldiers in Nesles

Some British soldiers and a Scottish sub-Lieutenant pose for the camera.

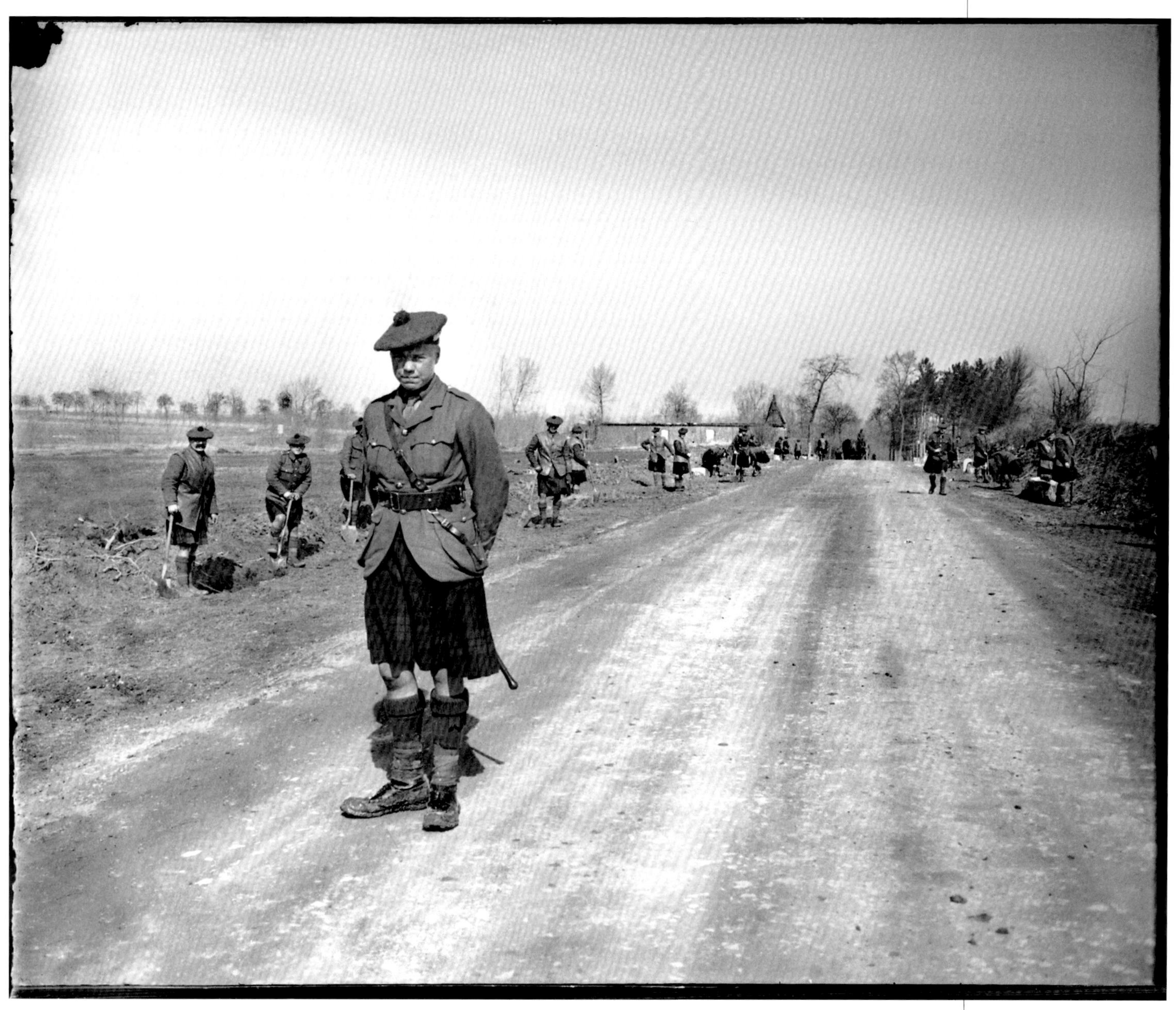

PHOT. 85
06/04/1917
Scottish soldiers in Nesles

A Scottish unit preparing a road.

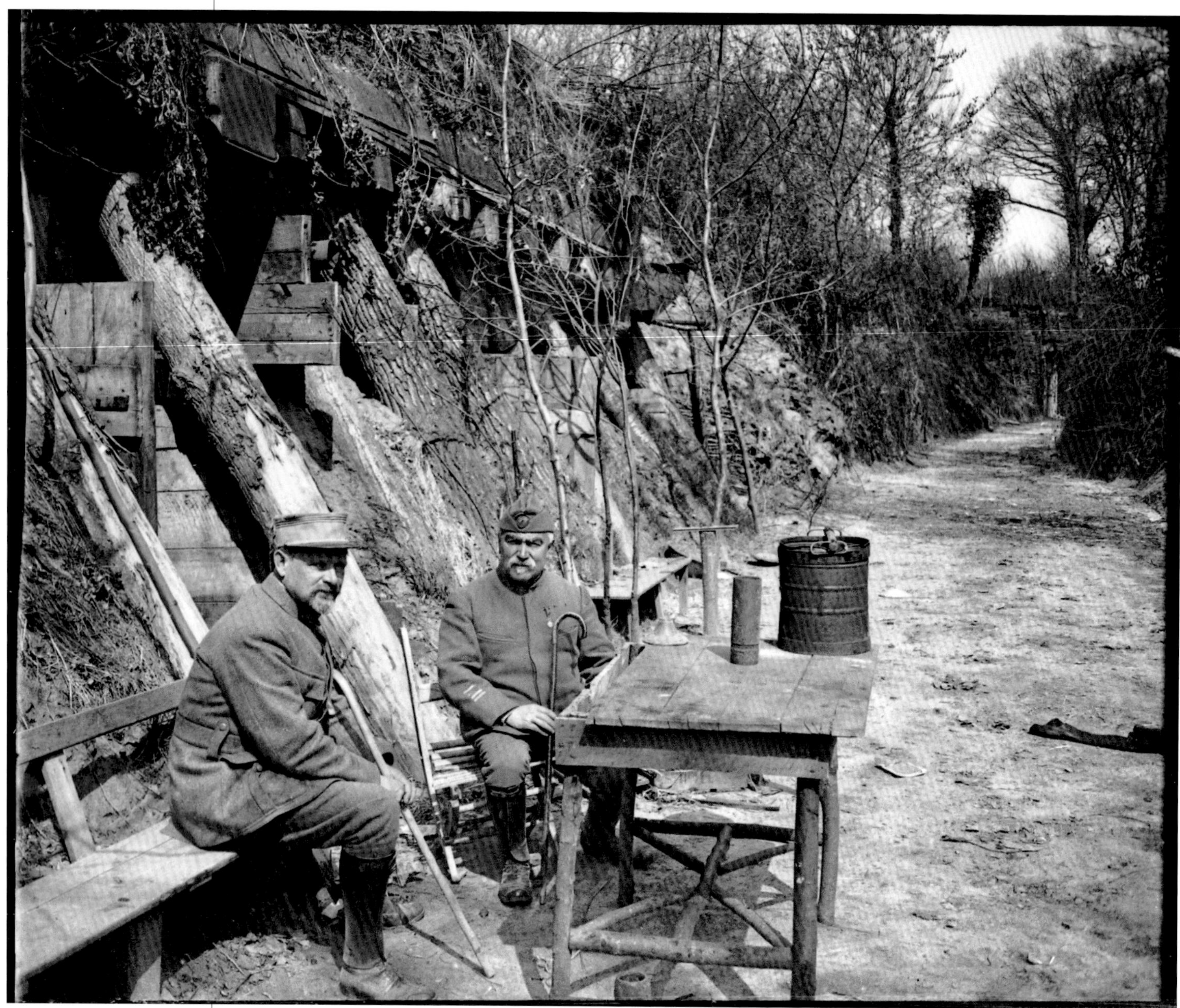

PHOT. 86
30/04/1917
Old Boche refuge

In general, German shelters were deeper and better built than the French ones. This corresponded with the German certainty that they occupied foreign land and to the French illusion that it was only a temporary situation before advancing to liberate the rest of France. Unfortunately it was not like that.

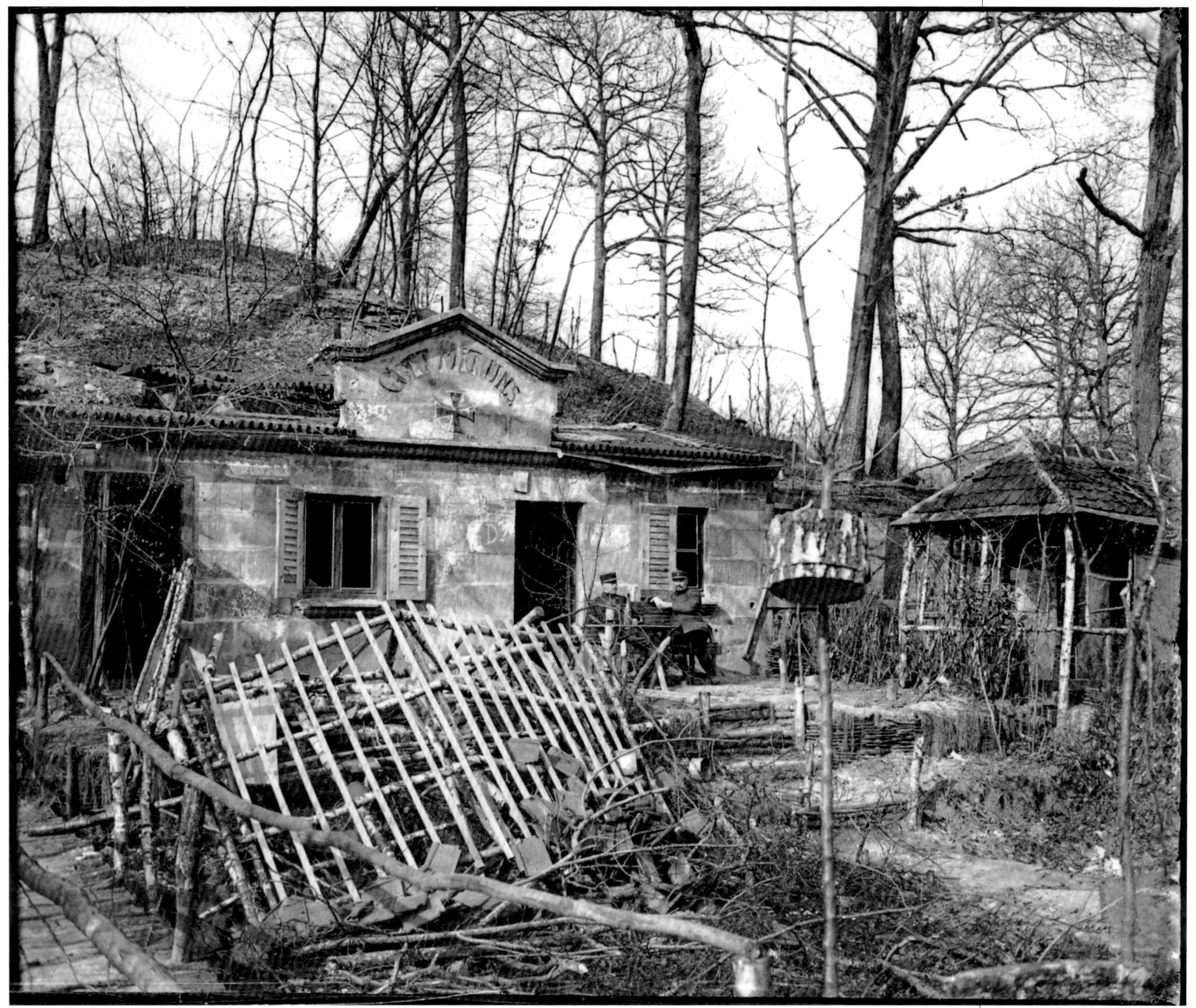

PHOT. 88
01/05/1917
Old Boche refuge

Quarters carefully dug in to the slope of a hill, in which the Iron Cross was sculpted on lintels and the German's Reich motto: *Gott mit uns* (God with us).

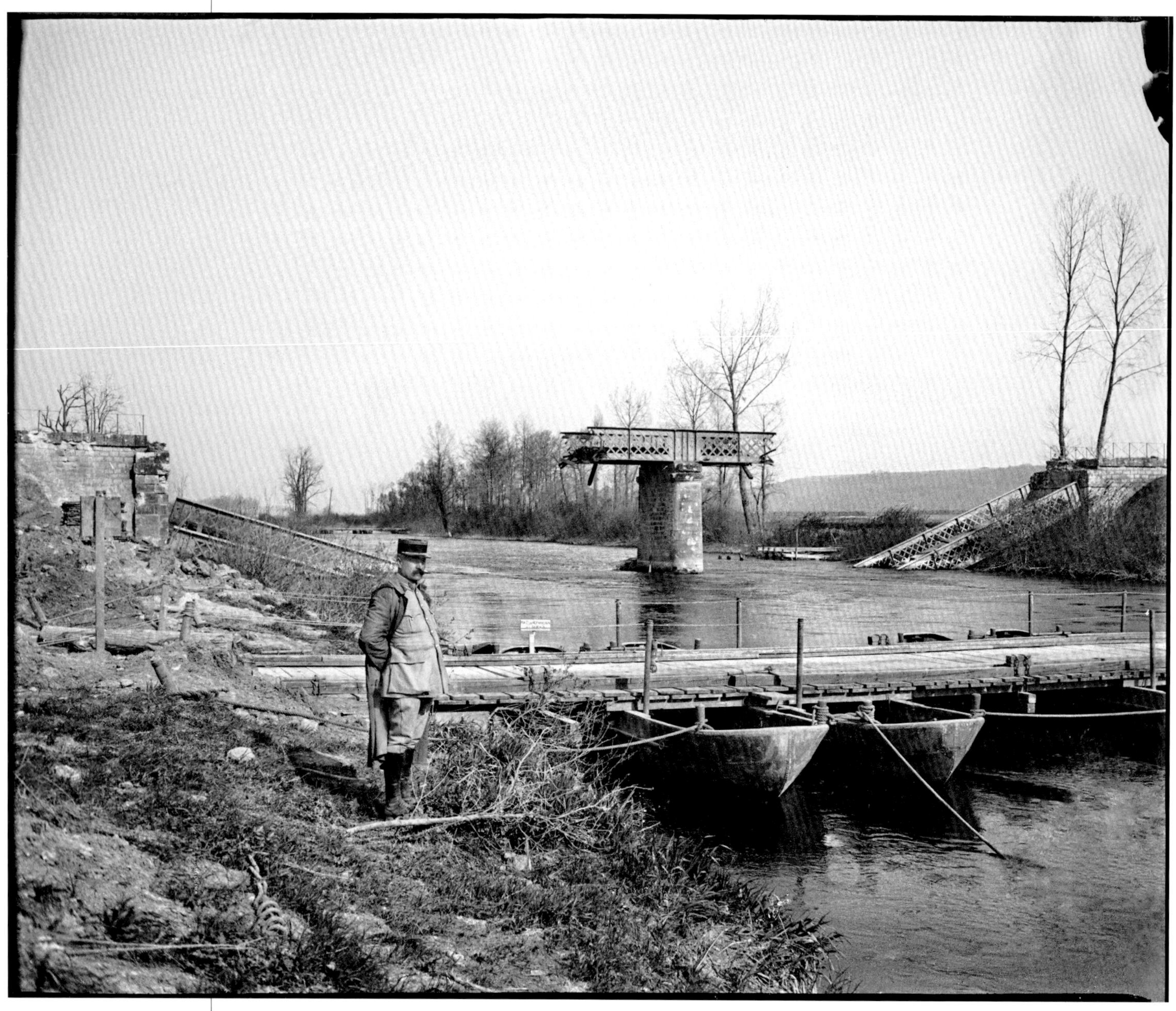

PHOT. 89
01/05/1917
Bridge over the Aisne at Soupir

Captain Givord poses beside a bridge of barges.

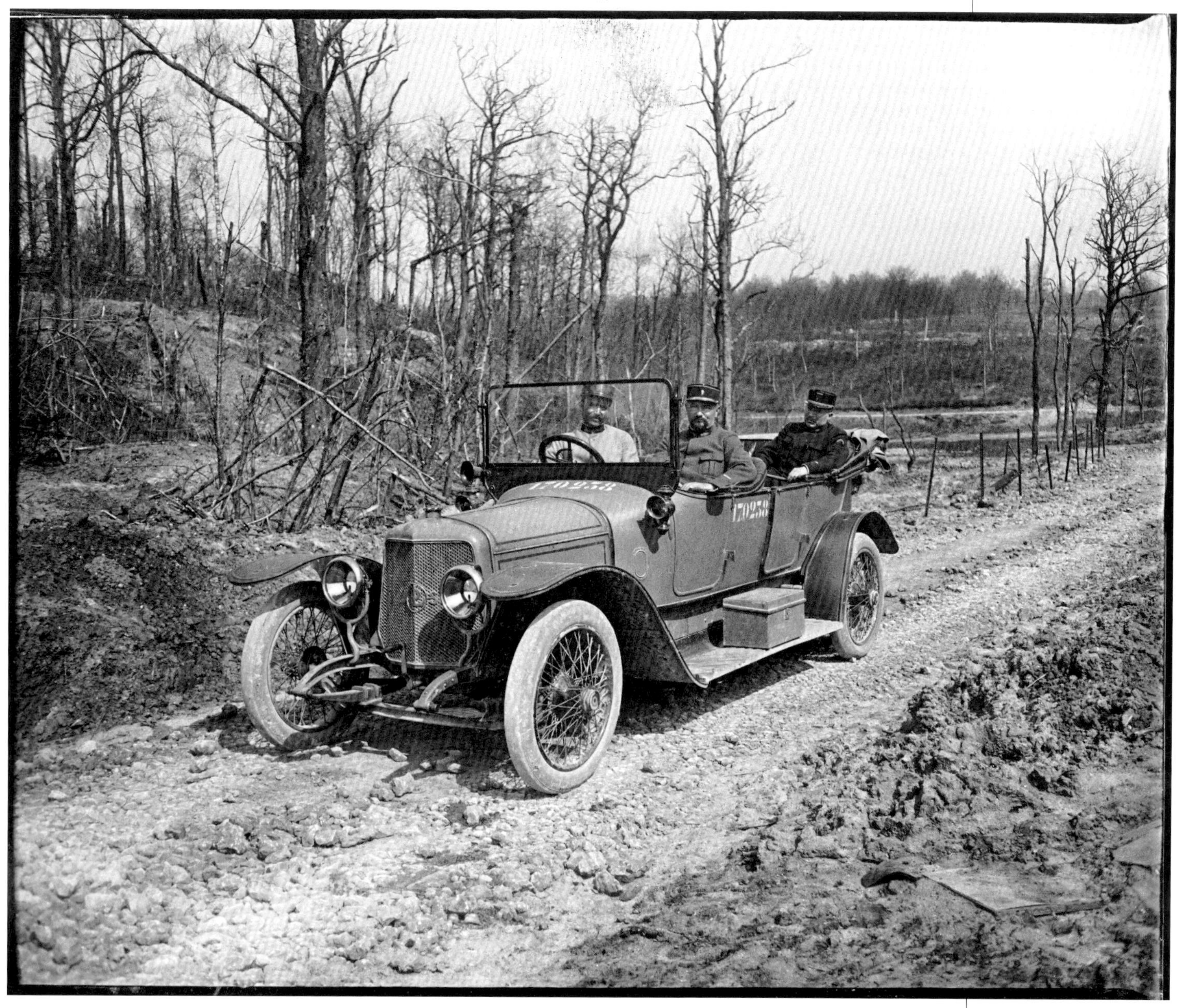

PHOT. 90
01/05/1917

The car that Givord was using, with military plate 170238, was a Panhard et Levassor type X 24 or 26.

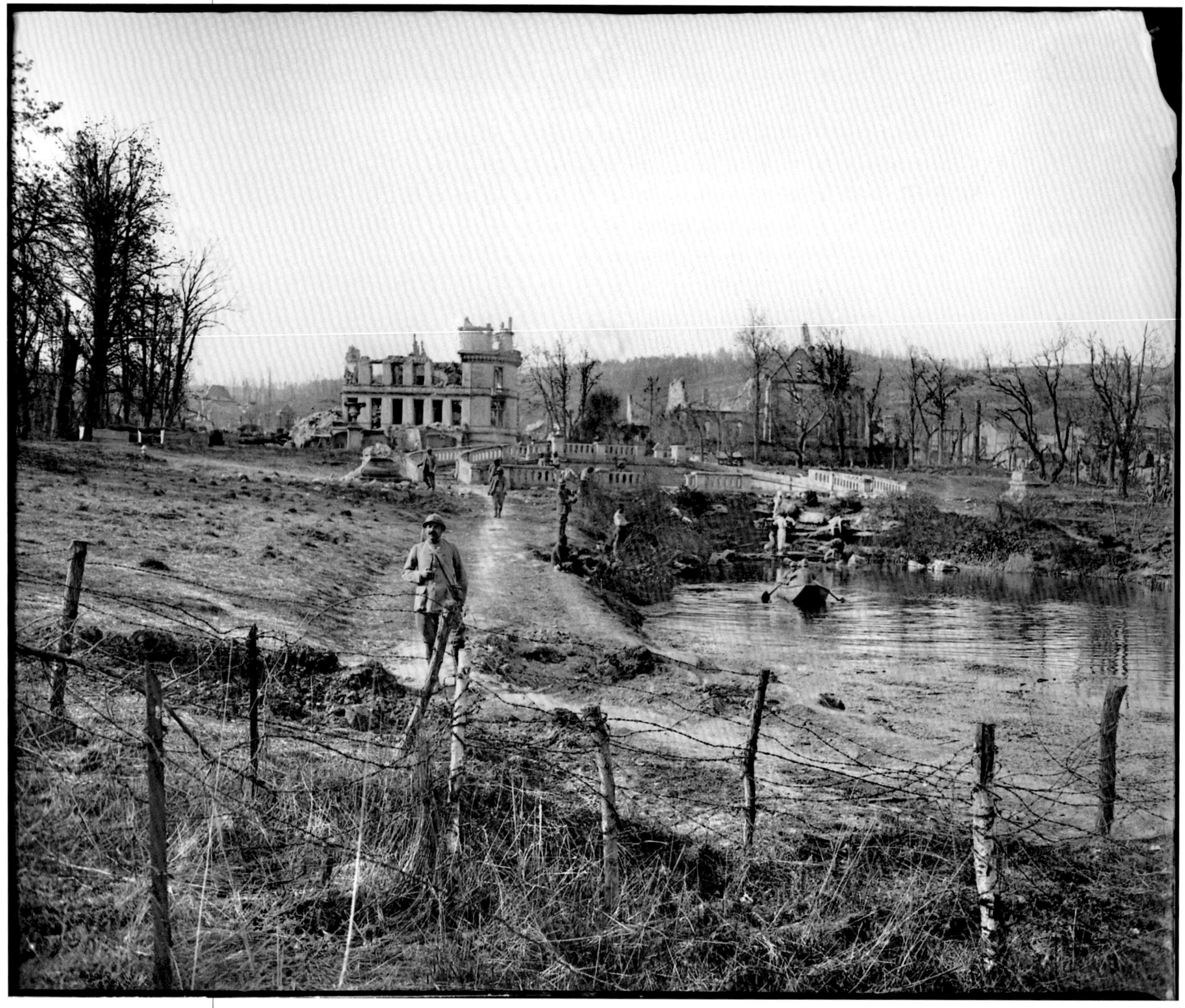

PHOT. 93
03/05/1915
Bridge over the Aisne at Soupir

Here we can appreciate what is left of the south façade of the 16th century *château* next to Soupir, seen from the park.

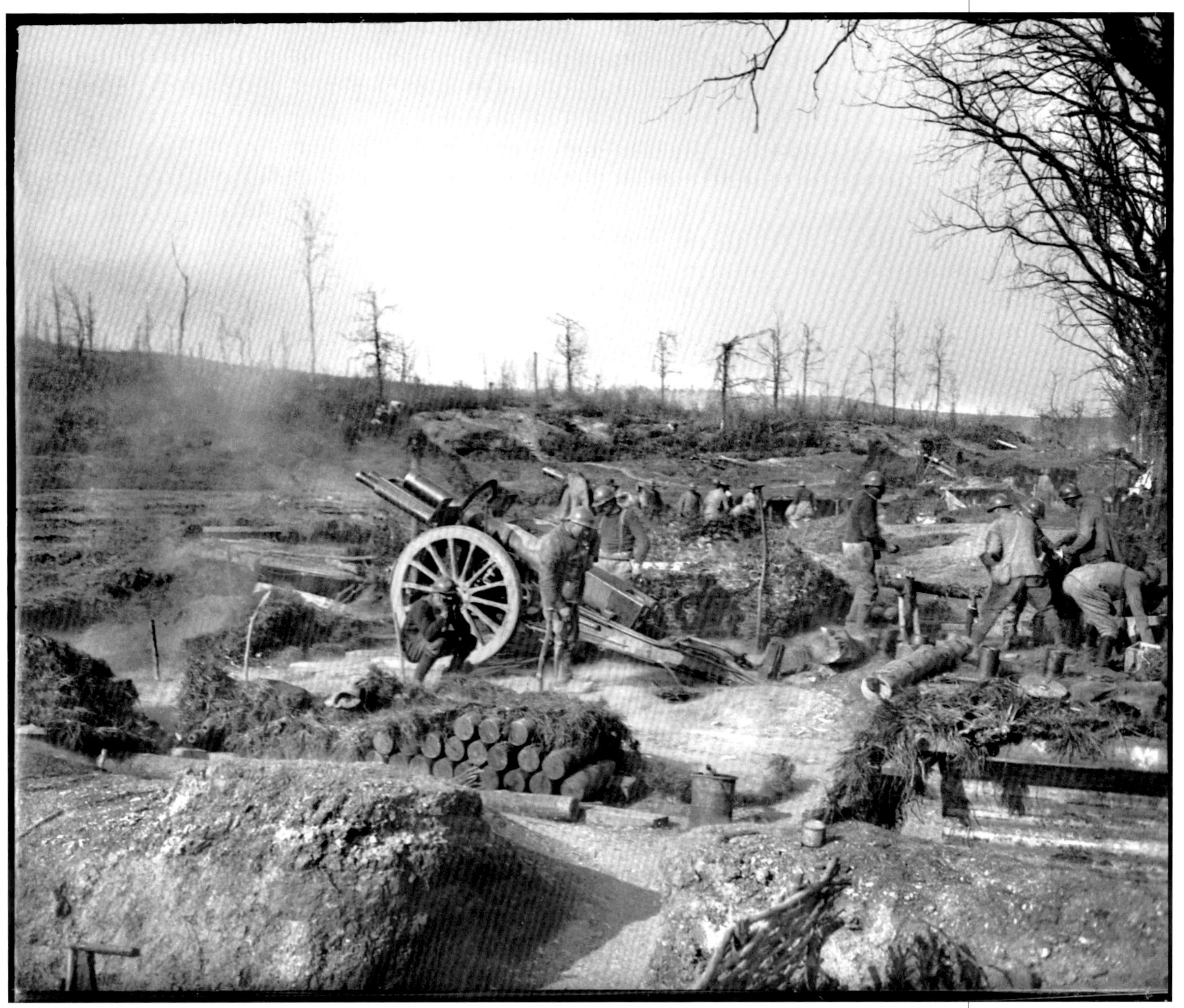

PHOT. 94
03/05/1917
Nearby Soupir

A battery of modern cannons, Saint-Chamond 155 mm calibre (1915 model), at the moment of firing.

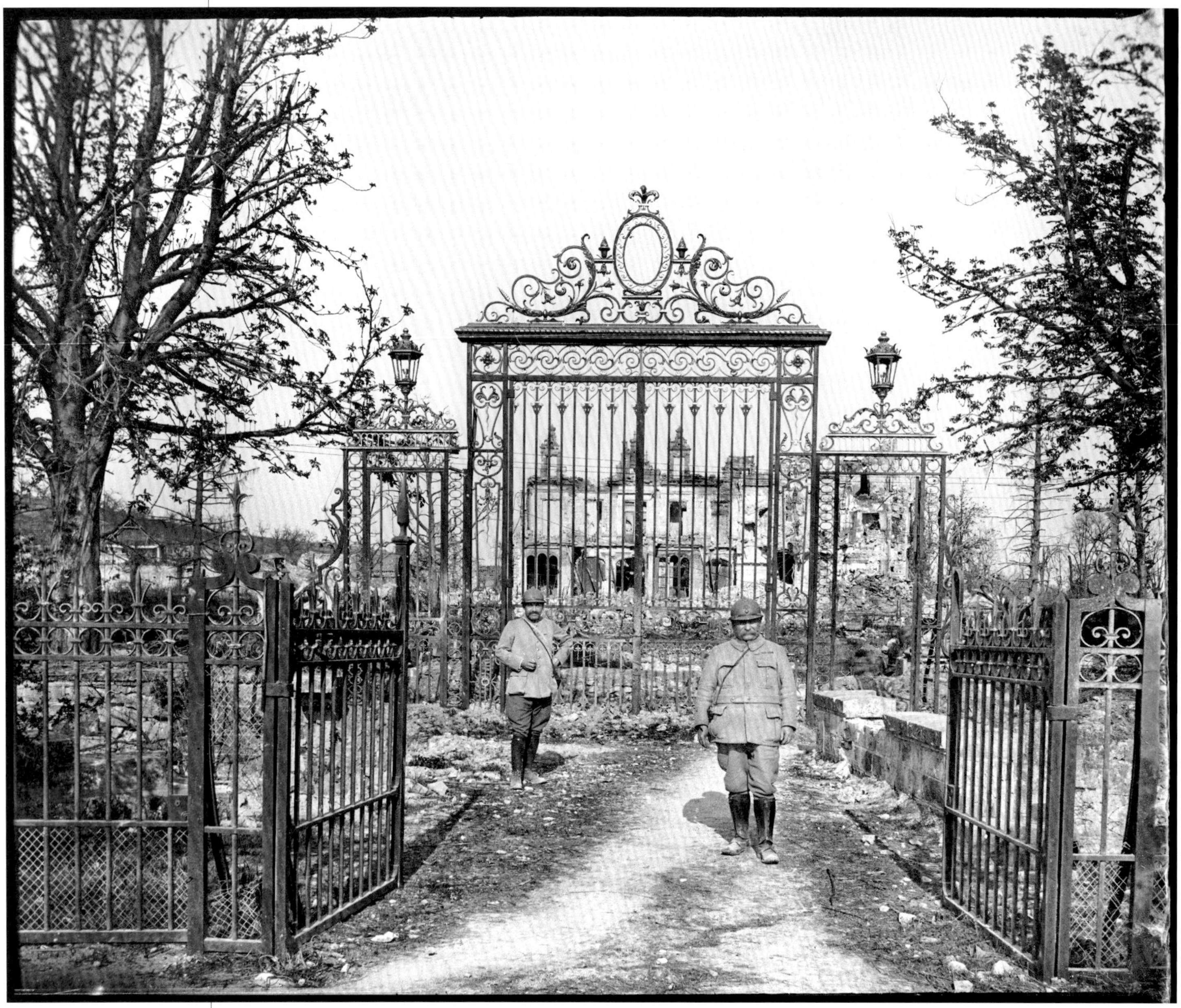

PHOT. 95
03/05/1917
Château of Soupir

View of the main façade of the small palace. Currently the forge gate is the only part remaining.

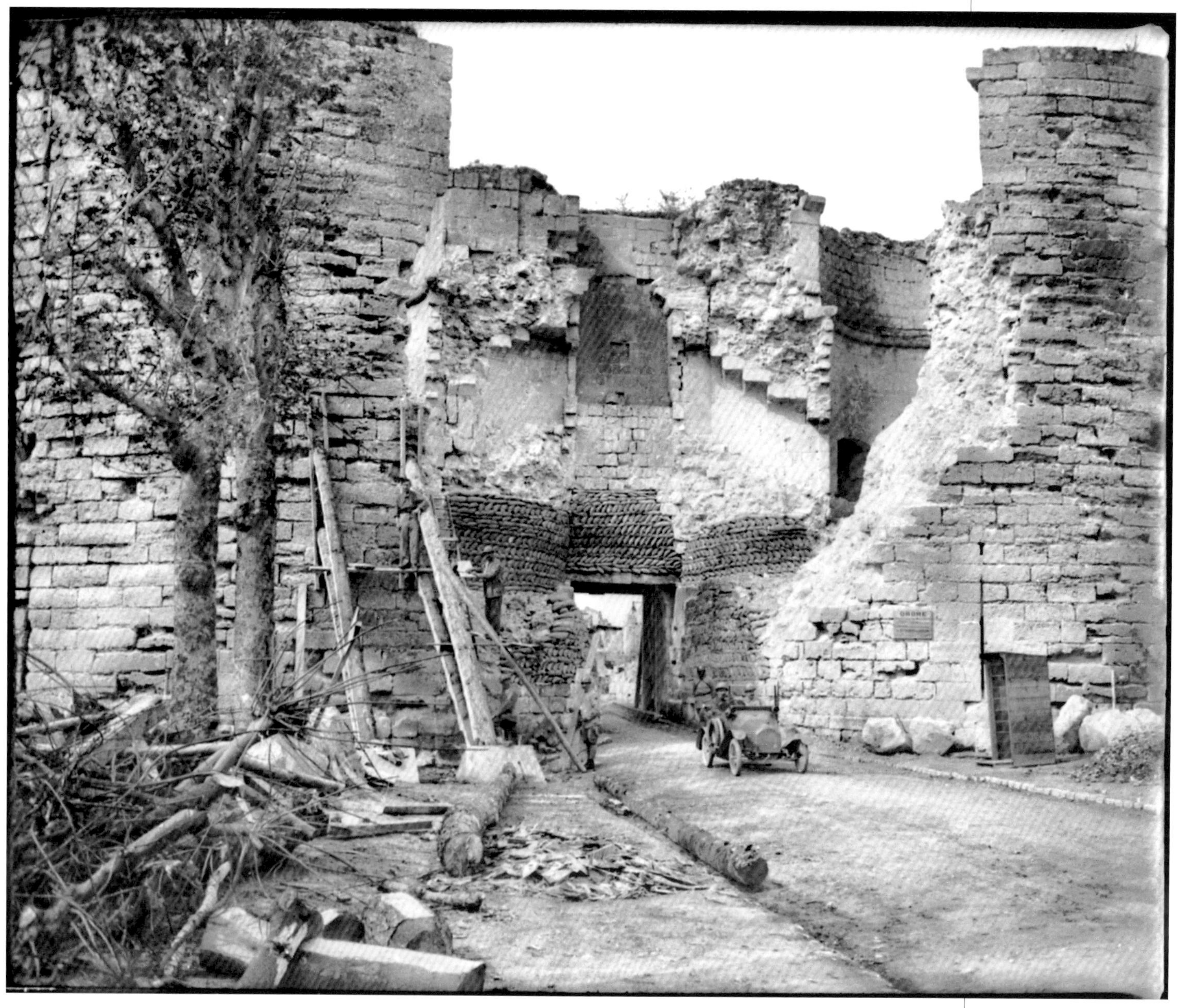

PHOT. 97
11/05/1917
Exterior door of Coucy-le-Château

The huge castle towers from the 13th century that give its name to the town were destroyed by the Germans with 38 tons of explosives on March 27th 1917 to avoid its use as an observation point.

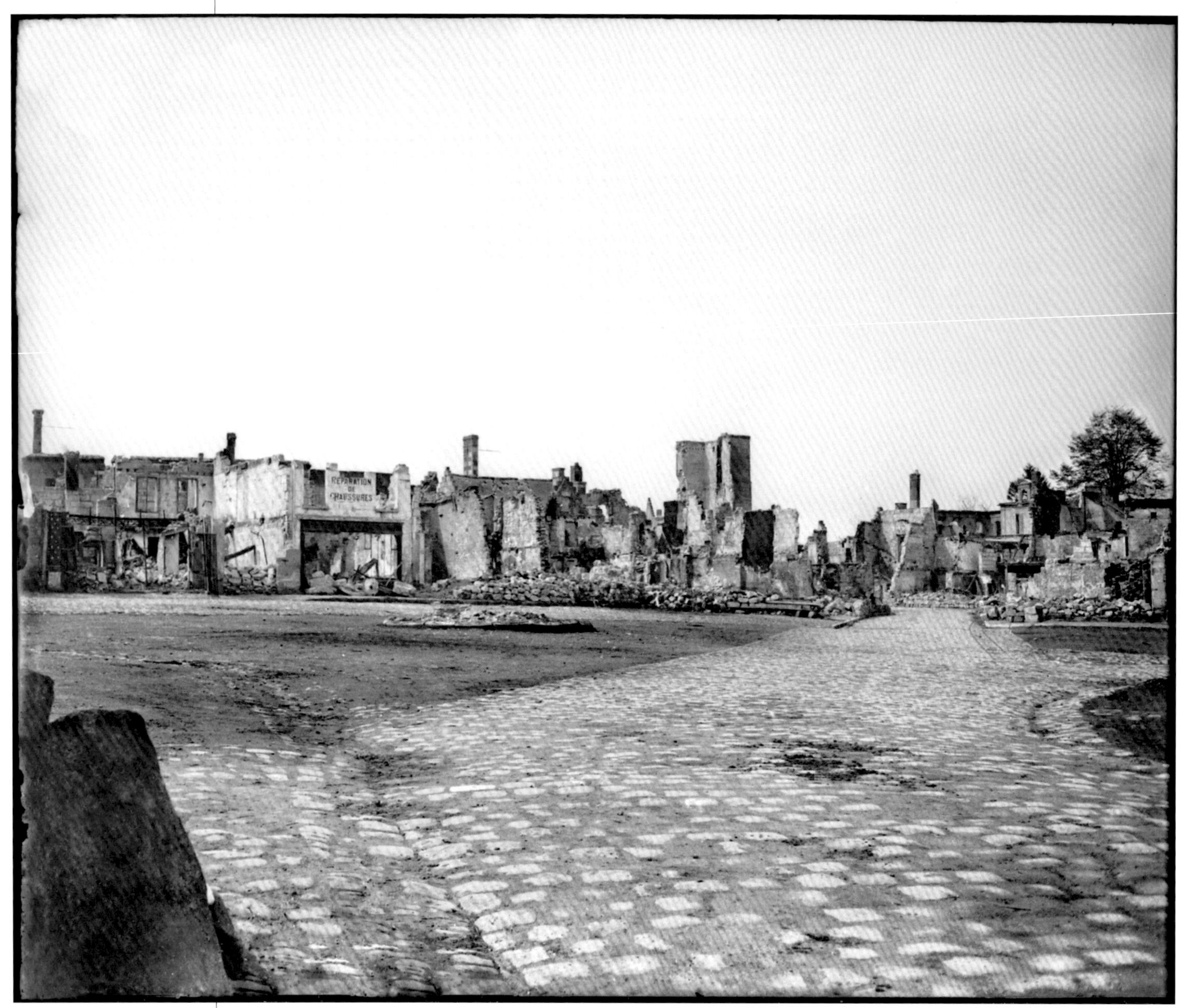

PHOT. 98
11/05/1917
Coucy-le-Château
Plaza

The town suffered a similar fate after an intensive bombardment on the same day.

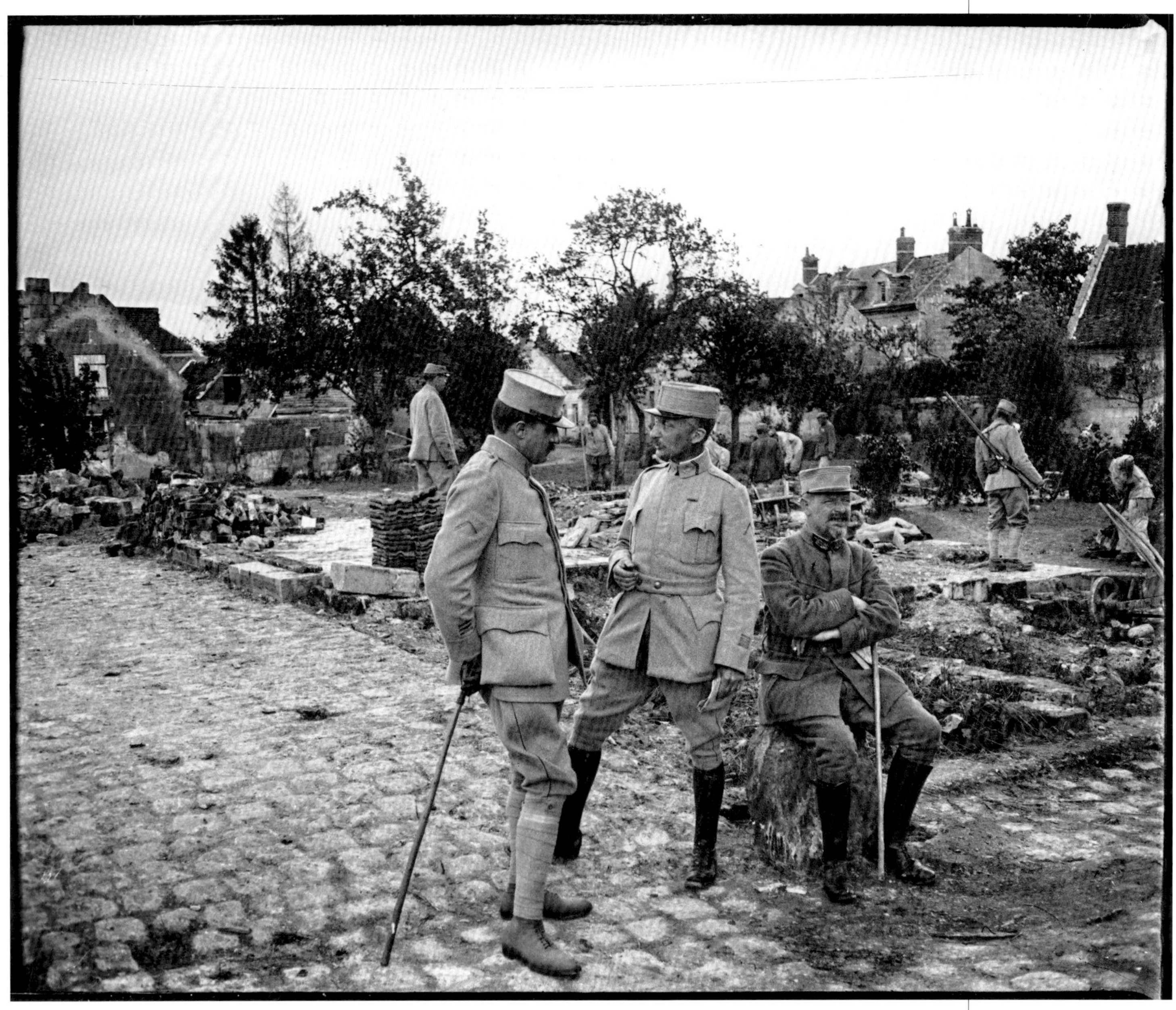

PHOT. 100
18/05/1917
Ribécourt

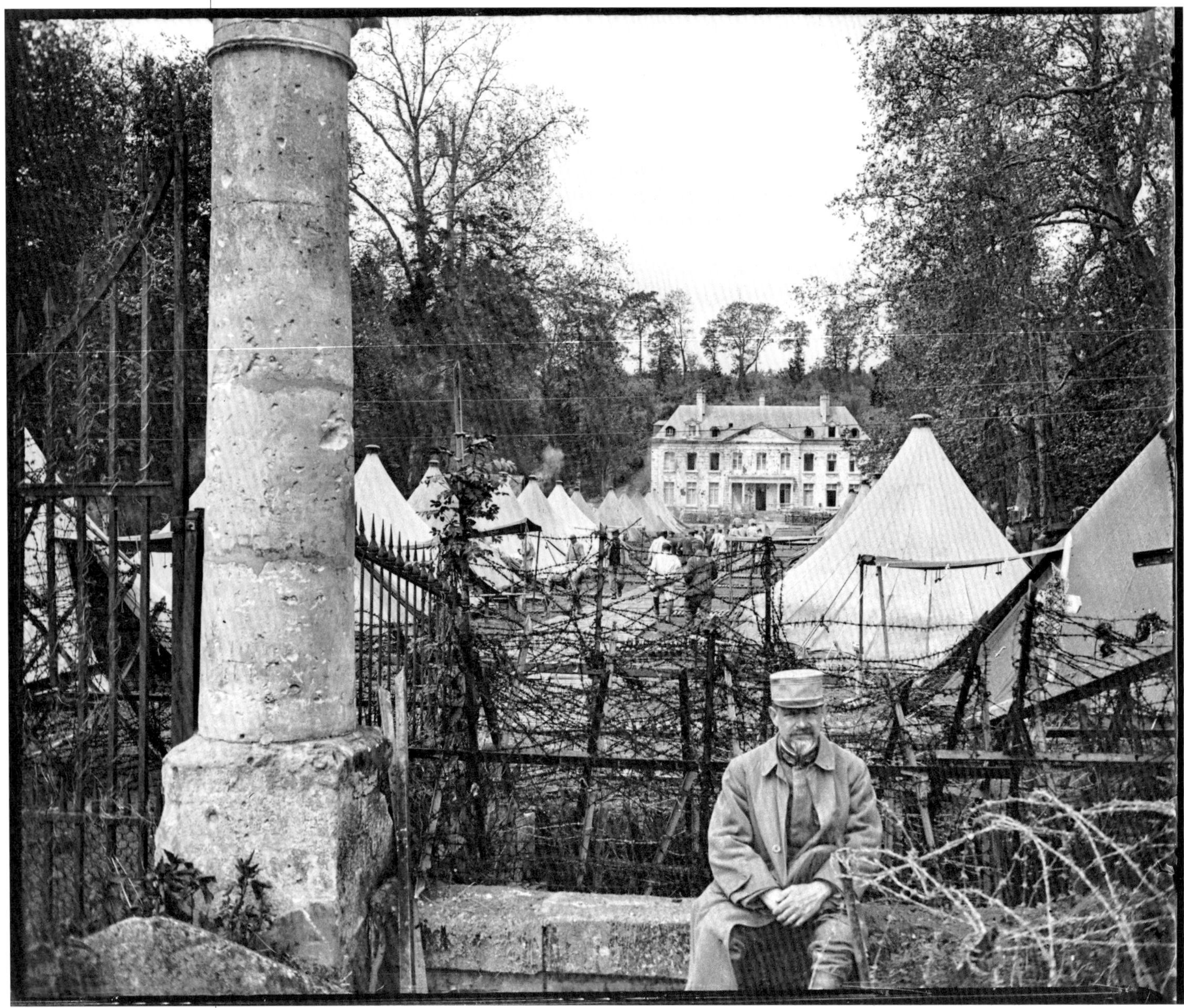

PHOT. 103
18/05/1917
Boche prisoner of war camp at Ribécourt

One of the missions assigned to territorial soldiers was guarding the prisoner of war camps, like this one set up in the 18th century château at Ribécourt.

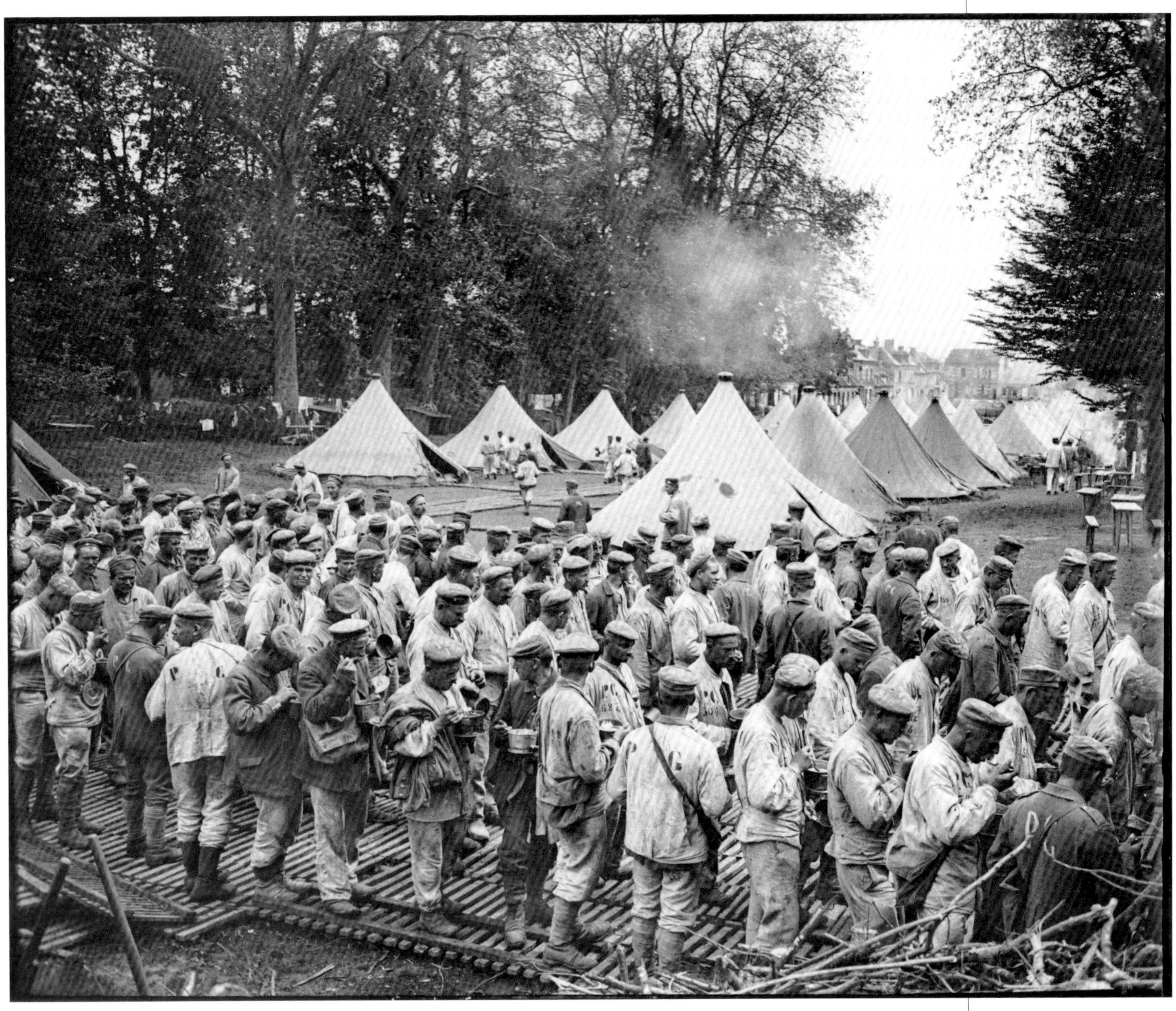

PHOT. 104
18/05/1917
Ribécourt

Lunch hour at the camp. The German prisoners, marked with a PG (*prisonnier de guerre*) on their backs, were forced to reconstruct the battered town close to the château.

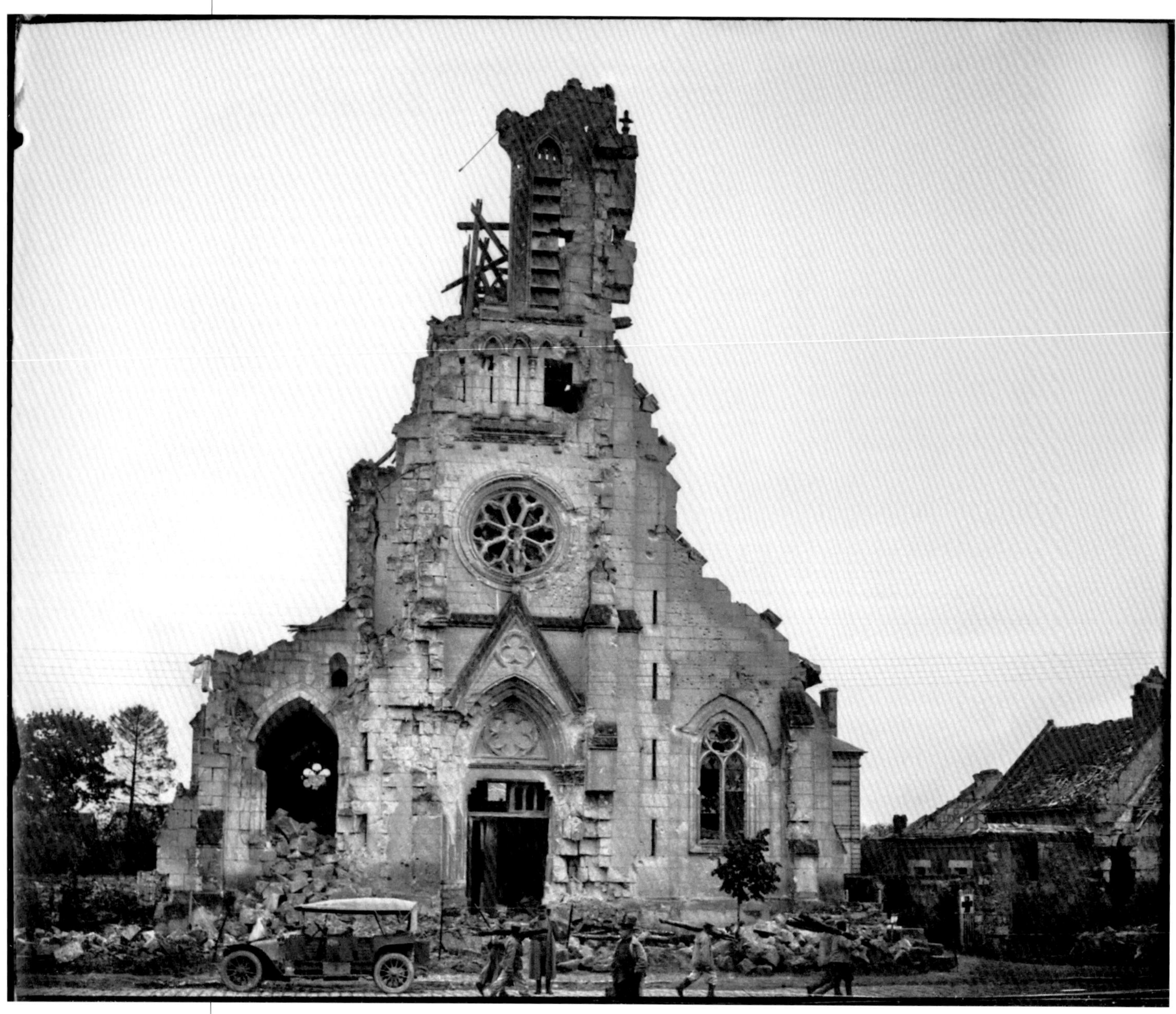

PHOT. 105
18/05/1917
Ribécourt, bell tower set for demolition.

The town's church, which was finished in 1887, had suffered bombardment by the French since 1914.

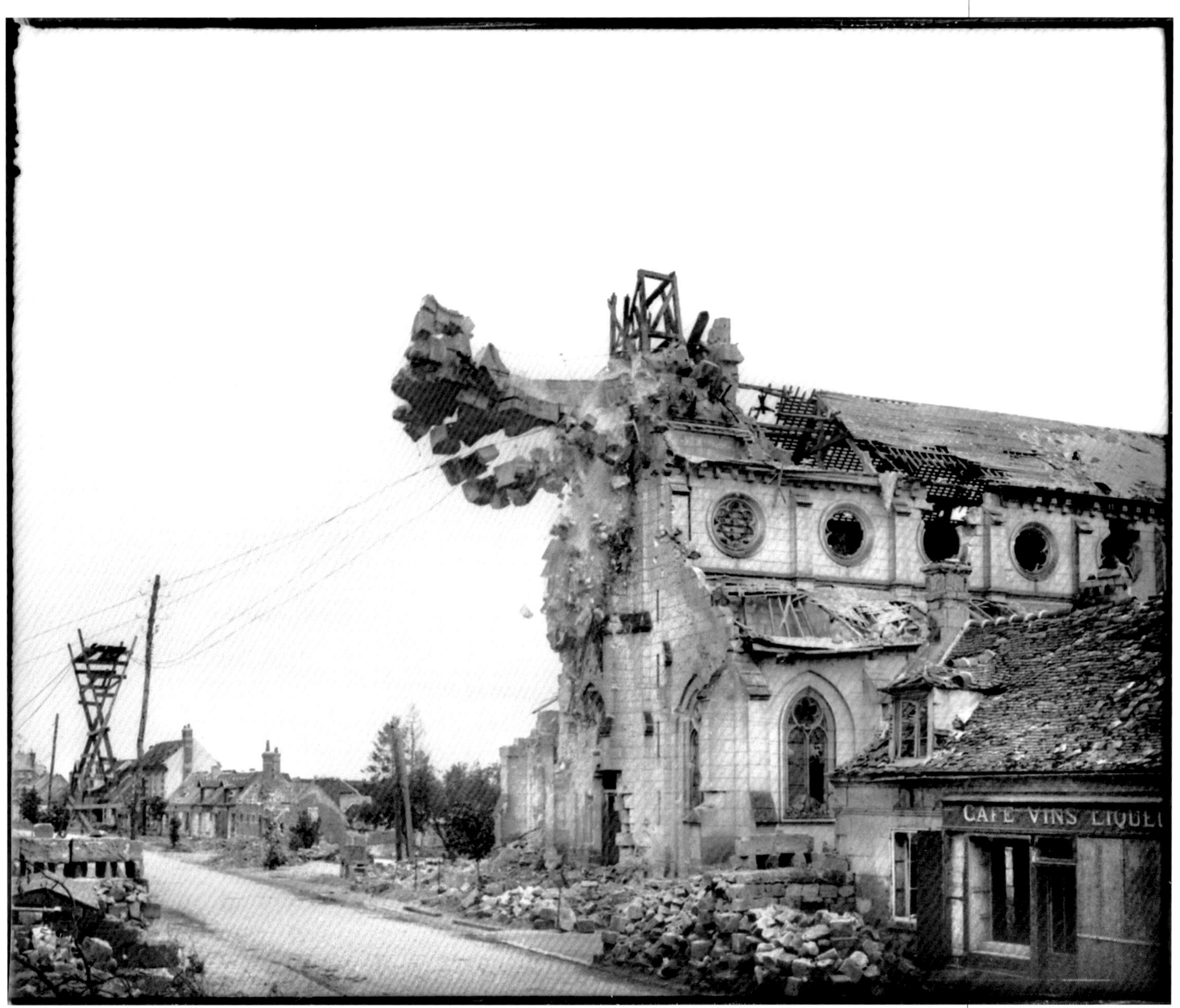

PHOT. 106
19/05/1917
Ribécourt
A precaution!

The tower was subsequently torn down, as it was unstable in addition to the danger it presented as a reference point for enemy artillery. The remains were used as barricades to block the main street which can be seen in front of the café.

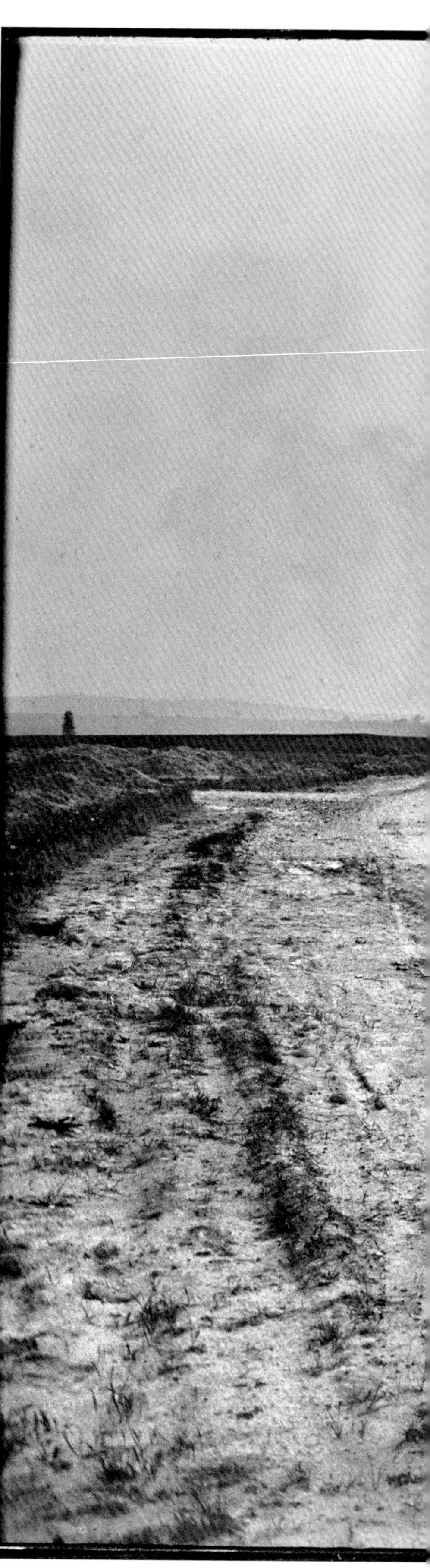

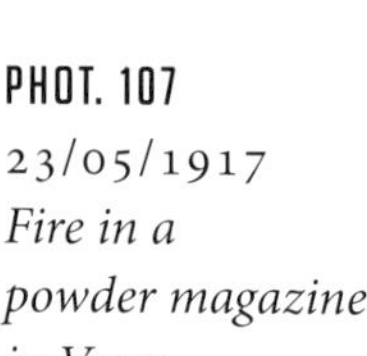

PHOT. 107
23/05/1917
Fire in a powder magazine in Vaux

In the nearby little town of Corbie a year later Manfred von Richthofen, the *Red Baron*, crashed over Australian lines.

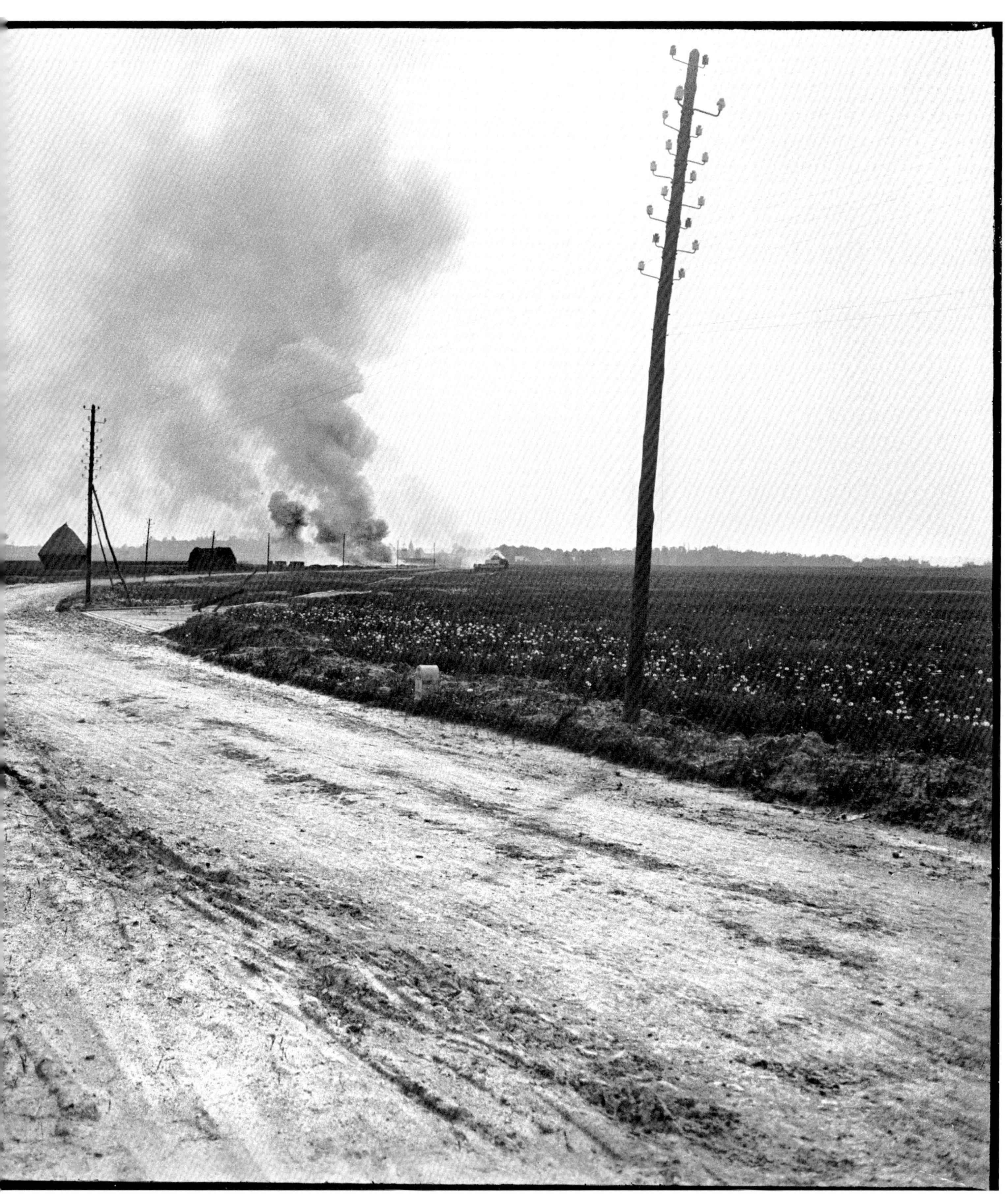

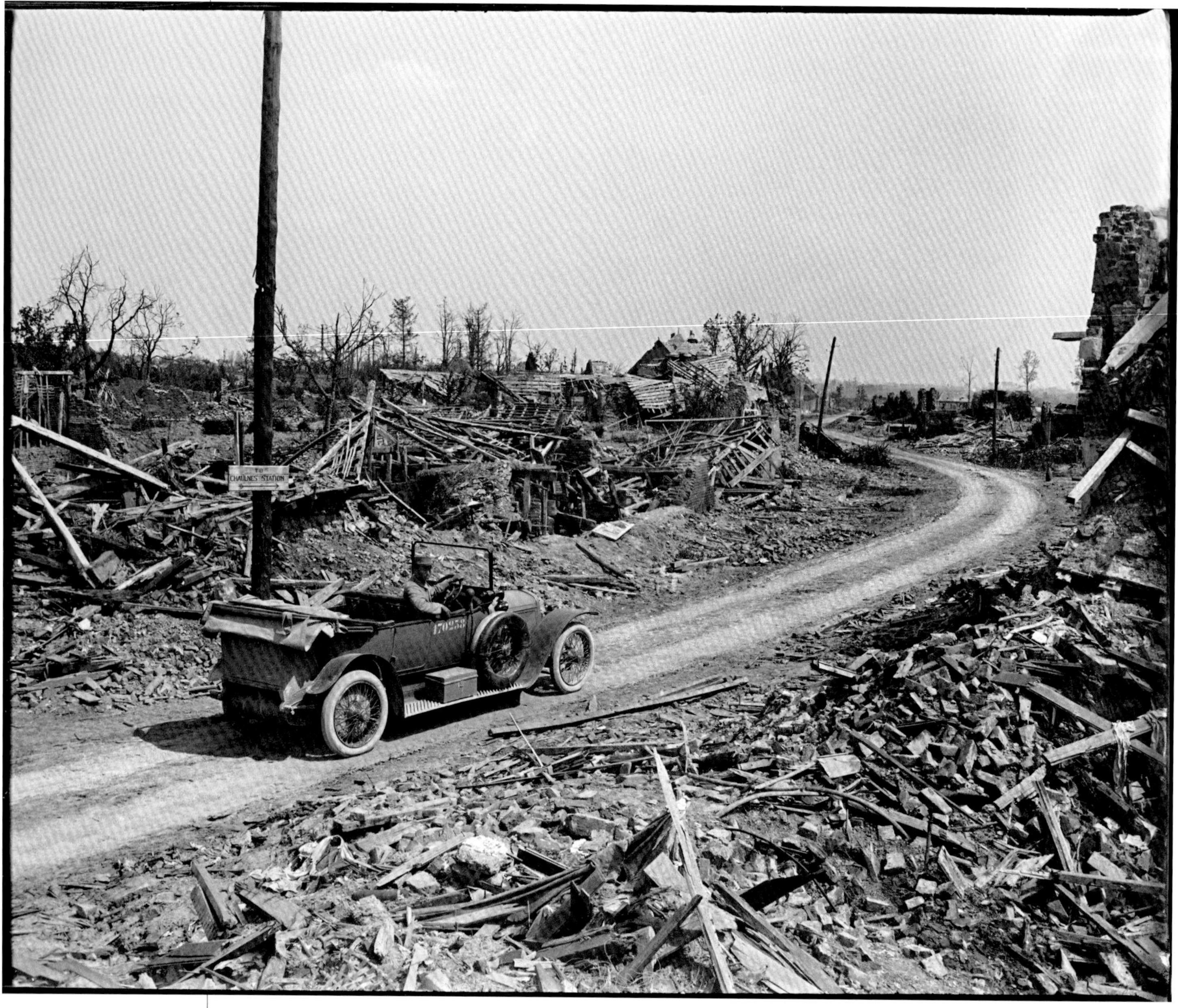

PHOT. 115
28/05/1917
Chaulnes (Somme)

Chaulnes was one of the priority targets for the French during the terrible battle of the Somme the year before. However, it was tenaciously defended by the Germans until their retreat to the Hindenburg Line in March 1917. The battle of the Somme cost in the region of 420,000 casualties to the British and Imperial forces, 208,000 to the French and somewhere between 465,000–600,000 to the Germans.

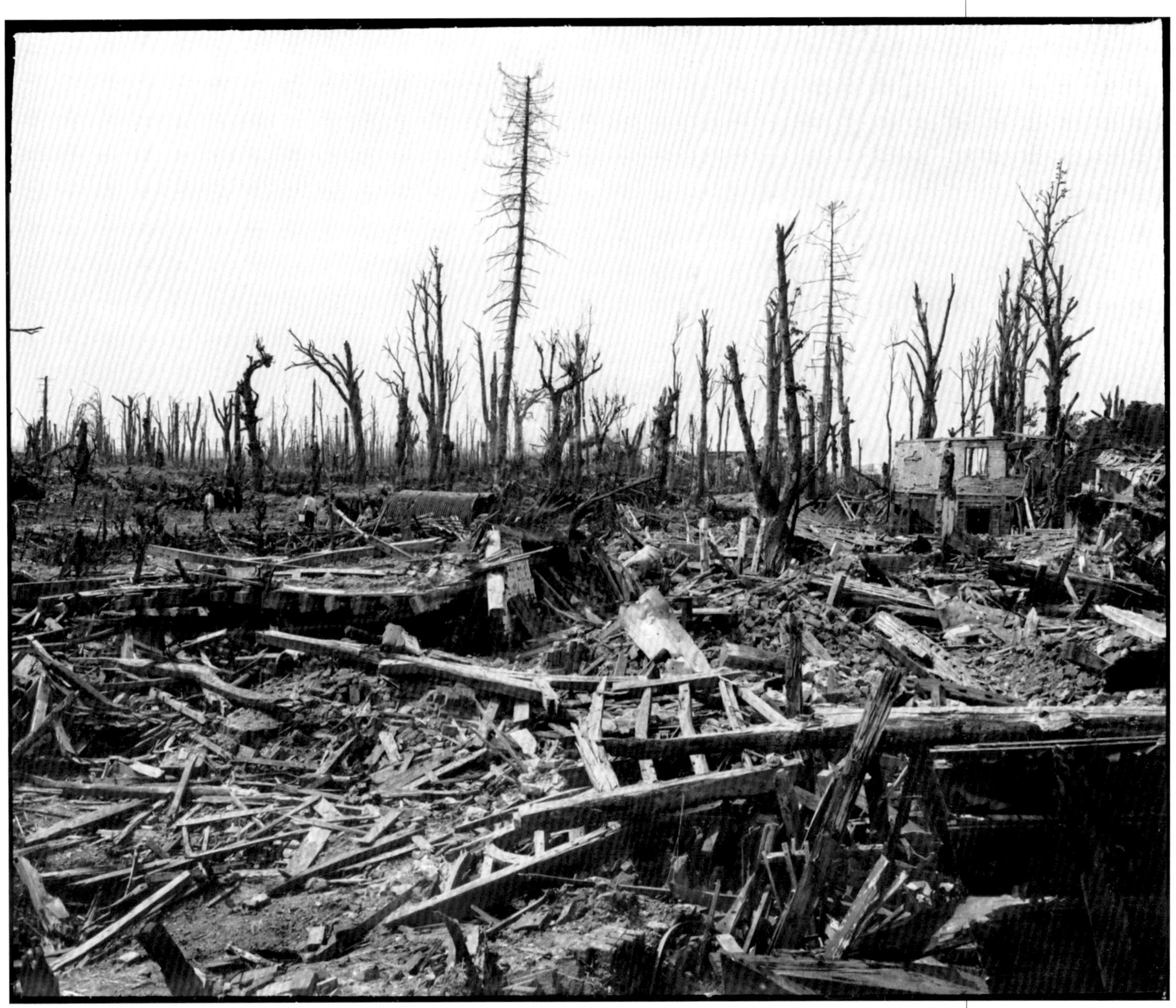

PHOT. 116
28/05/1917
Chaulnes (Somme)

Panoramic of what remained of the village of 1,200 inhabitants. After the war it was classified as *Red Zone*: totally devastated.

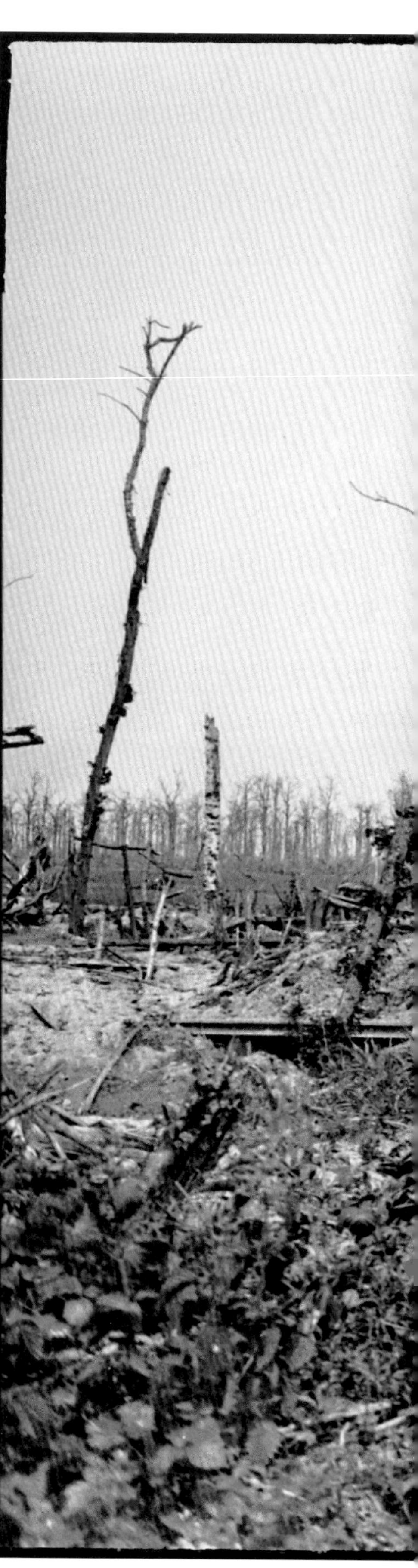

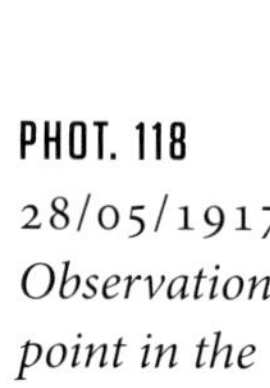

PHOT. 118
28/05/1917
Observation point in the British lines

The observation of enemy territory was essential, to monitor their movement and to direct artillery fire. The artillery fire was aimed in such way as to cover the most ground possible, destroying any positions in which the enemy could seek cover.

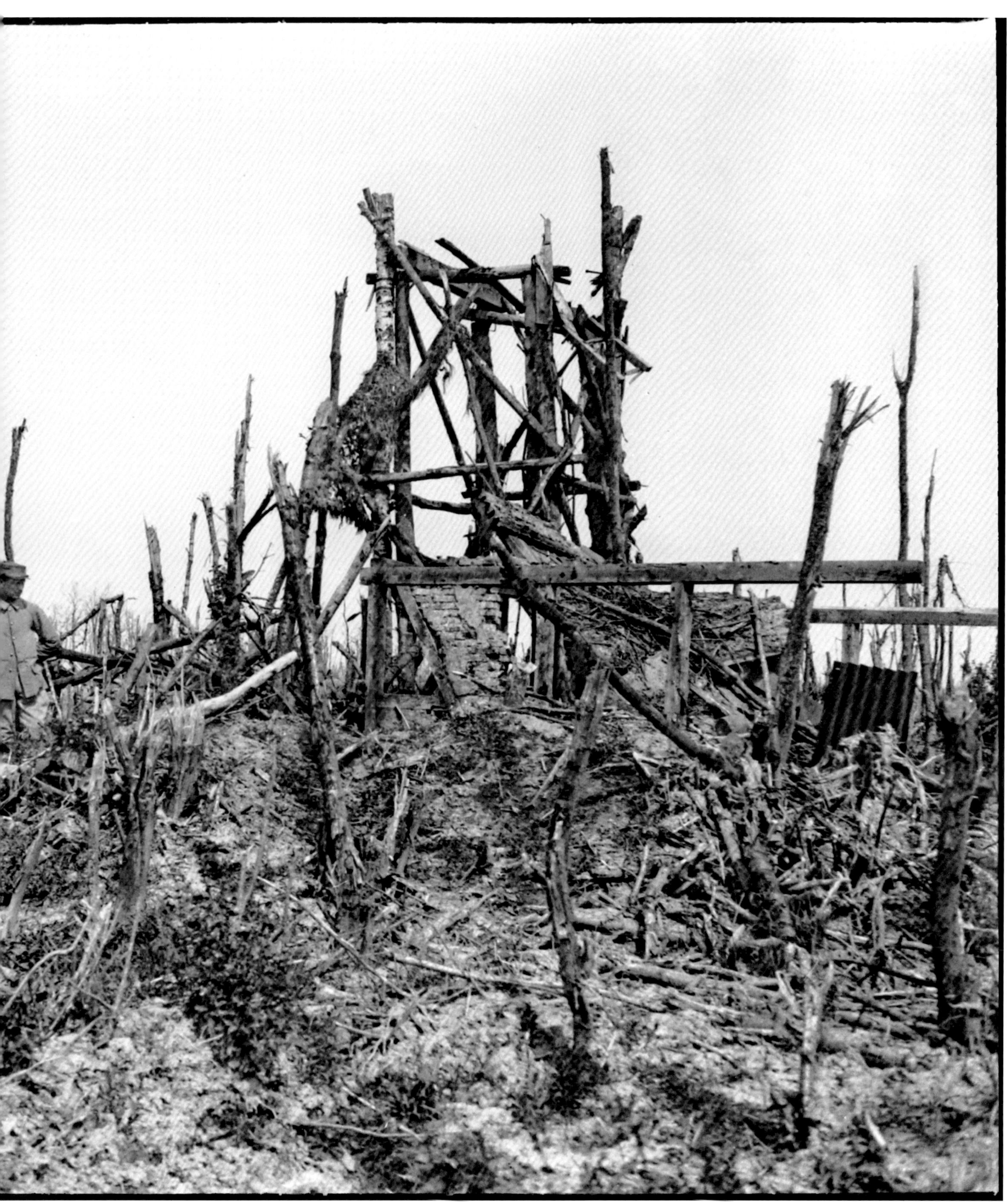

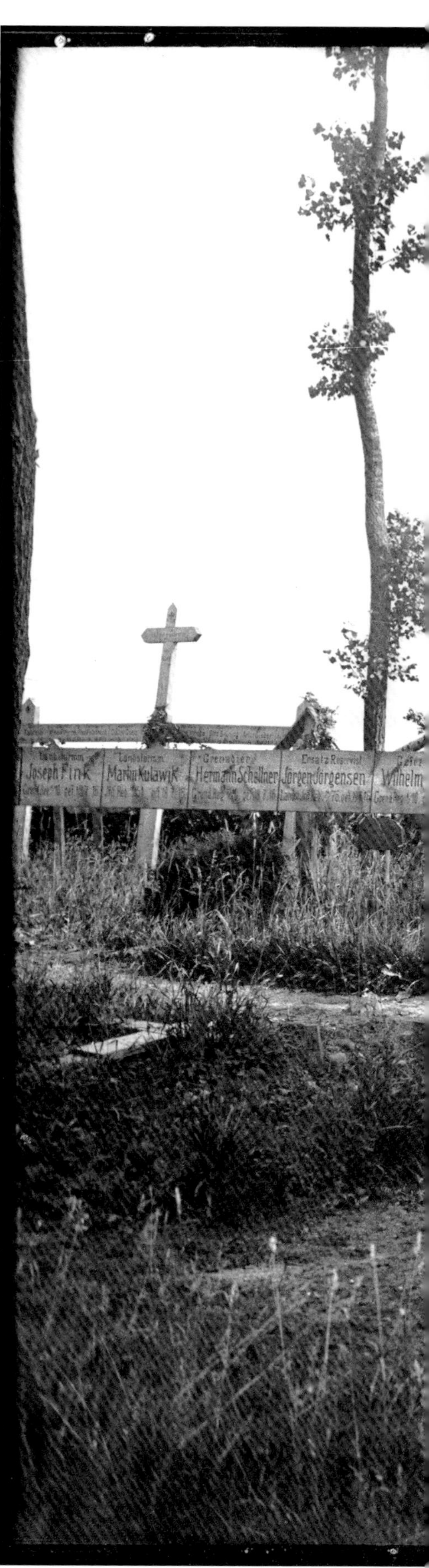

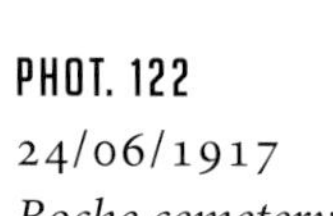

PHOT. 122
24/06/1917
Boche cemetery

The German graveyards became a recurrent subject for the Allies' trophy photographs.

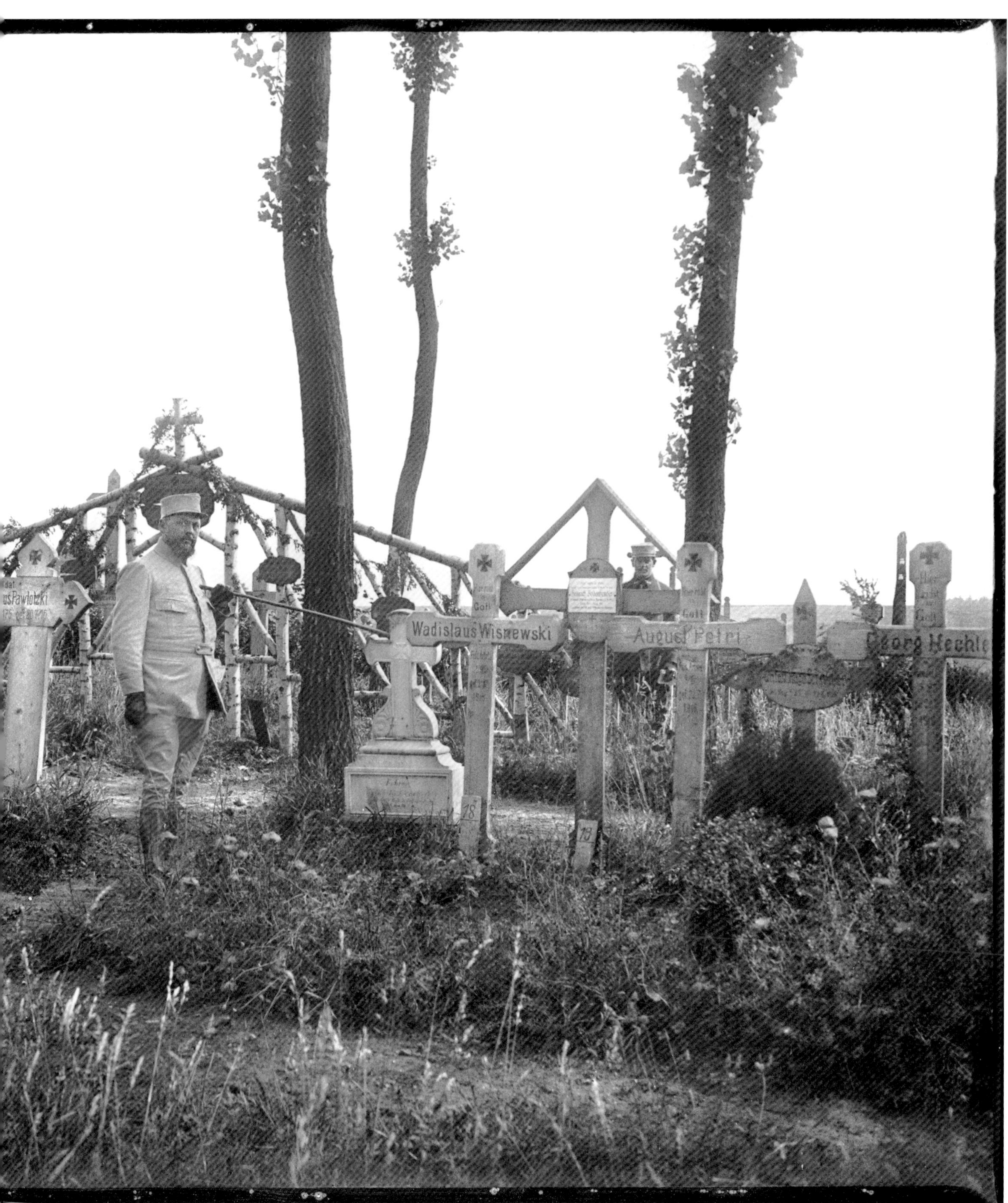
Wadislaus Wisnewski
Gott
August Petri
Gott
Georg Hechle

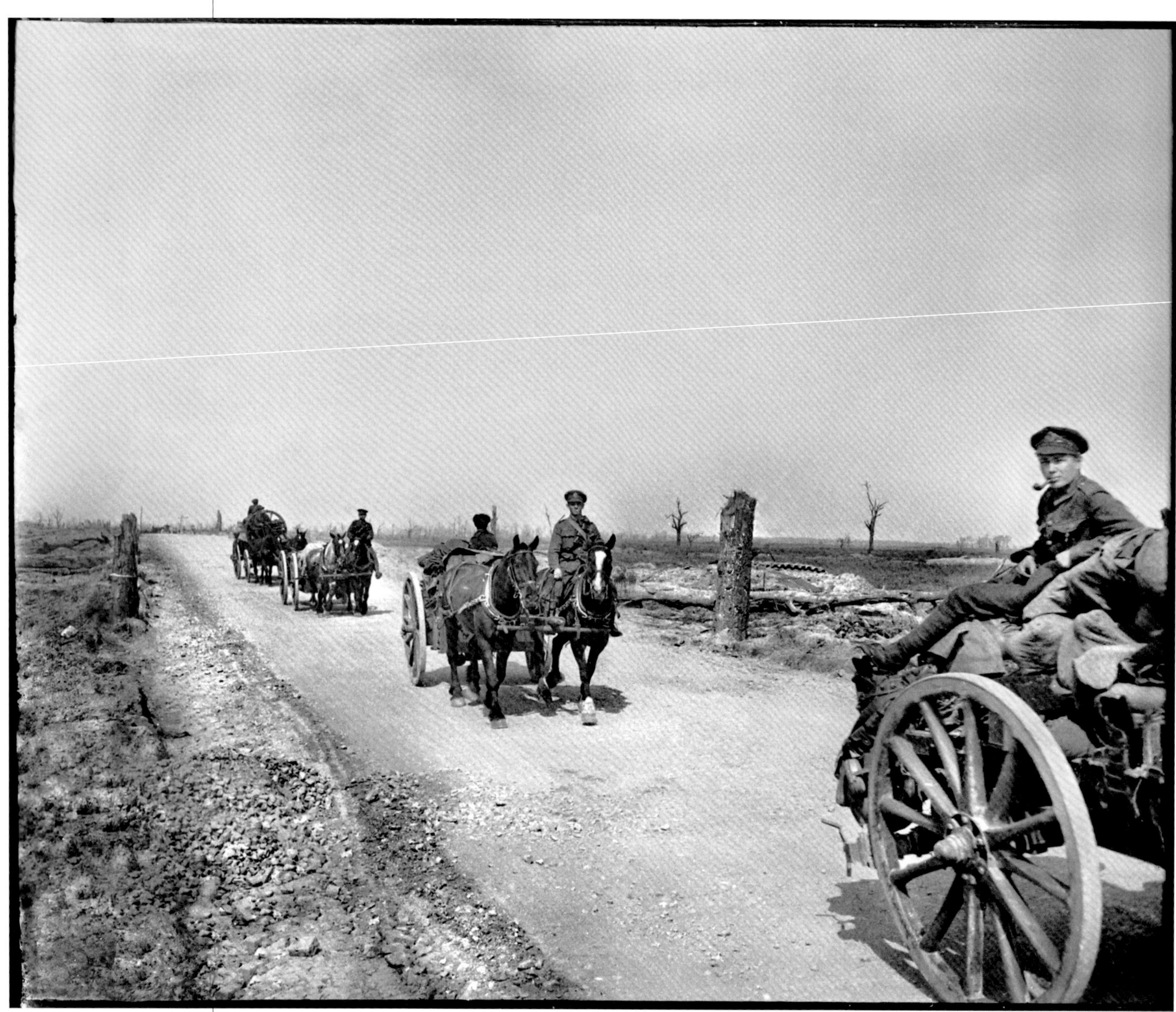

PHOT. 119
28/05/1917
A British convoy

Despite being the first mechanised war, animals were still fundamental for transport in the First World War. However, the cavalry did not recover its old tactical function and had to un-mount and line the trenches.

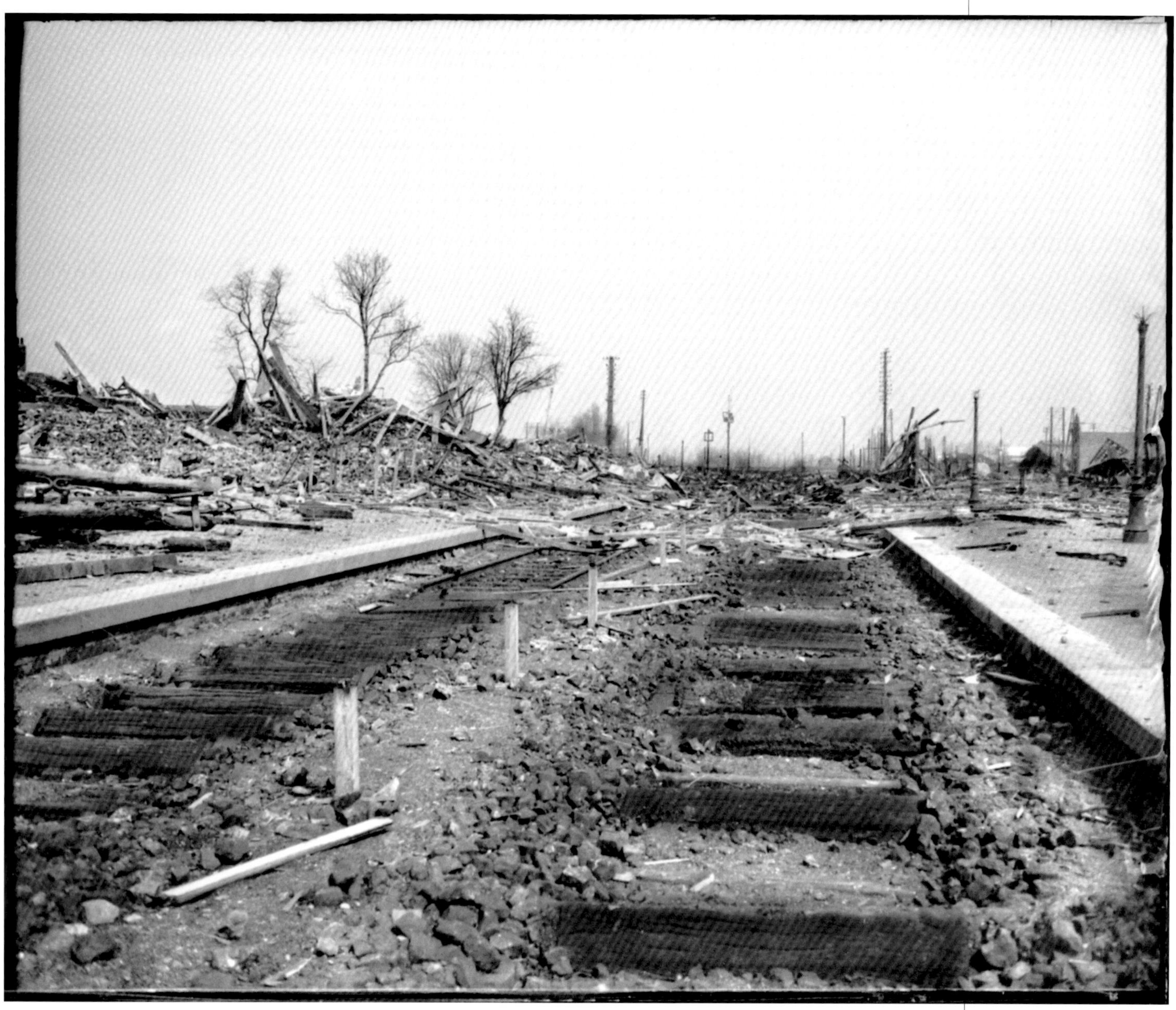

PHOT. 121
04/06/1917
The remains of a train station in Chauny

The state of the train station exemplifies the level of destruction achieved in this Picard town. The Germans even removed the rails before evacuating it.

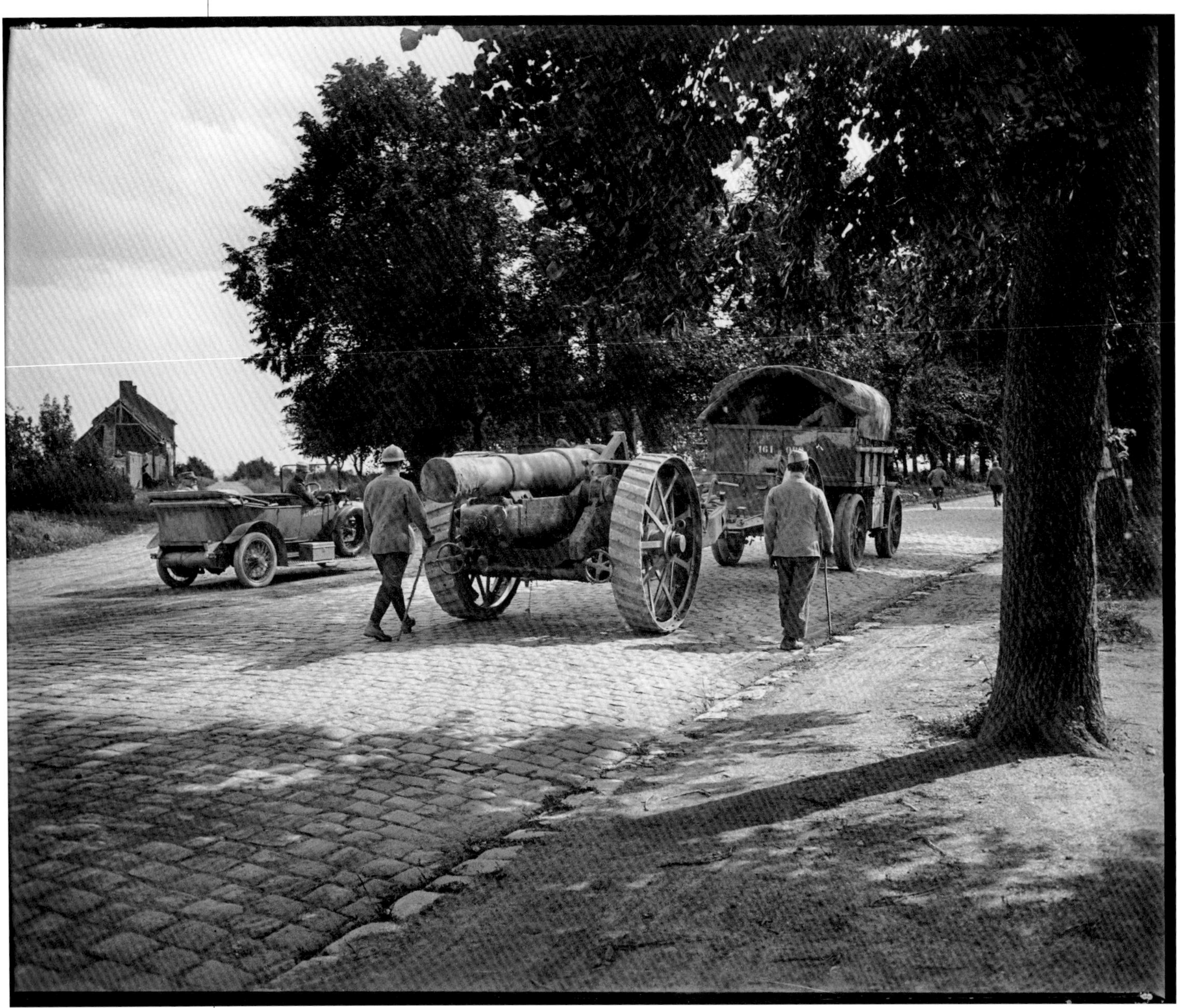

PHOT. 124
26/06/1917
Heavy artillery pulled by tractor at the exit of Roye

In front of Givord's car passes an English howitzer MK VII pulled by a French vehicle.

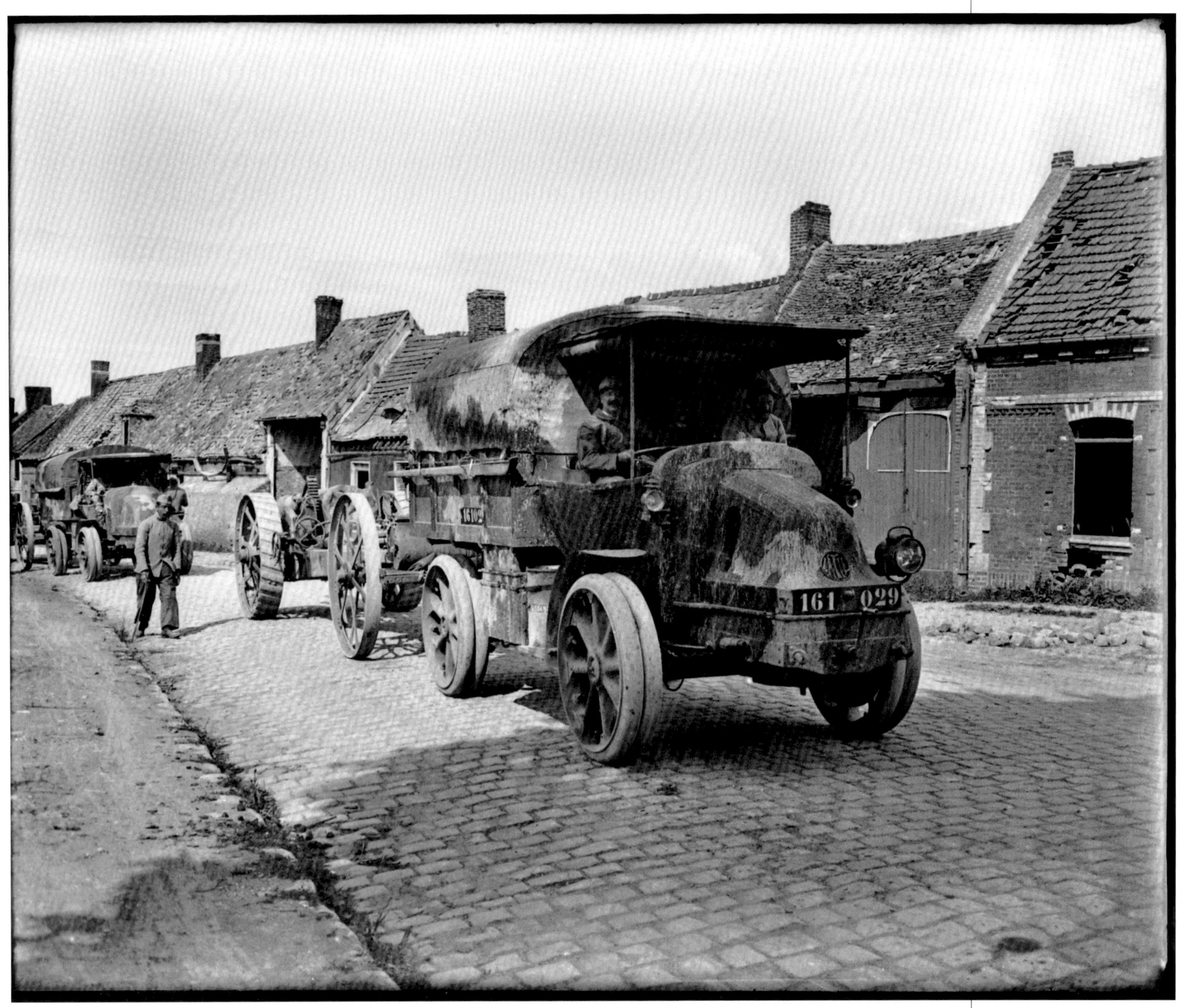

PHOT. 126
26/06/1917
Heavy artillery being pulled by tractor

A Latil artillery tractor equipped with four-wheel drive.

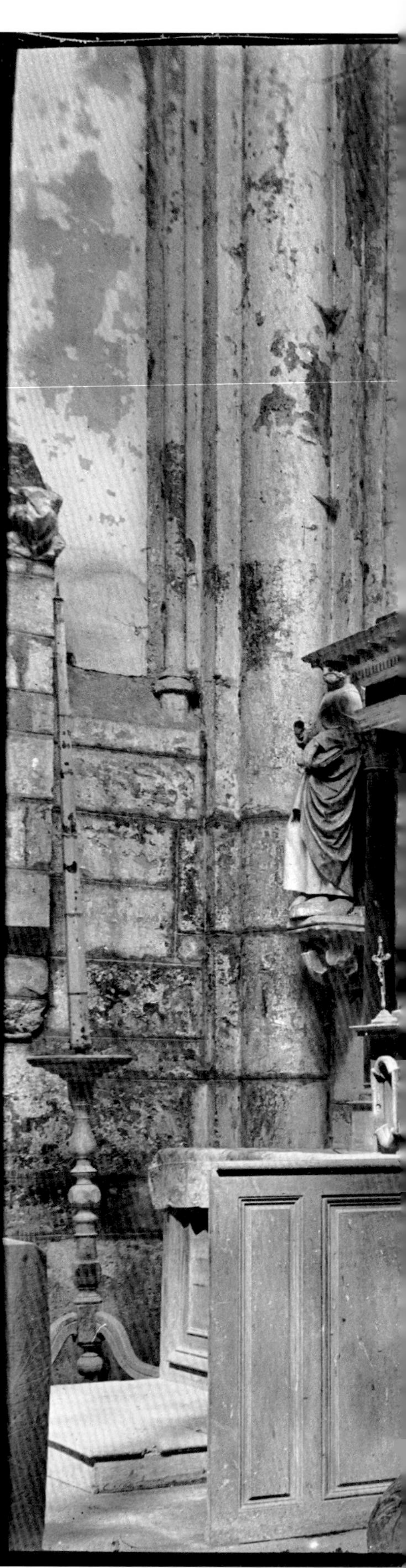

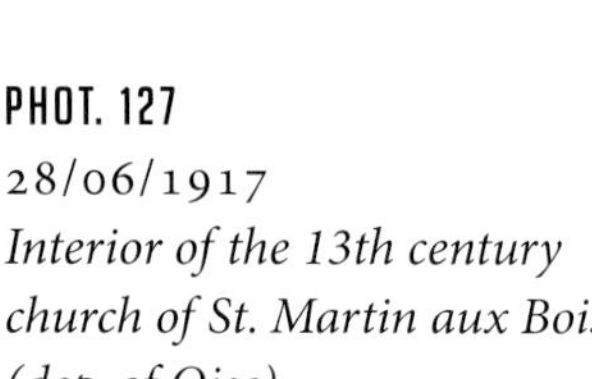

PHOT. 127
28/06/1917
Interior of the 13th century church of St. Martin aux Bois (dep. of Oise)

Captain Givord poses besides the gothic choir enclosure of this church. The wristwatch he wears is an accessory whose use was generalised during the First World War. The first to request it were the artillerymen. The pocket watch proved uncomfortable as a chronometer, and awkward to observe the projectiles trajectory at the same time.

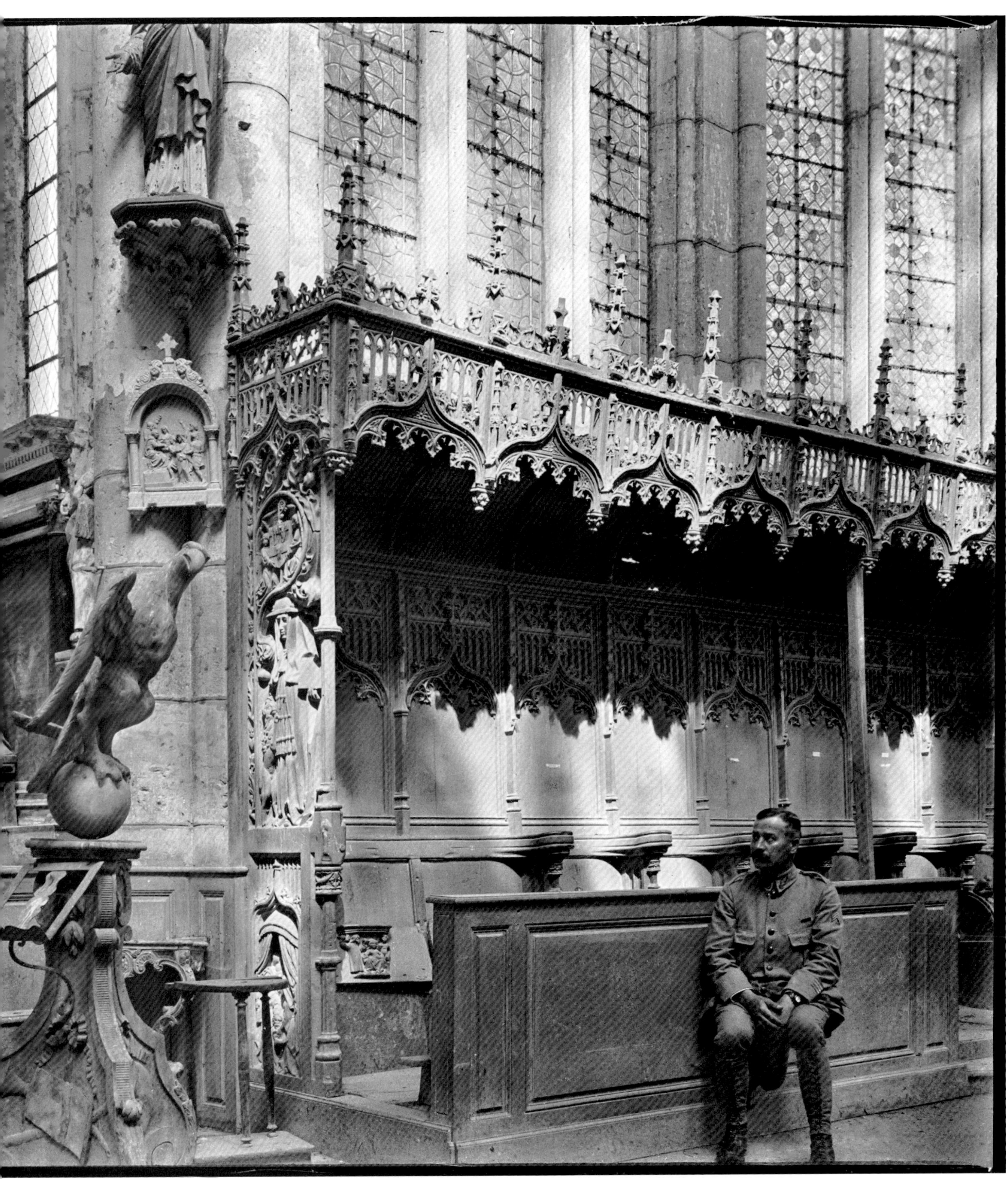

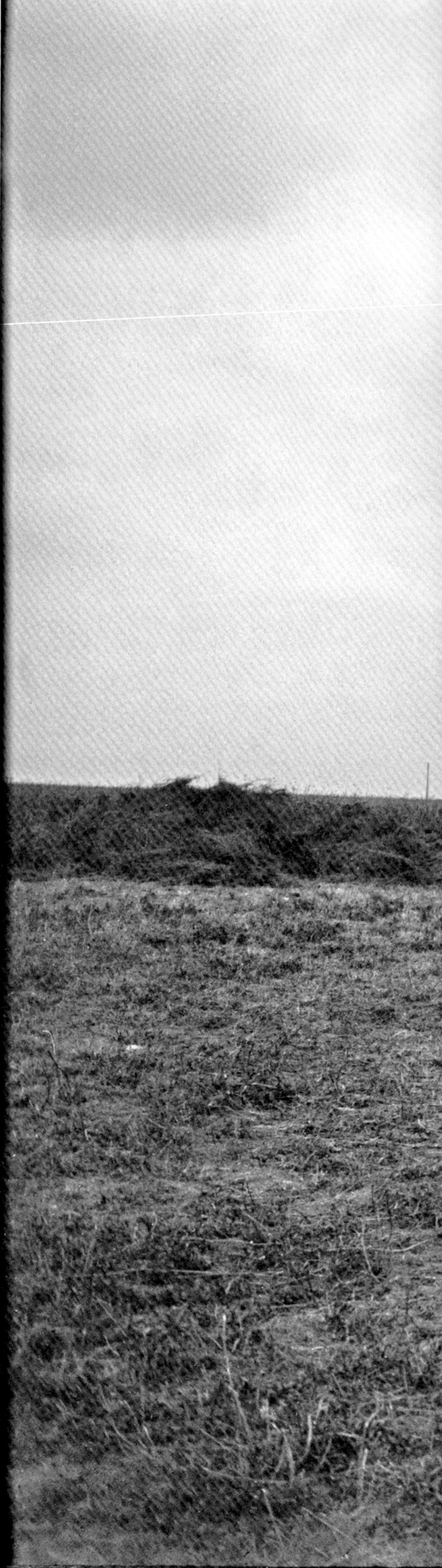

PHOT. 128
01/07/1917
An English plane in Faverolle!

An Airco DH. 5 of the Royal Flying Corps after a forced landing. It had a wing configuration with the upper wing placed slightly behind the lower wing; this left the pilot with an excellent field of vision. However, it was slow and not very reliable, hence it was active for only eight months. One of the aviation problems was the continuous demand for new planes, which led to combat designs that were not thoroughly tested.

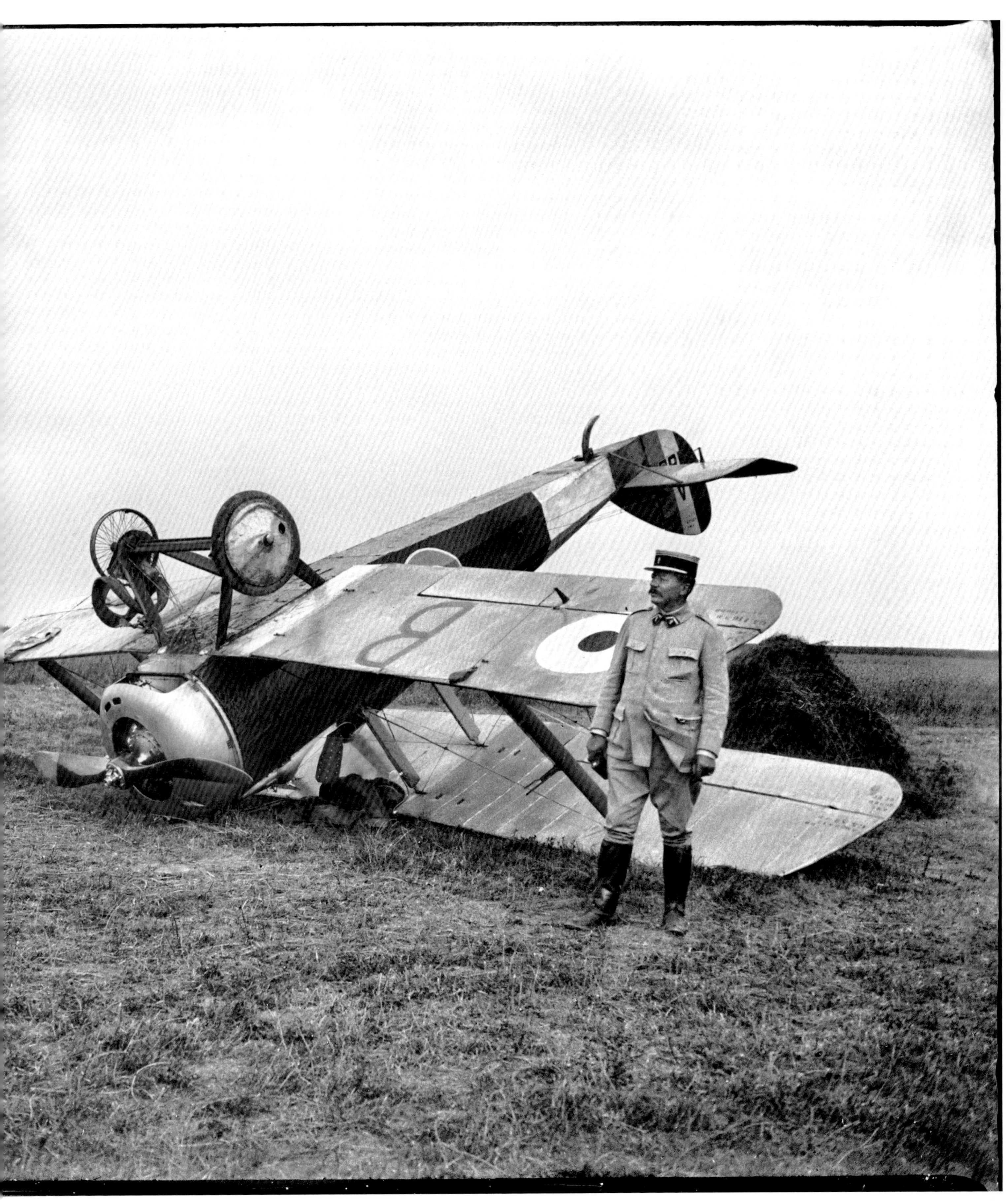

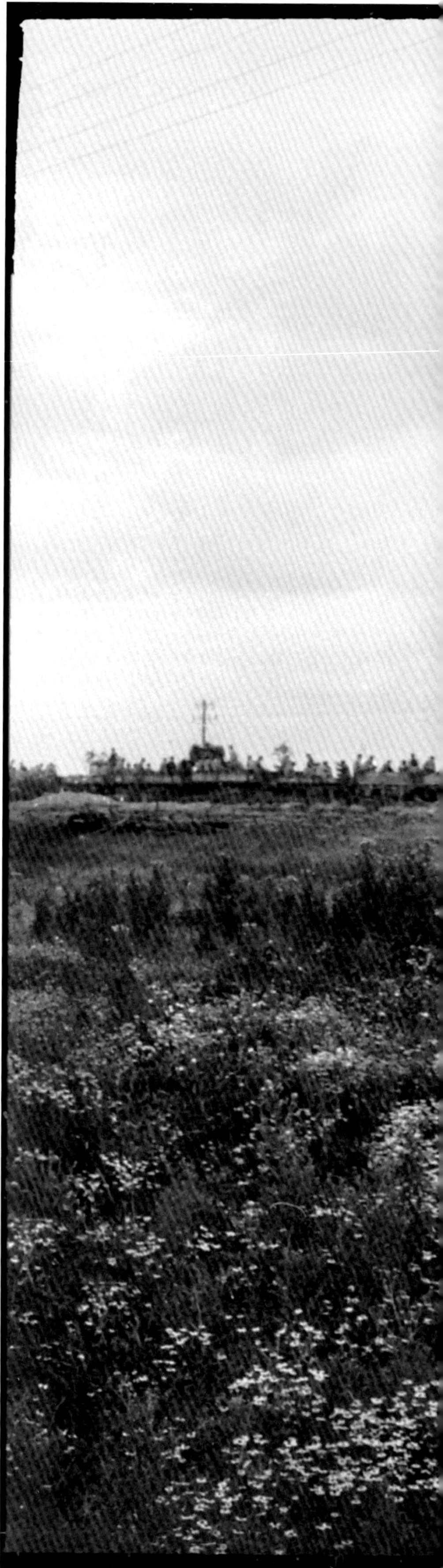

PHOT. 129
02/07/1917
A train of English workers

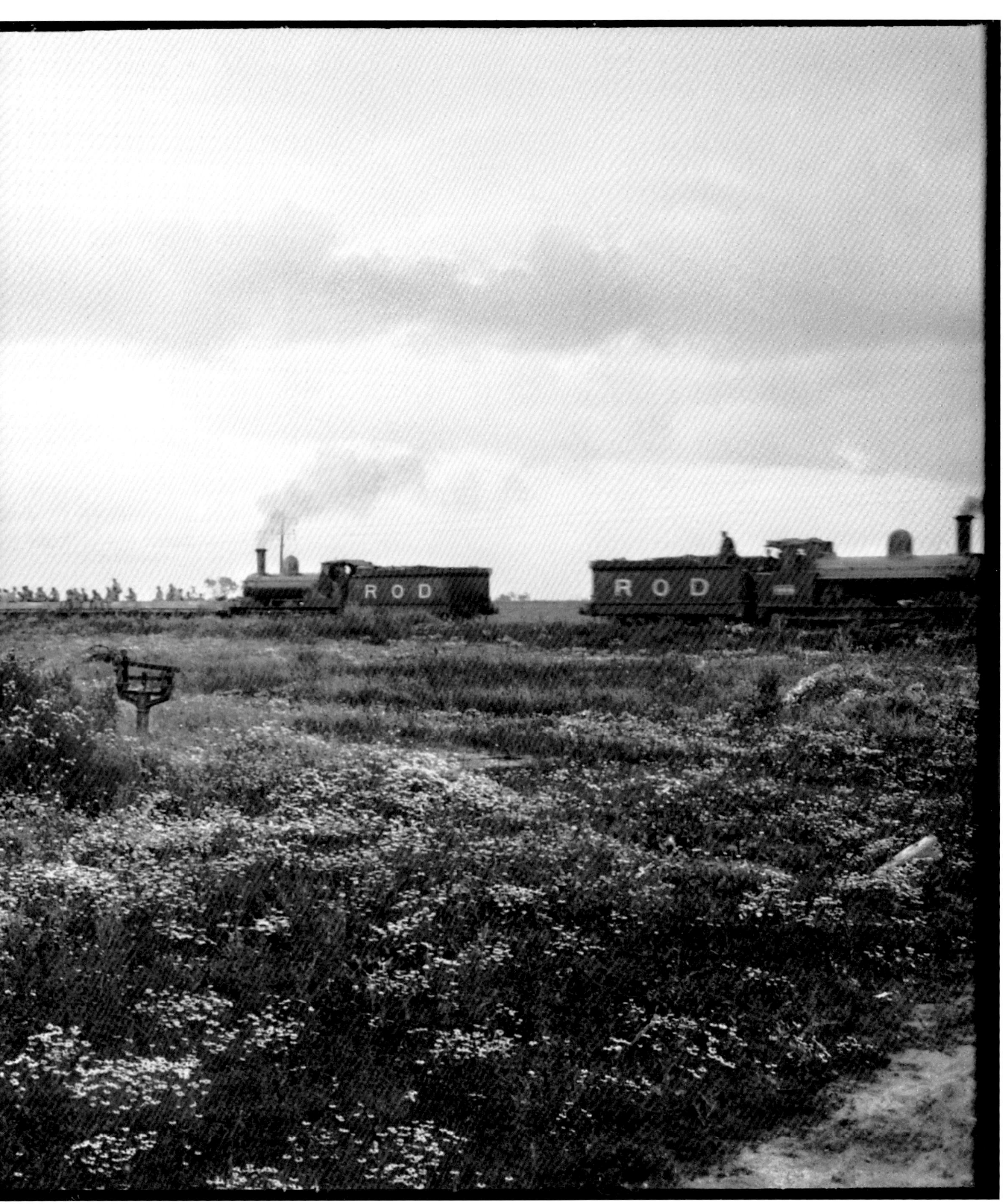
ROD
ROD

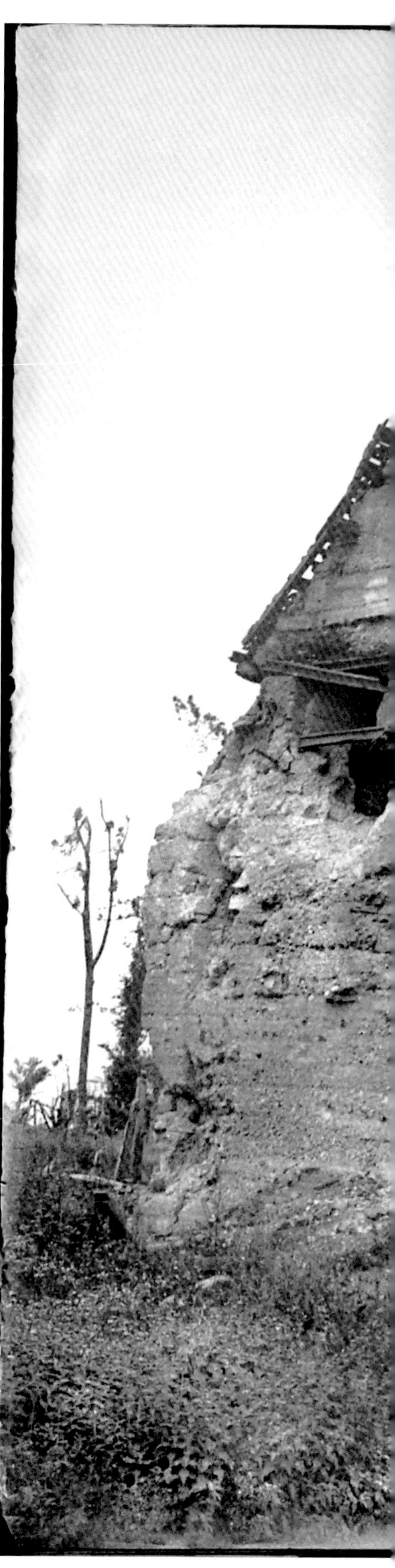

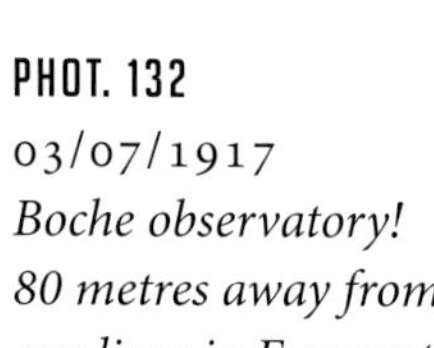

PHOT. 132
03/07/1917
Boche observatory!
80 metres away from
our lines in Fransart

The bombarded farms could be adapted to monitor the enemy, such as this one, close to the enemy lines which went undiscovered.

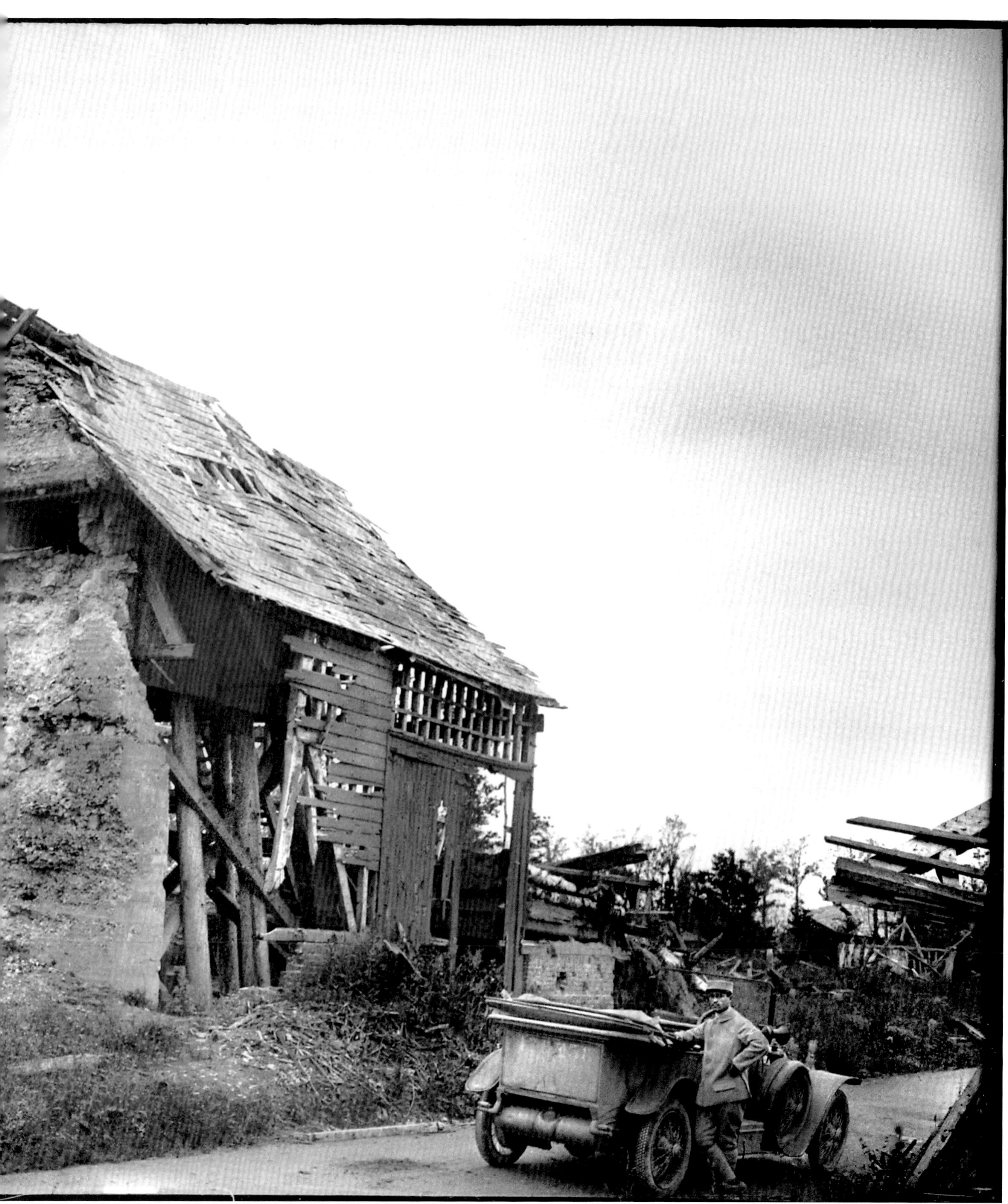

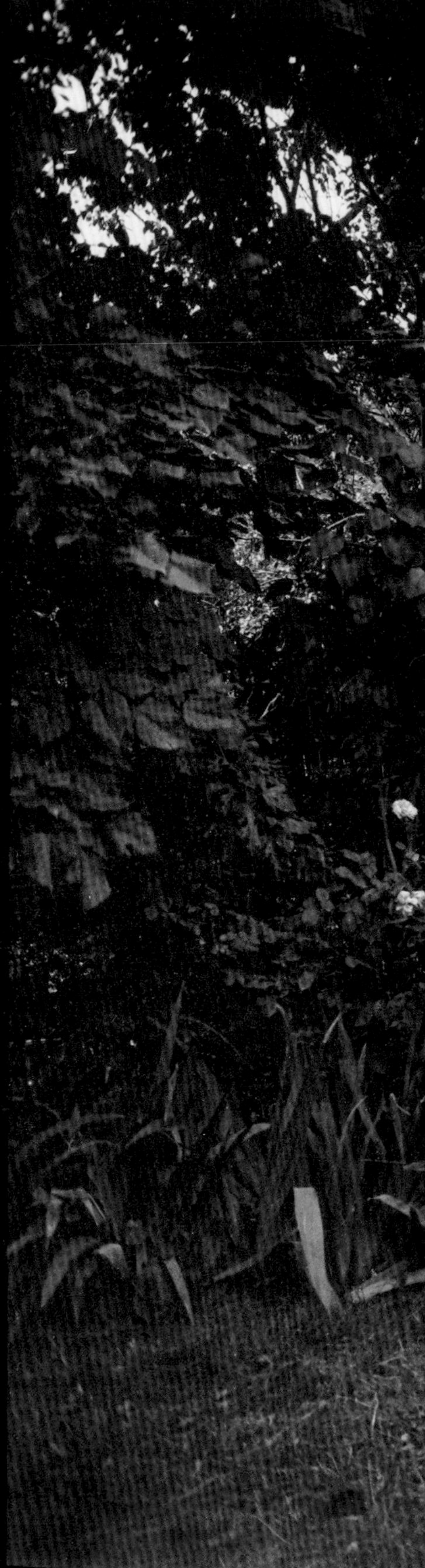

PHOT. 133
07/07/1917
General staff of the 99e Régiment d'Infanterie

Givord (left) poses with his old regiment comrades. Among them, his Commander Lieutenant-Colonel Borne (centre), his deputy the *chef d'escadron* Nativelle (between Givord and Borne), the band leader July (at the back, with his arms crossed) and two military doctors (on the right, with dark badges on the lapels).

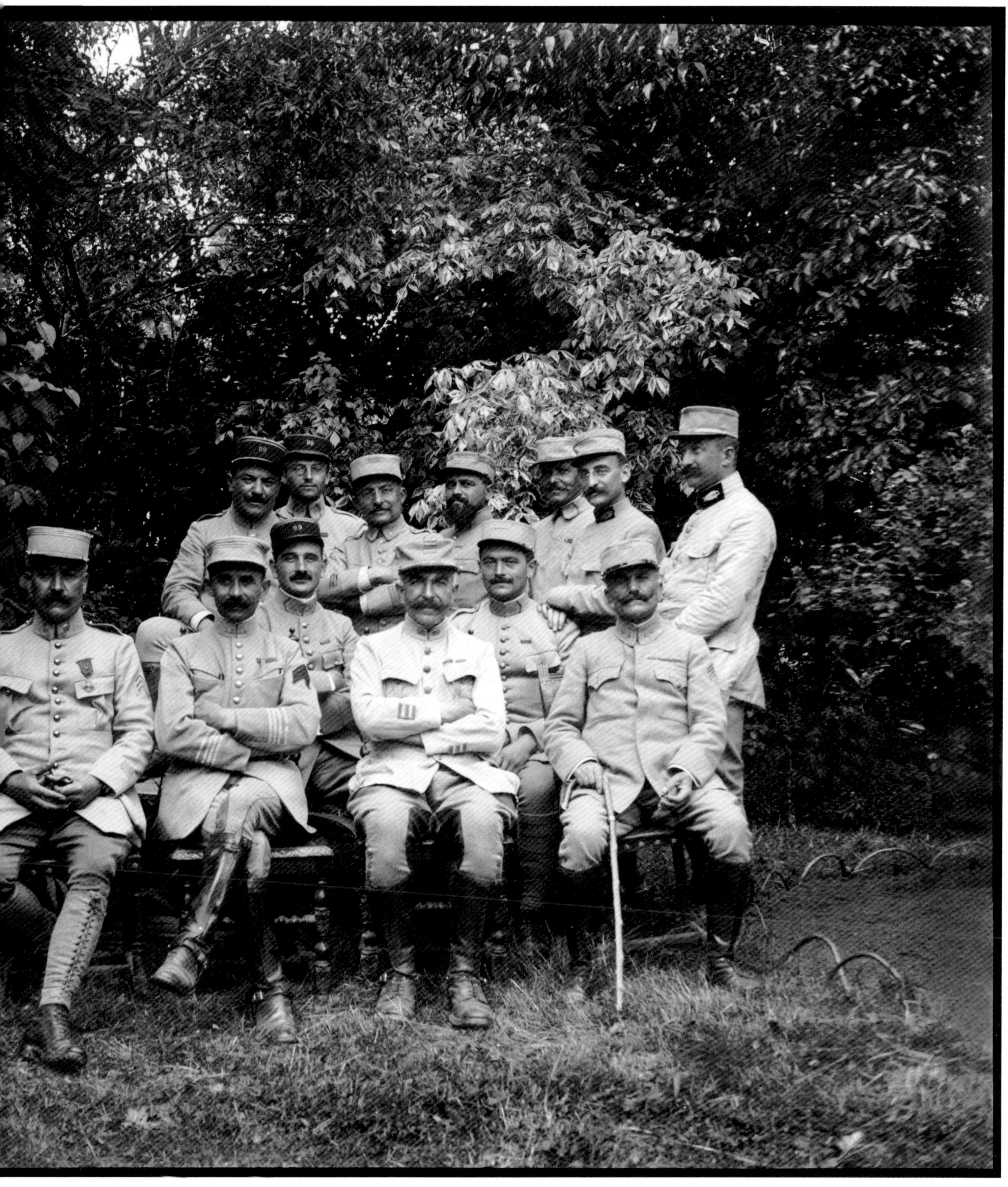
99
99
99

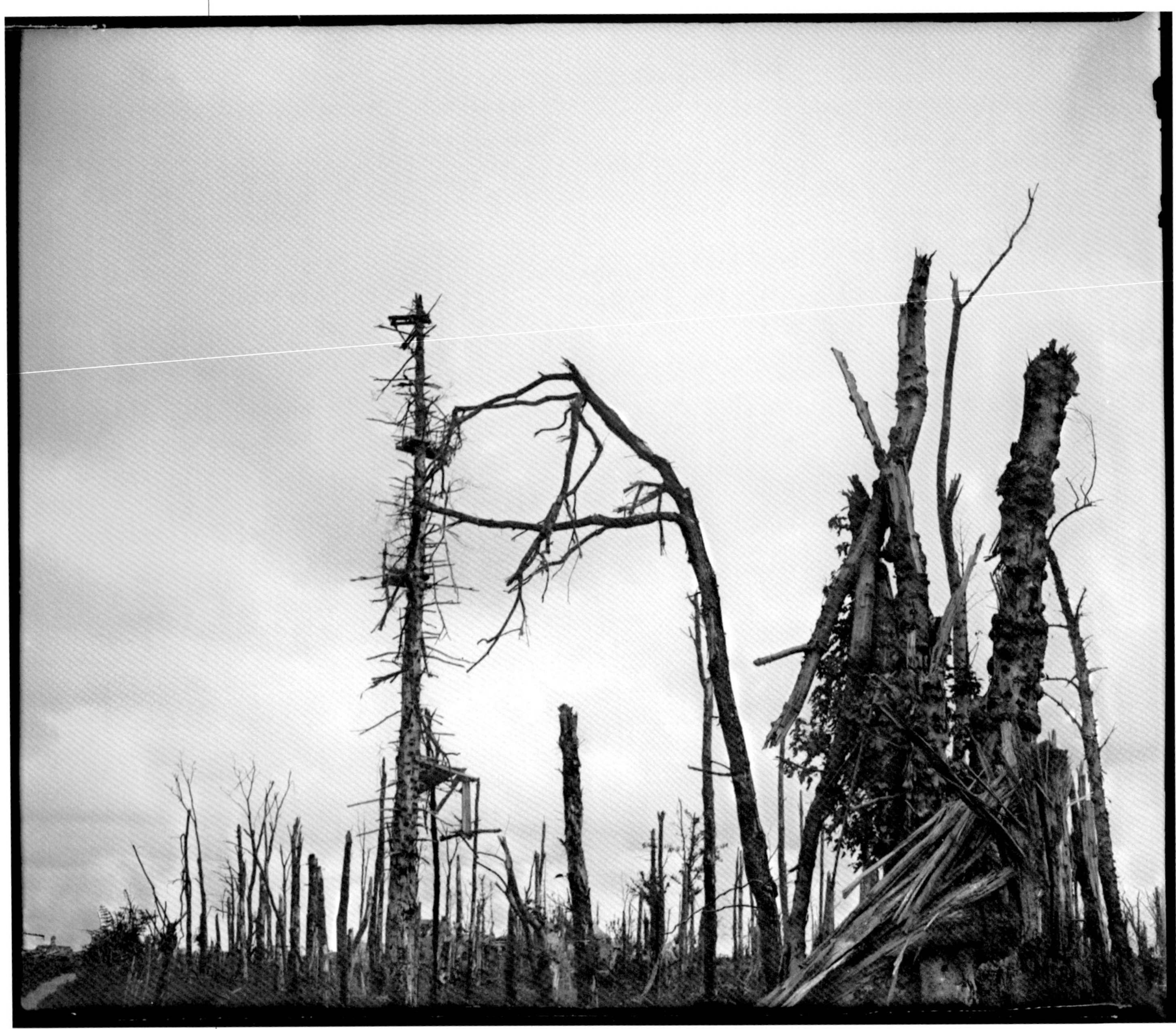

PHOT. 130
02/07/1917
A Boche observatory close to Chaulnes

The observation watchtowers could be disguised between the shattered trees.

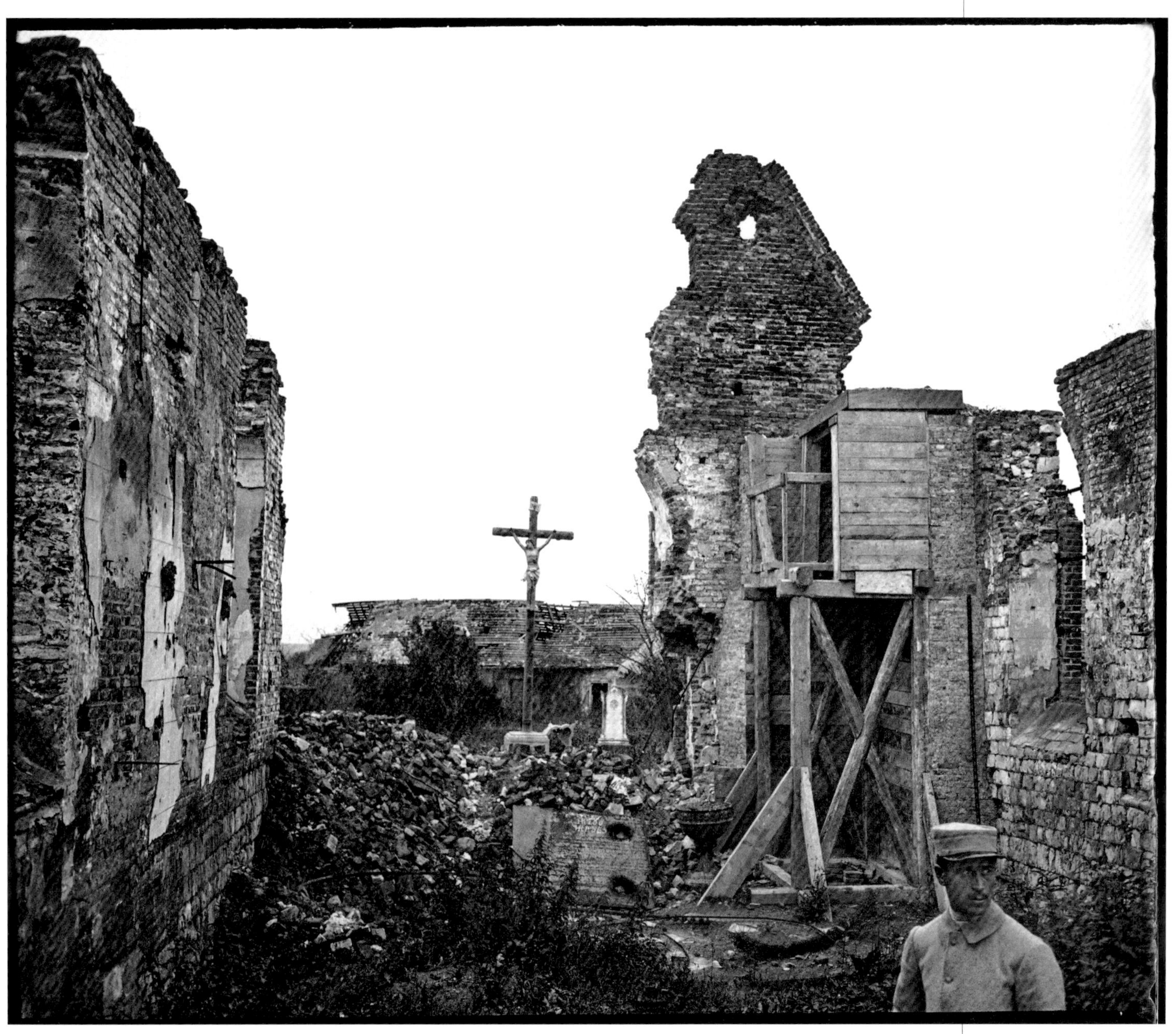

PHOT. 131
03/07/1917
Boche observatory in Fransart

The positions were also hidden in ruined churches.

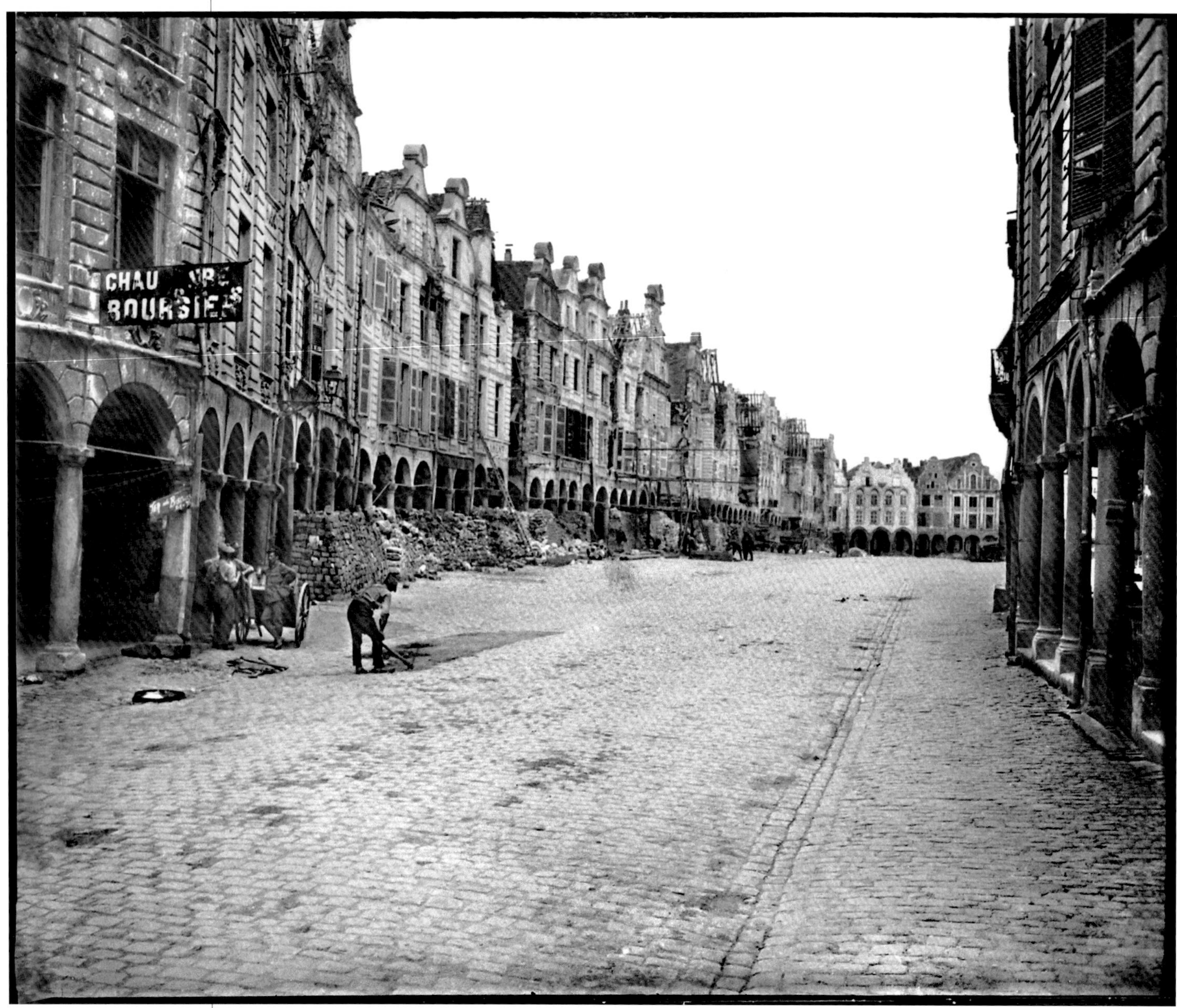

PHOT. 135
20/07/1917
Arras Market
Plaza

The Battle of Arras in 1917 was carried out by the British in two phases, the first one between April 9th and April 14th, and the second one between April 23rd and May 16th. Its intention was to distract the Germans whilst the French attacked at Chemin des Dames but in this effort the British received over 150,000 casualties, the Germans over 130,000.

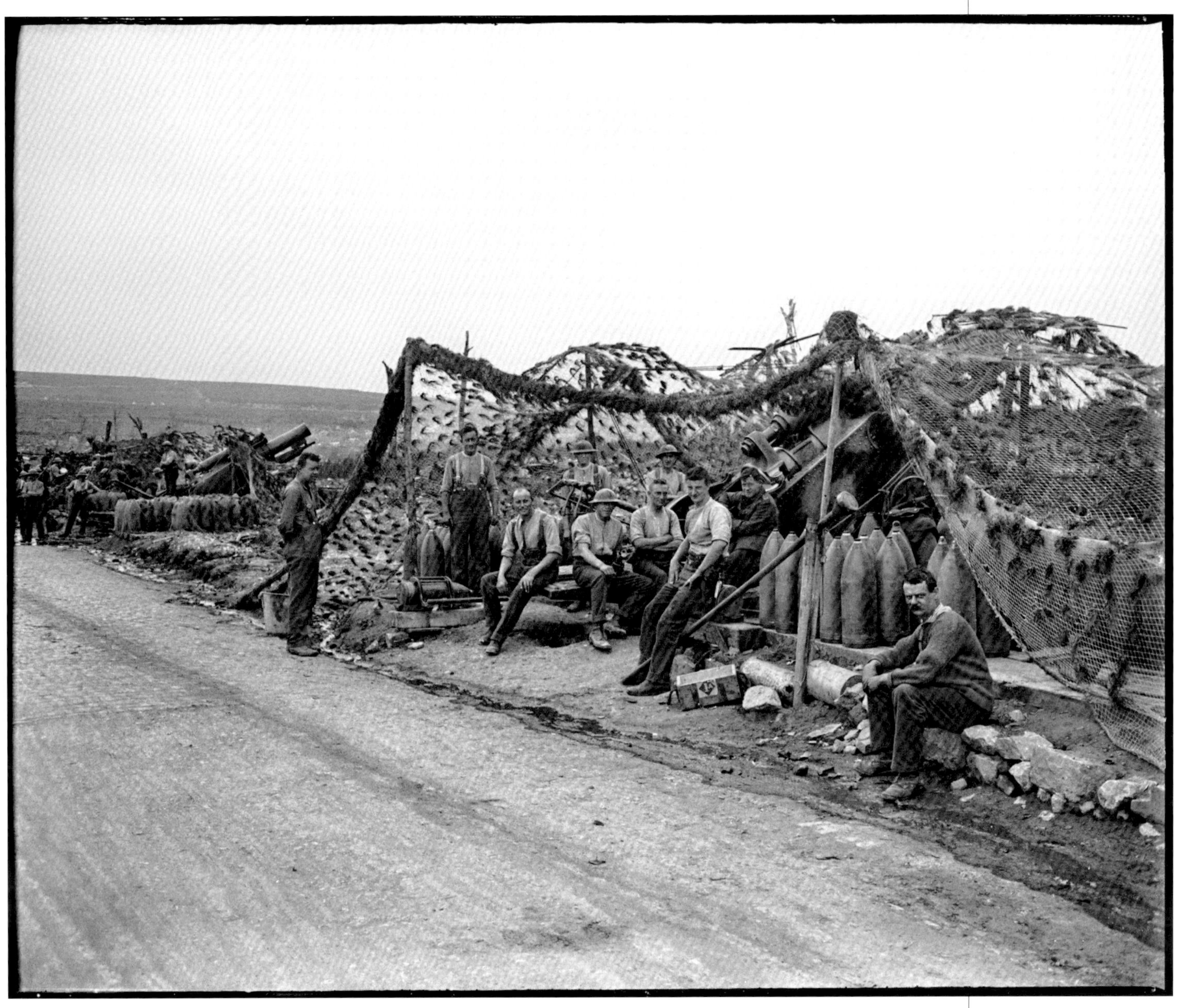

PHOT. 139
20/07/1917
English batteries close to Souchez (department of Pas-de-Calais)

These British cannons of 9.2 inches weighed 14 tons and it took 36 hours to disassemble them for transport.

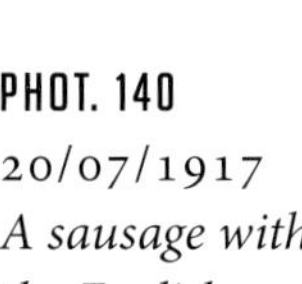

PHOT. 140
20/07/1917
A sausage with the English

The captive balloons, nicknamed sausages, had a fundamental role to direct the artillery fire. They were raised up to 50–1,500 metres by a steel cable, the anchor is set on a truck in the case of the photograph. Once there, the observer corrected fire by communicating by telephone. Its stillness, flammability and tactical importance made them the preferred objective for the enemy fighter planes equipped with rockets. In fact, these observers were the only 'pilots' equipped with parachutes.

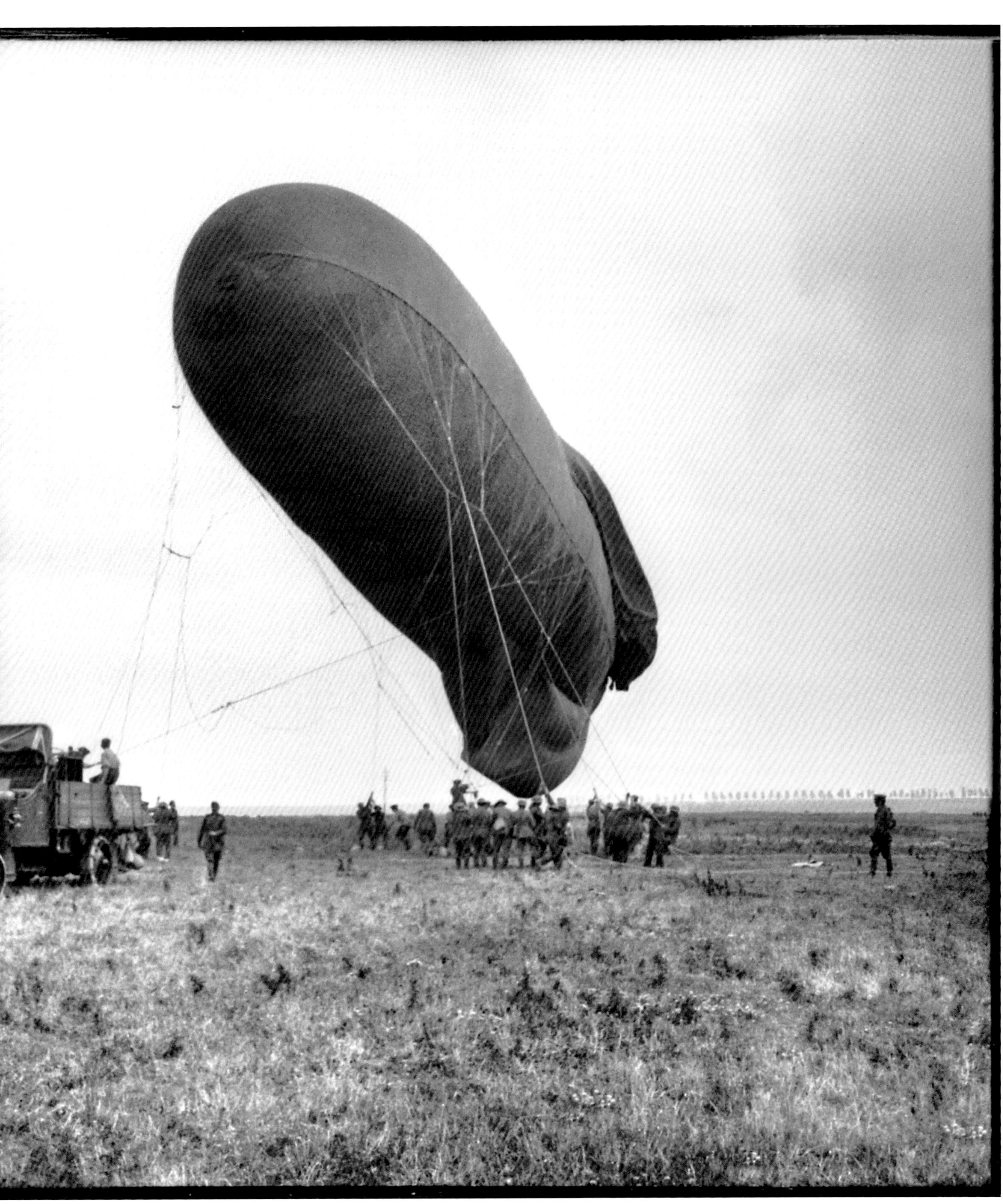

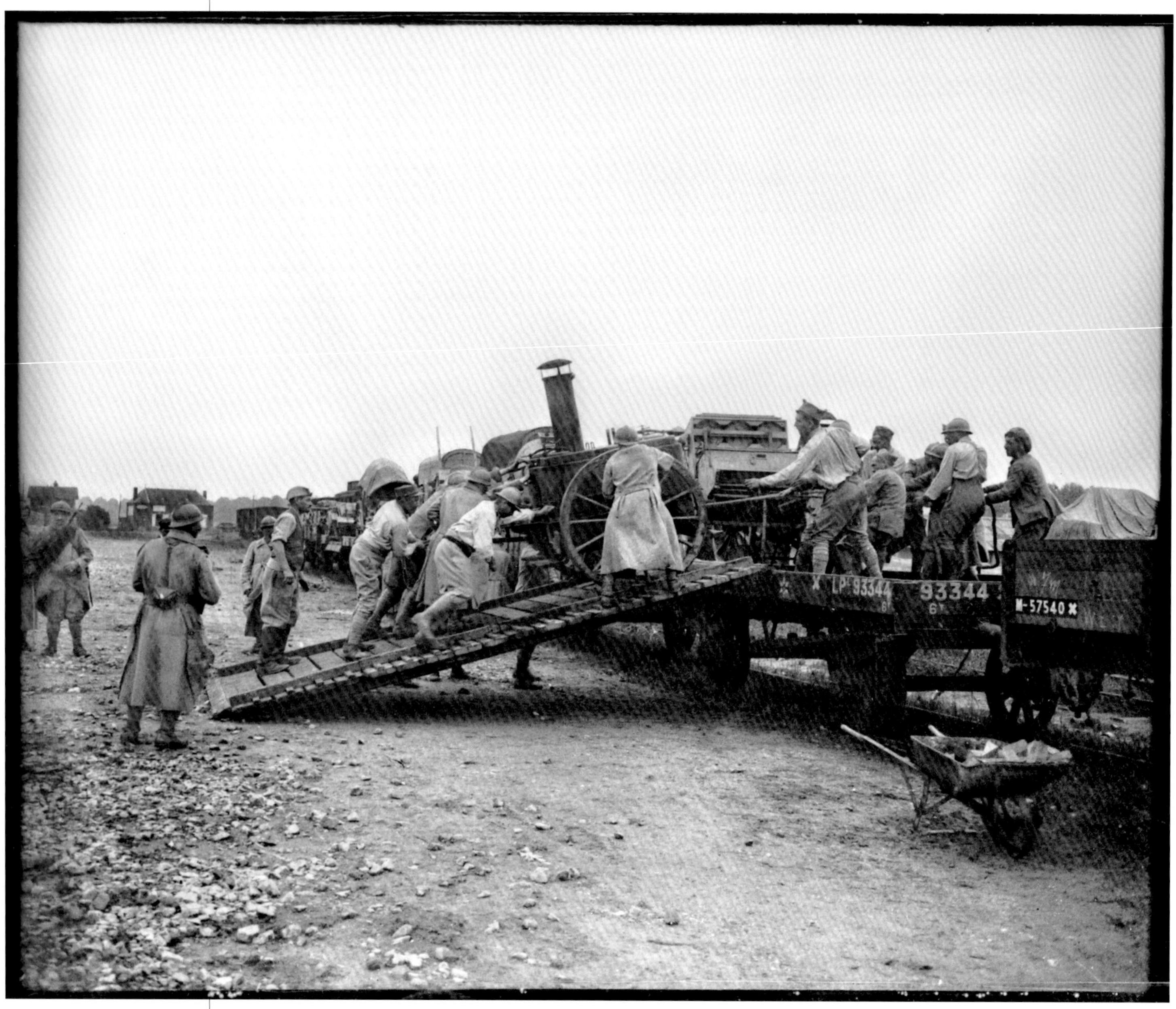

PHOT. 145
07/08/1917
Troops embarking
in Faverolles

Several men collaborate in loading a field kitchen.

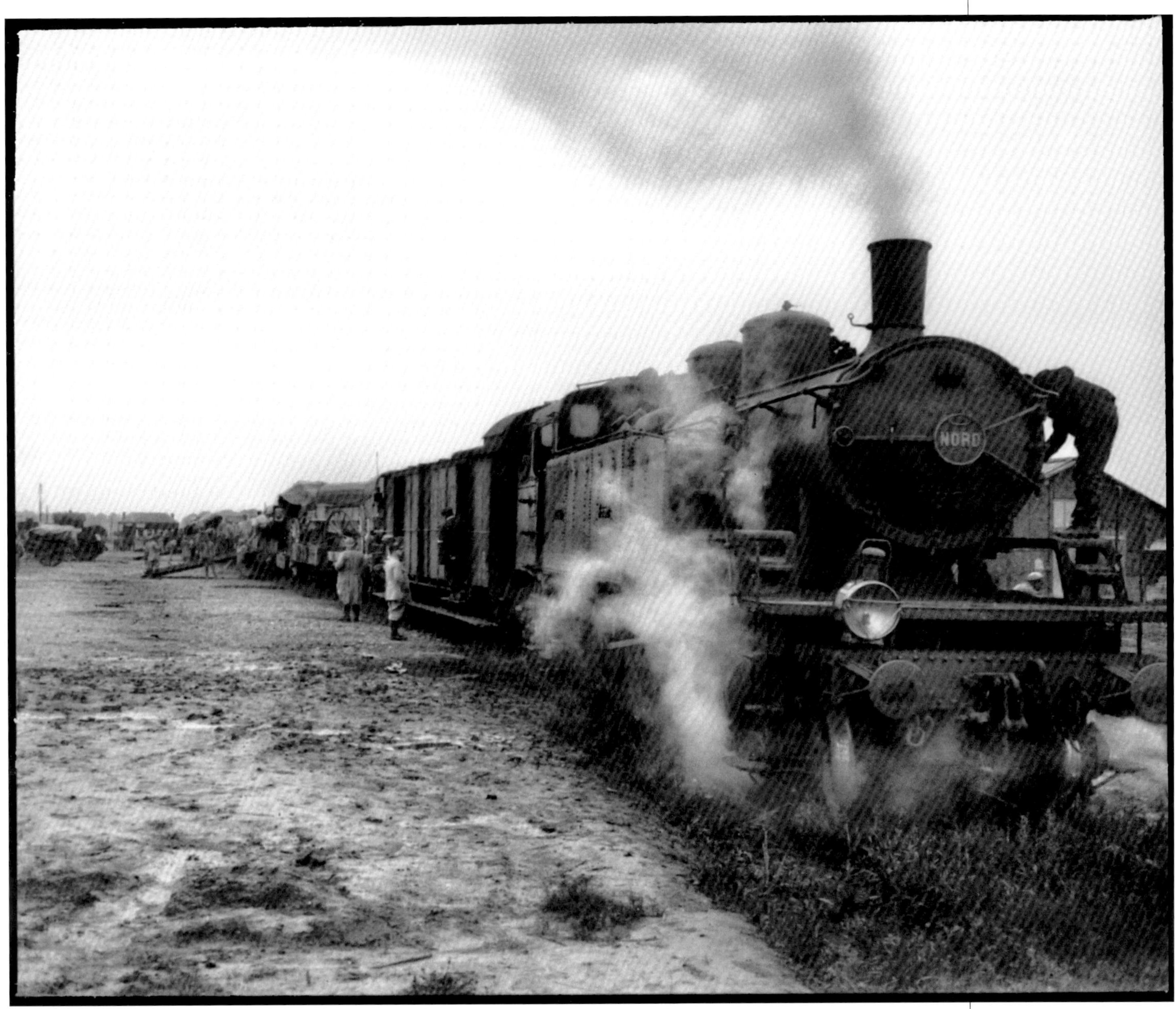

PHOT. 146
07/08/1917

The rail network had an influence on the stagnation of trench warfare, in a case of enemy incursion at any point on the front it could mobilise its reserves with rapidity to block a breach.

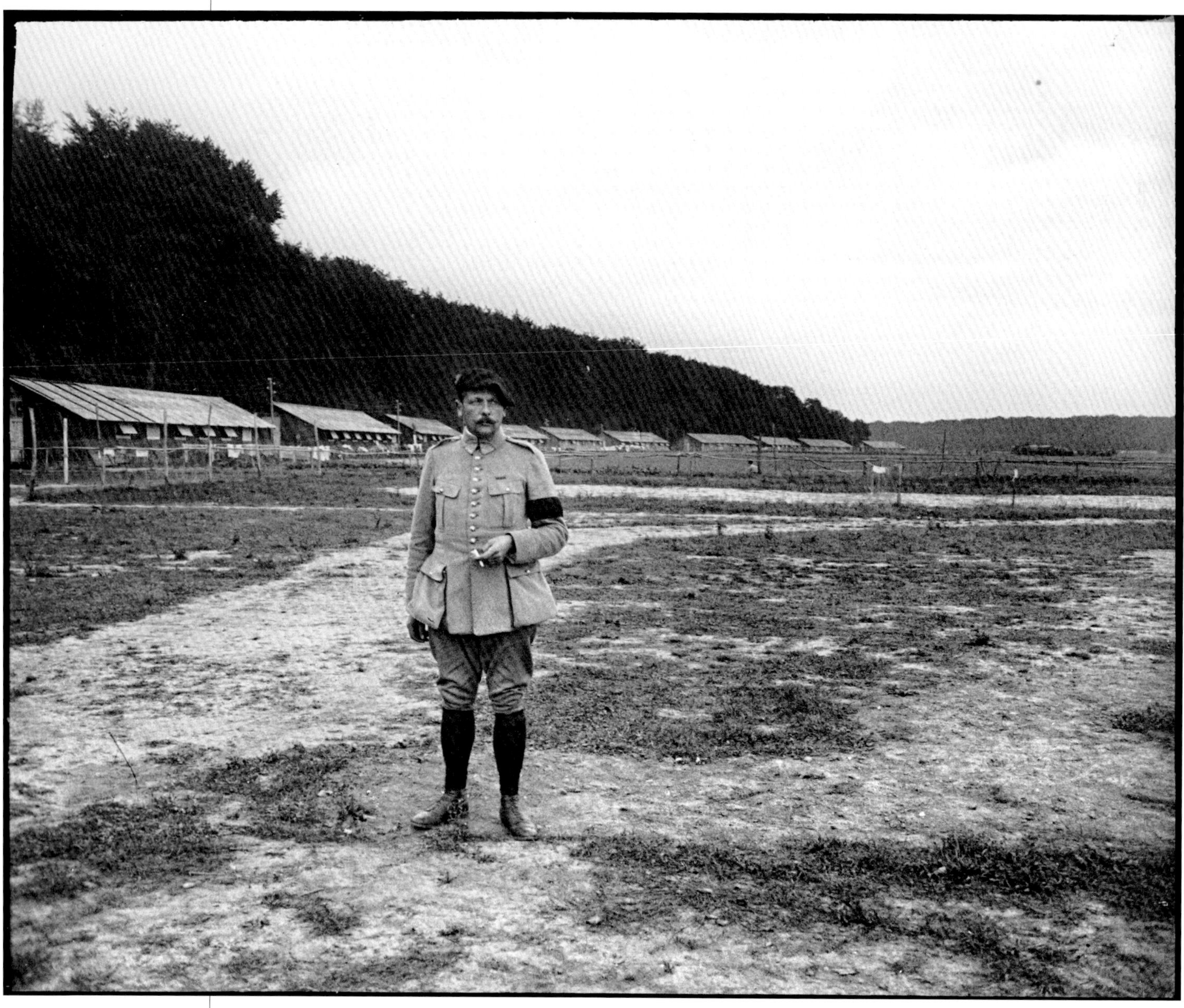

PHOT. 143
08/1917

A French captain of the General Staff in front of some barracks.

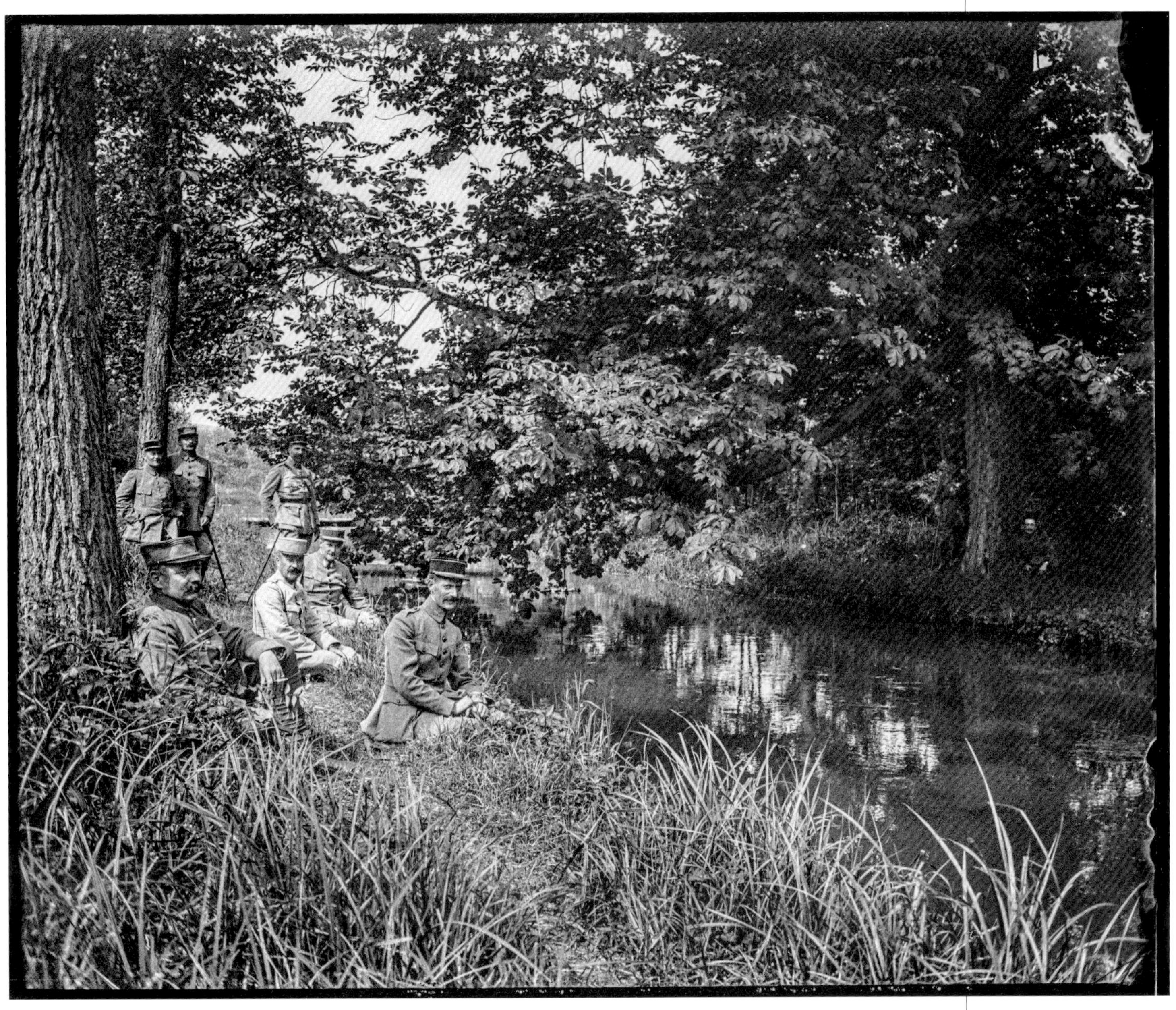

PHOT. 149
08/08/1917

The *Groupe Givord* enjoys enjoys a leisure day on the banks of the river in Monchy-Humières, in the department of Oise. Givord is sitting in the centre, with a lighter coloured uniform.

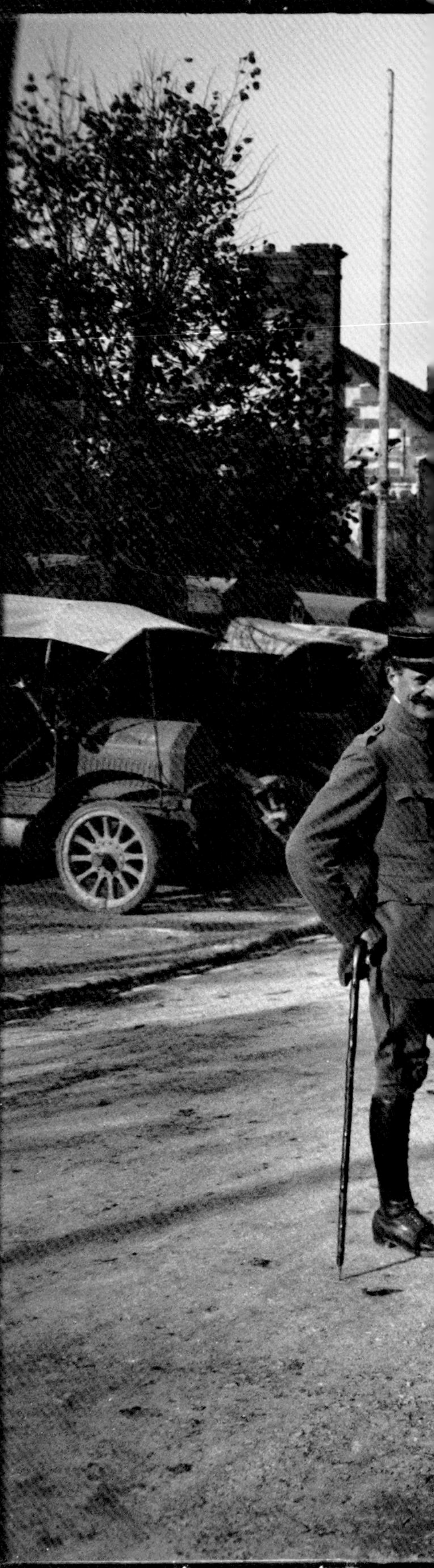

PHOT. 162
12/10/1917

Several members of the *Groupe Givord* joke in front of a section of the *Transport de Matériel.* Each *groupe* was formed of four sections of twenty vehicles. In this case it is the *section TM12,* whose emblem was a funny Alsatian.

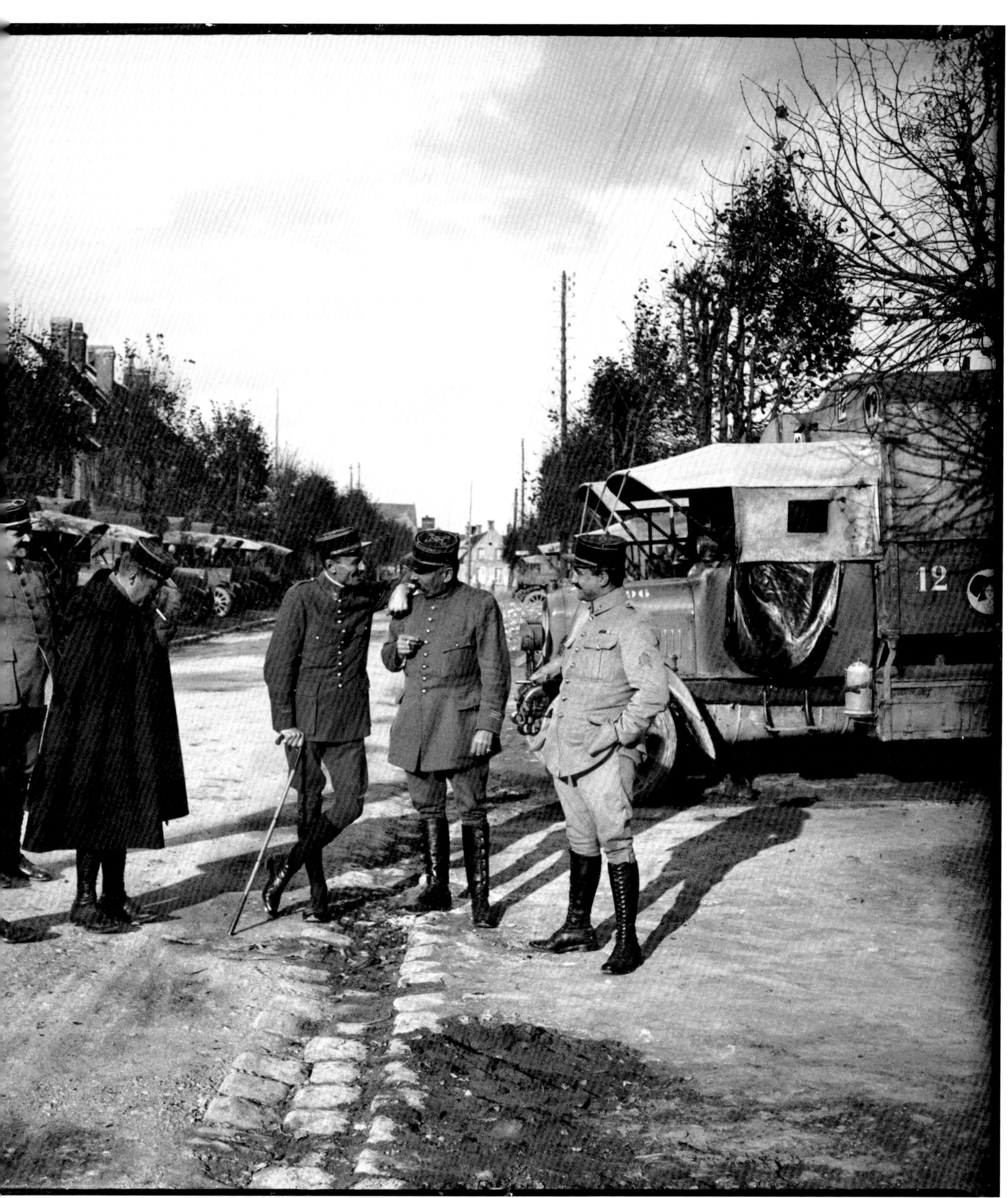
12

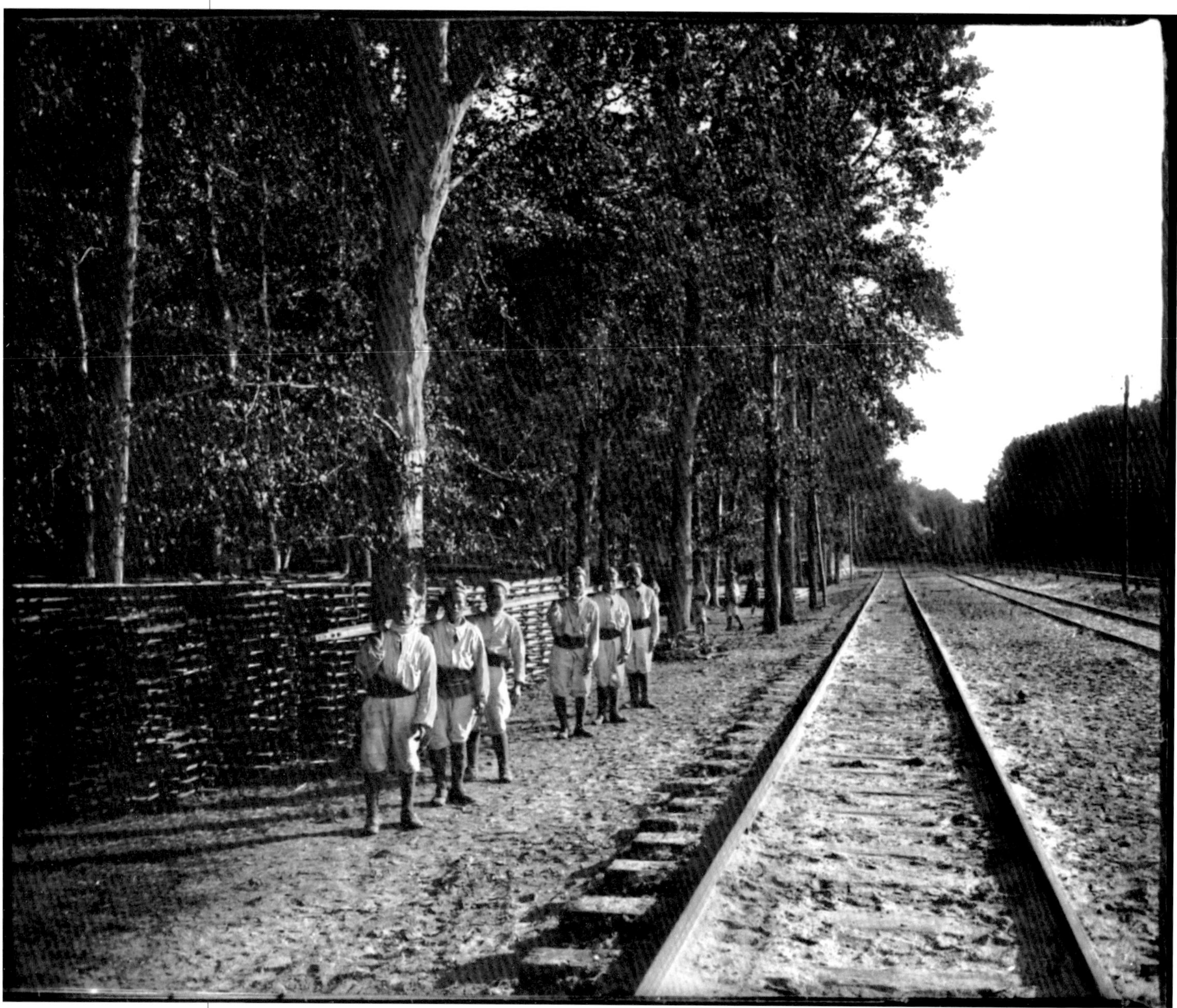

PHOT. 165
17/10/1917
At the woods of Compiègne

Indo-Chinese workers improving the rails where a year later the armistice was signed. The French companies could hire workers in their country of origin, China, to whom they paid between one and two francs per day. At the end of the war there were around 100,000 in the whole of France.

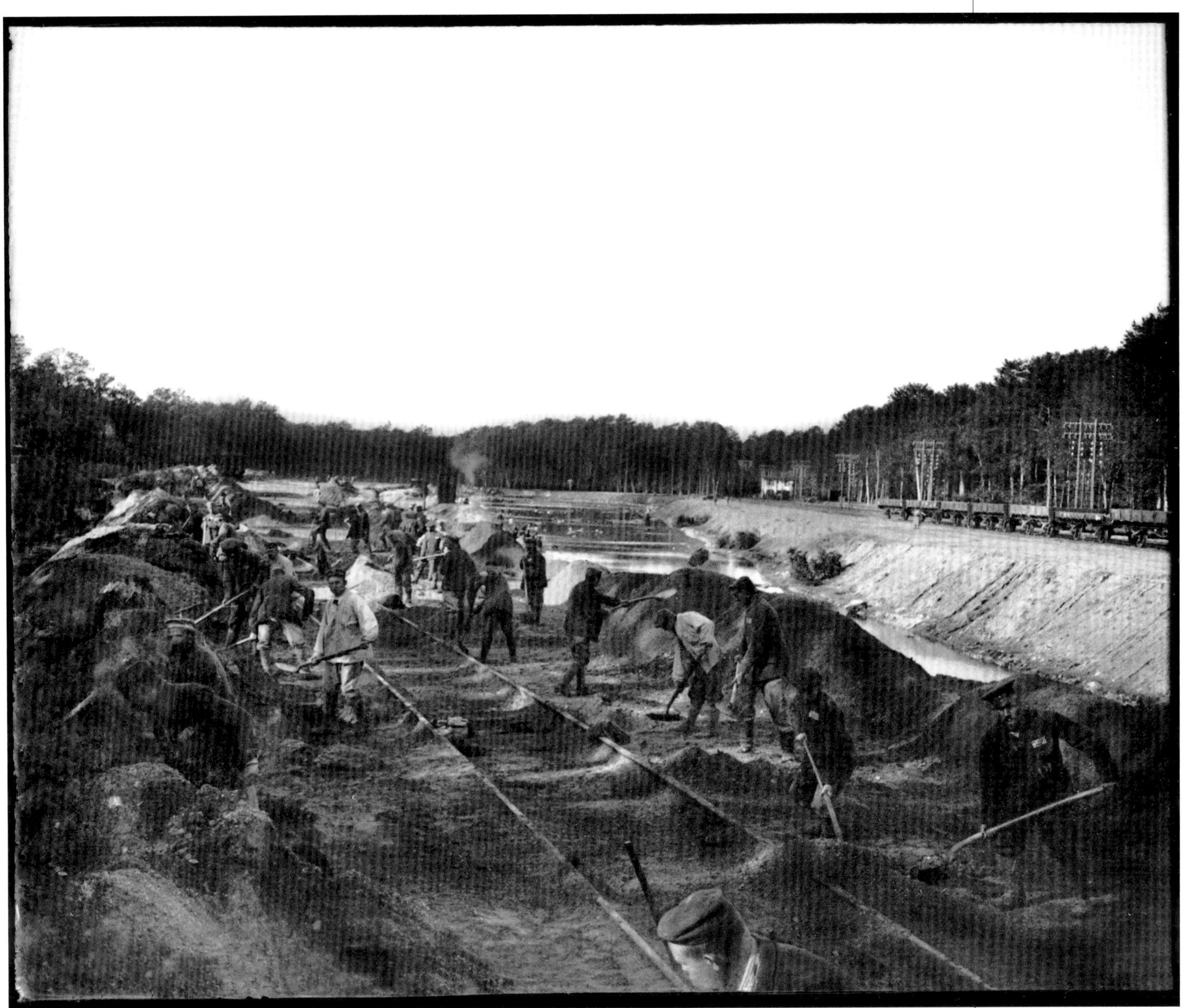

PHOT. 166
17/10/1917
At the woods of Compiègne

The German prisoners were also a recurrent workforce.

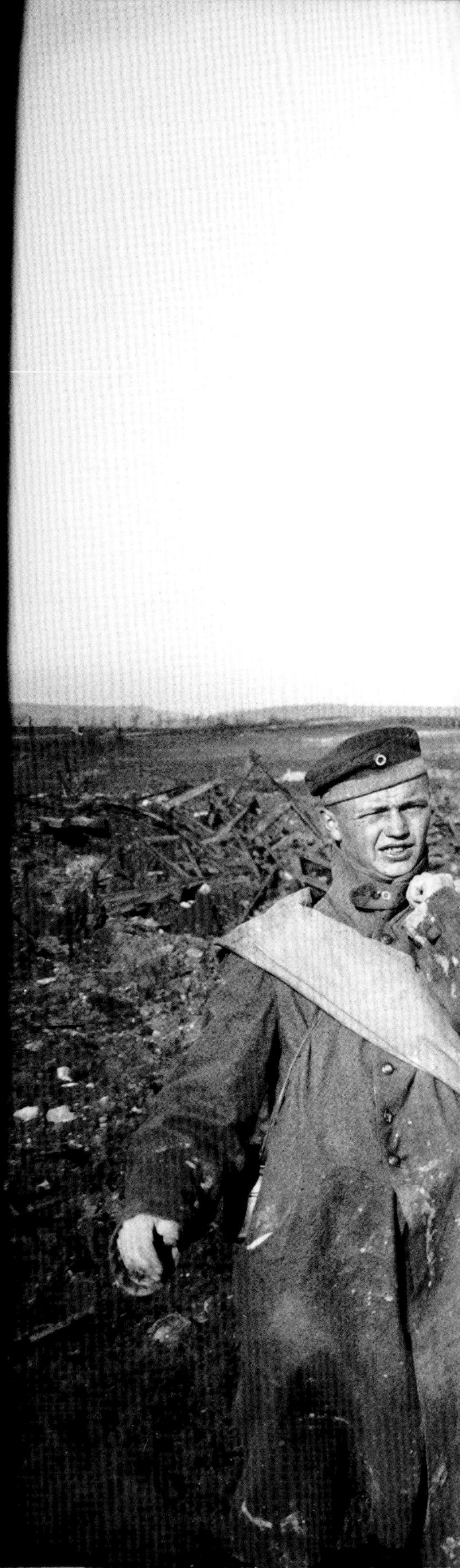

PHOT. 169
25/10/1917
Using the
Boche (…)
the battle fields

The German prisoners were useful to bury the dead, as these men are doing close to Laffaux after the battle. The battle also known as La Malmaison had begun on October 23rd and ended two days later on the 25th.

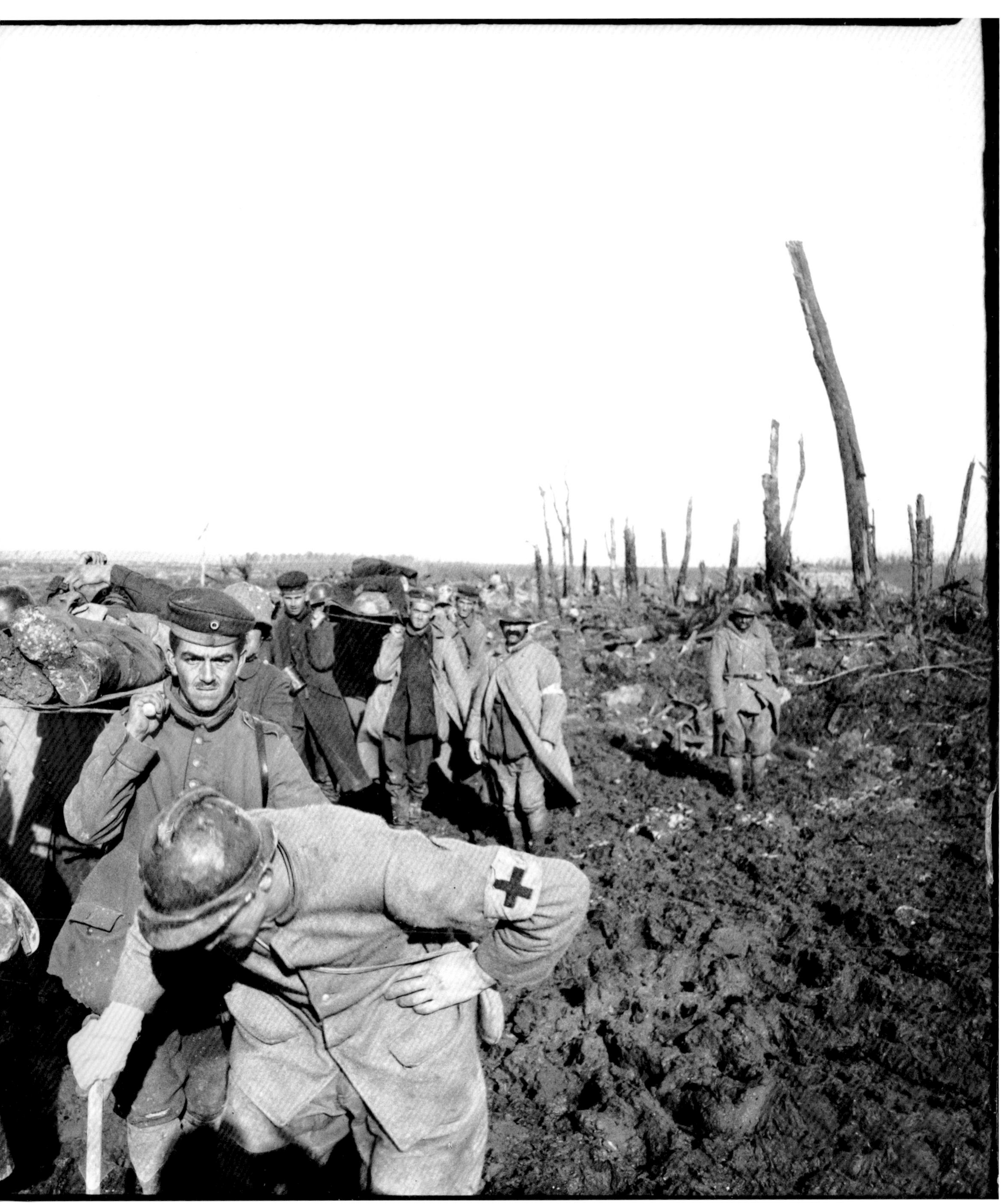

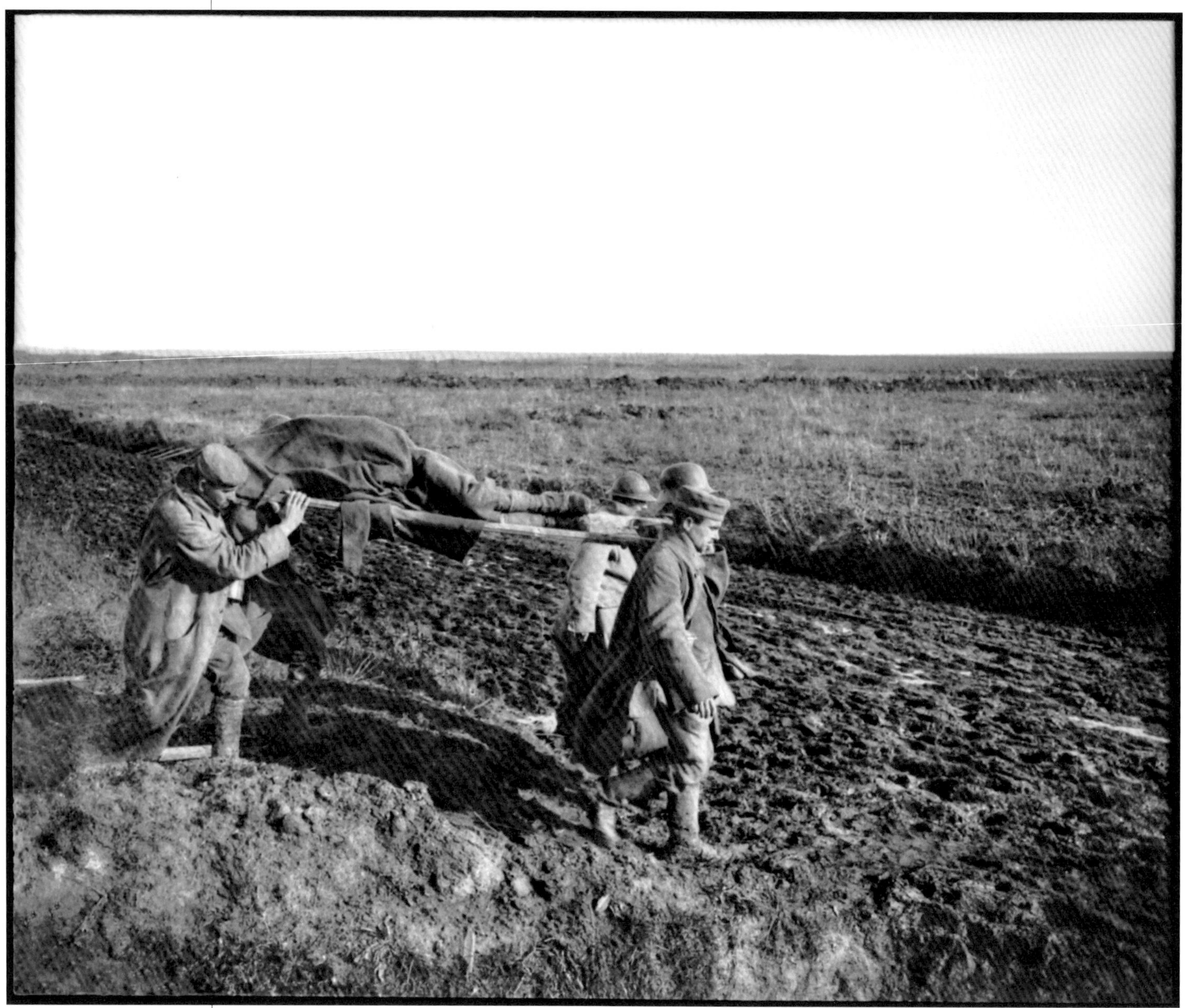

PHOT. 171
25/10/1917
Cleaning of the battlefields by the Boche

During the battle of La Malmaison the French captured 11,157 prisoners, 200 cannons and 220 heavy mortars.

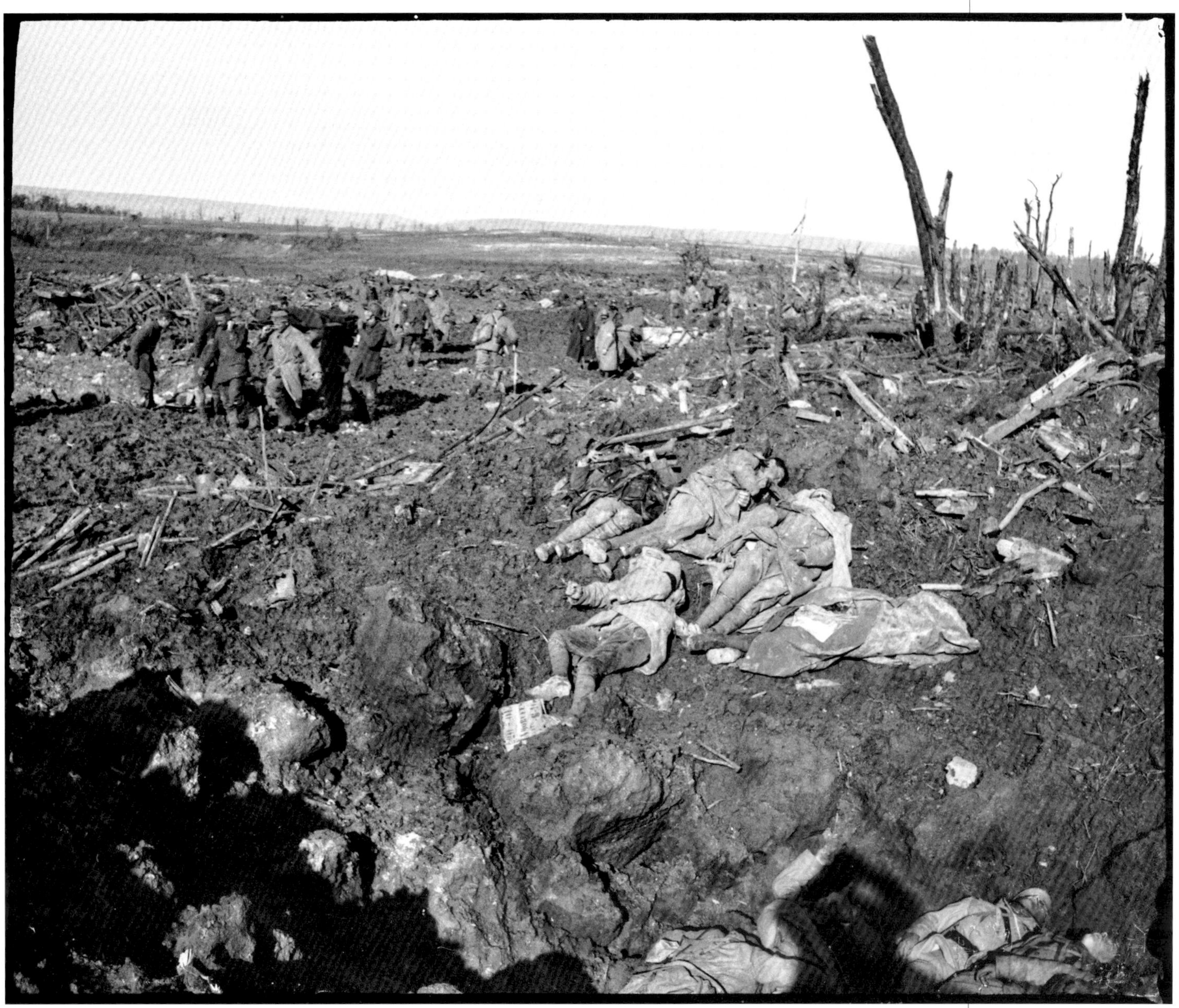

PHOT. 170
25/10/1917
Nearby the Moulin de Laffaux on the day after the attack

Despite the corpses we see in the foreground, the French casualties were relatively low: 2,241 deceased, 8,162 wounded and 1,460 missing in action.

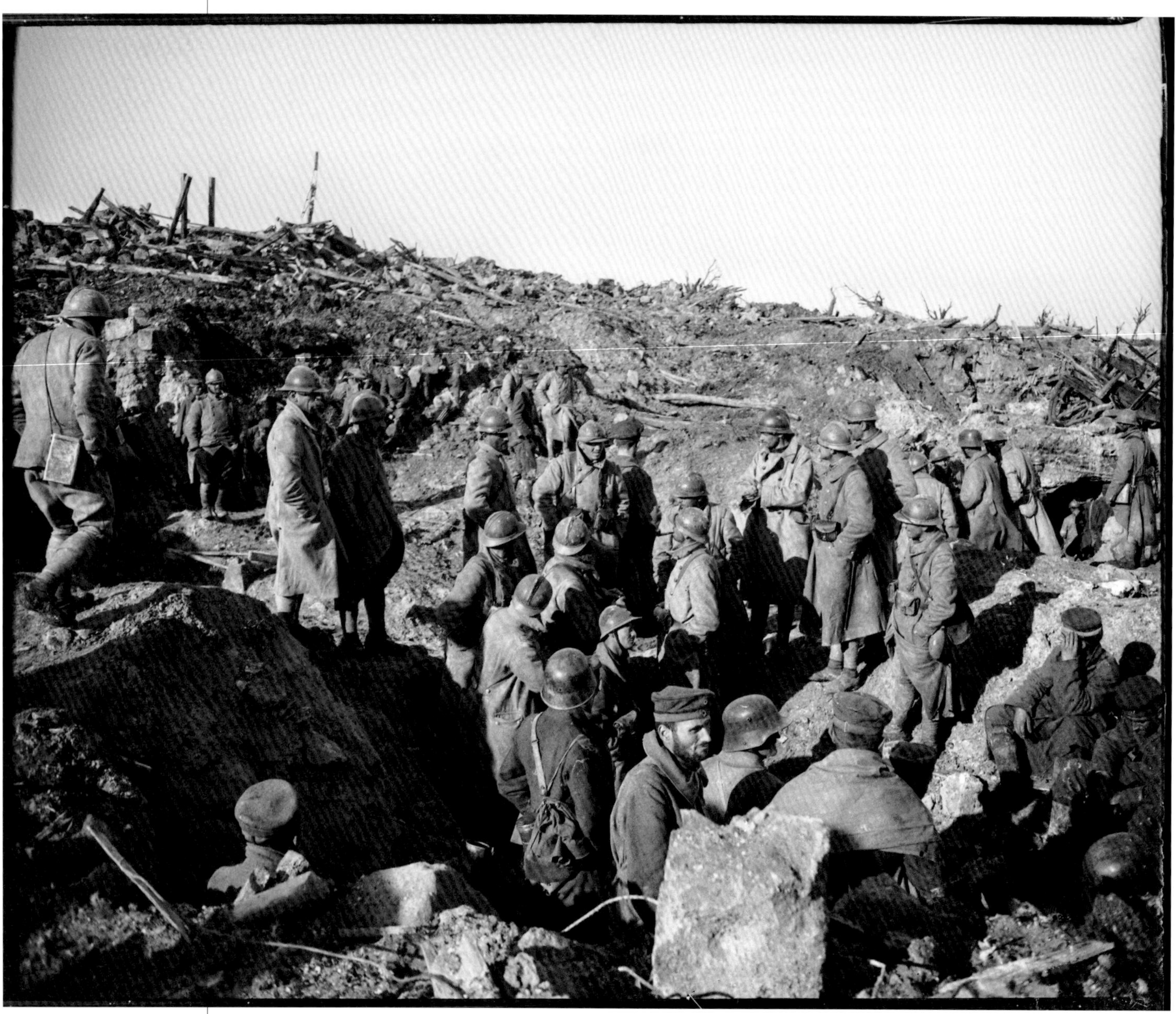

PHOT. 172
25/10/1917
The Château de la Motte!
Next day after the attack

The Germans counted around 8,000 dead and 30,000 wounded, being forced to retreat 10 km. The remains of the *château* of La Motte were one of the targets behind the German lines.

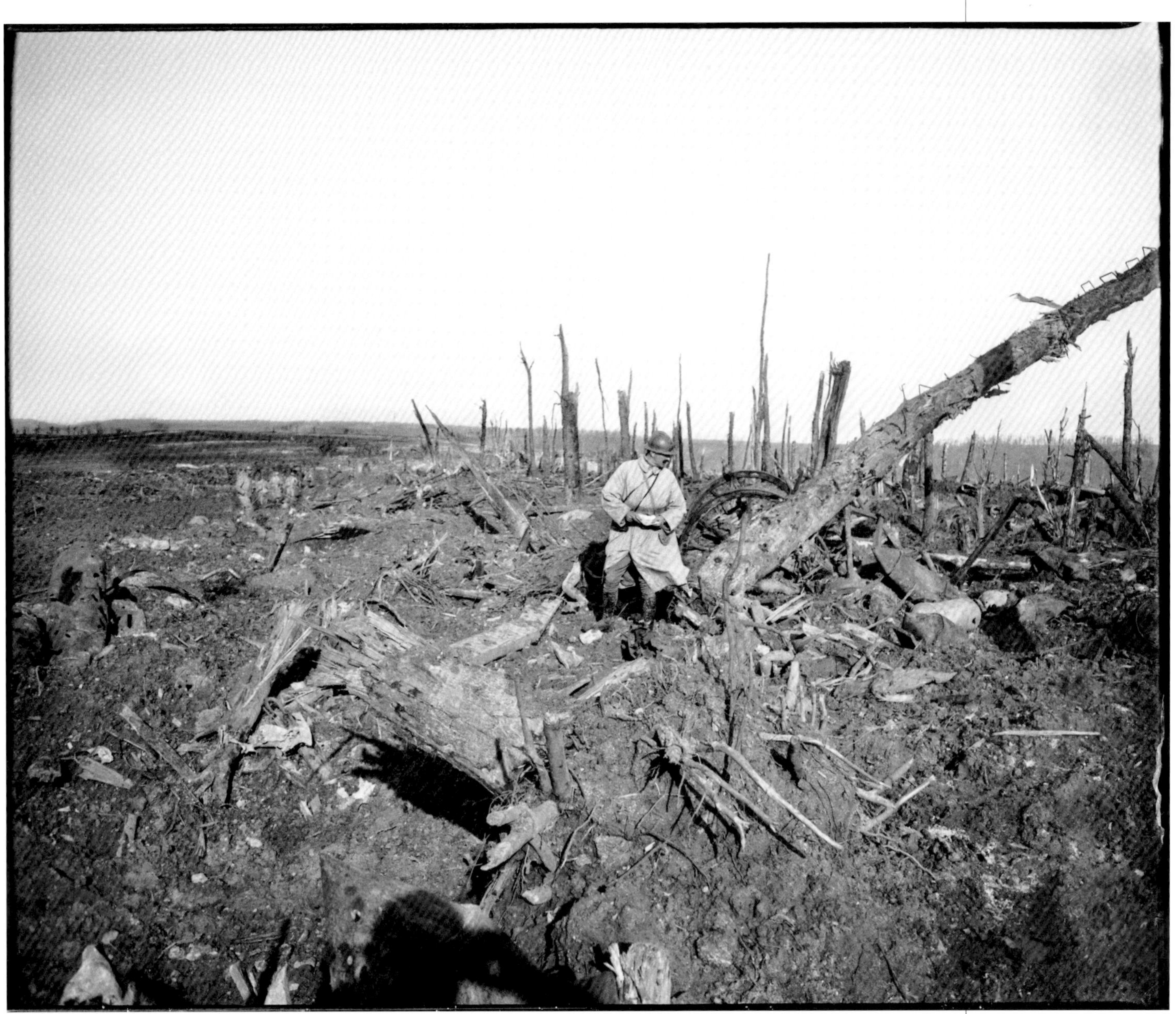

PHOT. 168
25/10/1917
At Laffaux

After the fighting there was nothing left of the little village of Laffaux. Although Louis Aragon would immortalise it in his verses: *Beacon of memories where to rise its flames / the dreams of twenty years to a sky that lied / and instead of love, the black Road of Dames / and the crackle of the red mill of Laffaux.*

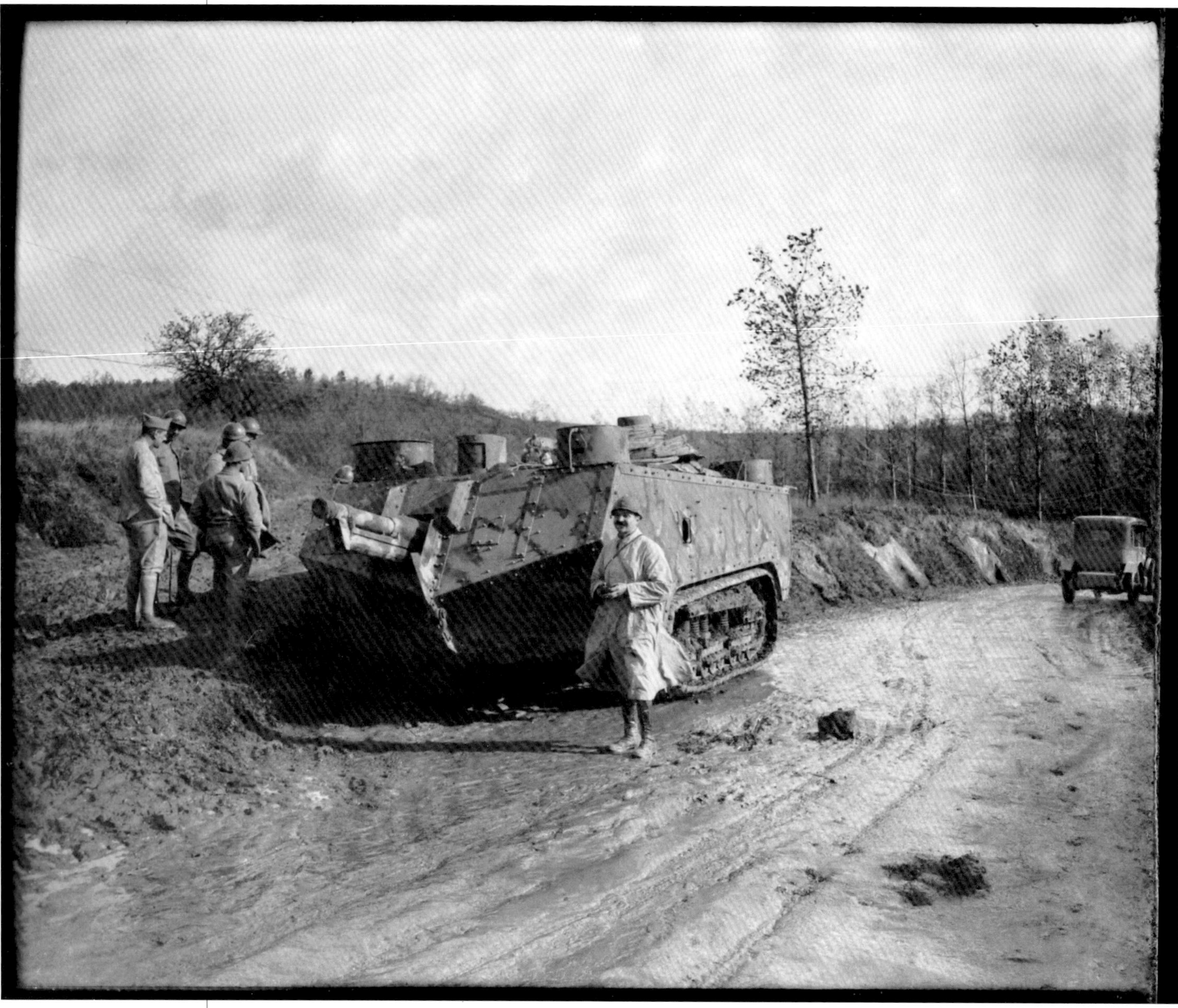

PHOT. 173
25/05/1917
A tank

The French used battle tanks for the first time in a coordinated way at La Motte, launching 63 on the first day of battle. When the day was over only 21 remained in use, between them the one in the photograph, a Saint-Chamond M1 belonging to the *Groupe AS (Artillerie Spéciale)* 33 of Captain Mottet de la Fontaine. This tank was commanded by Lieutenant Guy Edouard Frémont (which was the first tank of 1st battery of the AS33) and got stuck that very same day in a hole 500 metres north to the Moulin de Laffaux. Frémont died when trying to get out of the tank. Buried at the cemetery at the farm of Montgarni, his tomb remains still there. The Saint-Chamond was an inadequate tank, with a tendency to run aground due to its great hulk and small tracks. It had a maximum speed of 8 km/h.

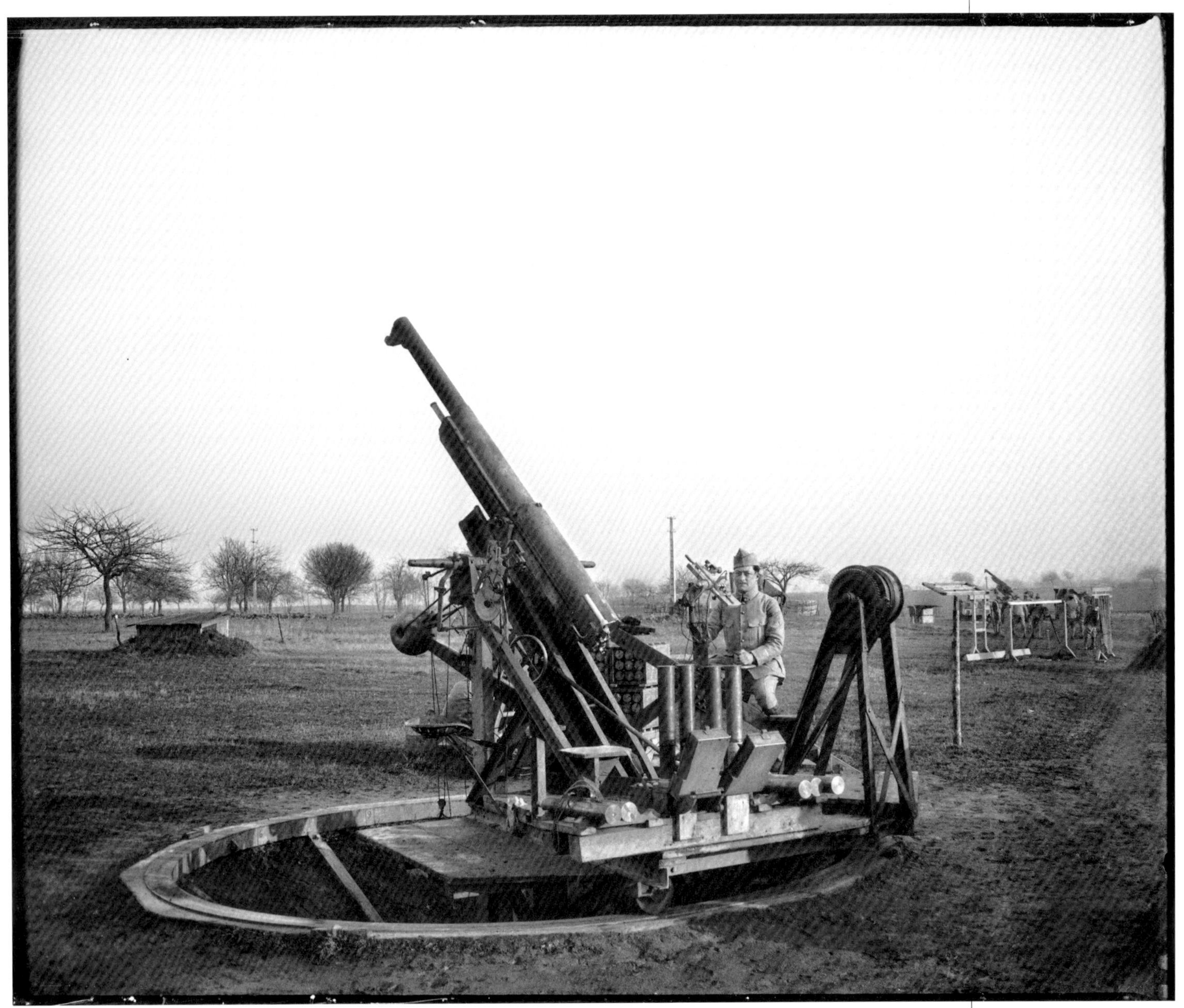

PHOT. 178
30/01/1918

The 75 mm campaign cannons **[PHOT. 13]** were converted into anti-aircraft guns, such as this fixed set up which defended a strategic point. It is an indicator of the increase of aerial power towards the end of the war.

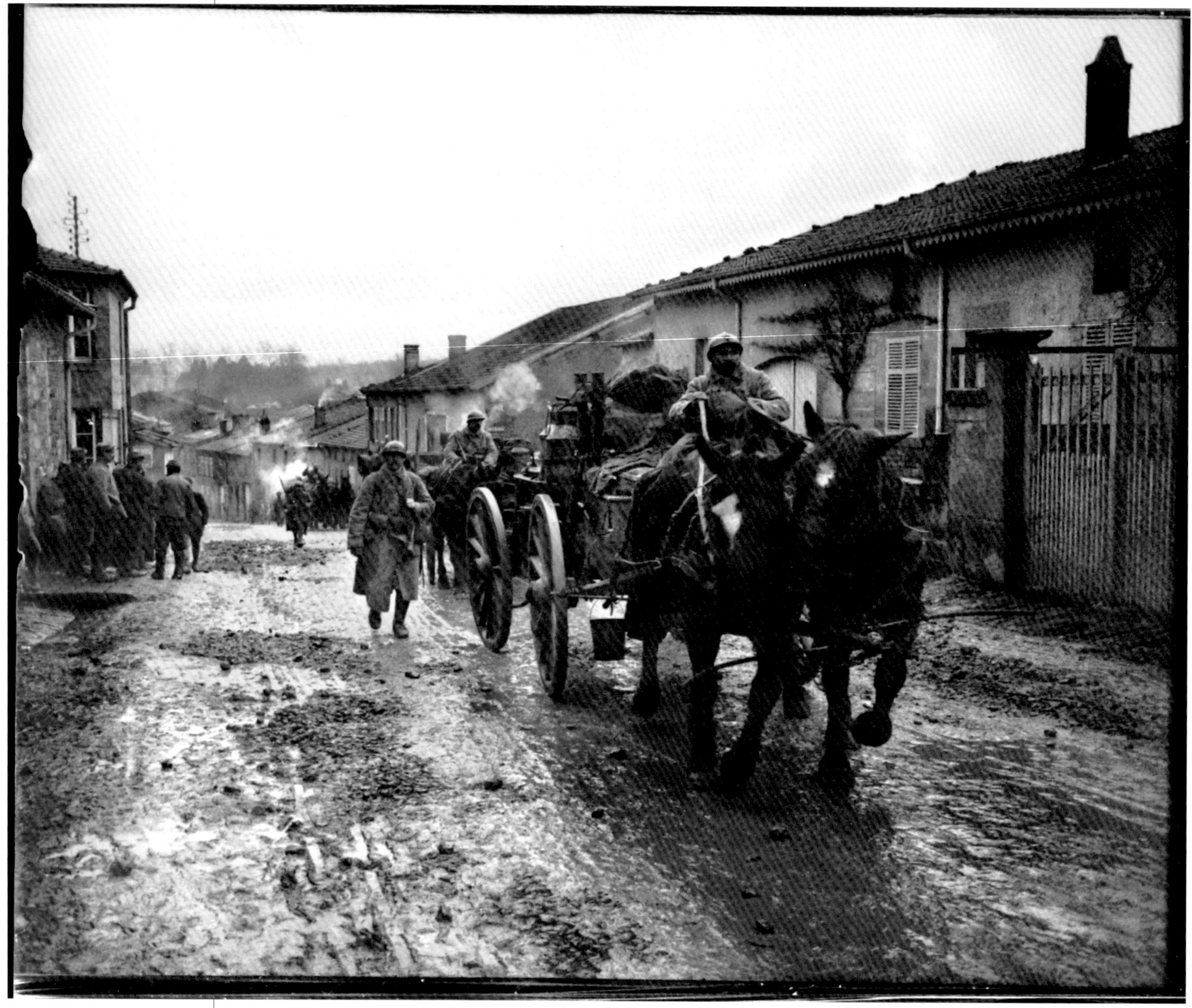

PHOT. 179
23/02/1918
The 147e *marching in Combles*

Givord spent the winter in the small Lorenese town of Combles-en-Barrois, photographing the units that passed by the *Grande Rue.* The buildings in the photograph are barely touched to this day.

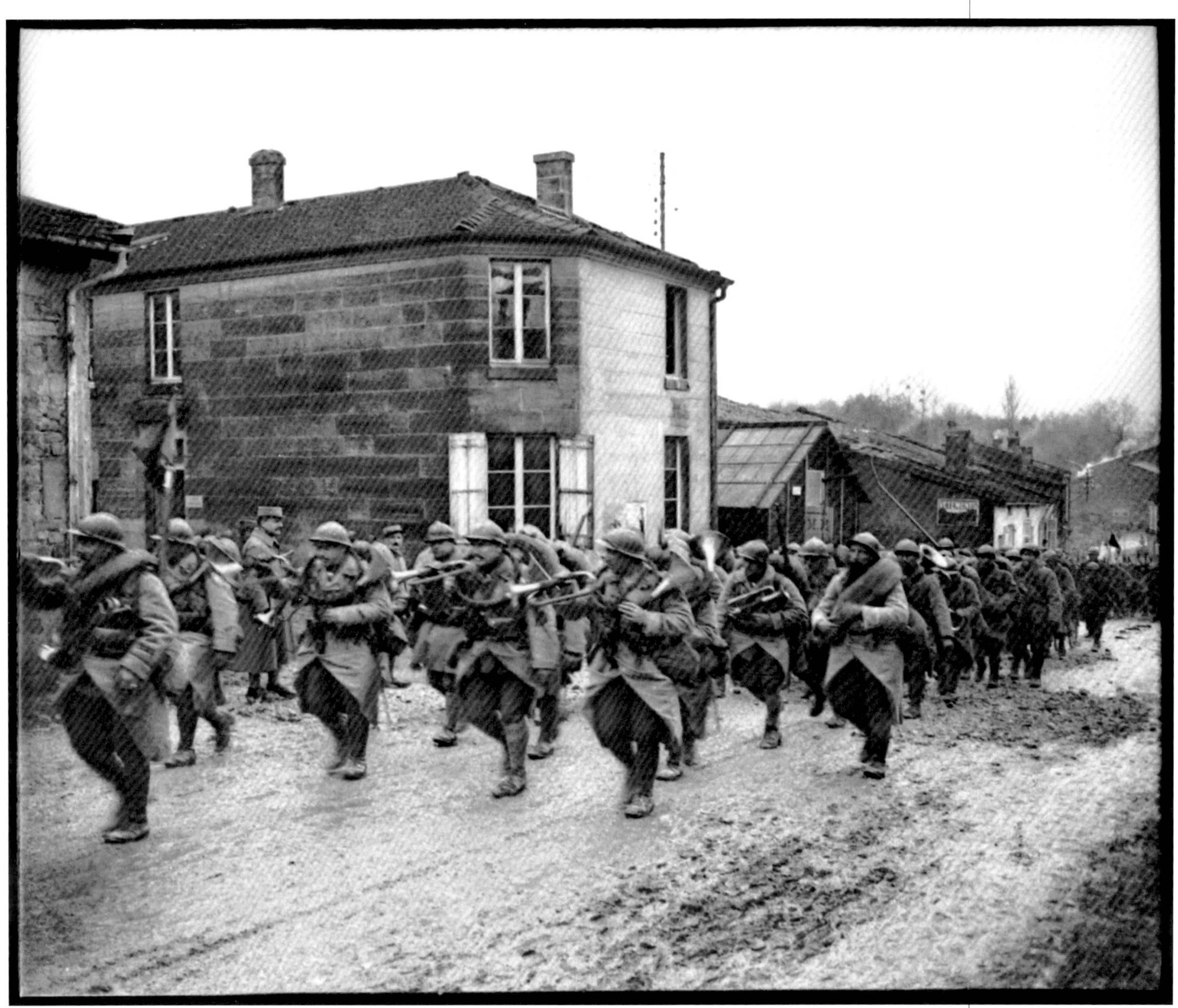

PHOT. 180
24/02/1918
Marching in Combles

This town is located near to Bar-le-Duc, which was the main point of supply for the Verdun offensive.

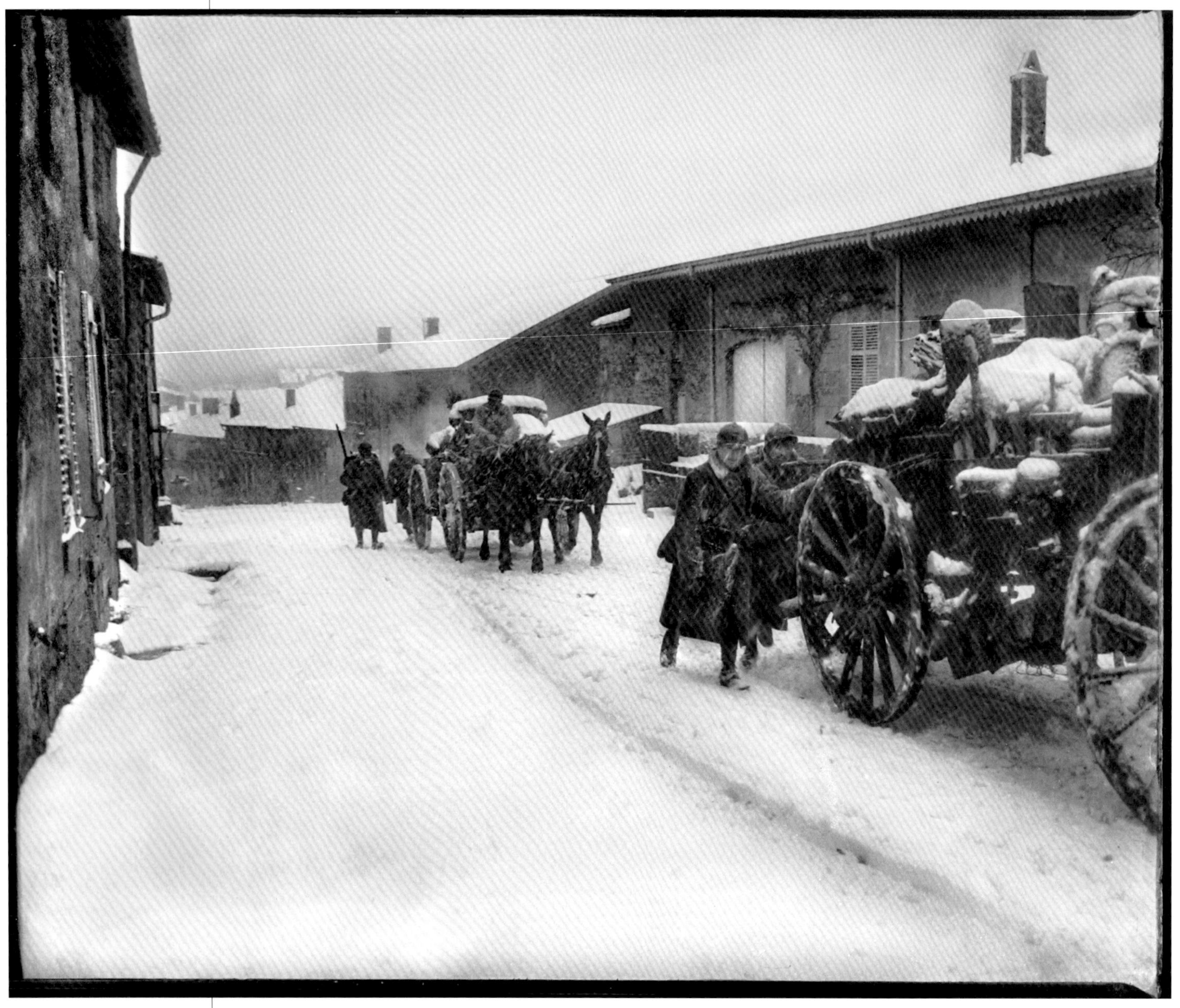

PHOT. 181
03/03/1918
March under the snow in Combles

Givord was probably billeted in this street, because almost all the photographs have the same framing.

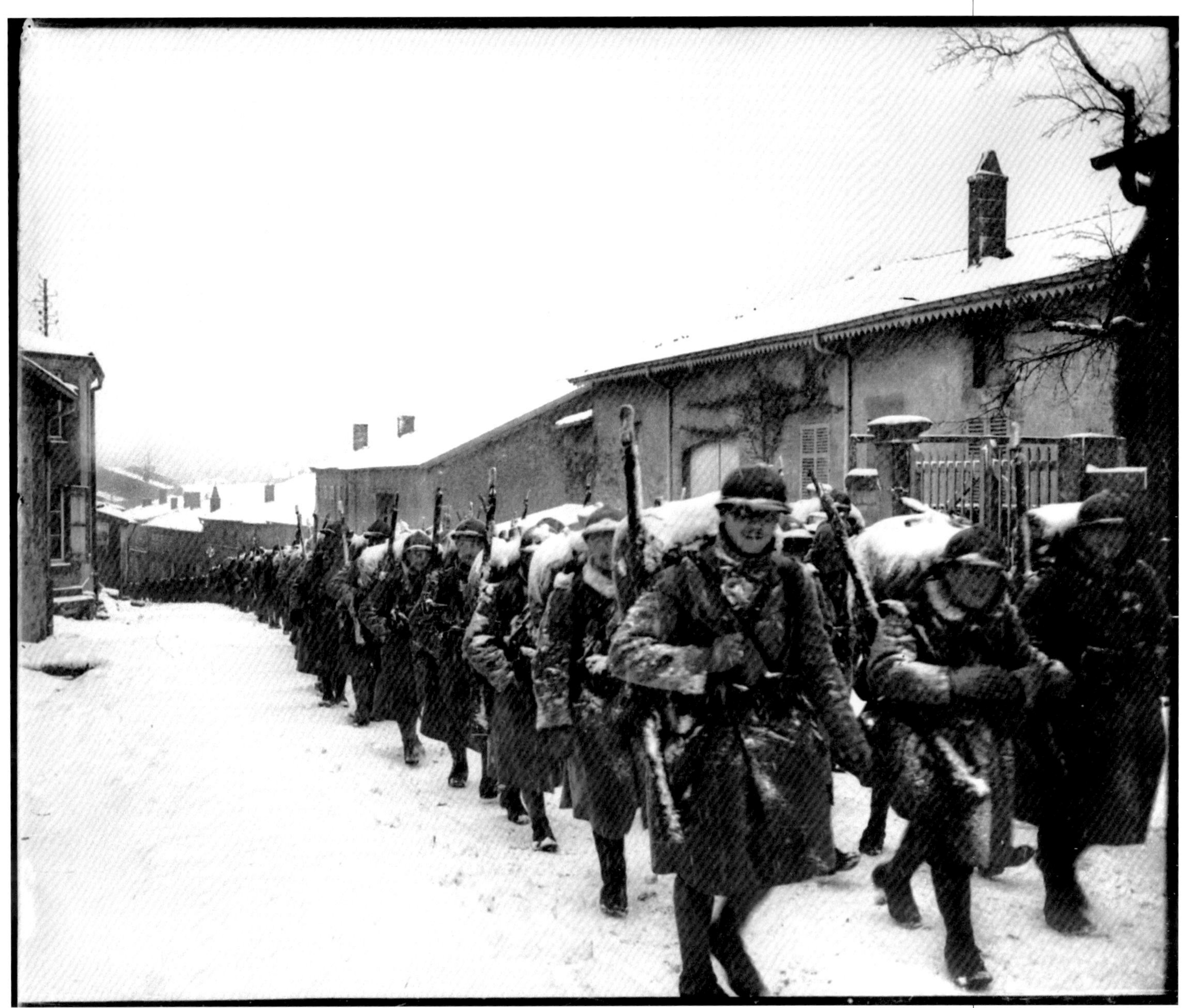

PHOT. 182
03/03/1918
March under the snow in Combles

A French column marches towards the front; 1,400,000 compatriots never returned. Twenty-seven per cent of the French male population between 18 and 27 years old died.

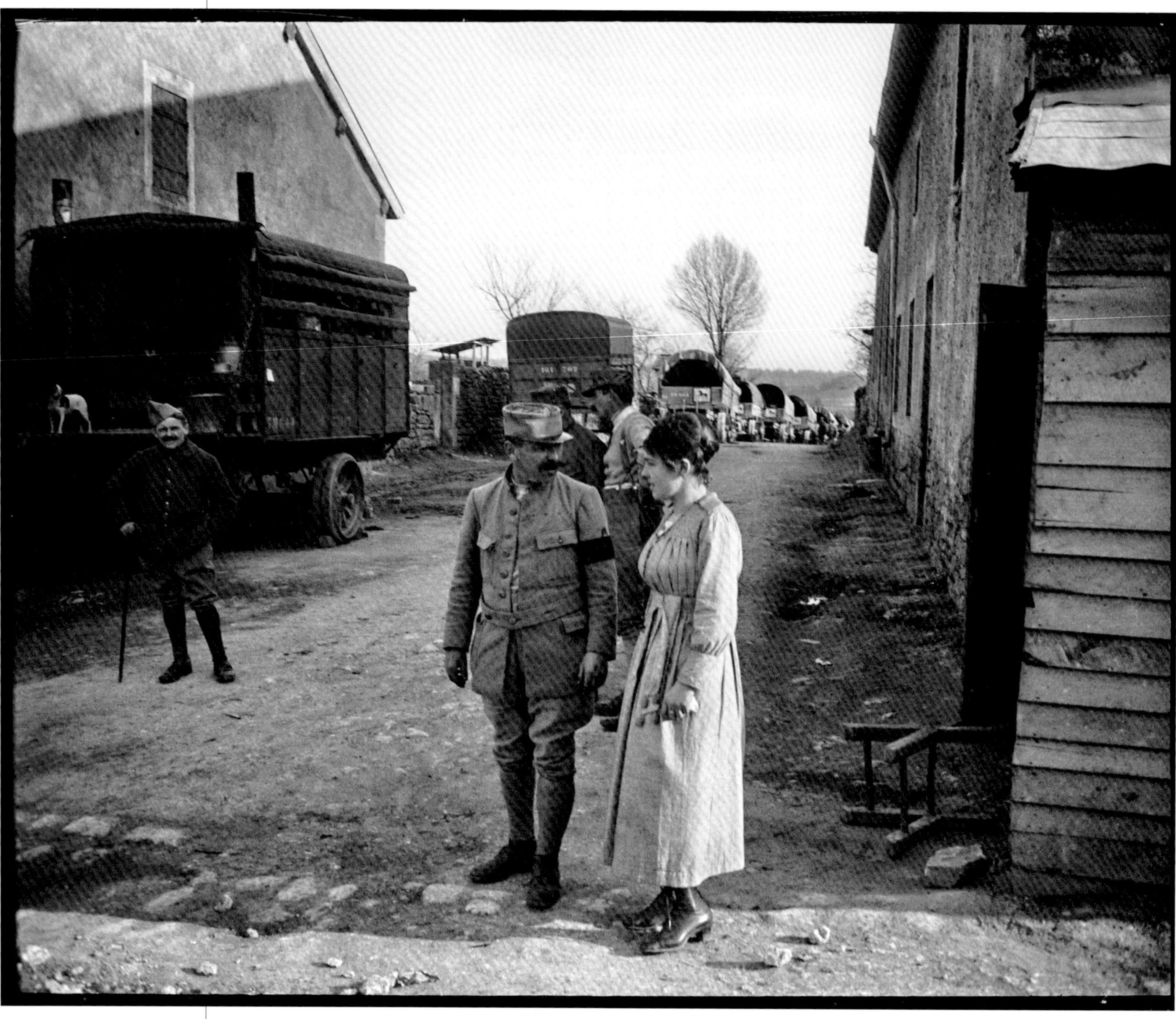

PHOT. 183
17/03/1918
A beauty in Combles

An officer of the General Staff ever the French gentleman. In the background we can see a column of trucks of the *644 TM*, whose emblem was a rocking horse.

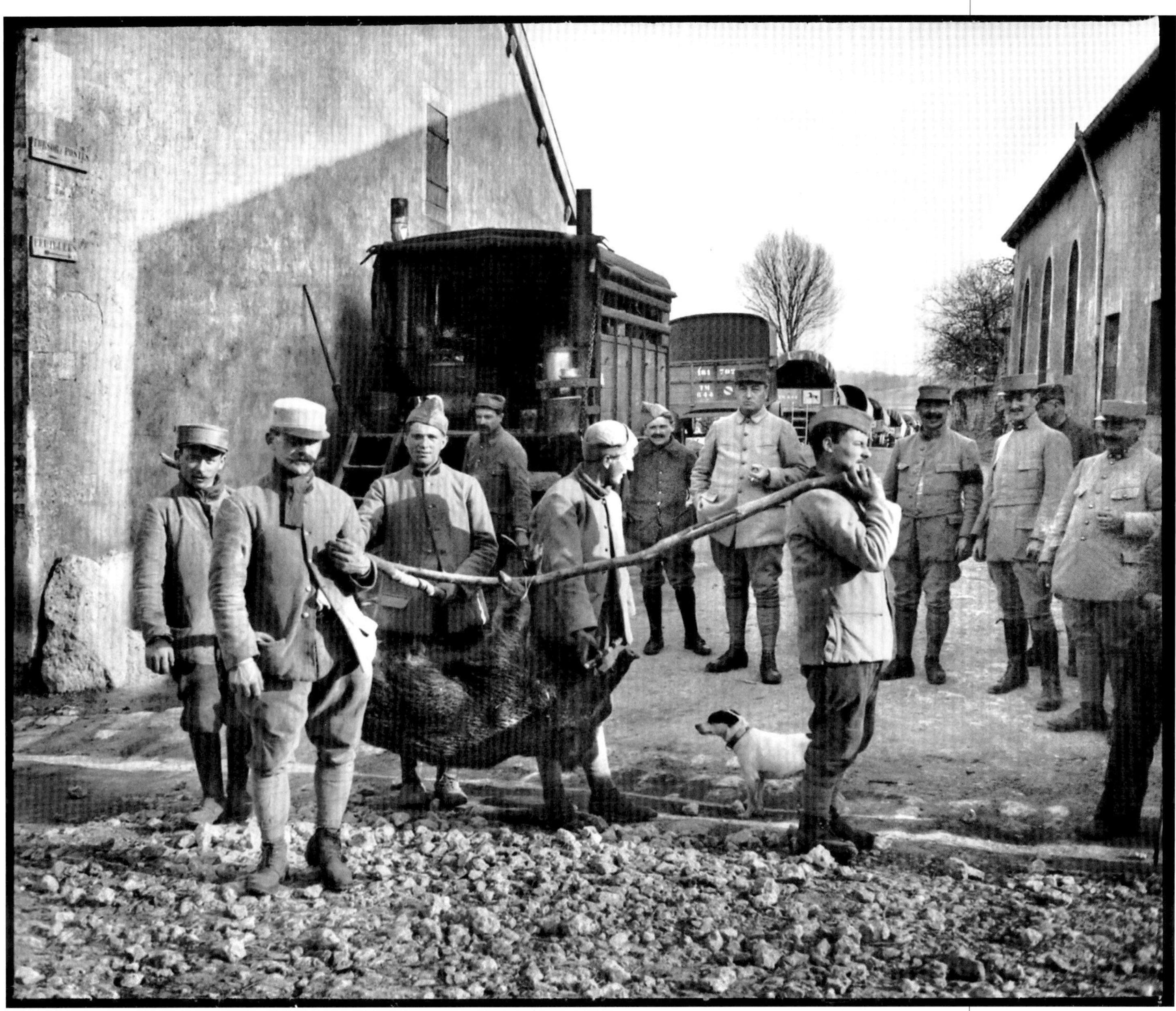

PHOT. 184
17/03/1918

A shot of the same street with a piece of meat to feed the mess that is going to be cooked in the motorised kitchen in the background. One of the reasons for the mutiny the year before was the soldiers' poor diet, a matter that improved with the guidelines from General Pétain.

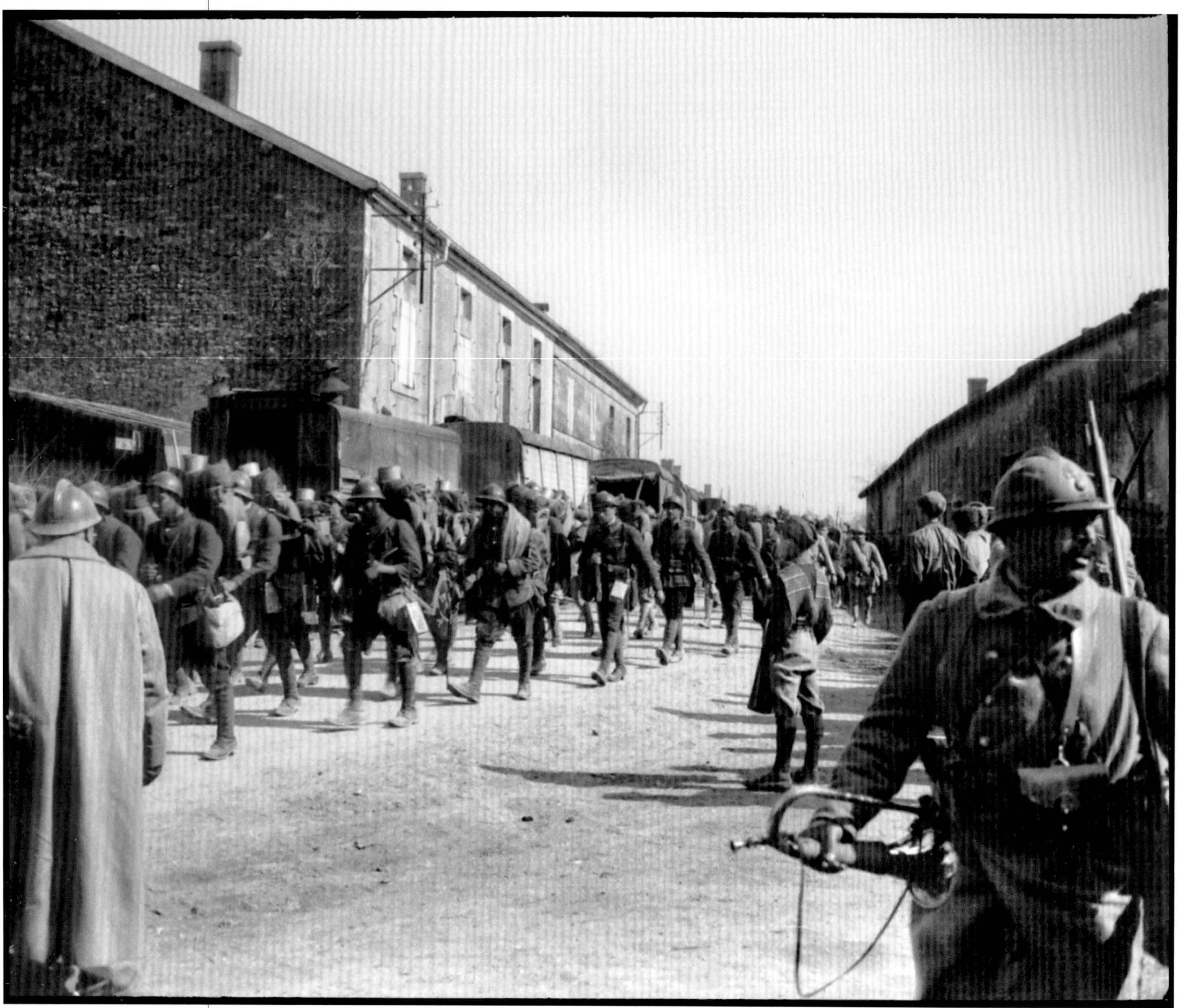

PHOT. 185
21/03/1918
Combles

Disembarkment of a regiment of Zouaves. The Zouaves belonged to the *Armée d'Afrique* (African Army) being recruited from men with French bloodline. These regiments attacked with a ferocity unknown by metropolitan units and they became elite units, although at the end of the war the losses reduced their fury.

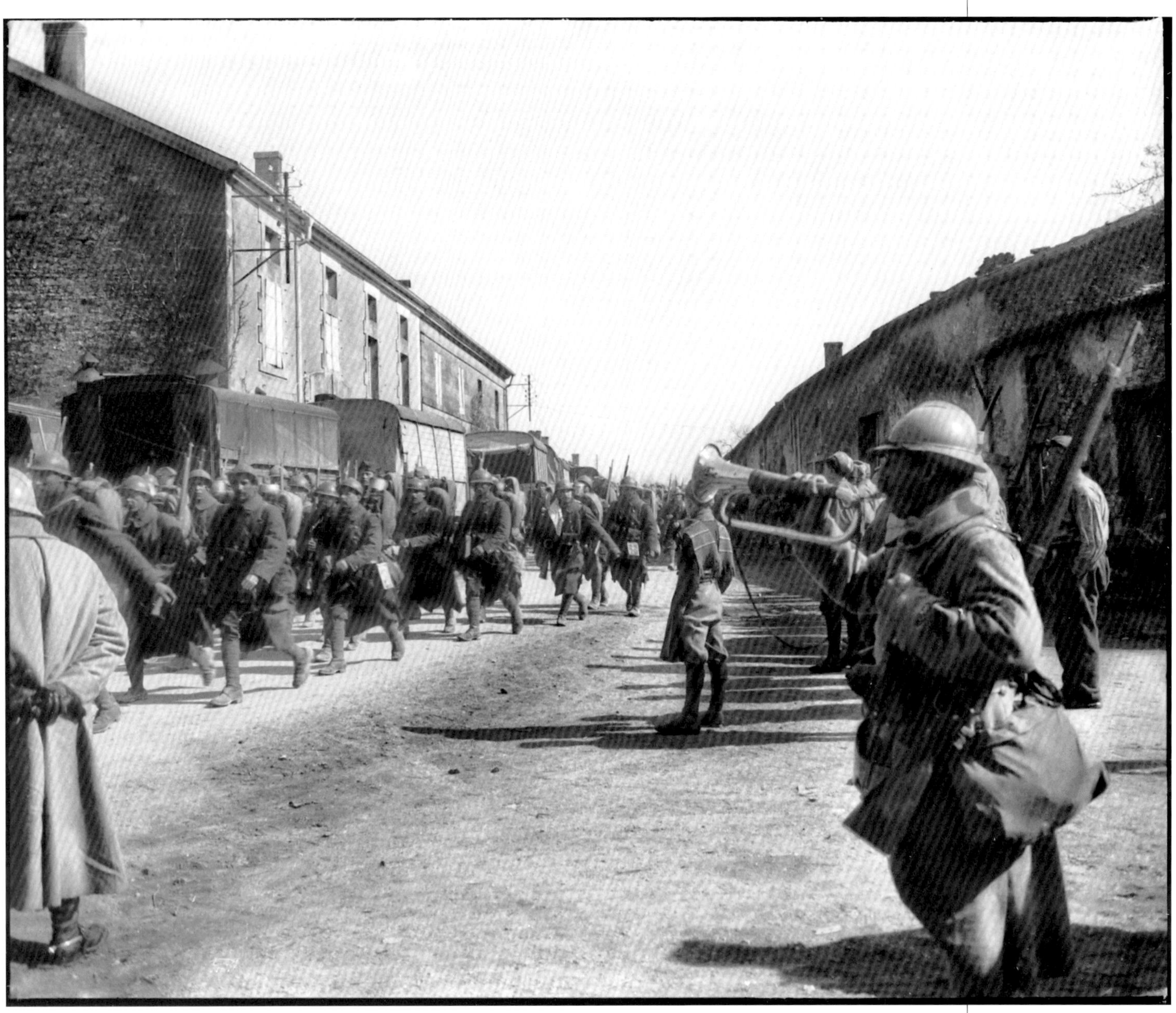

PHOT. 186
21/03/1918
(...) of a Zouaves regiment at Combles

The cornet player in the foreground carries a Berthier rifle, a weapon that only allowed three consecutive shots but which was an advance with respect to the one-shot Lebel.

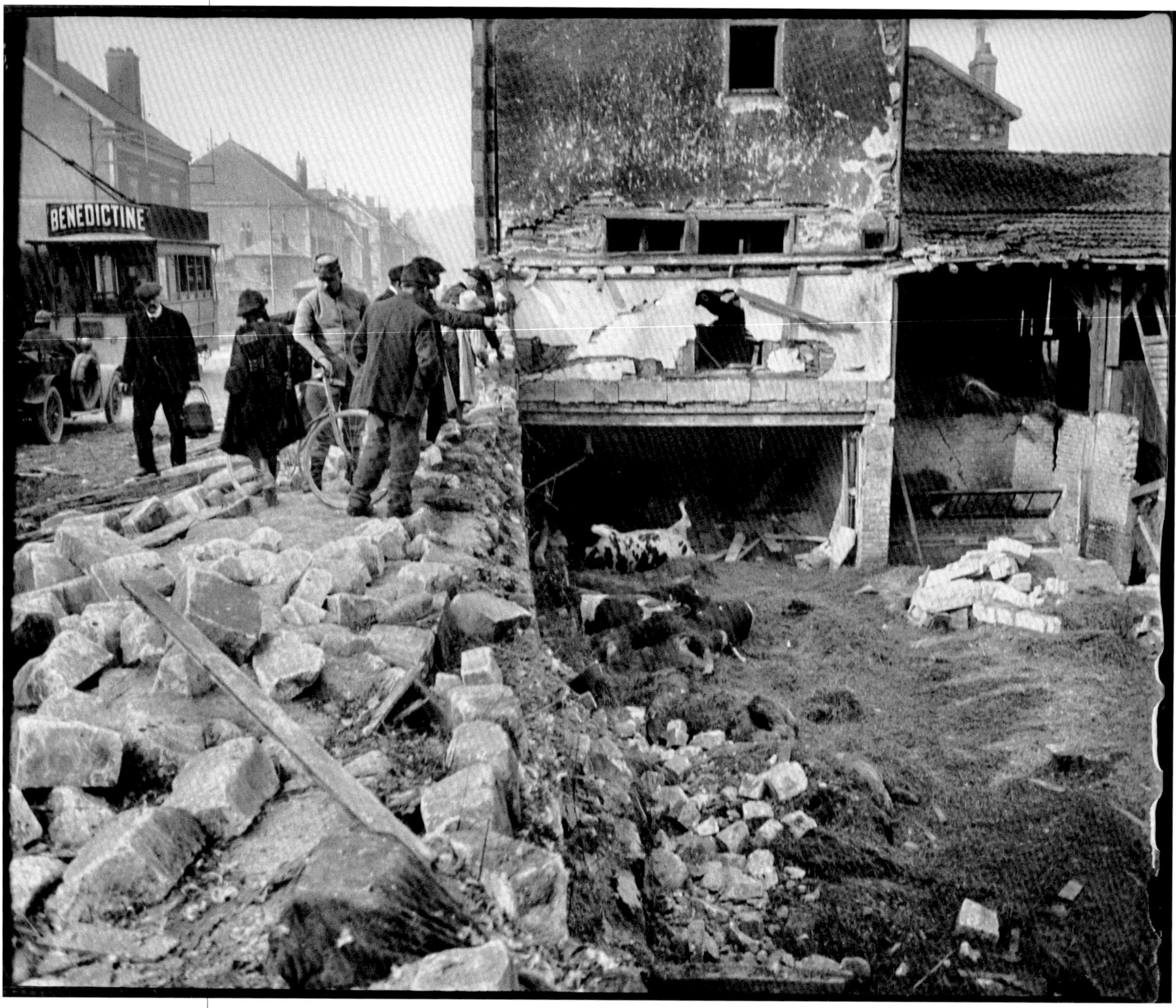

PHOT. 187
25/03/1918
The effects of
a Boche bombing
by plane in Châlons

Châlons-en-Champagne was a town of 30,000 inhabitants located at the French rear-guard nearby Reims, which made it a target for a new war concept: the indiscriminate aerial bombardment.

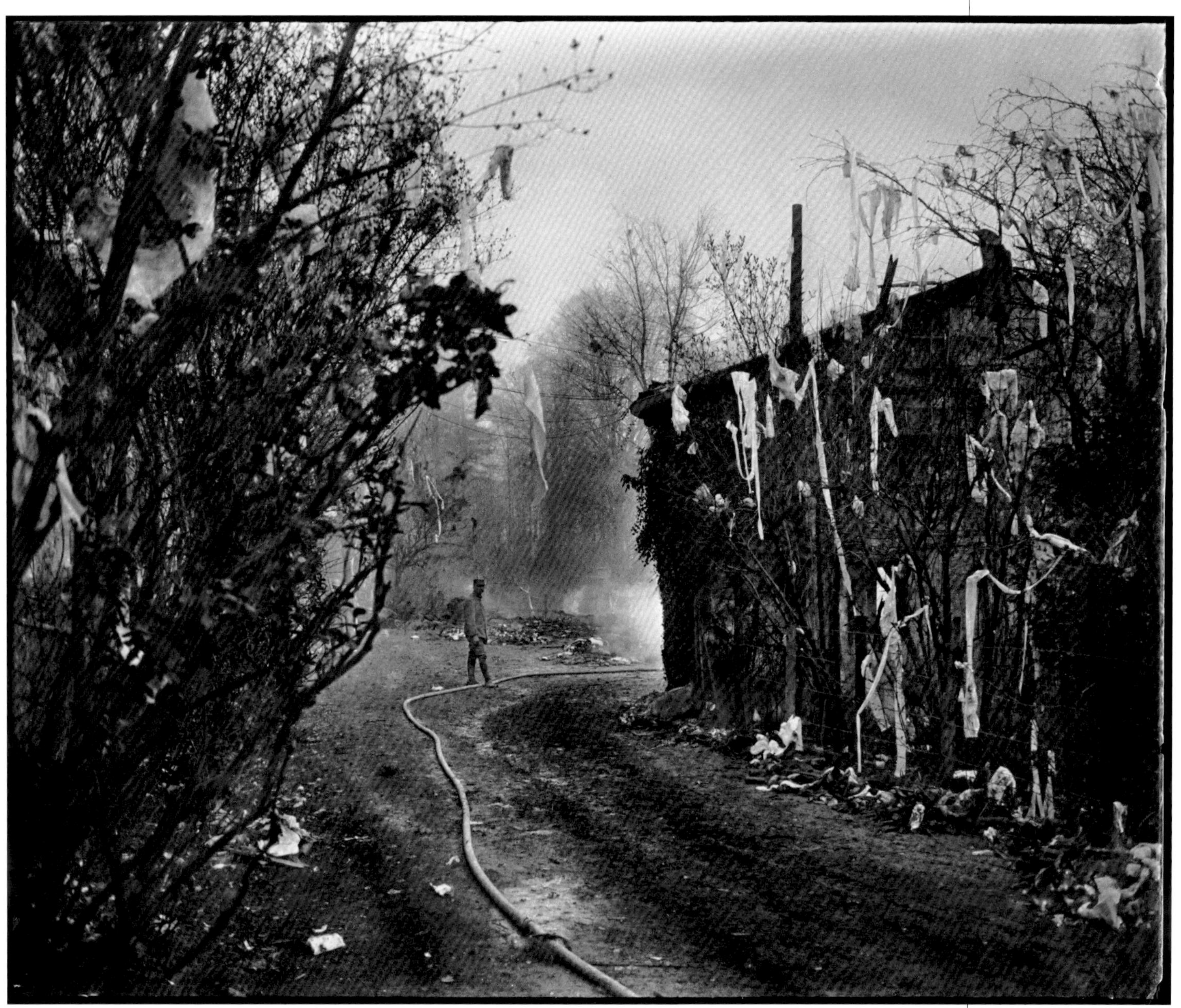

PHOT. 188
25/03/1918
Fire provoked by a Boche bomb in Châlons

Four days before the massive German Spring Offensive began, between the 25th and 26th Givord sets off with his unit towards the north, to Picard.

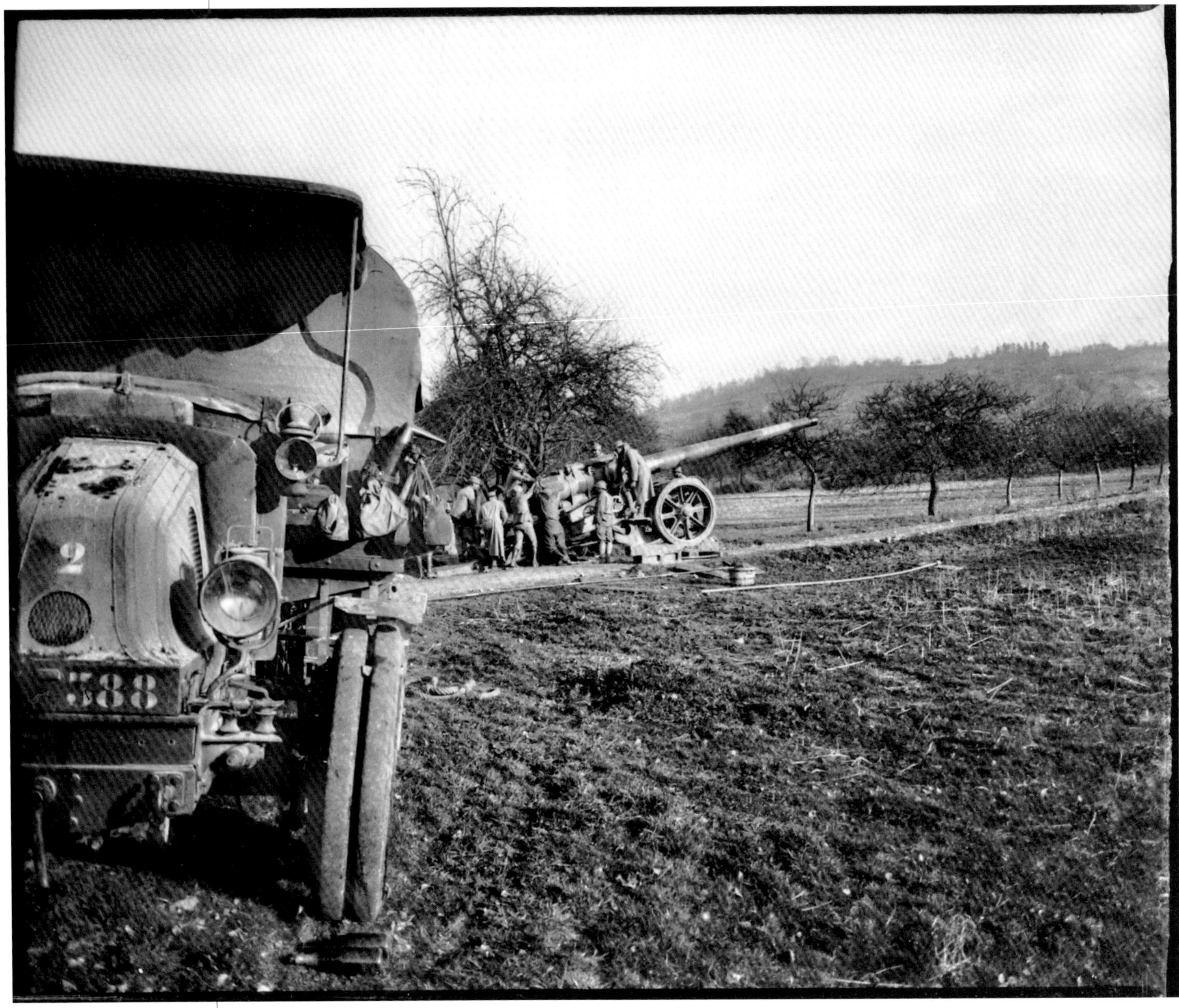

PHOT. 191
26/03/1918
On the route to Lassigny close to Machemont

Setting up position of a modern cannon 155 Long GPF. This type of cannon had a maximum range of 18 km. In the foreground, a Latil truck.

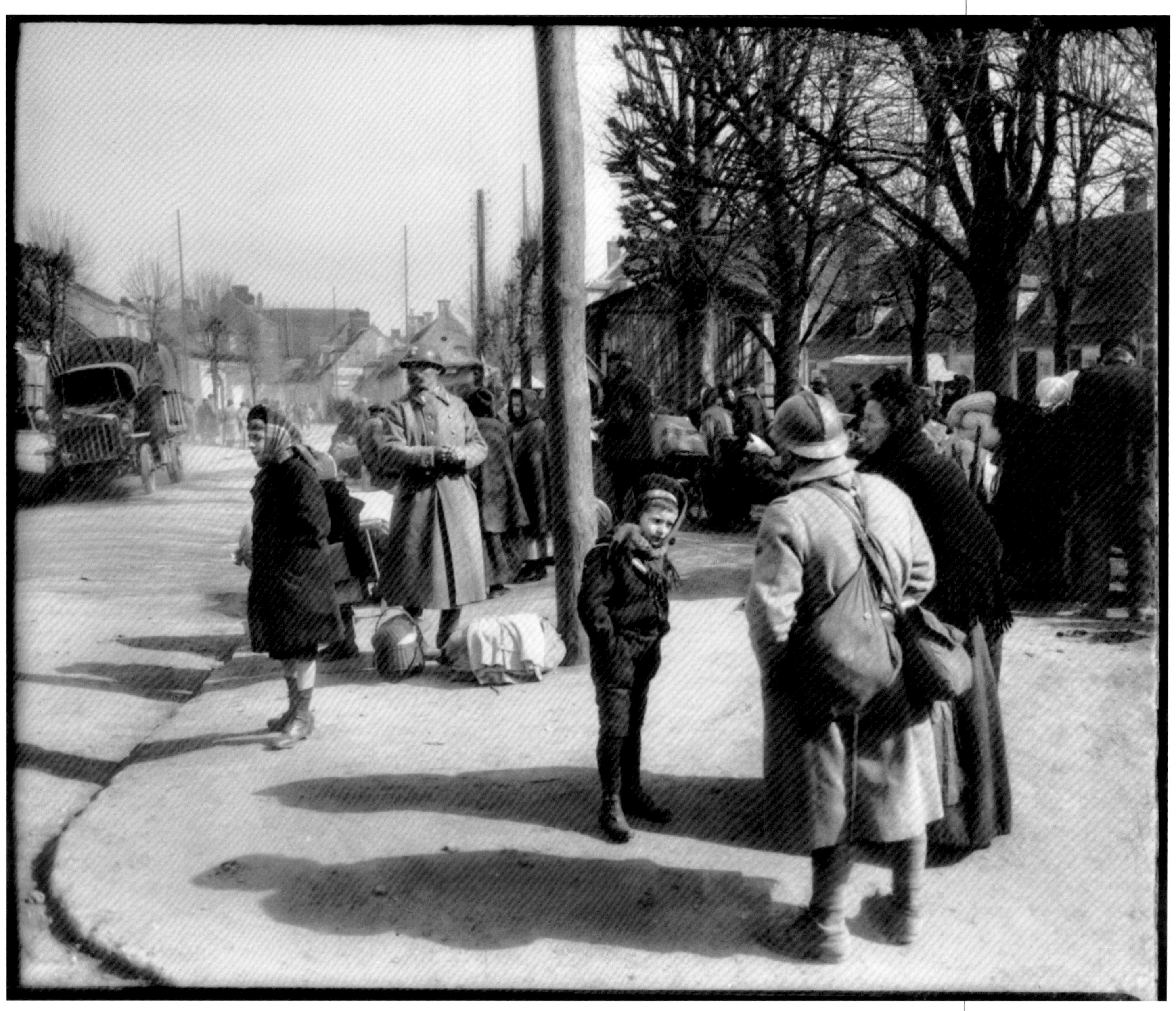

PHOT. 192
26/03/1918
The refugees at the Ressons-sur-Matz plaza

The tremendous German push provoked the massive evacuation of civilians, similar to that seen in 1914.

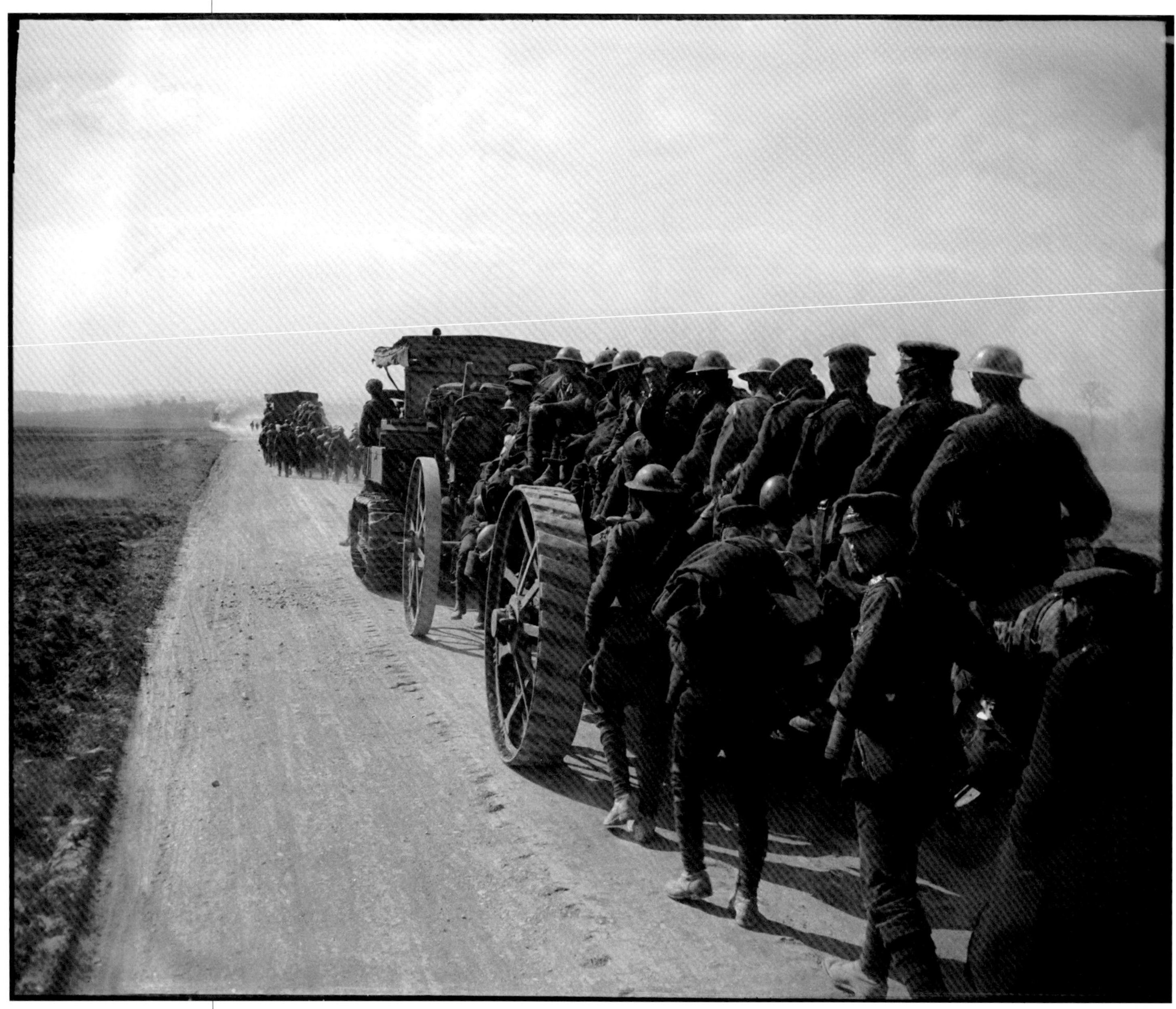

PHOT. 193
26/03/1918
The Boche advance!
The English in retreat!

The German Offensive focused on the British lines that were weaker, to the west of Cambrai. Here we see how some Canadian heavy artillery is pulled away by caterpillar tractors.

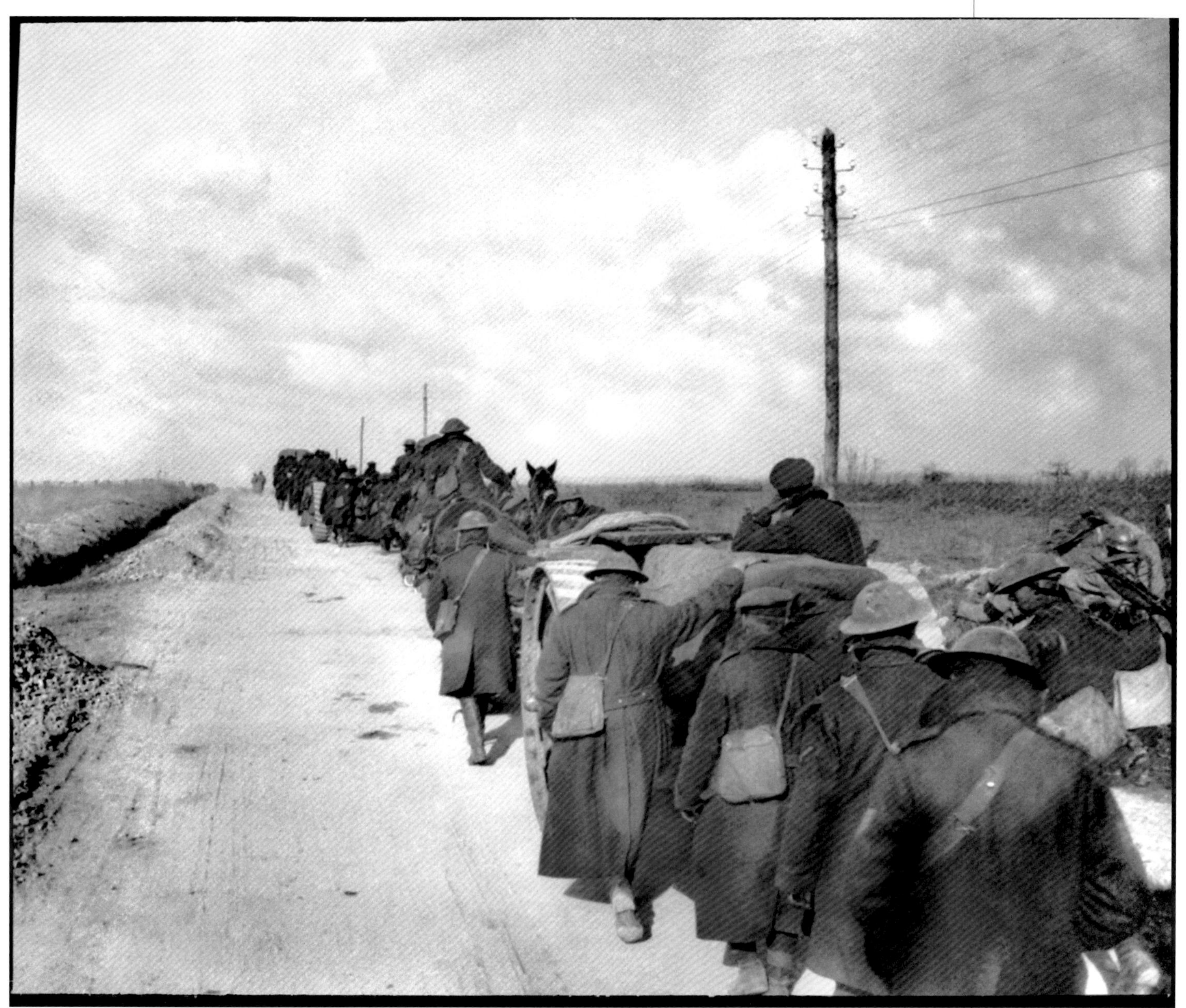

PHOT. 194
26/03/1918
The English retreat!

Around 4 pm on March 21st 10,000 German cannons and mortars crews open fire simultaneously in a bombardment 70 km wide. In five hours the German army spent 1,160,000 shells, each piece discharging between 200 and 600 shots.

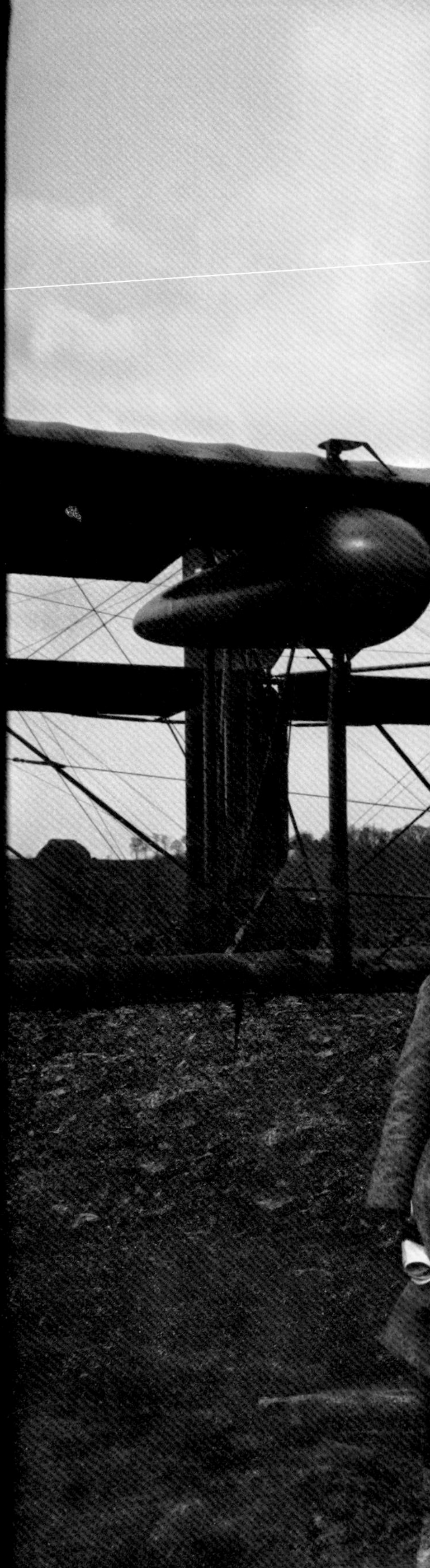

PHOT. 195
28/03/1918
A plane nearby
Estrées-Saint-Denis

A French two-seater biplane Voisin X with Renault engine, painted in black for night time bombing. In the foreground there are American and French officers mingling.

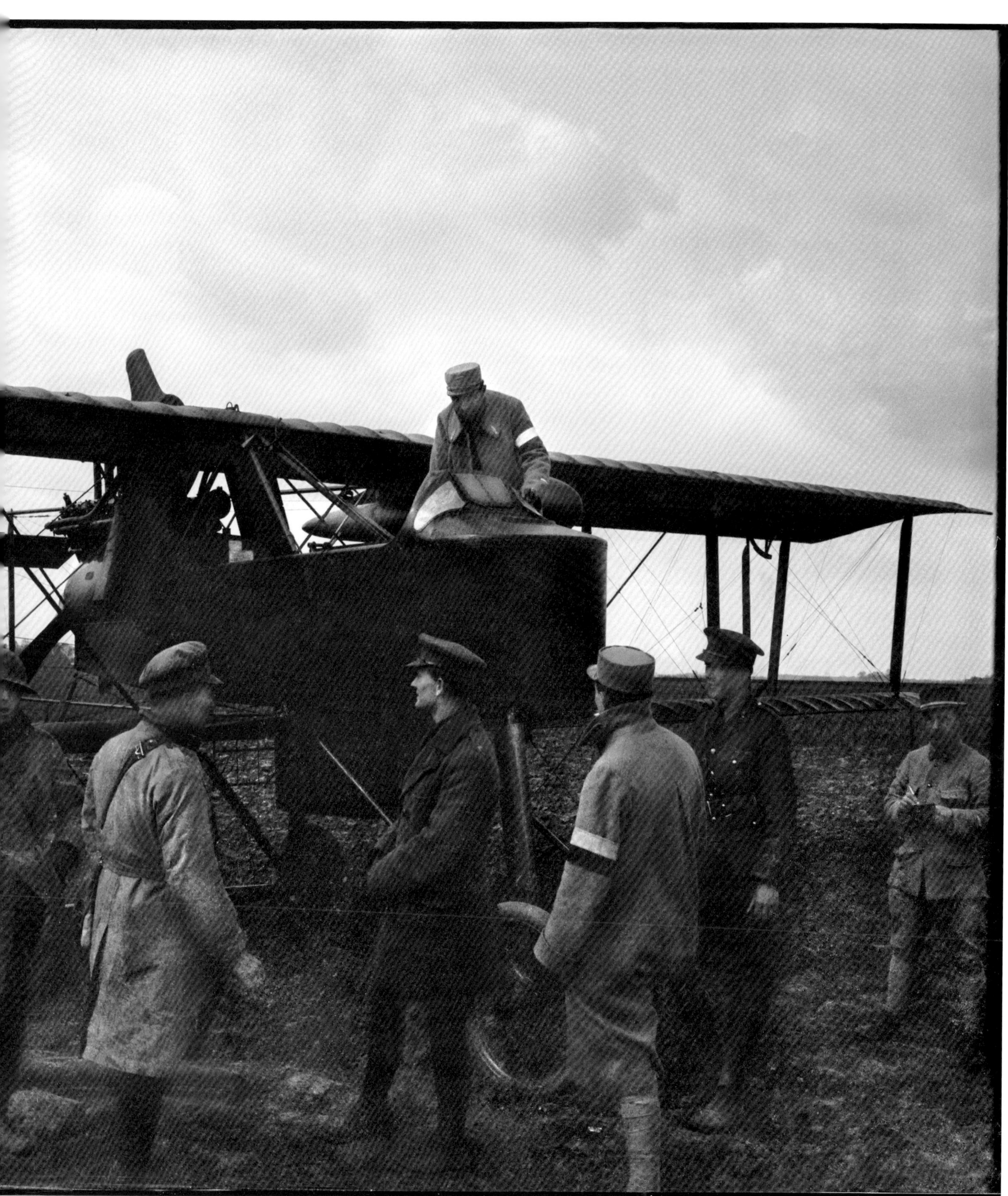

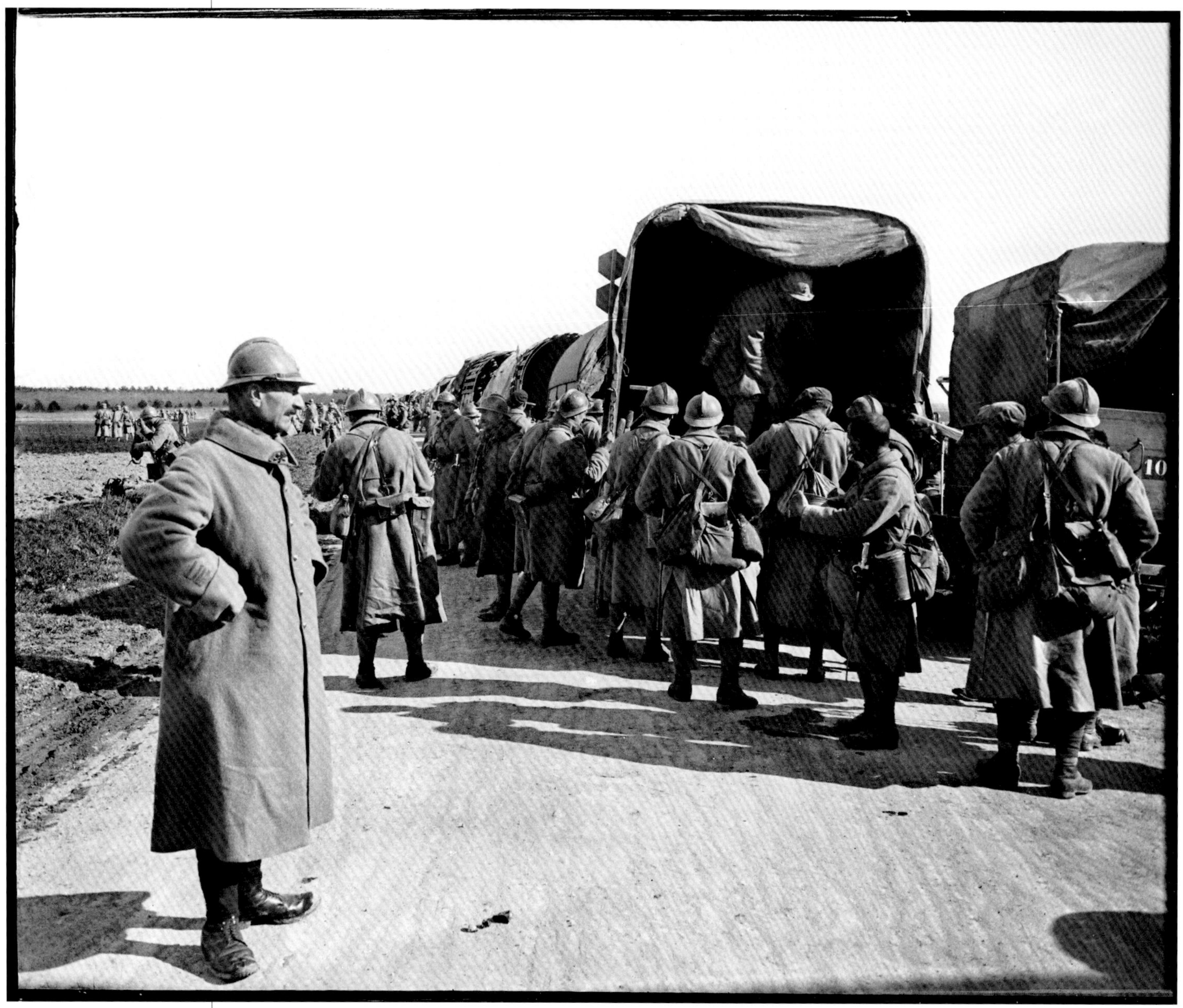

PHOT. 196
11/04/1918
Commander Rouchon of 359

In the foreground appears Commander Camille Rouchon, of the *359e Regiment d'Infanterie.* Born in Gap in 1870, he probably met Givord before the war.

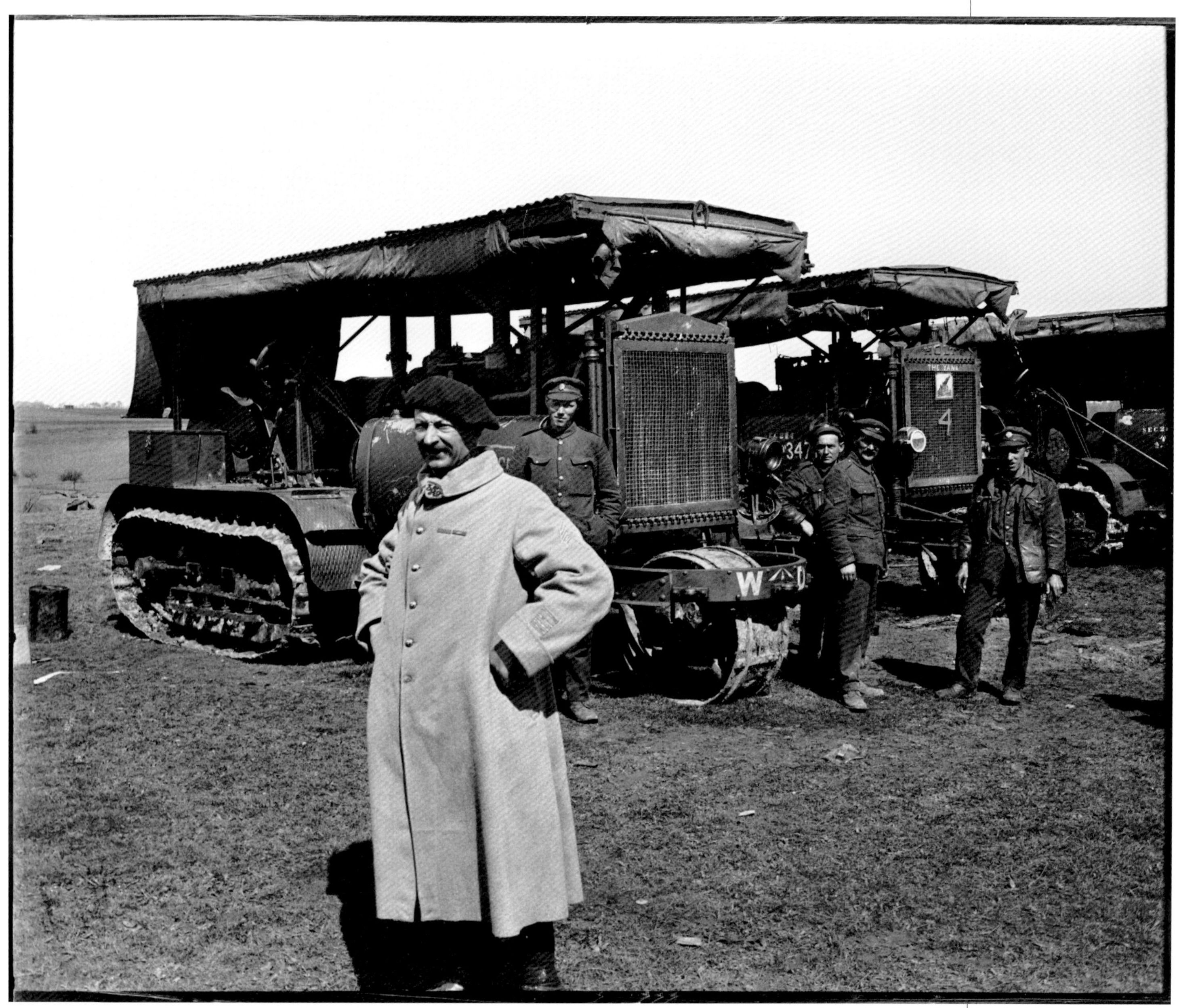

PHOT. 197
11/04/1918
English tractor on the route from Poix to Amiens

During the move of 359e RI, Commander Rouchon finds a moment to be photographed besides some Holt artillery tractors. The second one at the back was baptised as 'The Yank'. Within the period of the war the transportation of heavy pieces was mechanised, replacing horse and manpower in less than four years.

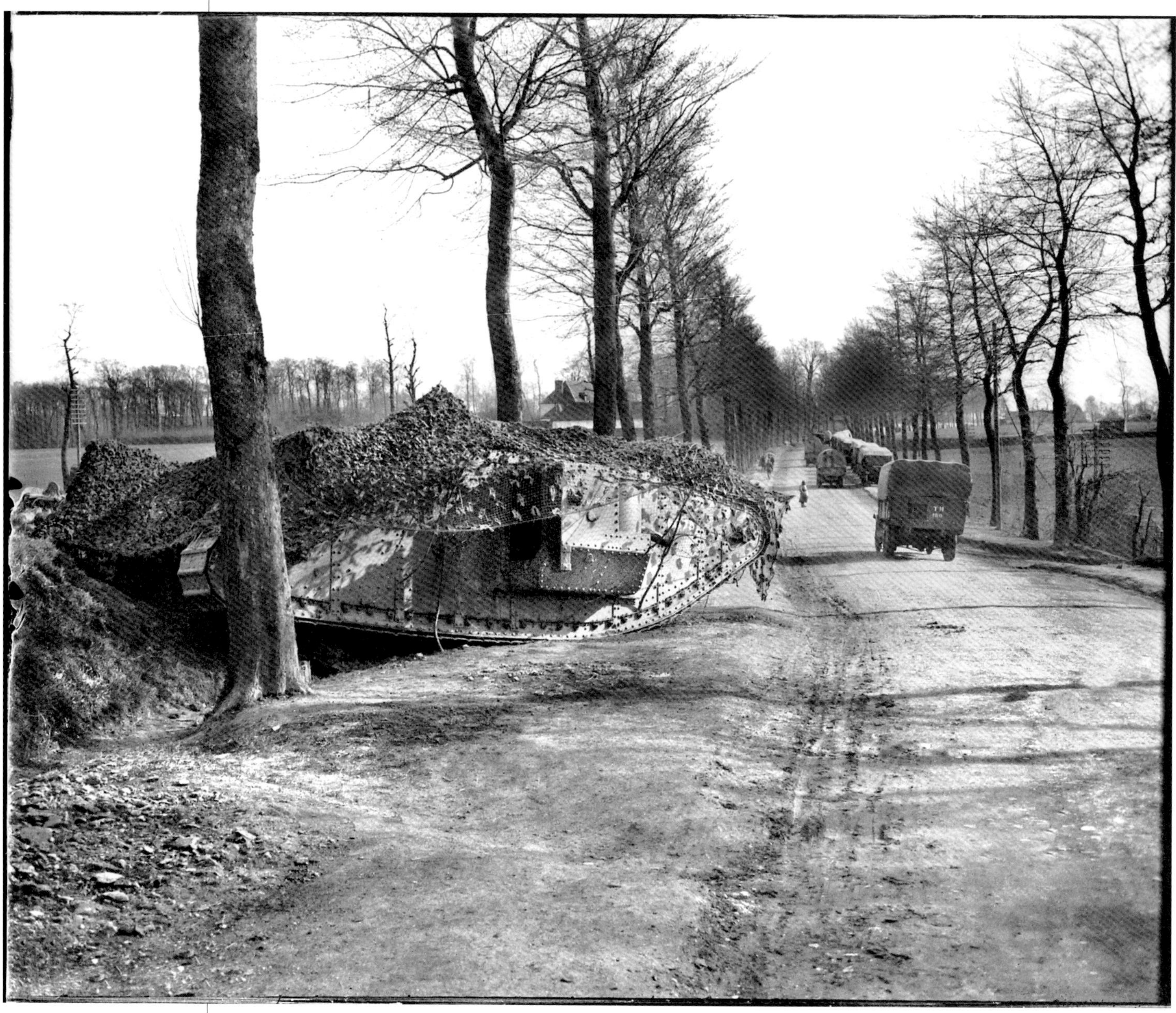

PHOT. 198
12/04/1918
English tank

Some trucks of the *Transport de Matériel* pass by a camouflaged British Mark IV tank. The one in the photograph is the *male* version that had two 6 pounder cannons and 3 machine guns, while the *female* version was equipped with 5 machine guns, designed to protect the male tanks on their approach. Going into battle inside a tank was a real torture. The 8 men crew suffocated from the fumes of the cannon and the 105 CV engine, although its peak speed did not exceed 6 km/h. The term *tank* was the result of an English strategy to hide the true mission of these machines, which is why they made them look like mobile water deposits.

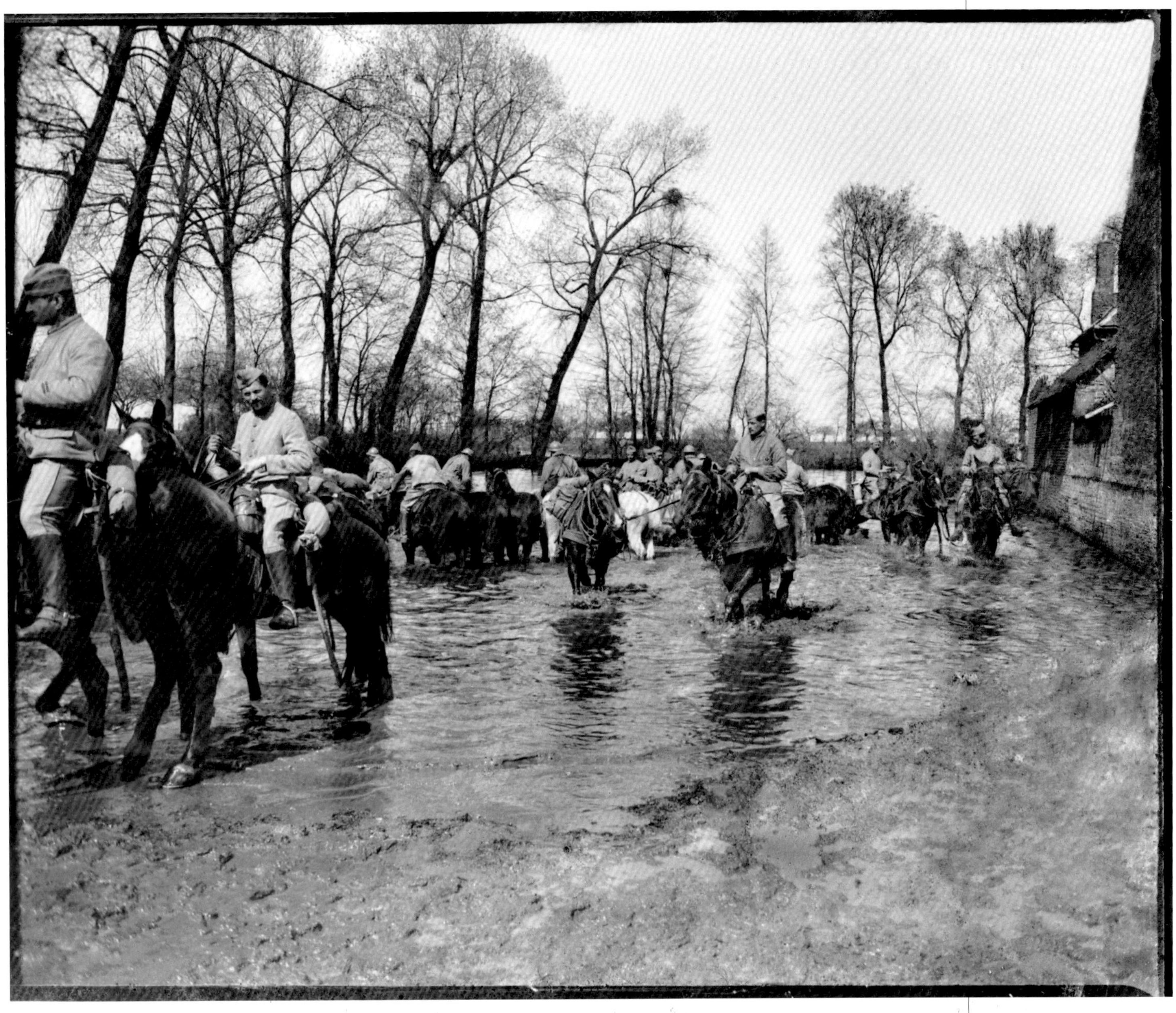

PHOT. 199
15/04/1918

A cavalry section tries to wade across a flooded area. On this day in April Givord finished the evacuation of the hospital in Ressons-sur-Matz.

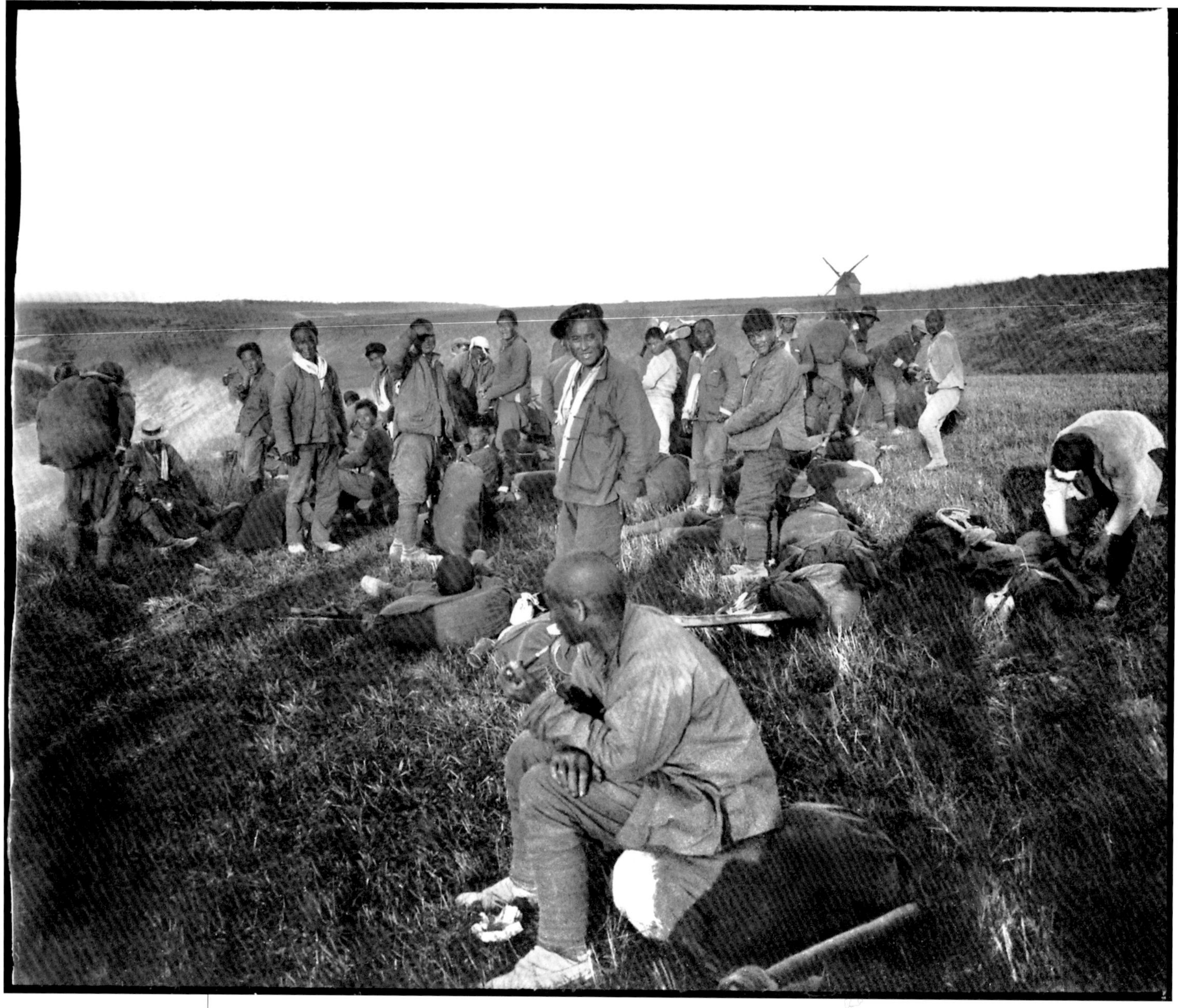

PHOT. 200
15/04/1918

The colonial empires called on their vast populations to collaborate in the war effort. For instance, the French called on the Annamites (Vietnam, Cambodia and Laos) to bolster the labour corps.

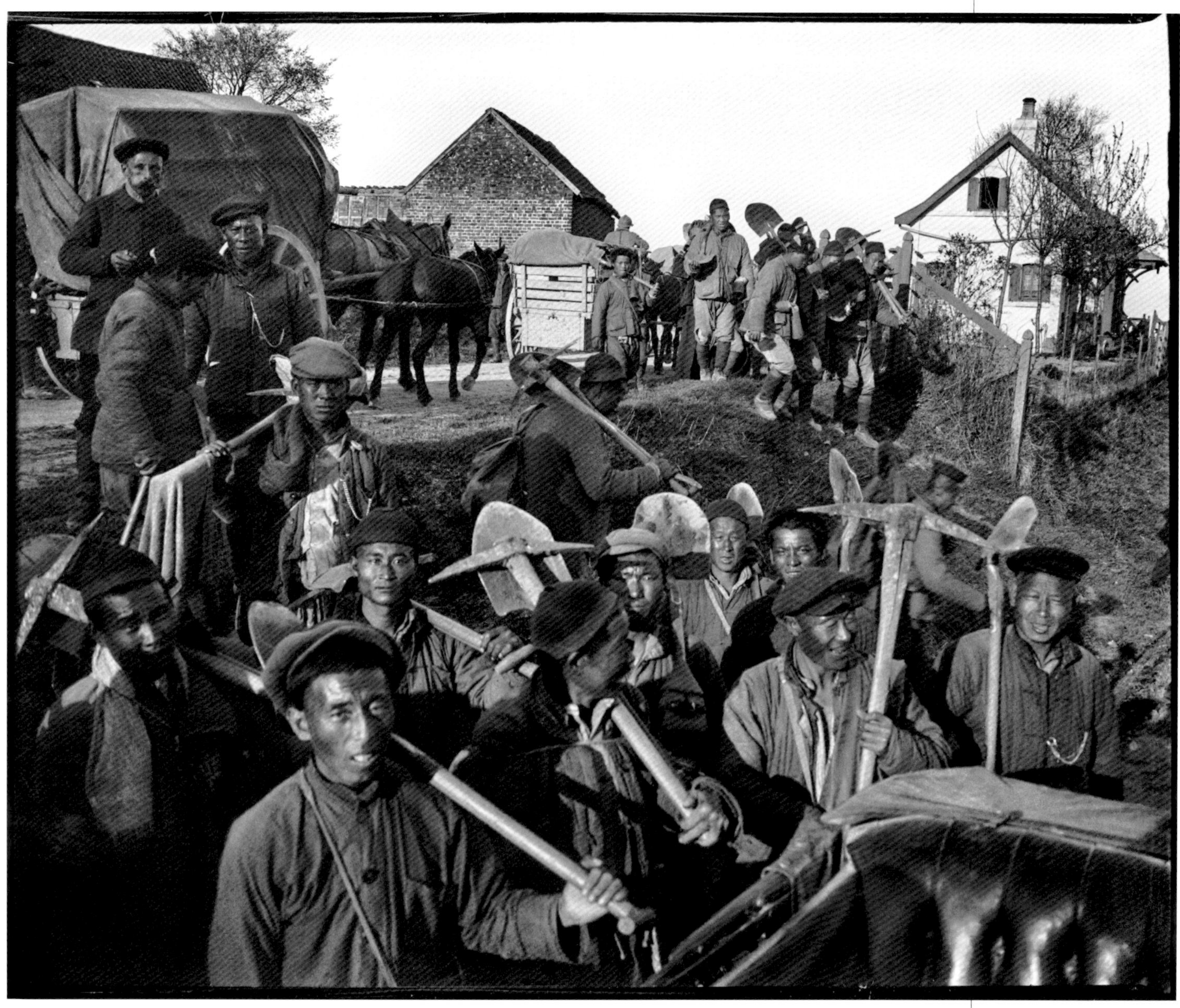

PHOT. 201
23/04/1918

Around 90,000 Indo-Chinese from French colonies were deployed within the army workforces and at the ammunition factories.

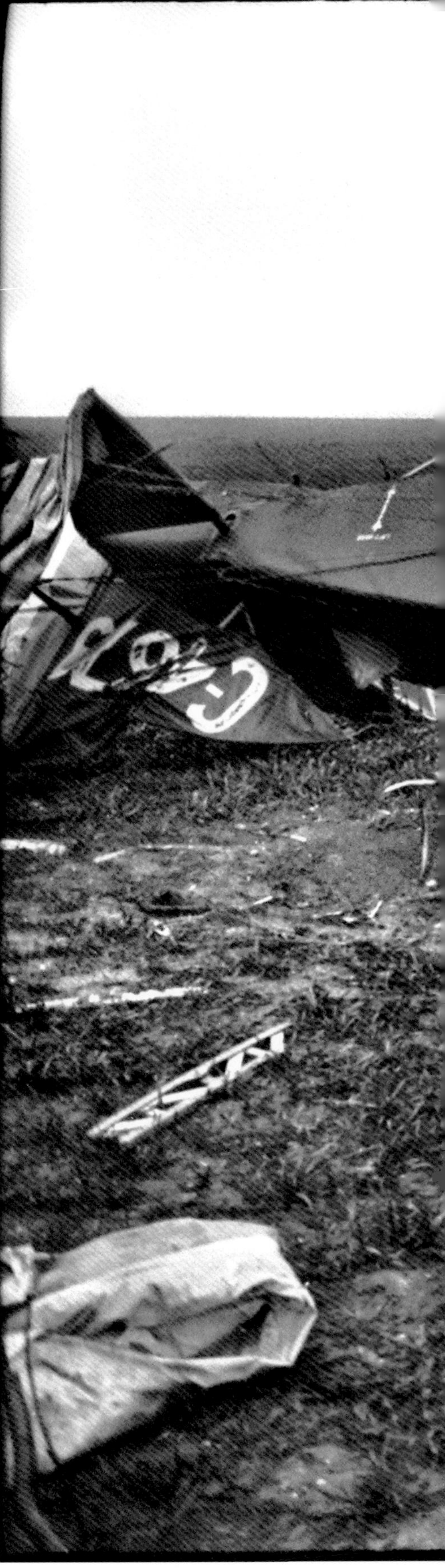

PHOT. 202
25/04/1918
British plane crashed at Heuzecourt

Remains of a Bristol Fighter F.2b numbered C4673 of 11 Squadron of the recently created Royal Air Force. It had crashed the day before after skimming some trees whilst it was on a reconnaissance mission at dusk. The pilot and observer died in the impact, Edward Woollard P. Lamb (born in 1892) and Bertie Joseph Maisey (born in 1898). Both rest at the nearby cemetery in Doullens.

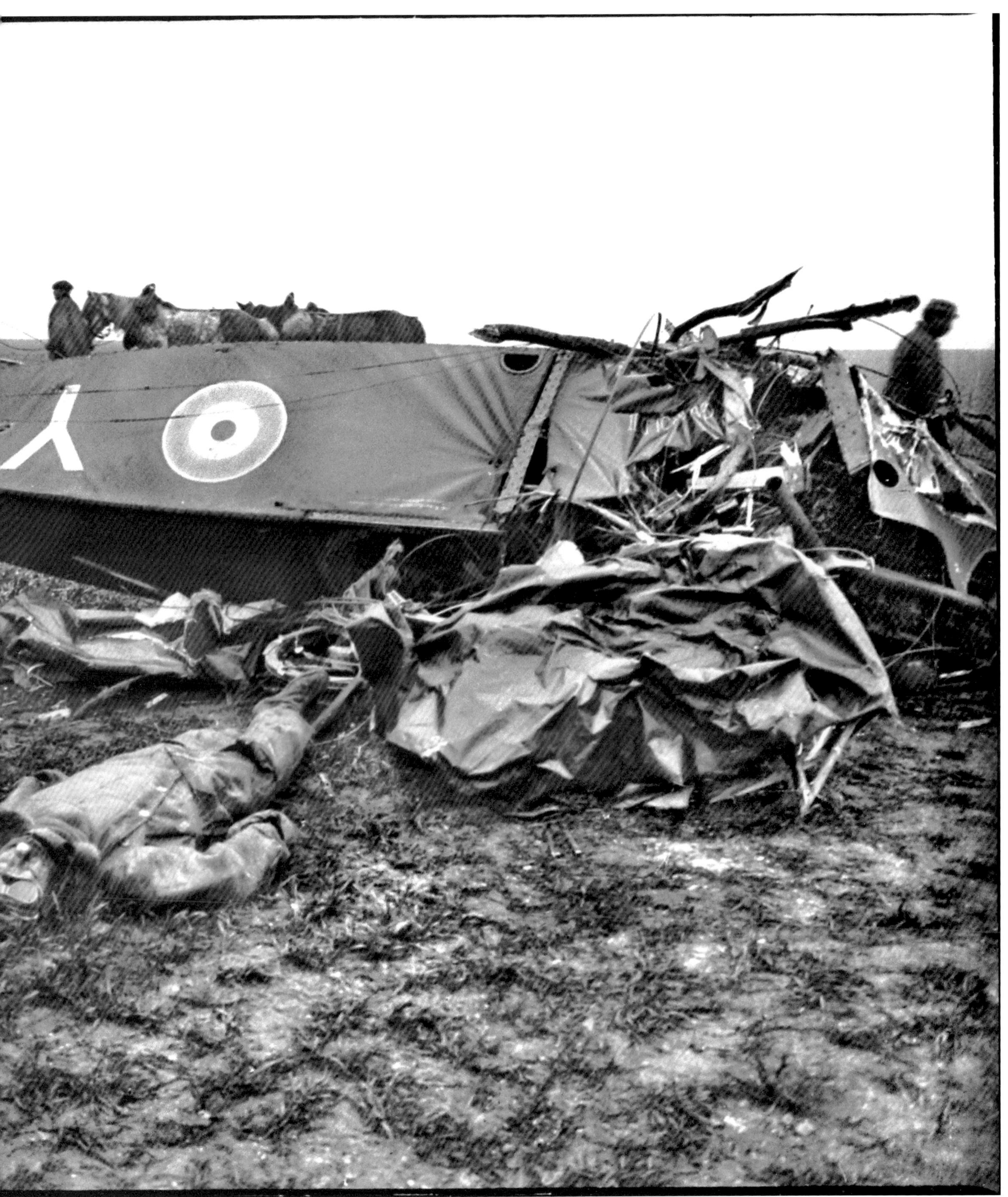
Y

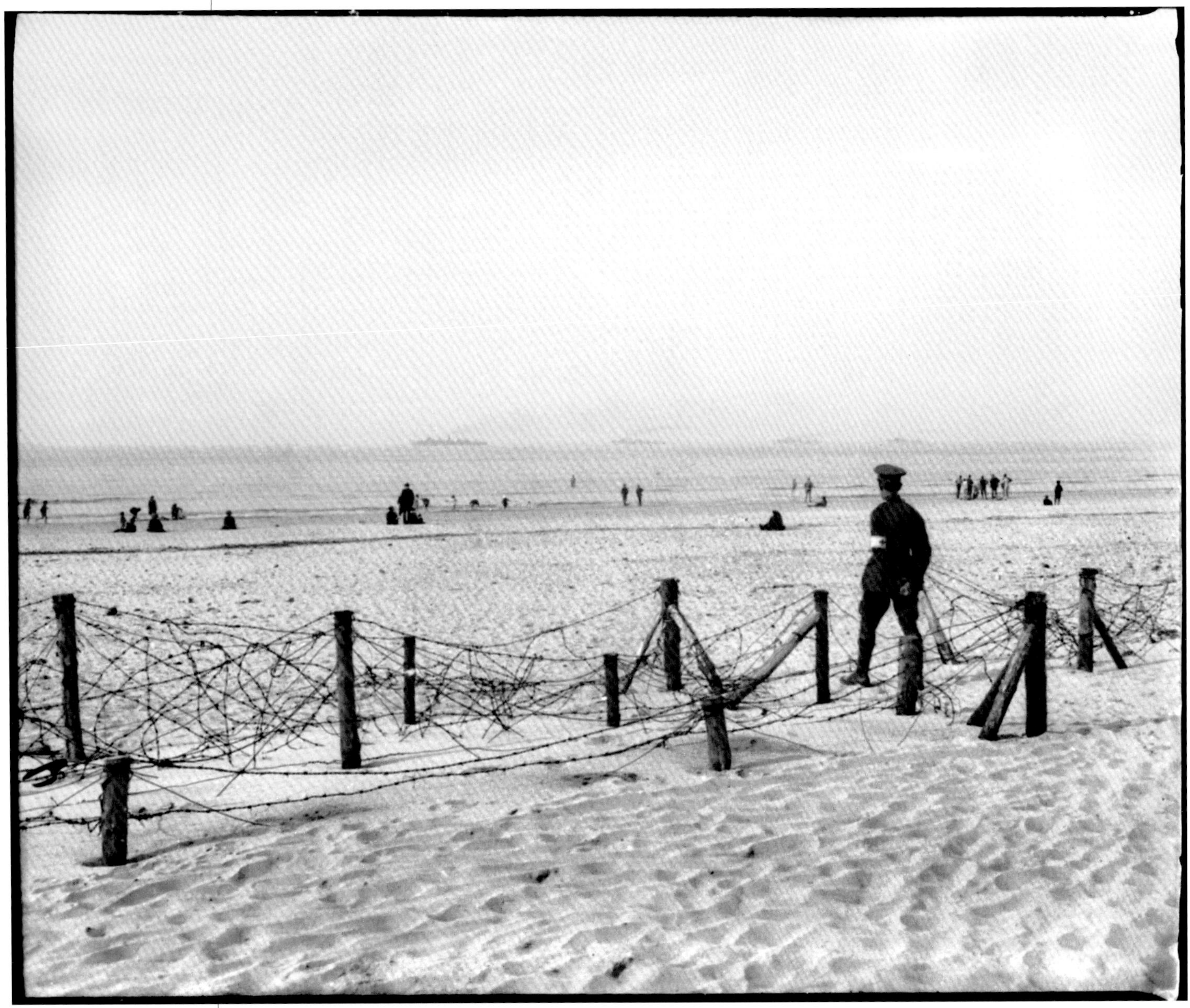

PHOT. 209
18/05/1918
The beach of Malo les Bains in times of war

This beach is at Dunkerque, operation base of the British Army, on the coast of the English Channel.

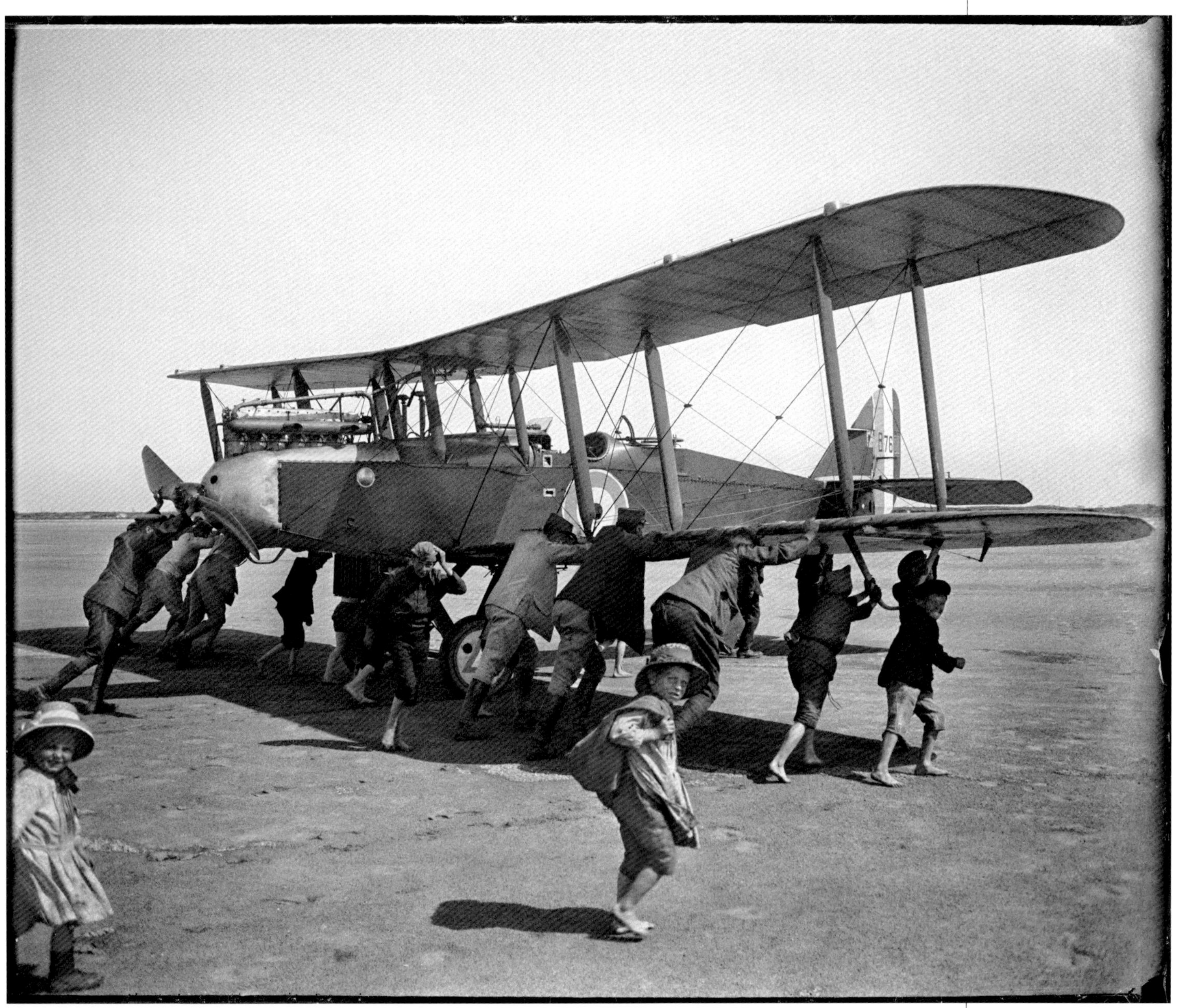

PHOT. 212
04/06/1918
An English plane at the beach of Mardyck

This kind of biplane Airco DH.9 had poor performance in combat due to its deficient engine. The plane in the photograph with plate B7601 belonged to the RAF 218 Bombing Squadron, stationed nearby at Dunkerque. A week before it had been damaged by an engine failure while it was flown by Lieutenant B. H. Stata.

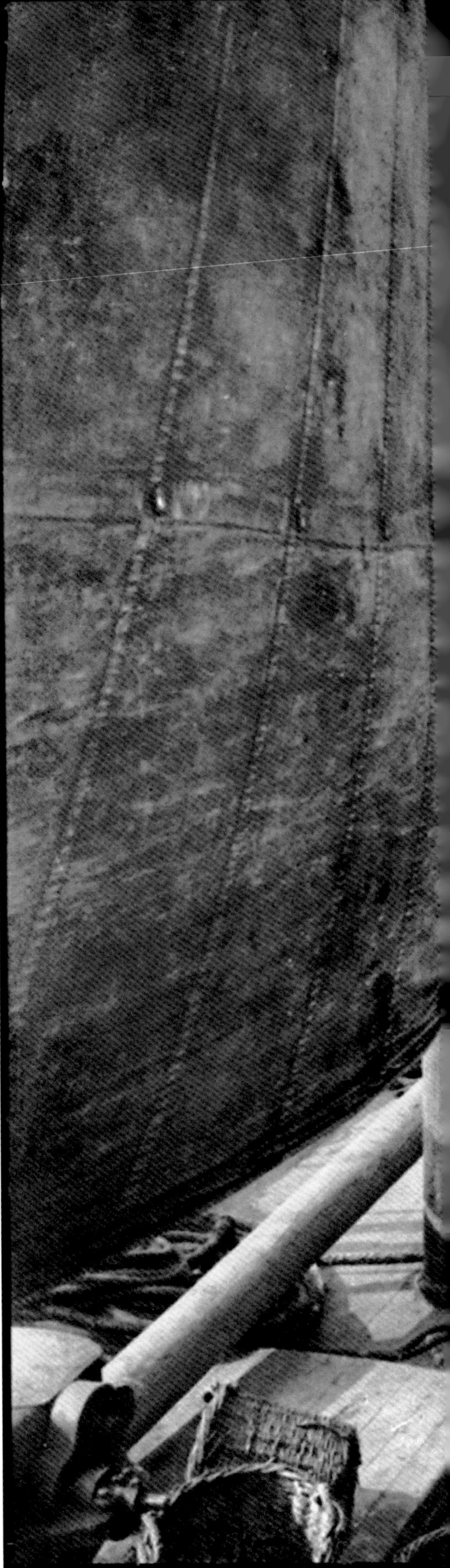

PHOT. 211
23/05/1918
Fishermen at Dunkerque's dockside

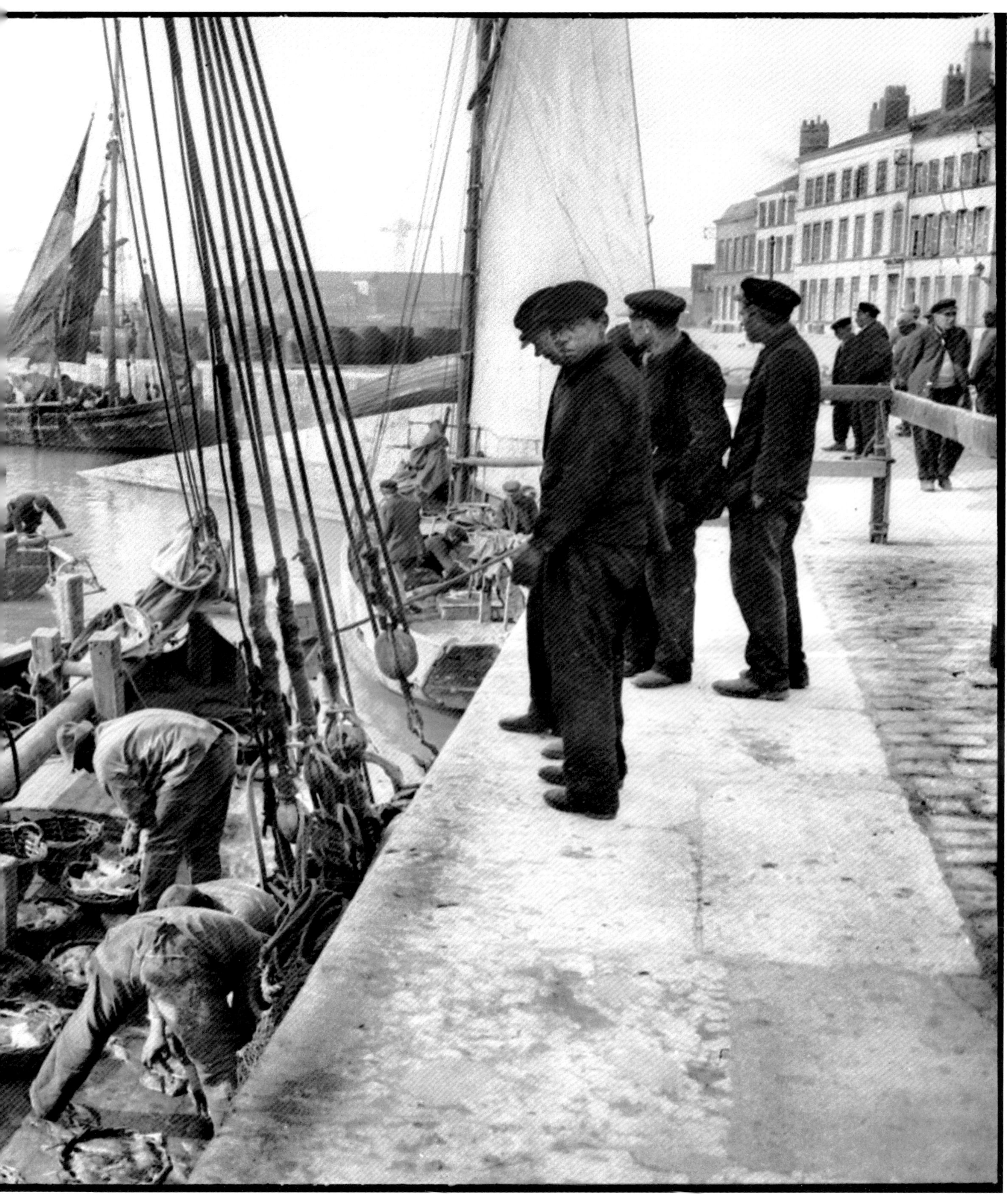

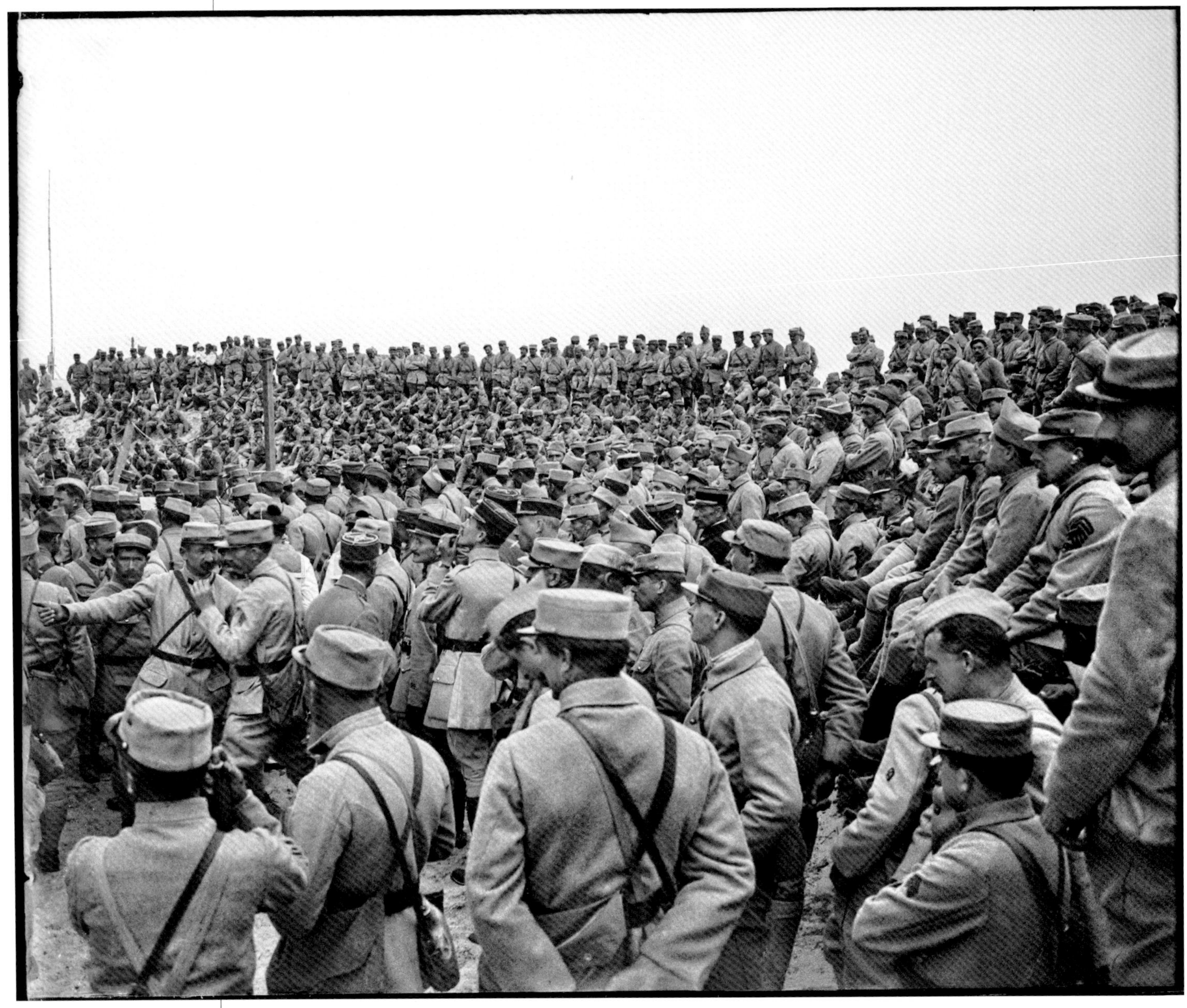

PHOT. 215
20/06/1918
In Clipon (department of Nord-Pas-de-Calais)

Clipon is placed in Loon-Plage, very close to Dunkerque.

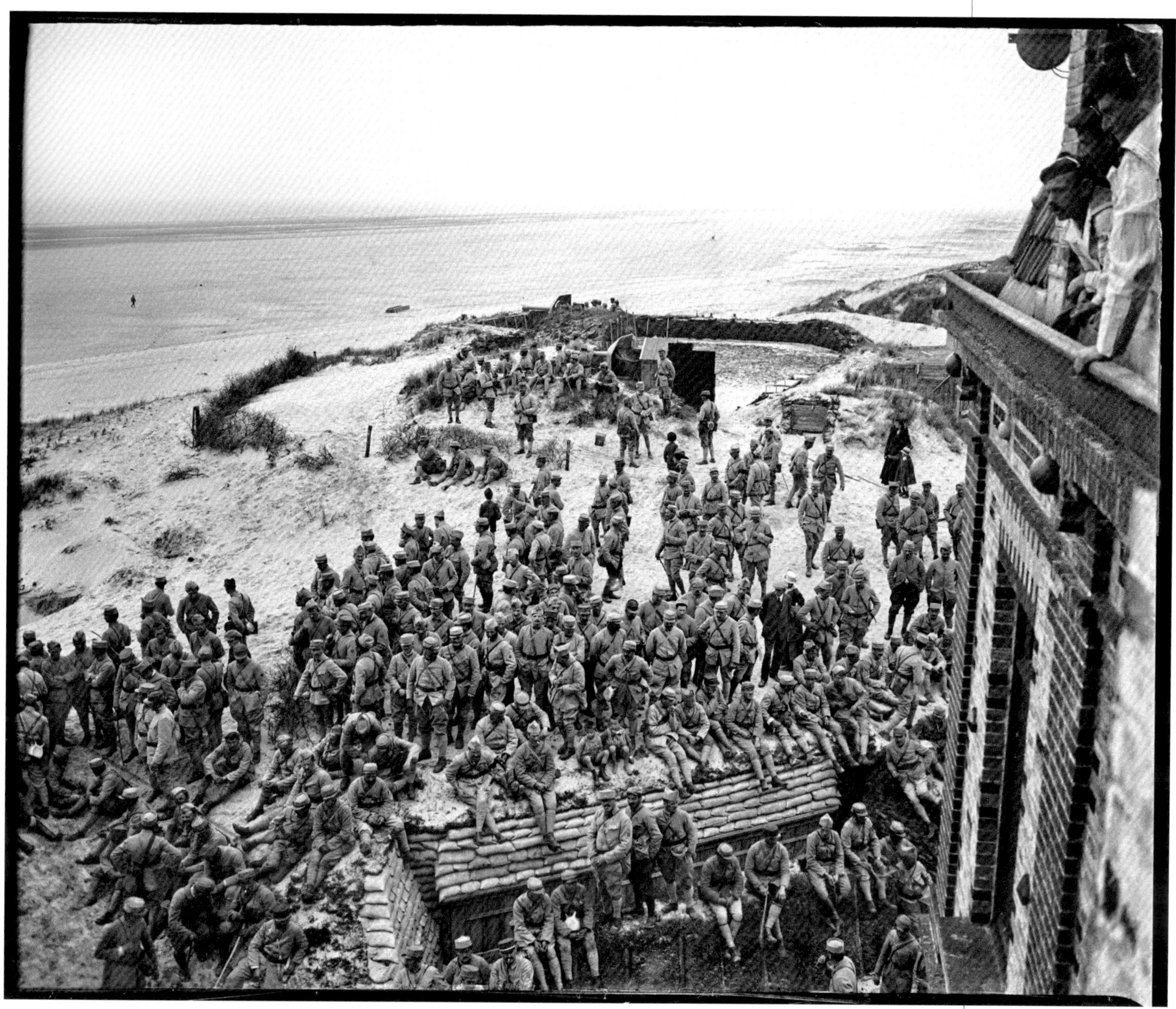

PHOT. 216
20/06/1918
The men from the regiments at the casino in Loon-Plage, going for a walk!

In the background we can see the emplacement of two naval cannons, while on the right hand some sailors observe the meeting.

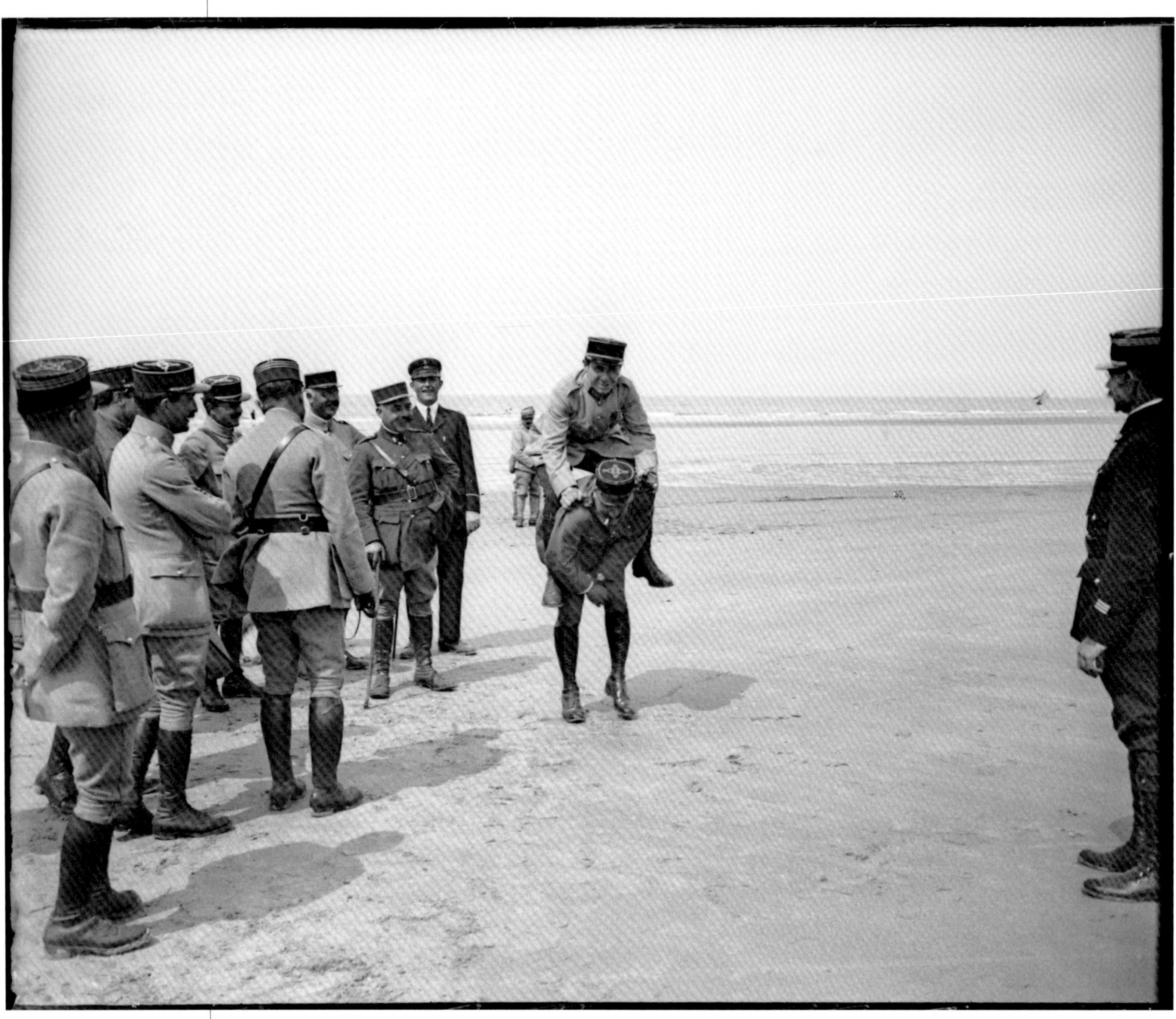

PHOT. 217
20/06/1918

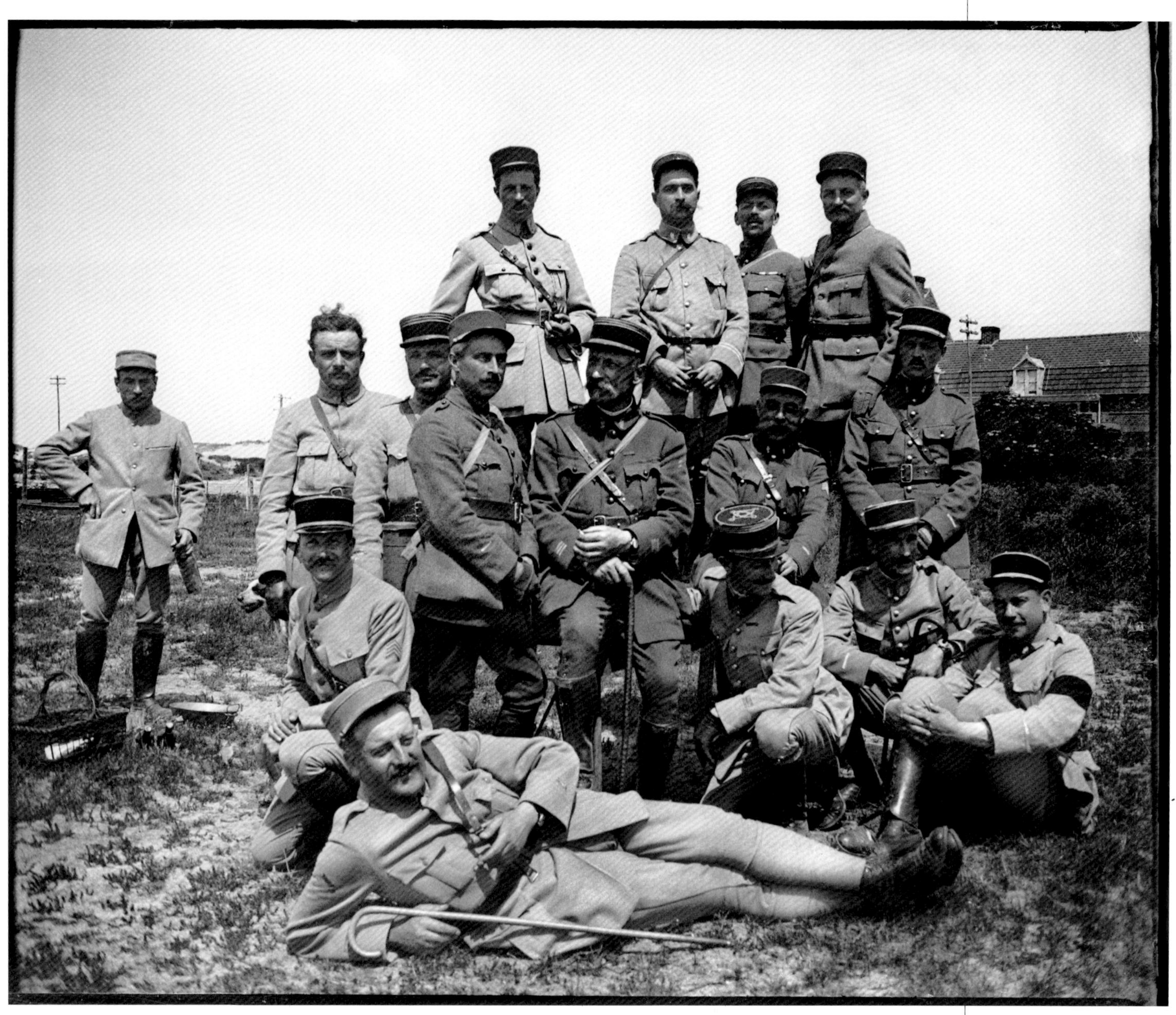

PHOT. 218
20/06/1918

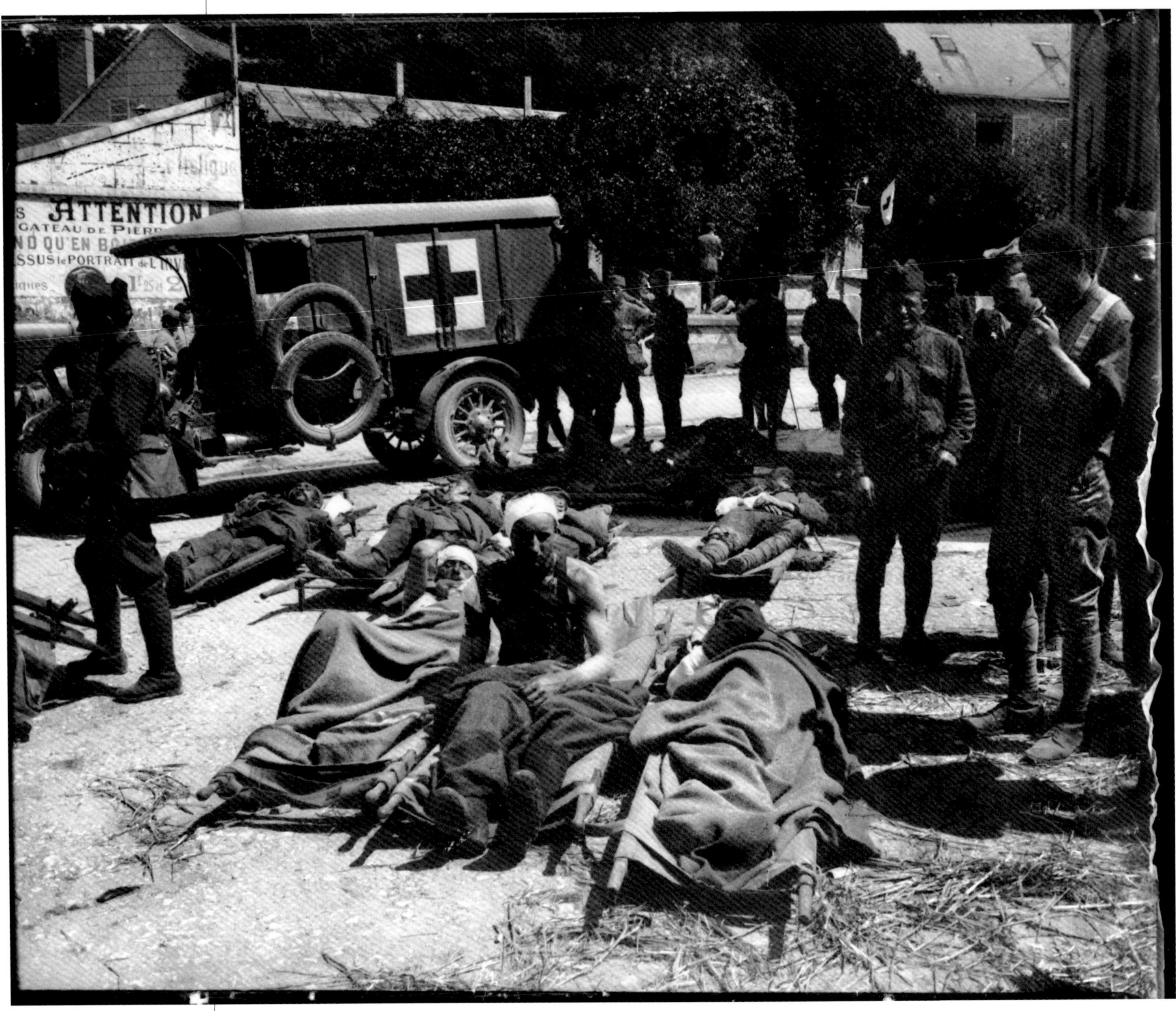

PHOT. 222
JULY 1918
American wounded
at Pierrefonds (sic)

The Americans entered fighting during summer 1918, as it can be appreciated in the photograph. The image is taken in the Picardian town plaza close to Compiègne, famous for its castle, where the front moved to after the German attack. In the background you can see the Red Cross symbol which features again in another photograph.

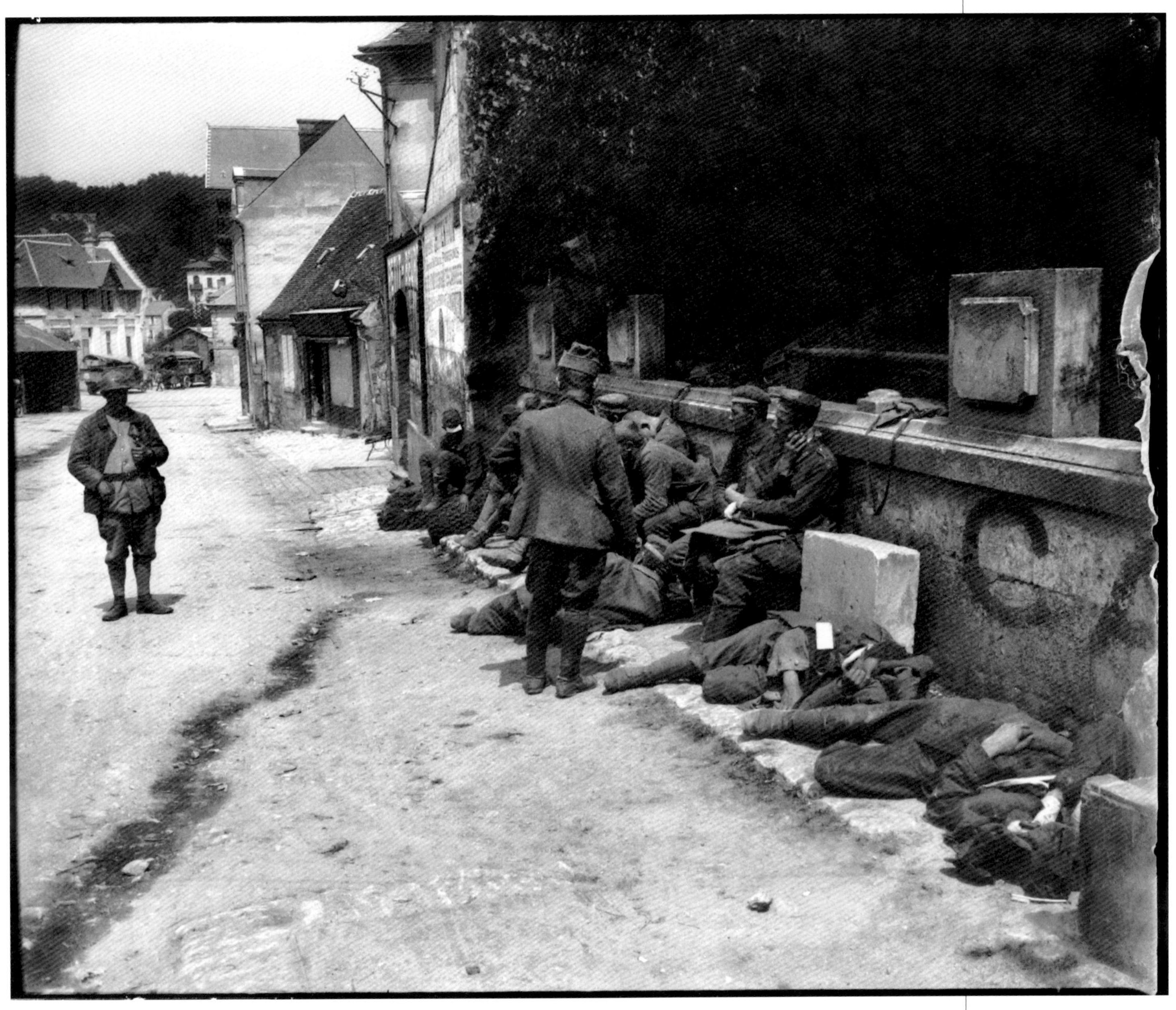

PHOT. 223
JULY 1918
Boche wounded
at Pierrefonds (sic)

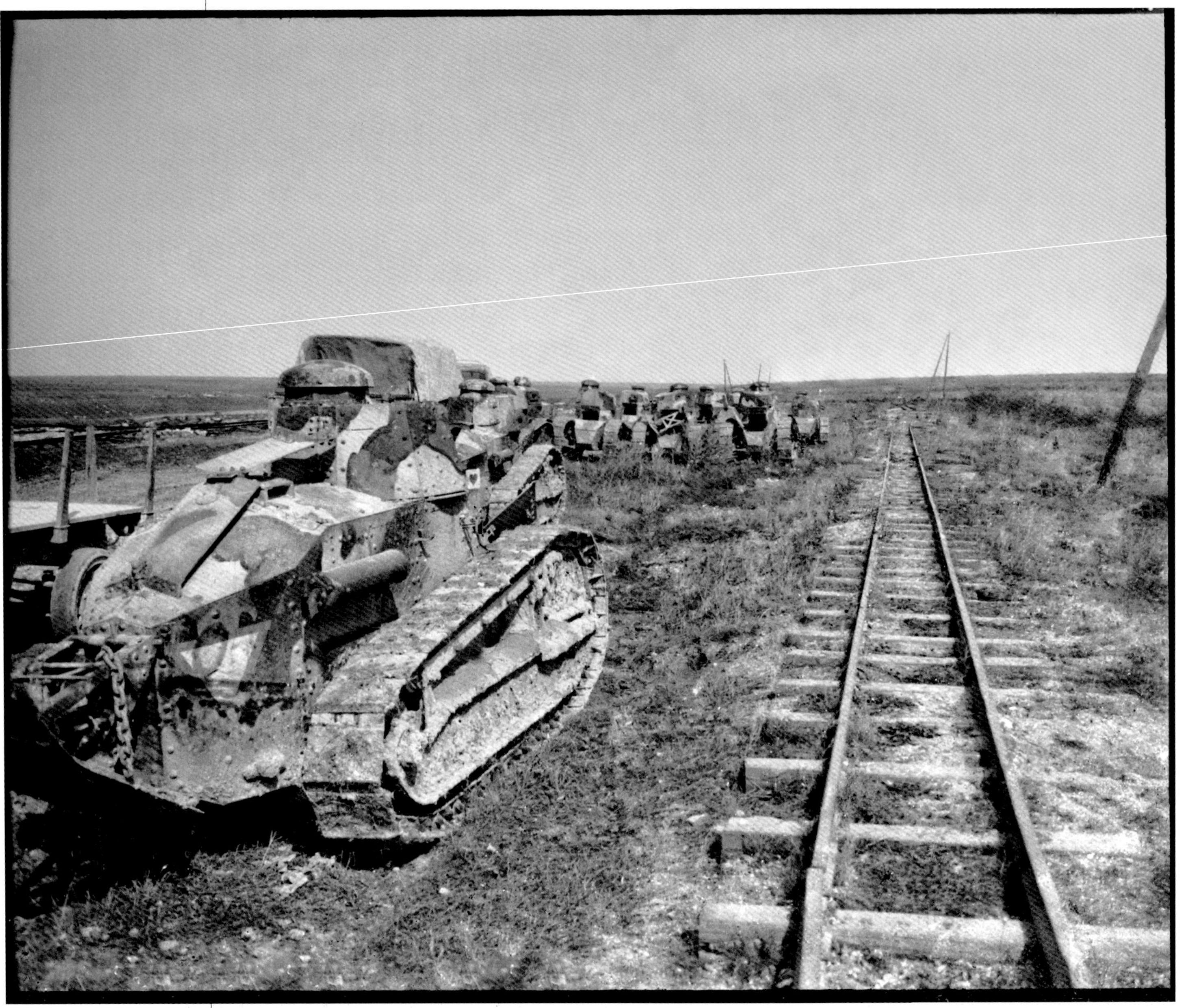

PHOT. 224

SEPTEMBER 1918

Small tank for (...)

Several Renault FT-17, probably needing a repair. This light tank is the predecessor of modern tanks with its layout of rotatory turret and rear engine. It only weighed 6.5 tons and had two crewmen: driver and commander, who also had to fire the cannon and move the turret by hand.

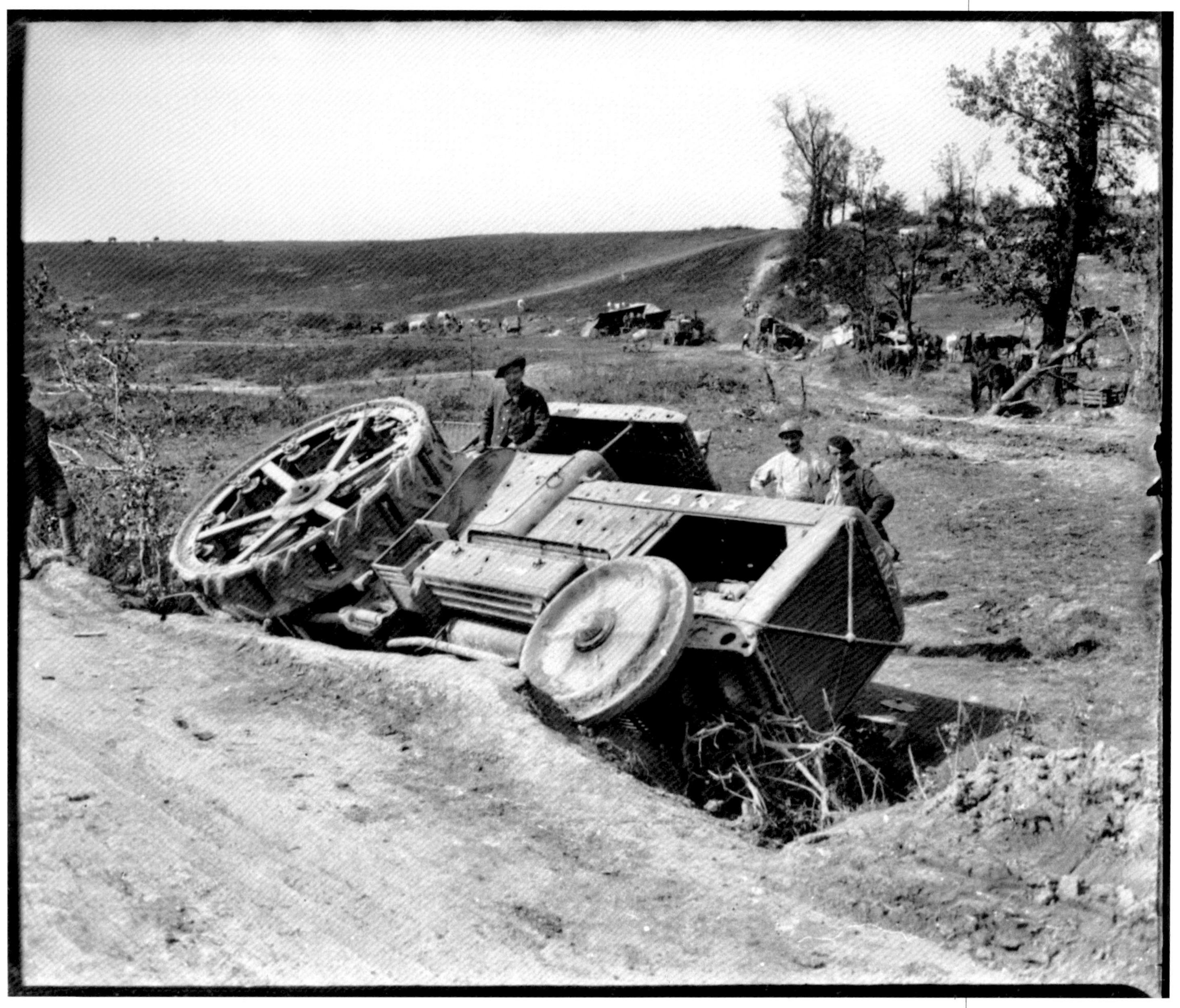

PHOT. 225
07/07/1918 /5/

A German Lanz artillery tractor.

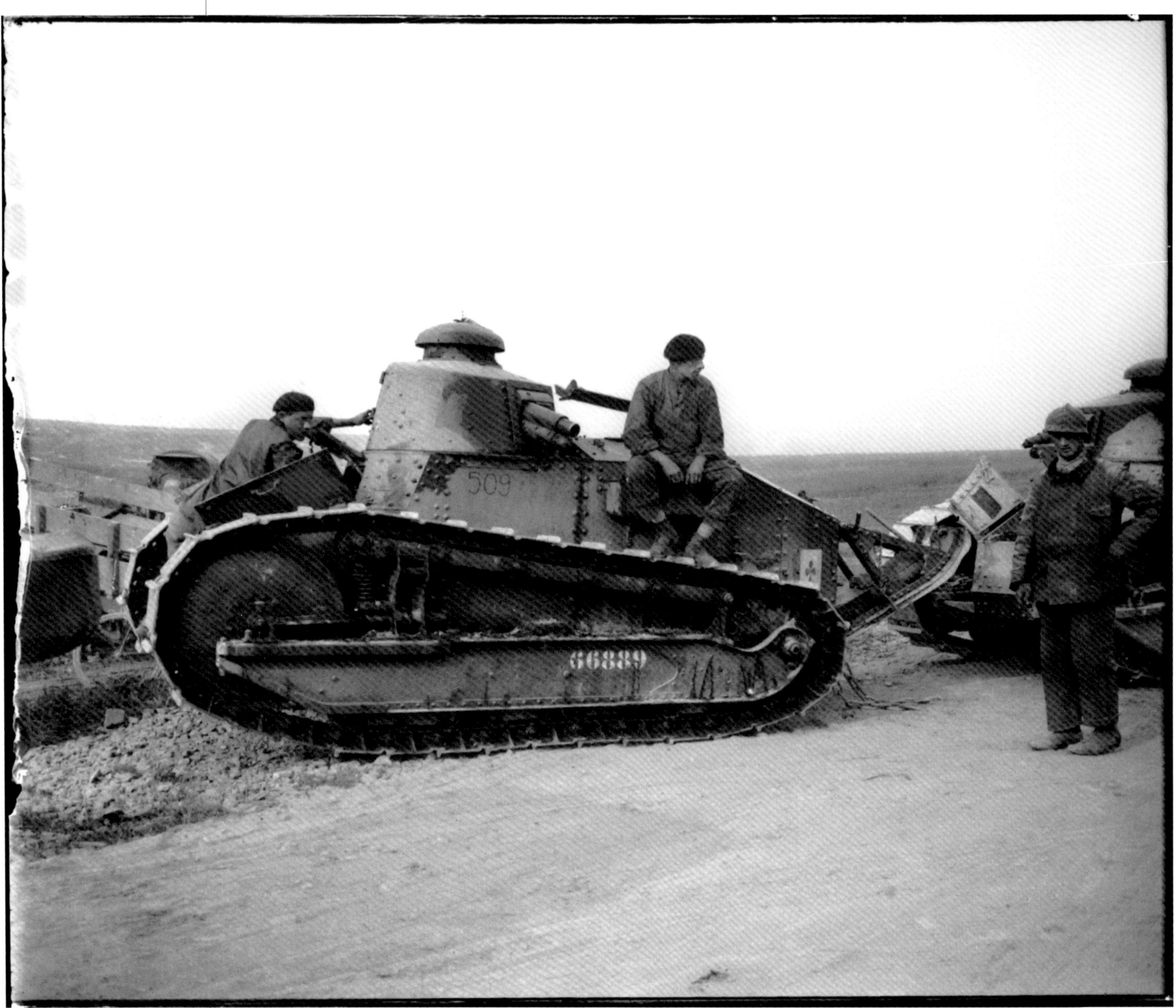

PHOT. 227
August 1918
A tank
nearby Moreuil

The Renault FT-17 number 66889, photographed in a road close to Moreuil. The allied attack in this sector was carried out on August 8th and 9th. If the picture was taken during this period, it is very probable that this tank belonged to the *504e RAS (Régiment d'Artillerie Spéciale)*. The identification of these French tanks was done by a combination of colours, geometric figures and playing card symbols: an ace of clubs inside a square indicates it was posted to the 4th section of the 2nd company. On August 8th the allies had begun the offensive in nearby Amiens, achieving such a success that the German Commander Erich Ludendorff baptised it as a *black day for the German army*.

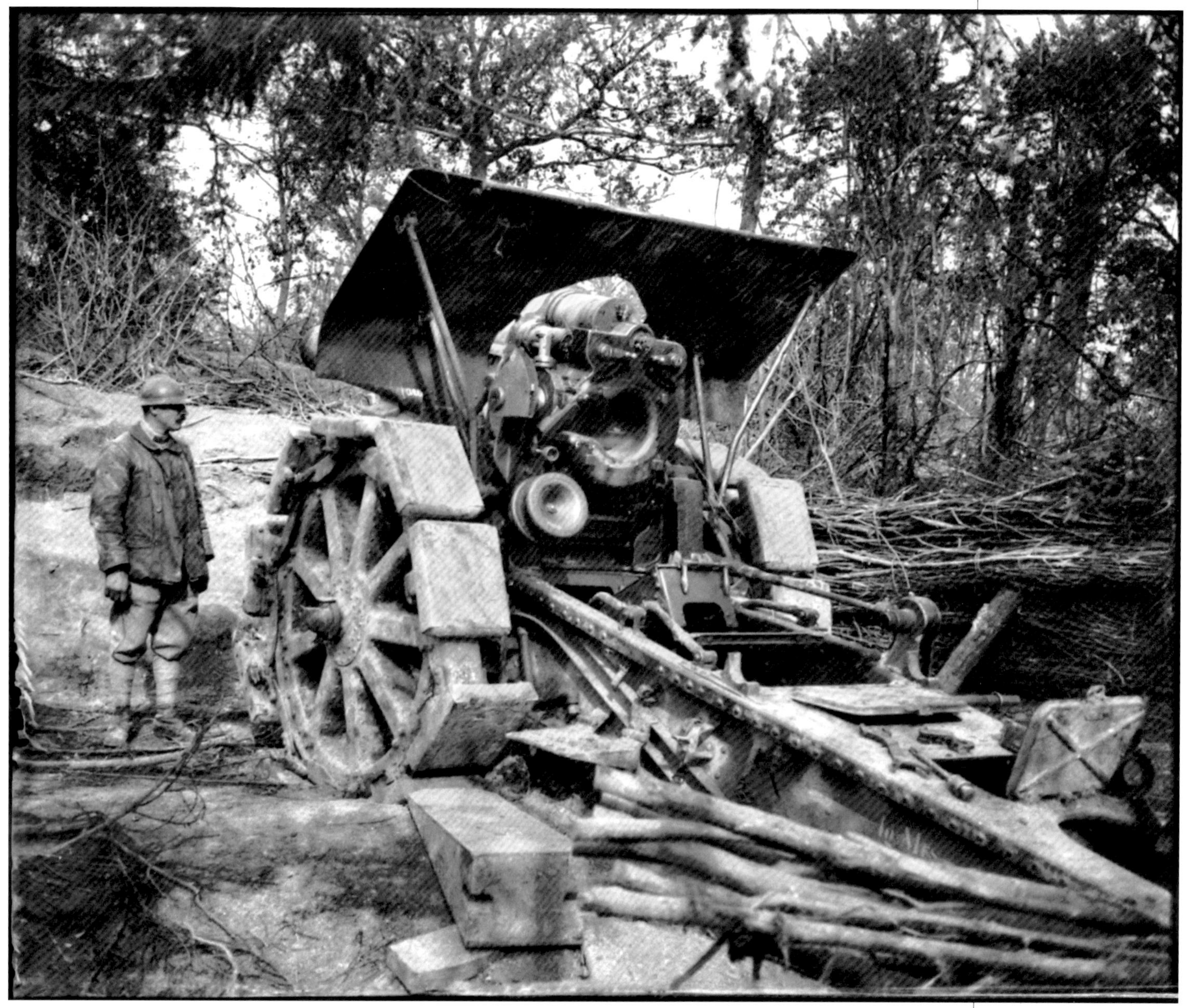

PHOT. 229

August 1918

A 220 mm Boche taken close to Moreuil

Here we must correct Givord and point out that this heavy cannon captured from the enemy really is a 21 cm Mörser 16. This cannon designed by Krupp used two kinds of projectiles, the 21 cm Gr 18 (HE) that weighed 113 kg and the 21 cm Gr 18 Be (anti-bunker) of 121 kg and an explosive load of 11 kg of TNT. It had a maximum reach of 11 km.

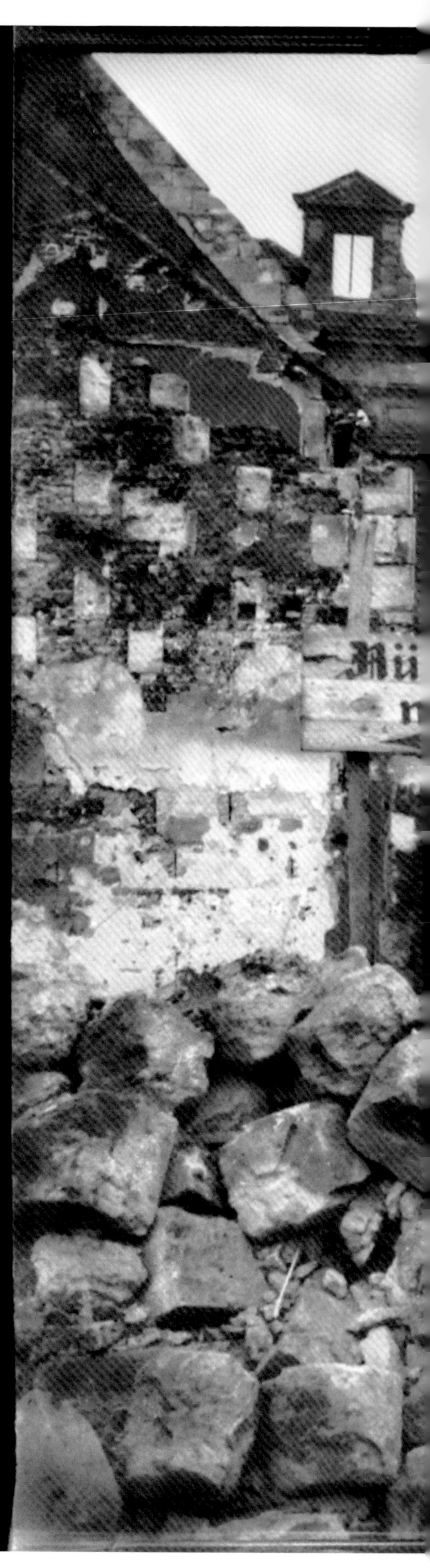

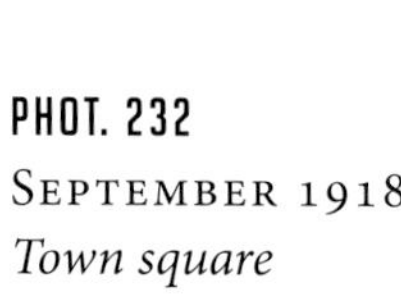

PHOT. 232
September 1918
Town square
of Noyon

This Picard town had been finally liberated by the French on September 30th after being subjected to a tremendous bombardment to hamper the German advance. On the signs written in German are displayed the directions of retreat towards Ham and a campaign hospital.

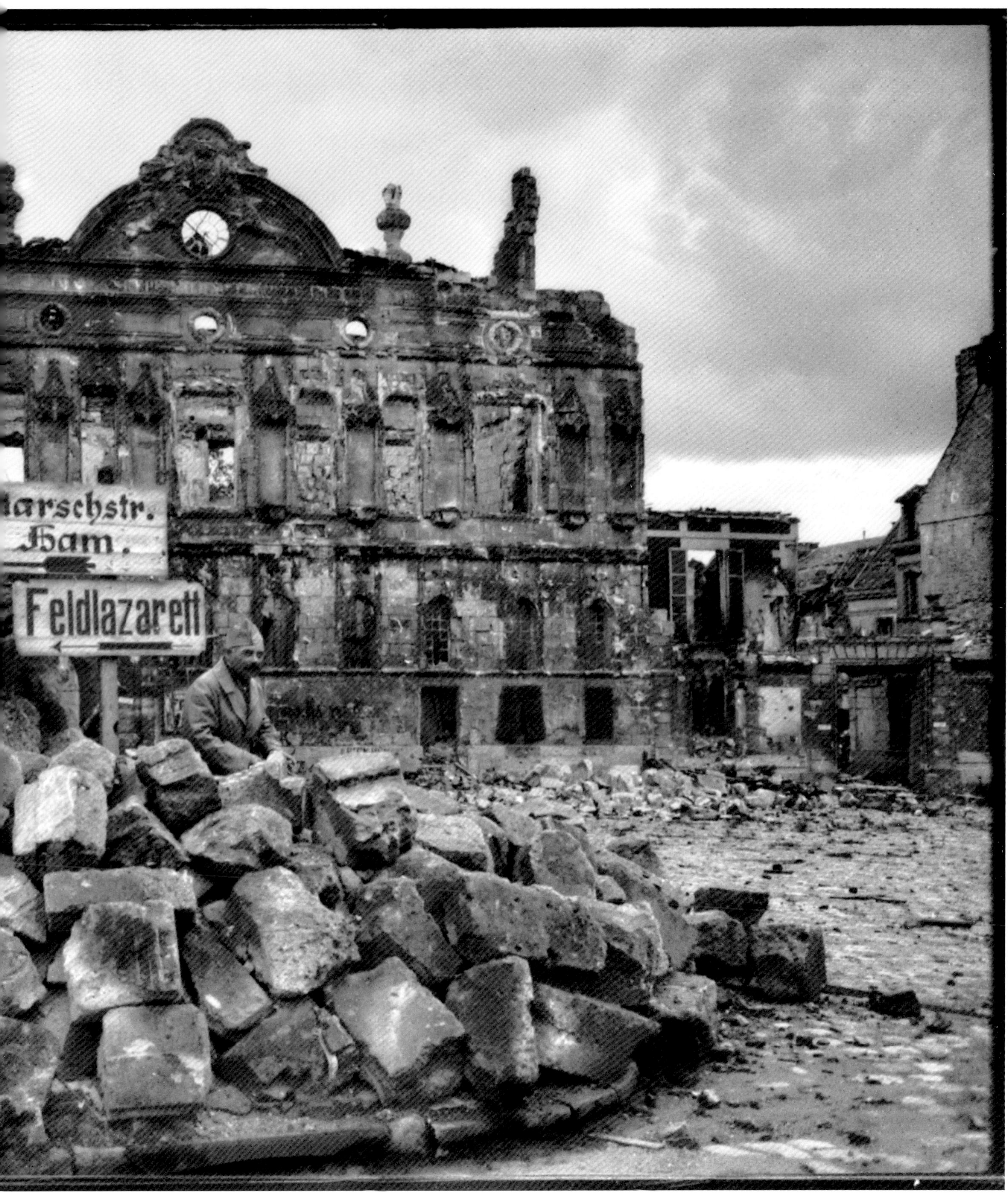
arschstr.
Ham.
Feldlazarett

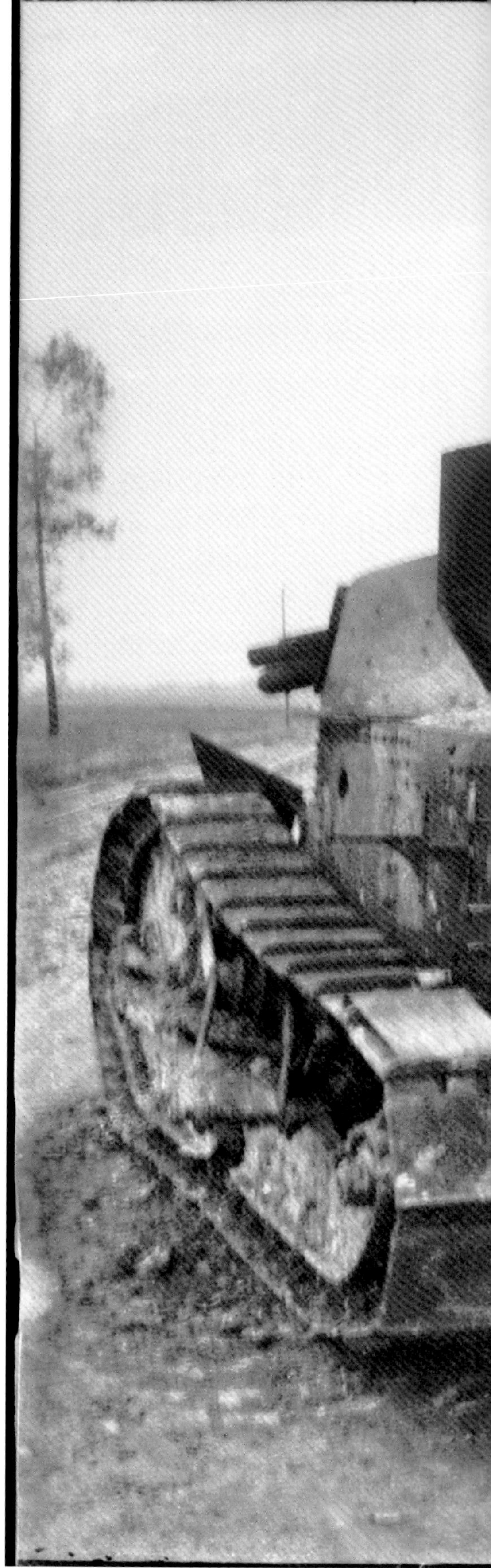

PHOT. 239
10/1918
Burnt out tanks nearby Roulers (Belgium)

With the unstoppable allied advance, Givord is assigned to the North of Flanders. These battered FT-17 belonged to the 1st battalion of light tanks of the *501e RAS* or to the 12th of the *504e RAS*, these were the only units with this model in Belgium. These small tanks were essential in breaking the stagnation of the trench war by overrunning the German defences.

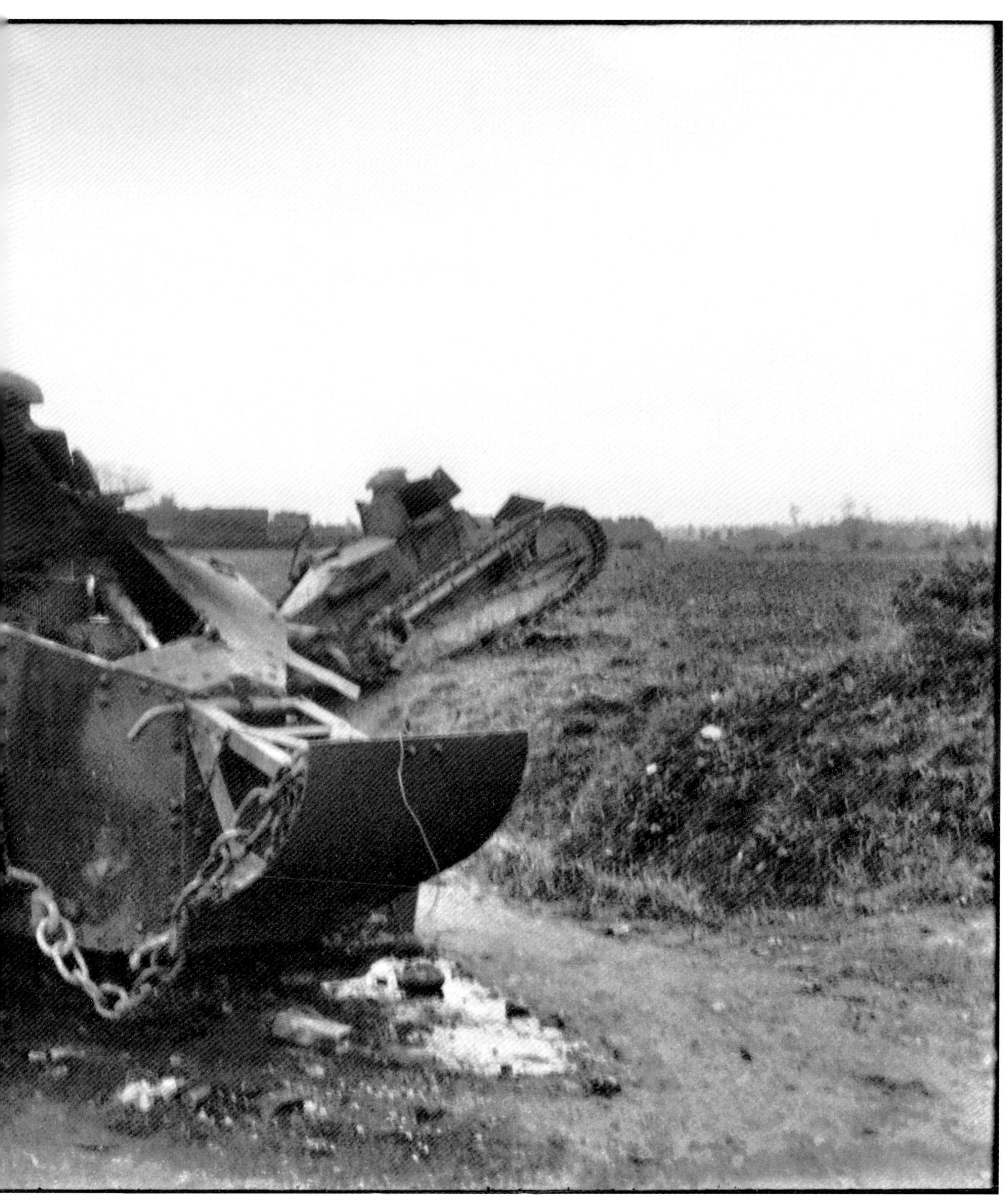

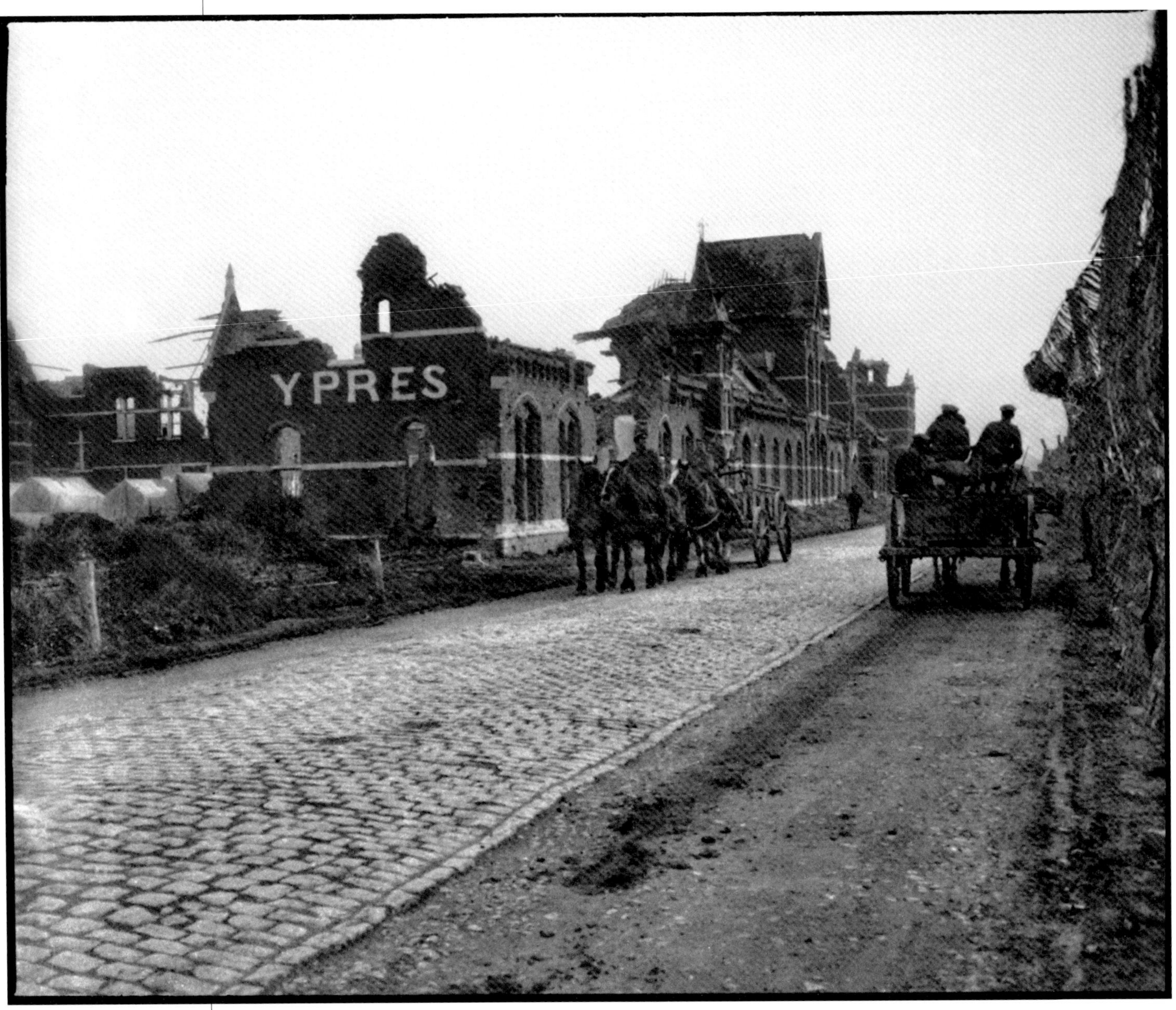

PHOT. 240
10/1918

Entrance to the town of Ypres, heroically defended by the British during four years of conflict, being an important salient in Belgium not occupied by the Germans. The net on the right hid movements on the road.

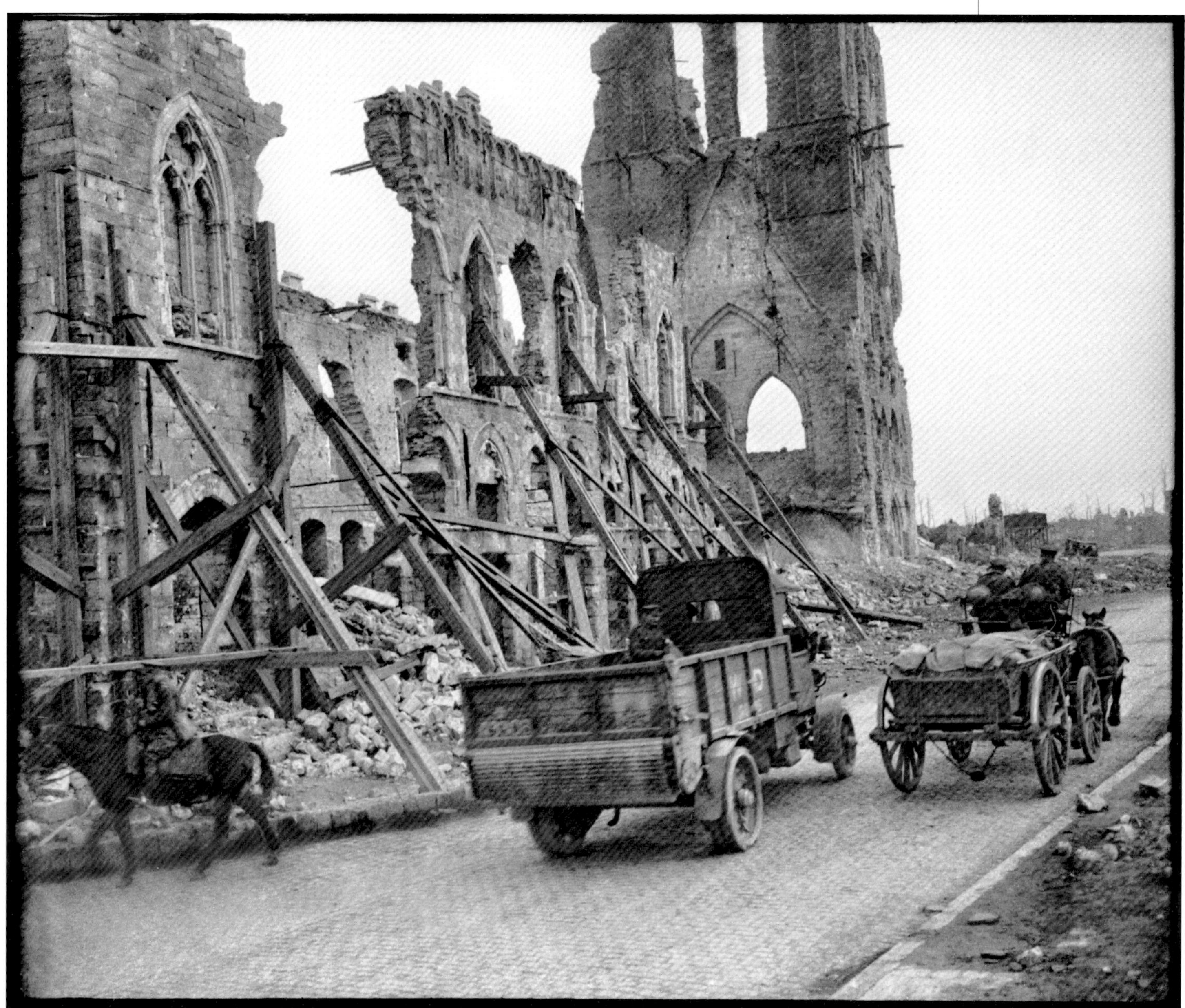

PHOT. 241
10/1918
Ypres

The *Lakenhalle* (Cloth Hall) from the 13th century was erected again as a symbol of the continuous destruction of the city.

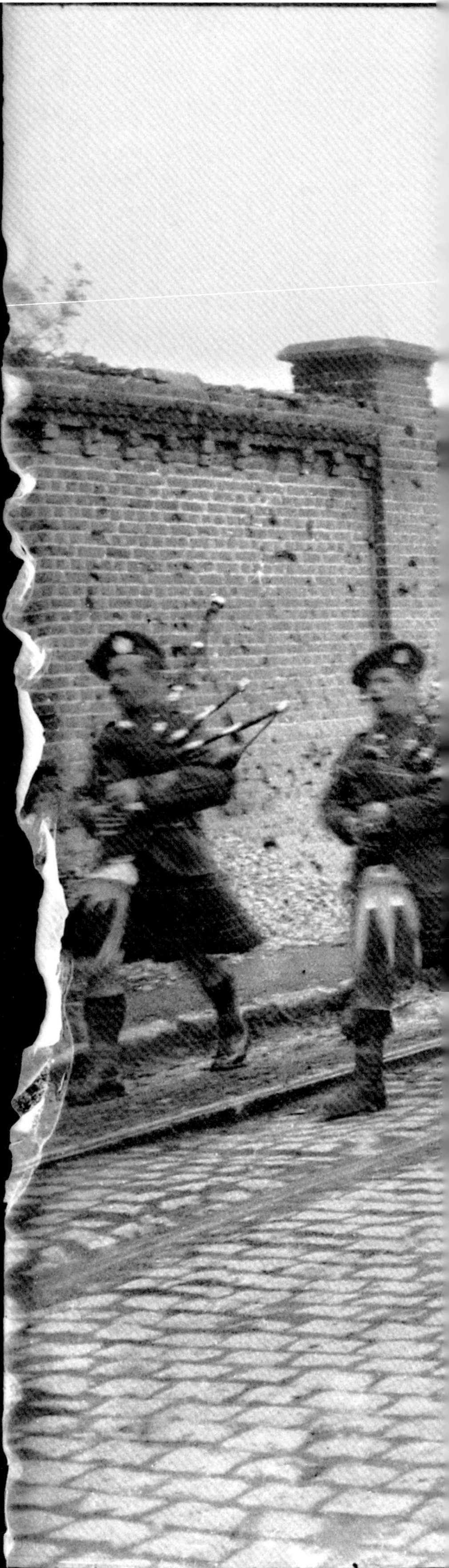

PHOT. 242
10/1918
In Ypres

The band preceding the march of a Scottish unit.

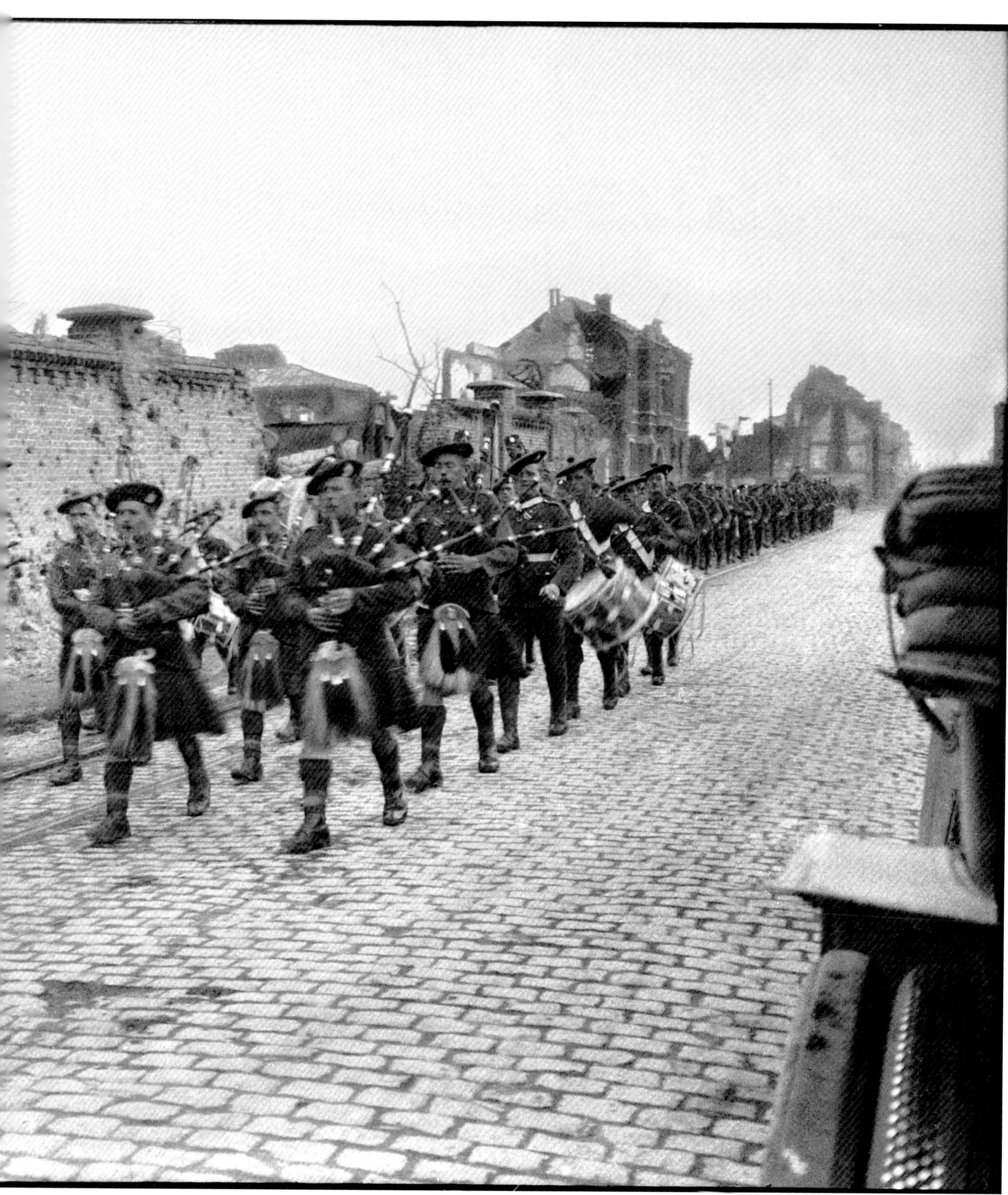

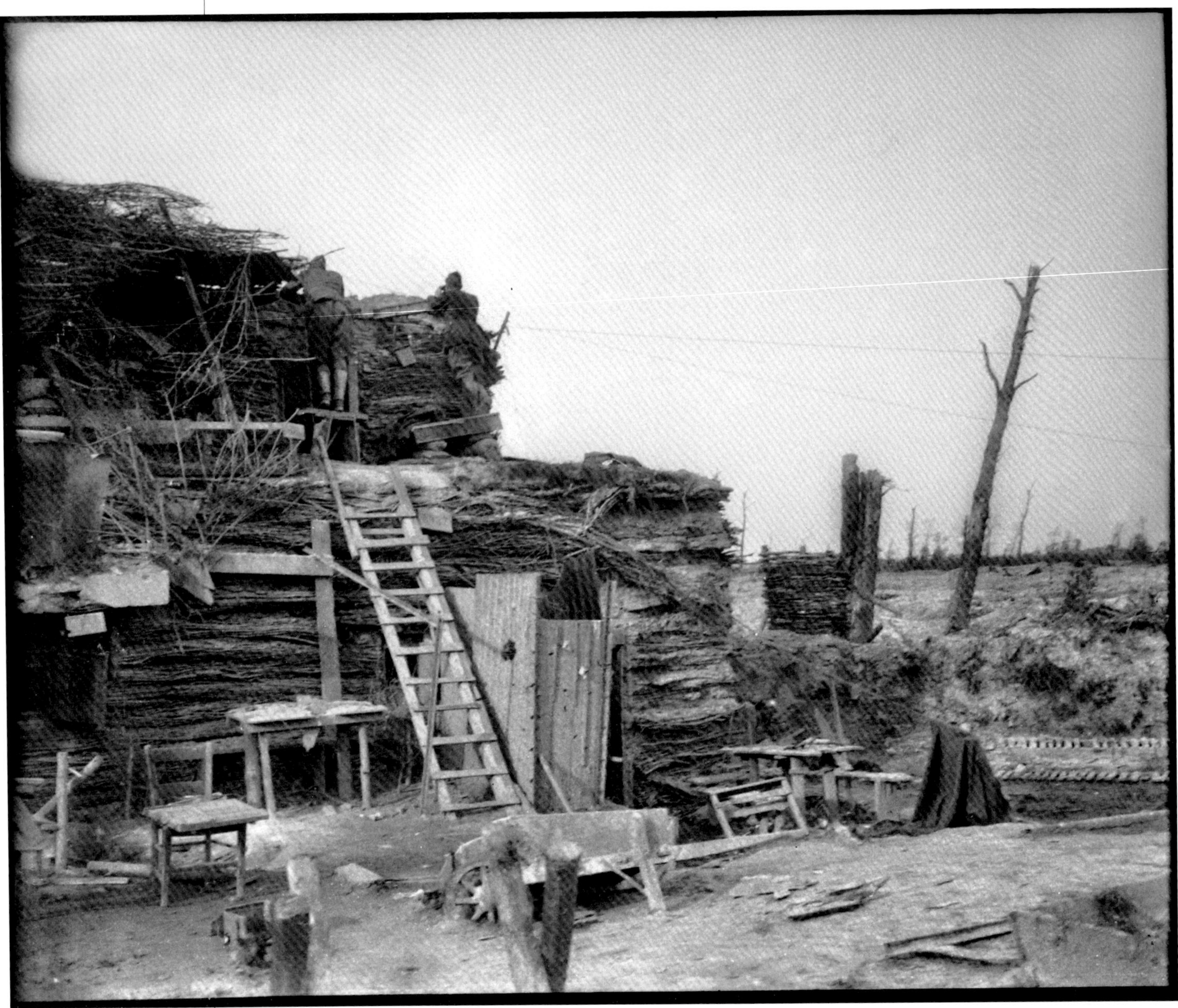

PHOT. 243
10/1918
At the Yser

British observation post in the region of the Yser River, which crosses France and Belgium.

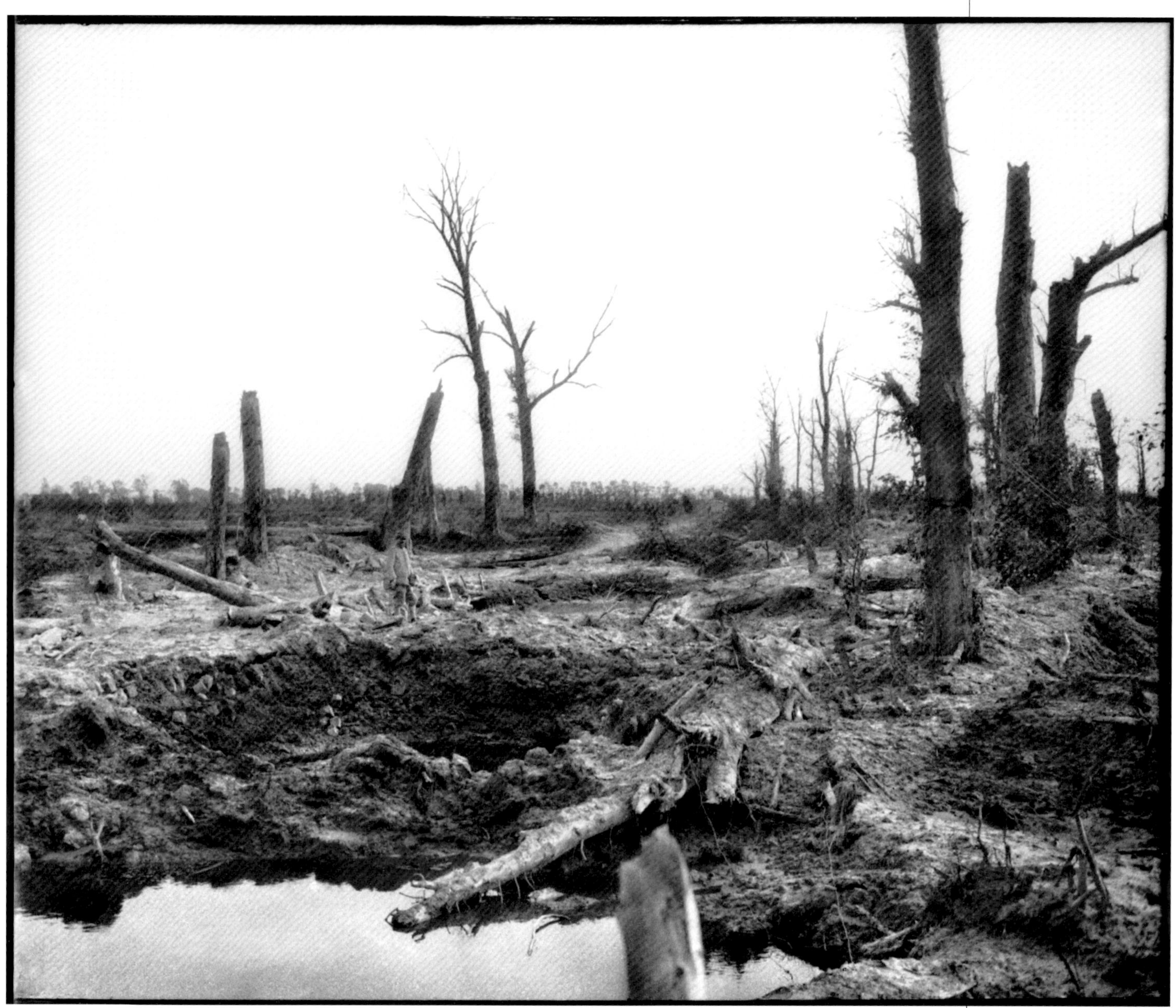

PHOT. 244
10/1918
Yser region

In this area of the front the mud was an enemy as dangerous as the Germans, swallowing indiscriminately material, mules and soldiers who were never seen again.

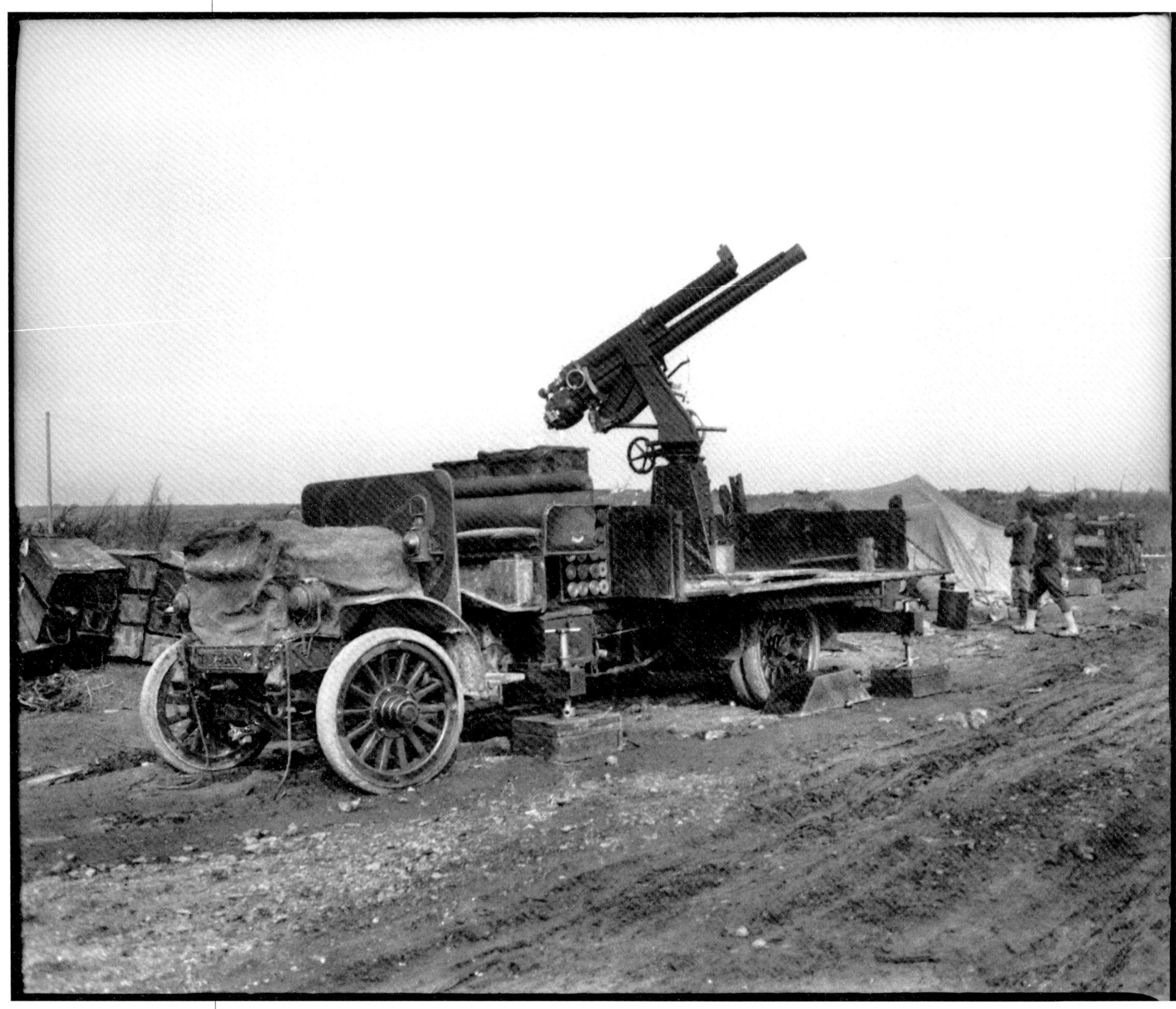

PHOT. 245
10/1918
British cannon against planes

The 13 pounder cannon was the British army standard for anti-aircraft defence and frequently was set up on the back of trucks. Its rate of fire was about eight shells per minute.

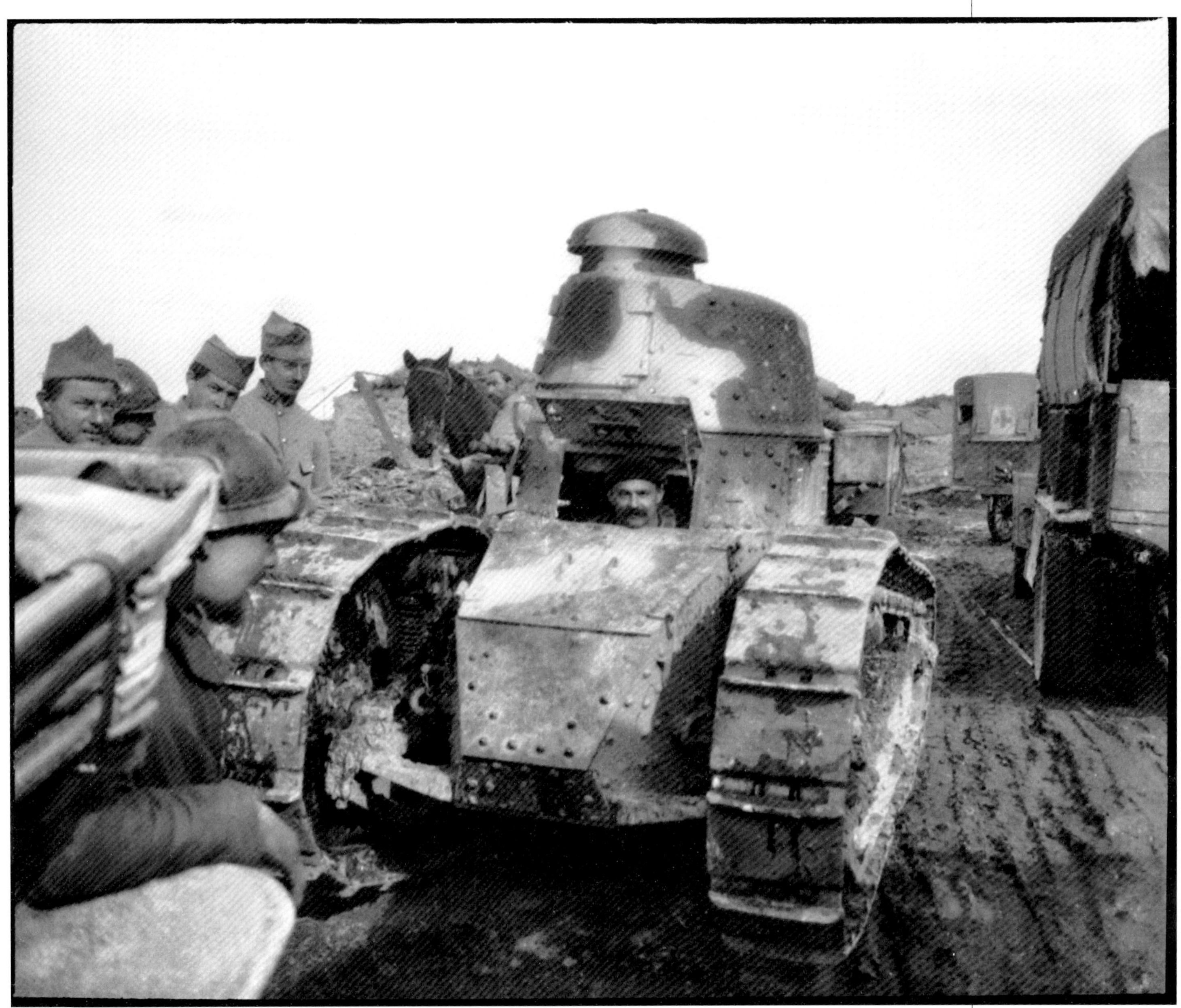

PHOT. 246
10/1918

A smiling driver pops up from the porthole of his FT-17. The men on the left belong to the *177e RI*.

PHOT. 248
21/10/1918
Last resistance of the Boche in what remains of a machine gun post in Hooglede (Belgium)

At the end of the war, this German bunker was taken by assault and the defendants corpses looted, as can be seen on the body in the foreground with the unbuttoned jacket and missing boots. The scattered masks indicate they were gassed.

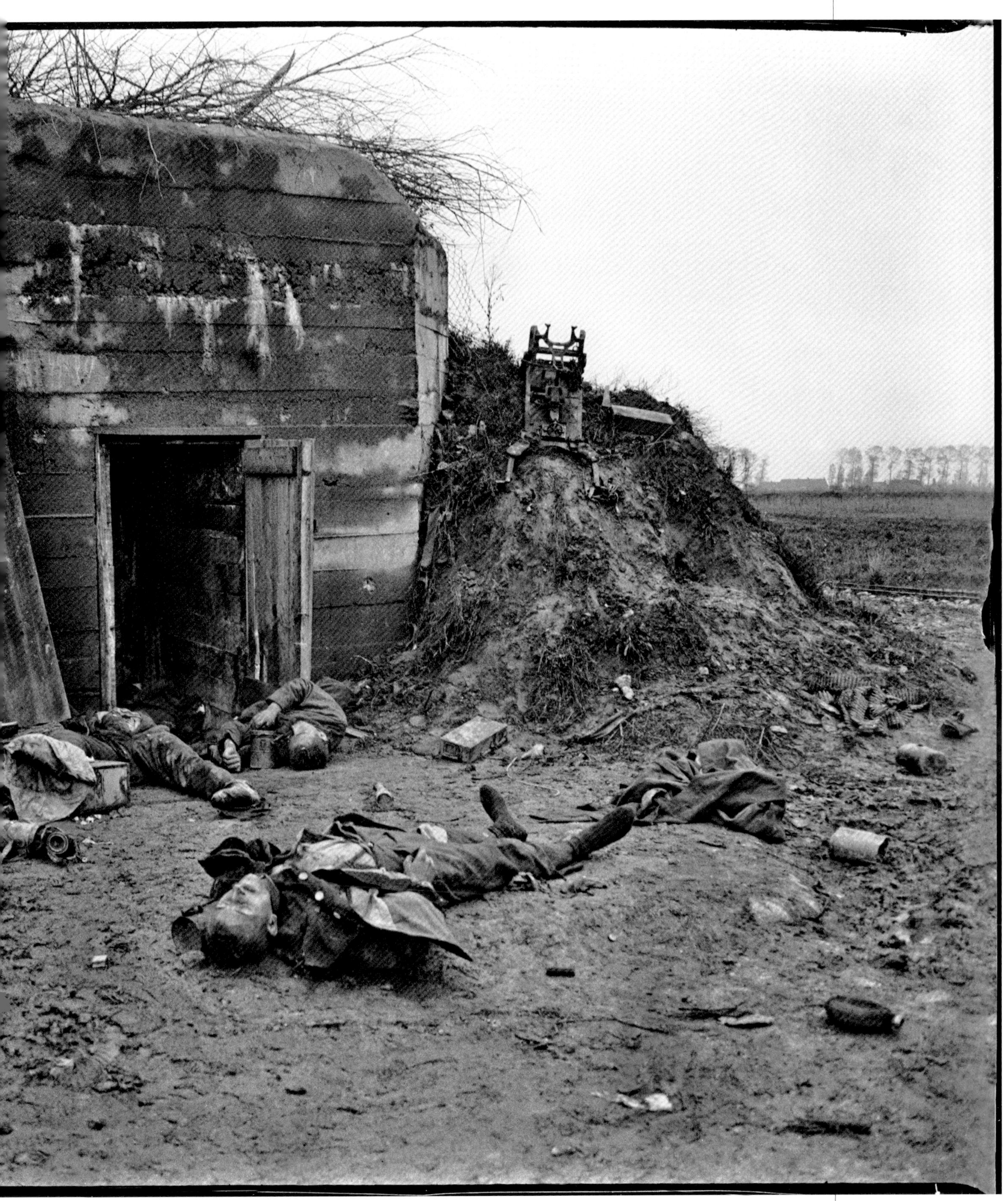

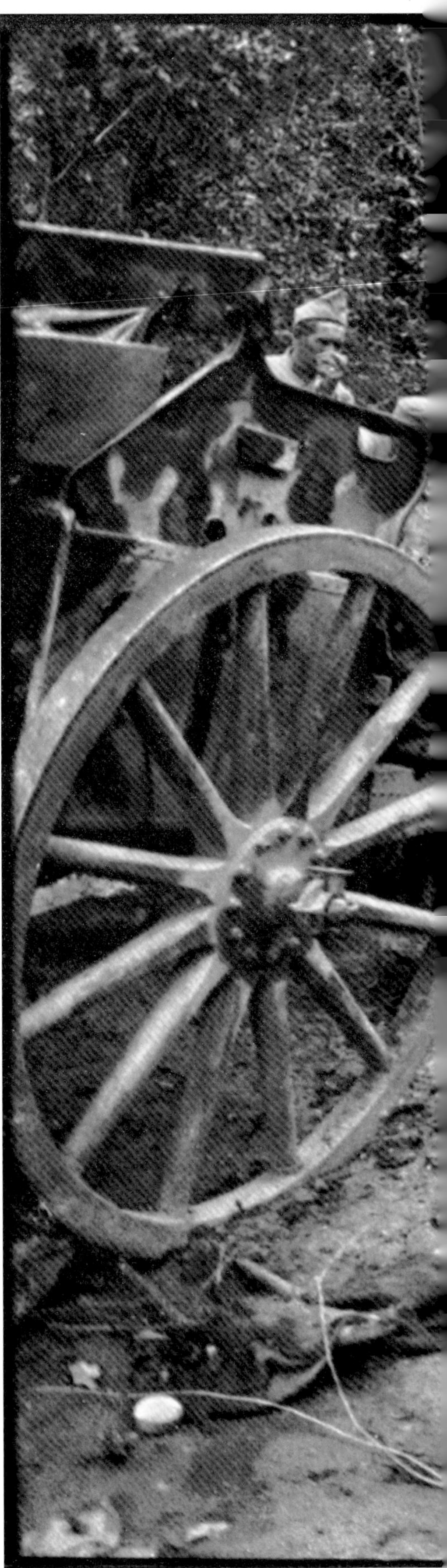

PHOT. 252
S/F

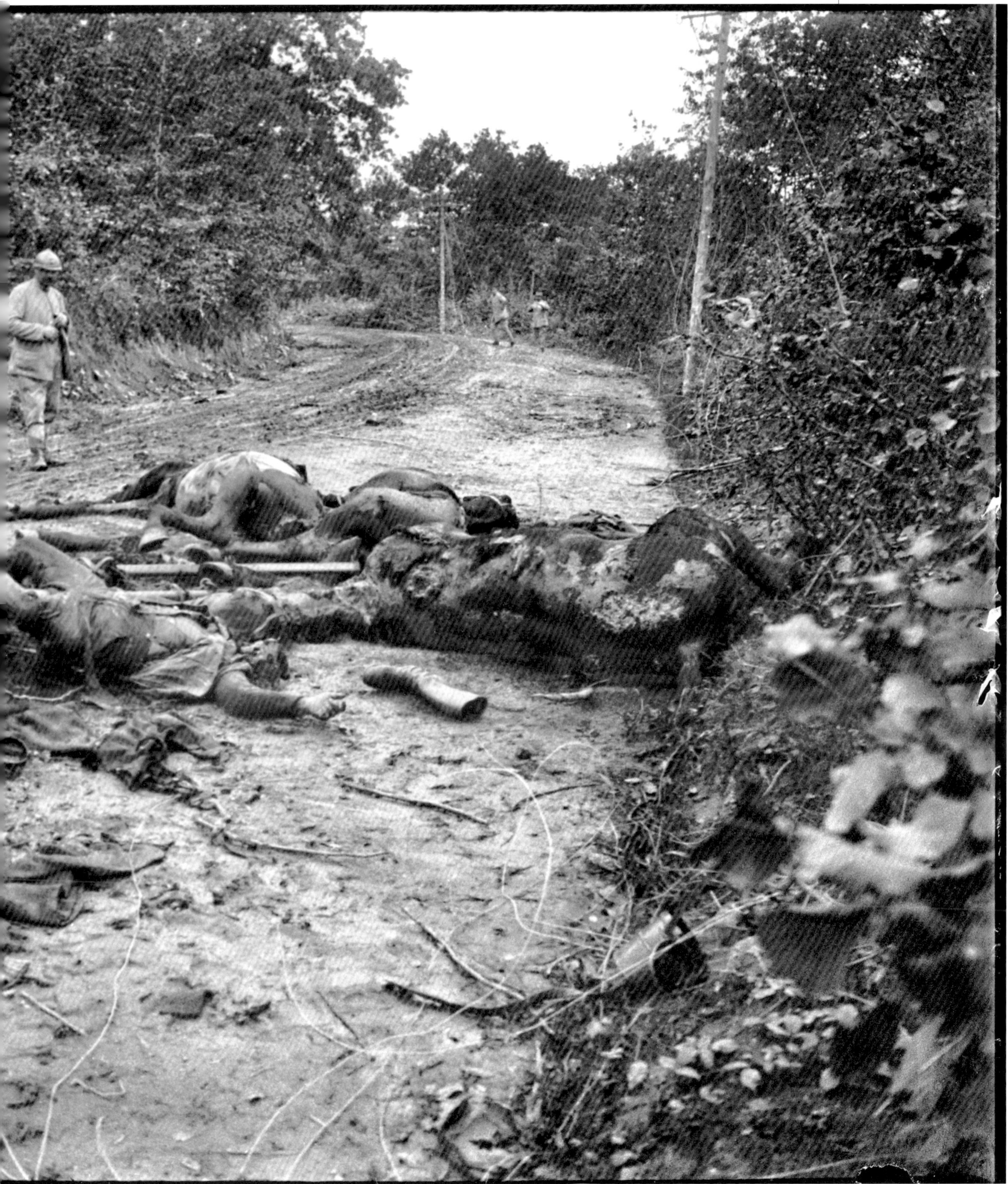

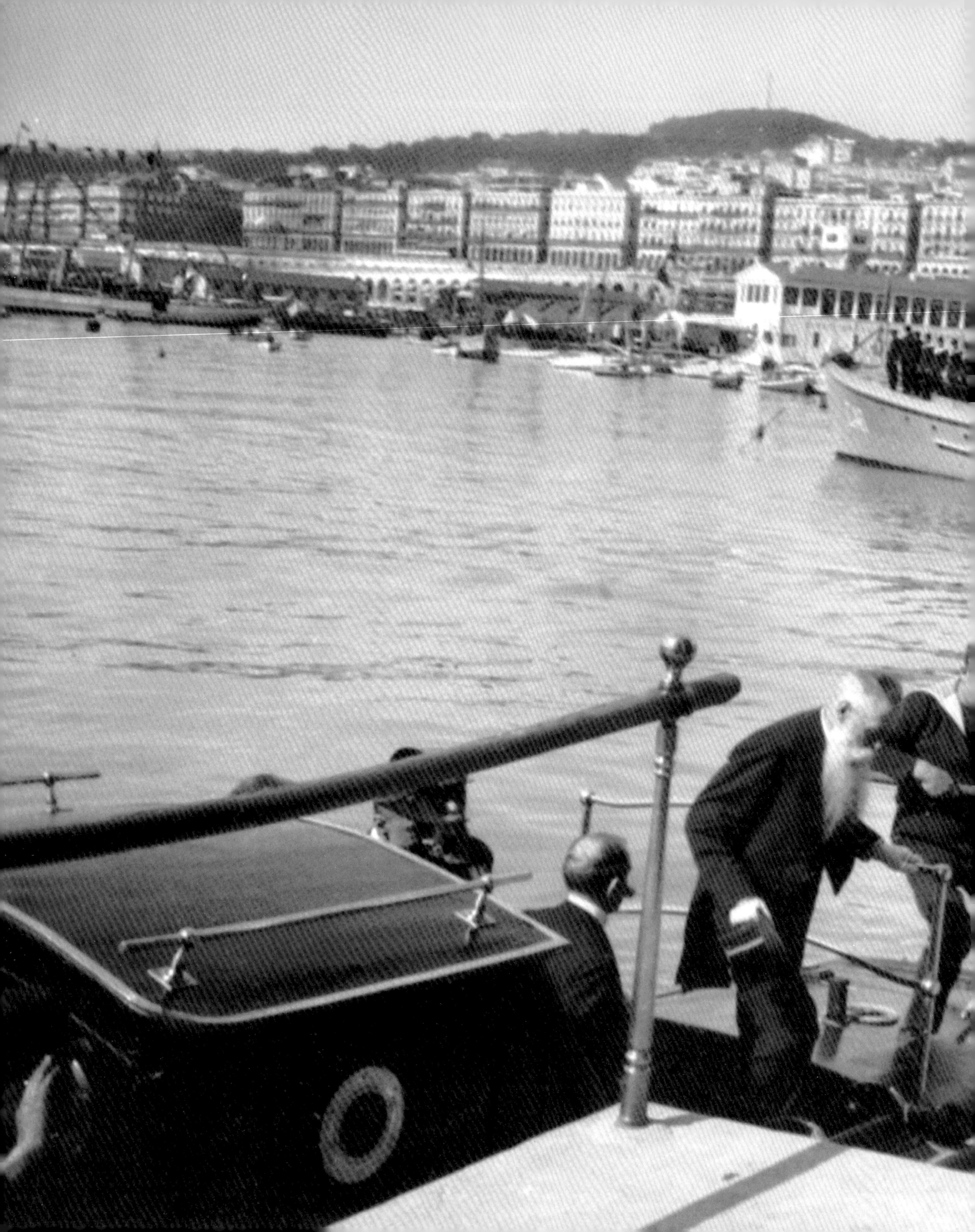

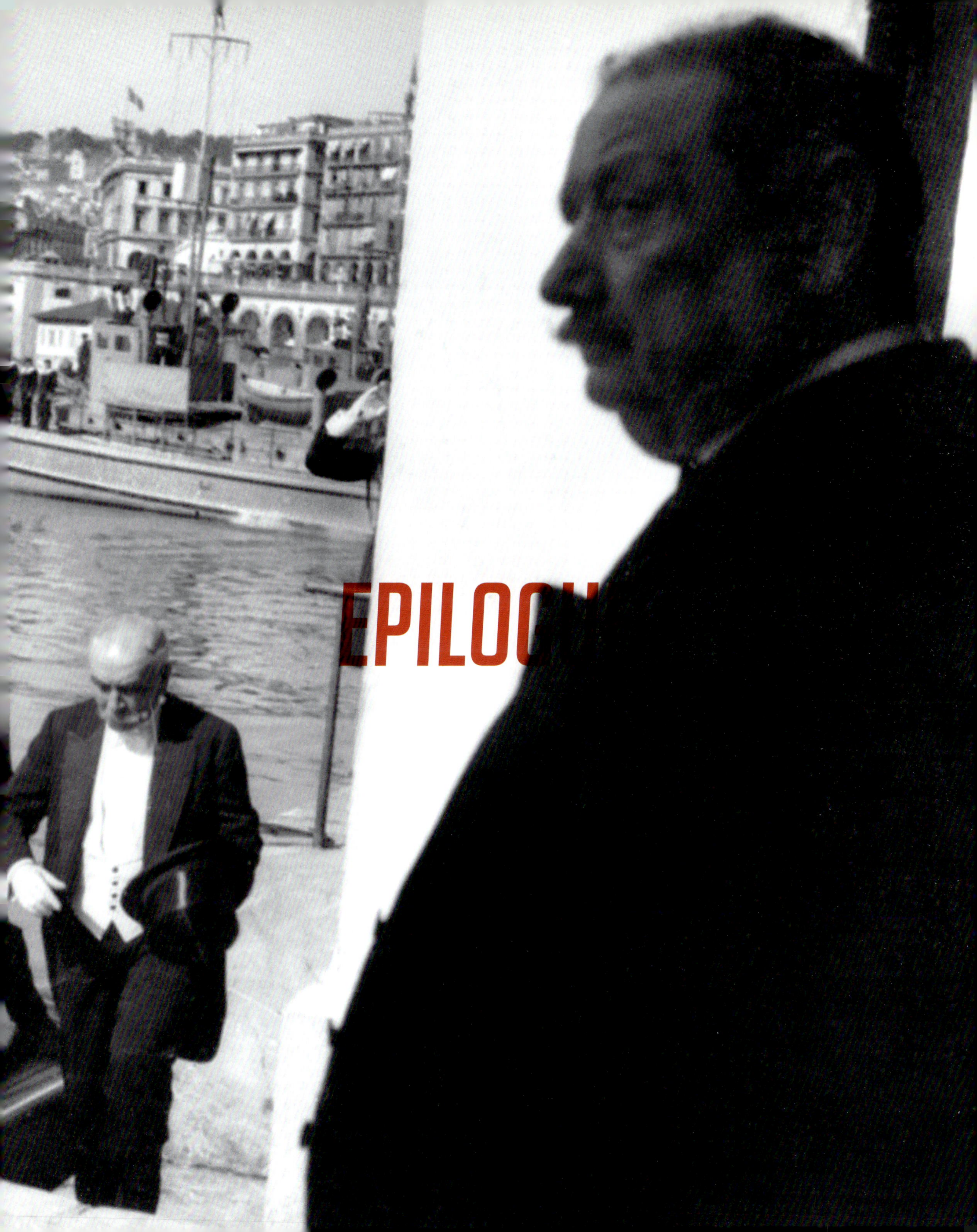
EPILOG

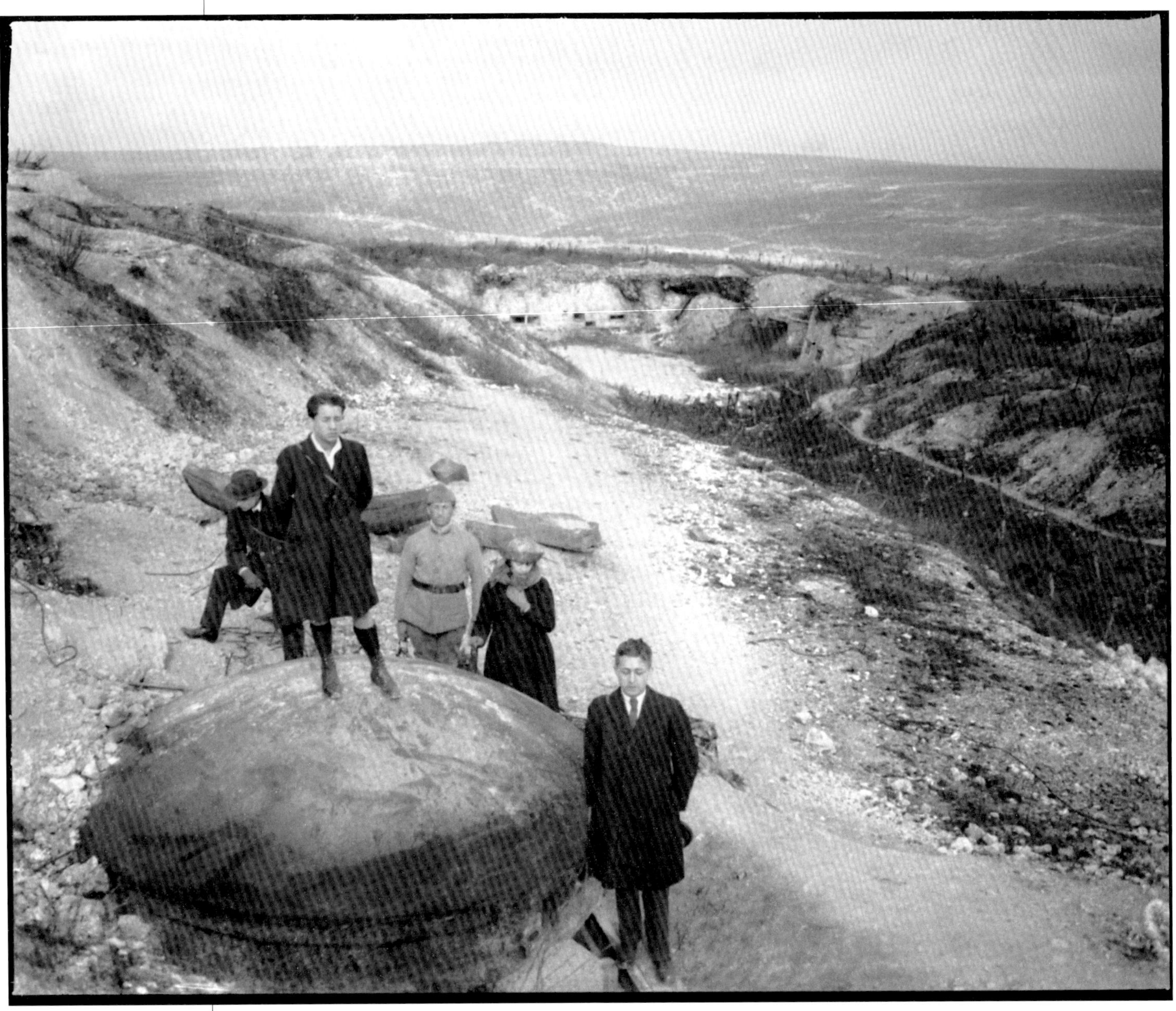

28 March 1921
On the dome of the fort of Vaux in Verdun

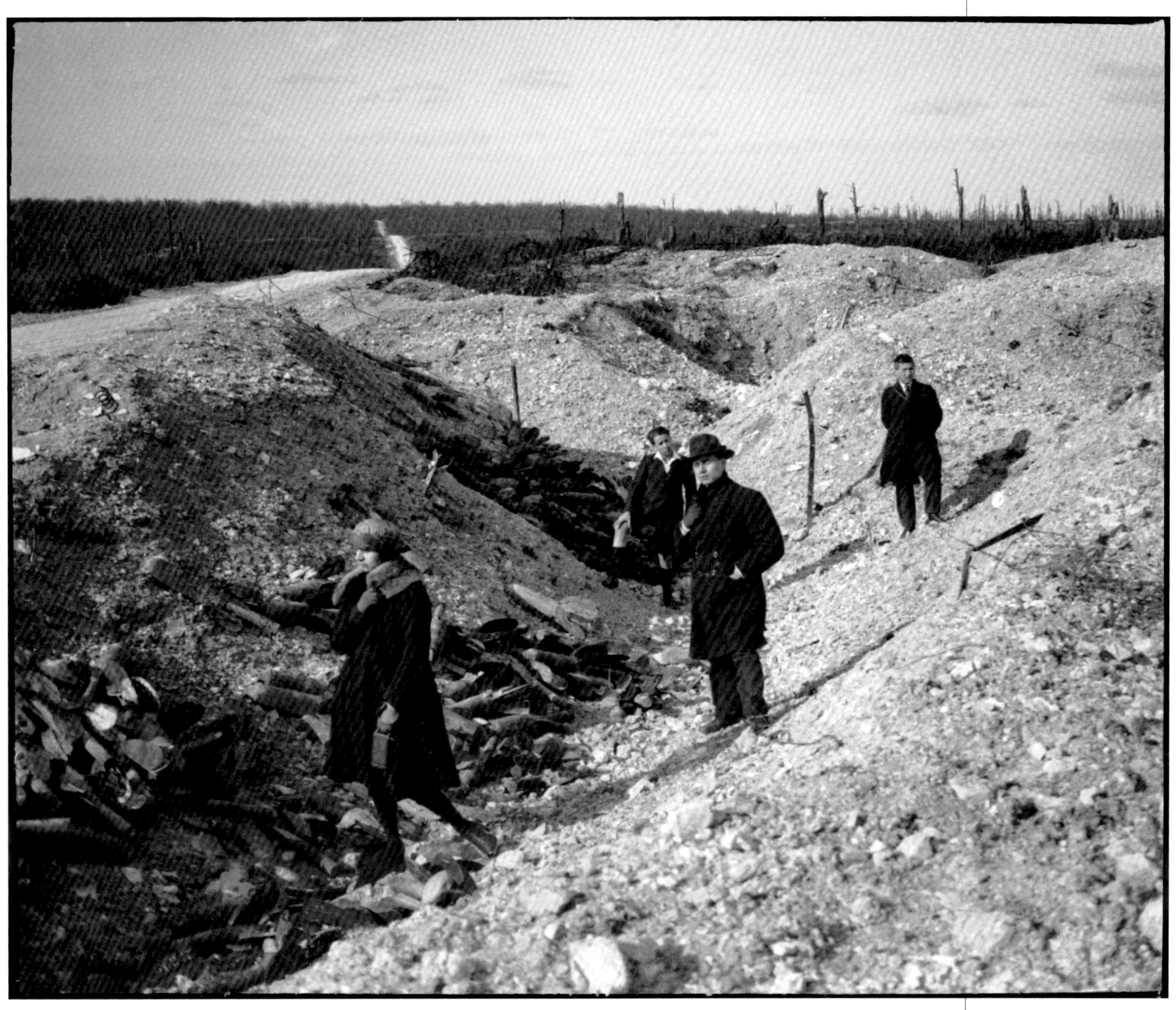

27 March 1921
At the trench of Calonne

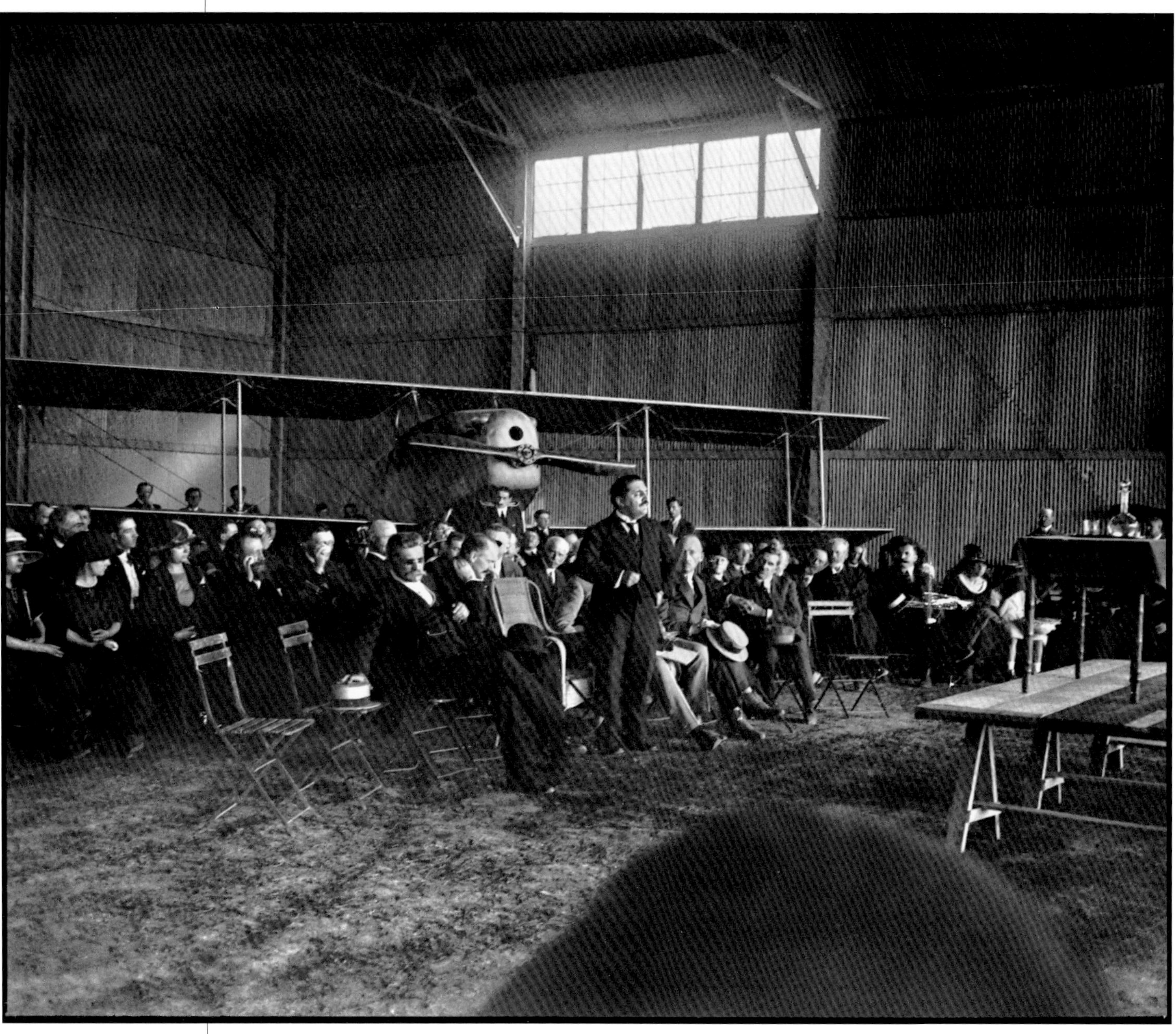

09/07/1921
The Under Secretary of State for Aeronautics Laurent Eynac at Le Bourget

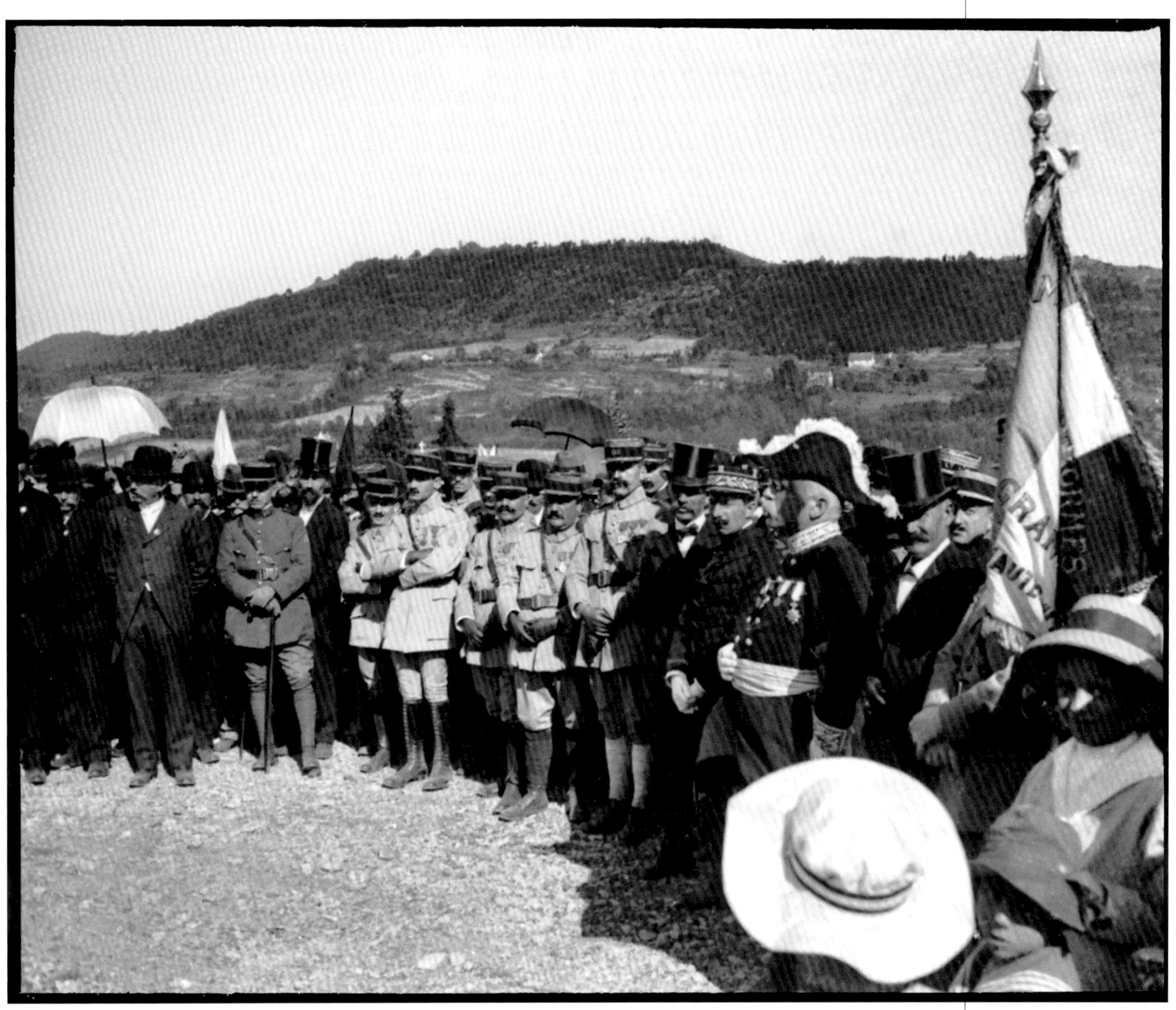

13/07/1919
Commemoration of the dead soldiers at the cemetery of Gap

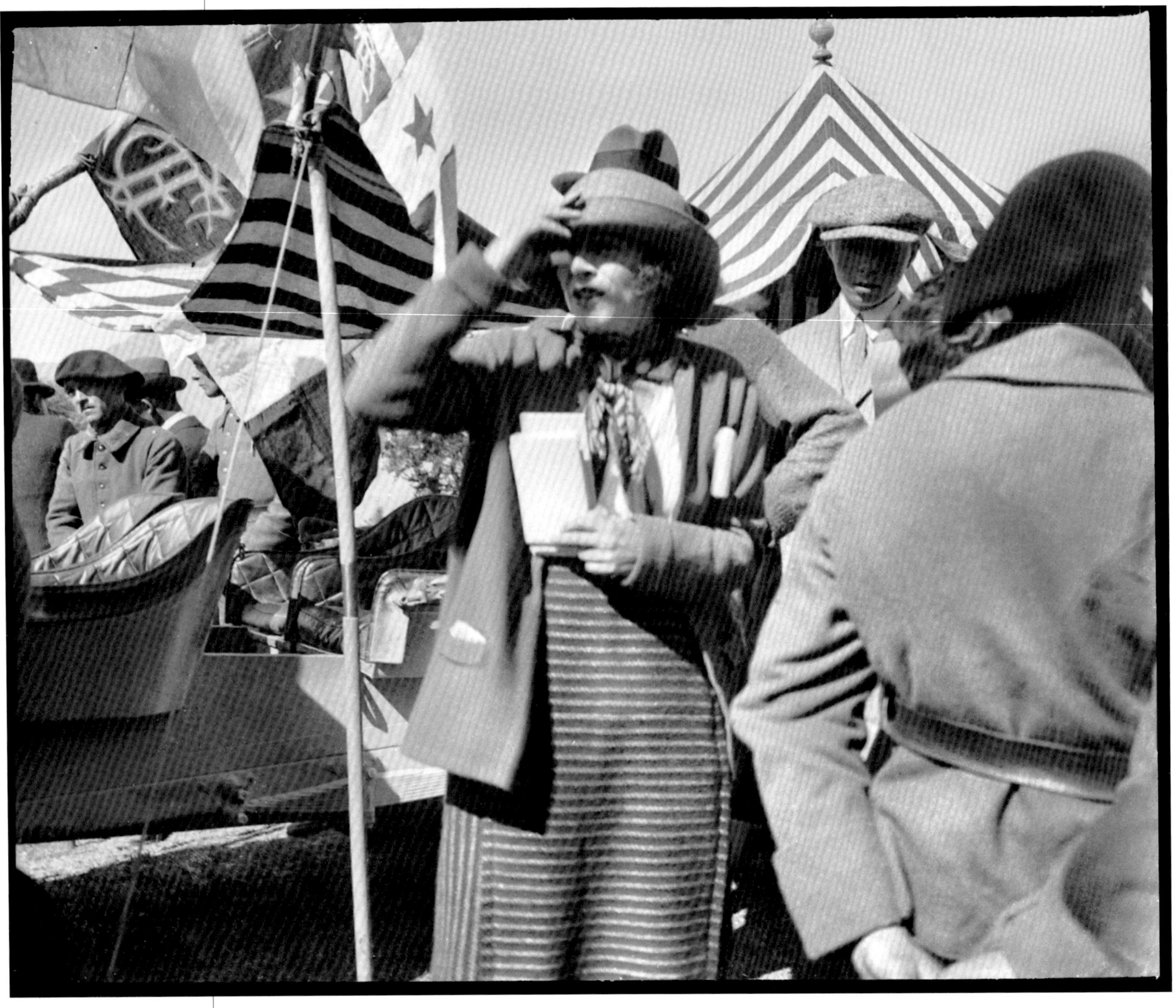

27/08/1922
At Sommet Bucher
(department of Hautes Alpes)

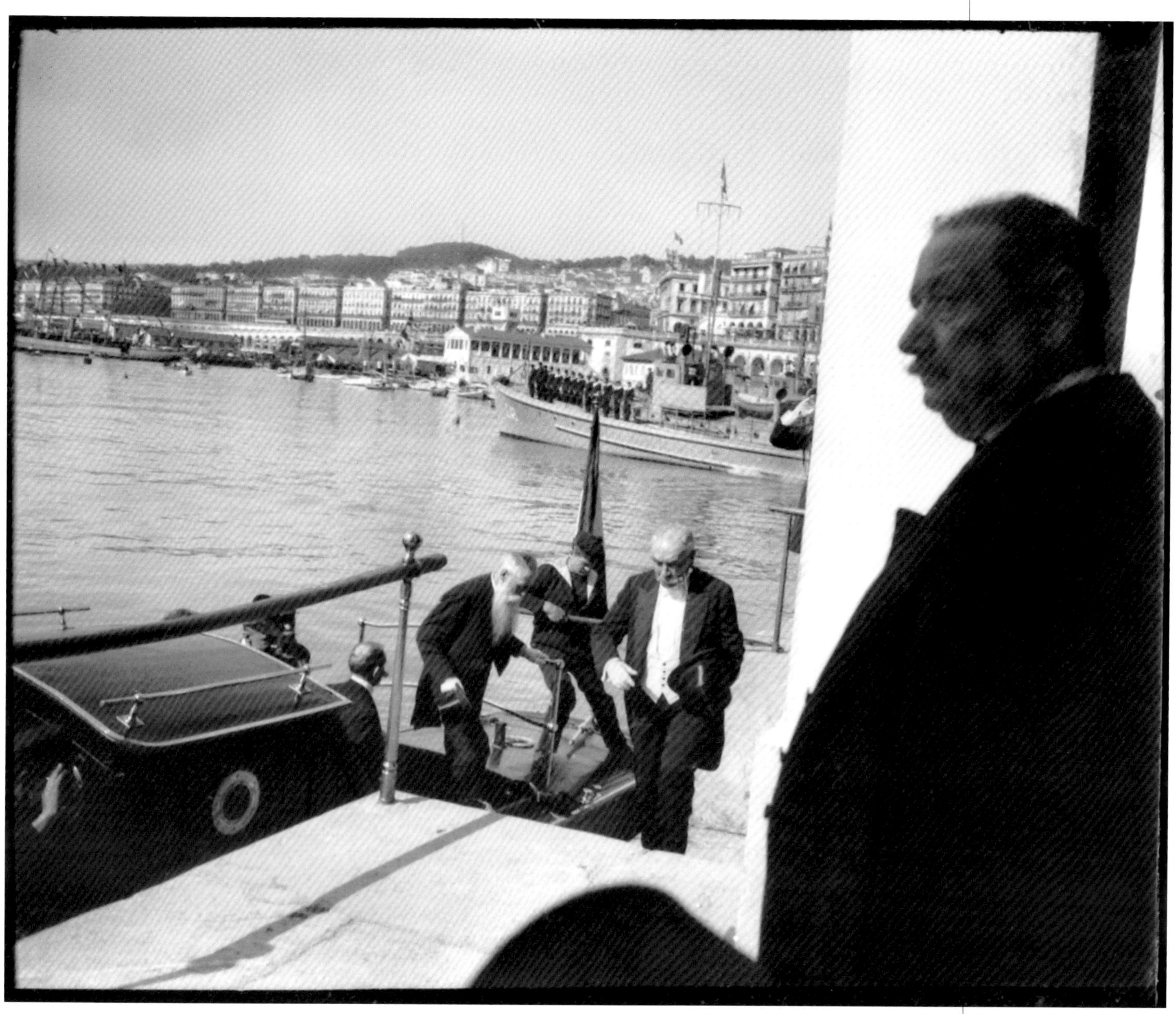

April 1921
The Minister of the Navy Gabriel Guist'hau disembarks in Algiers.

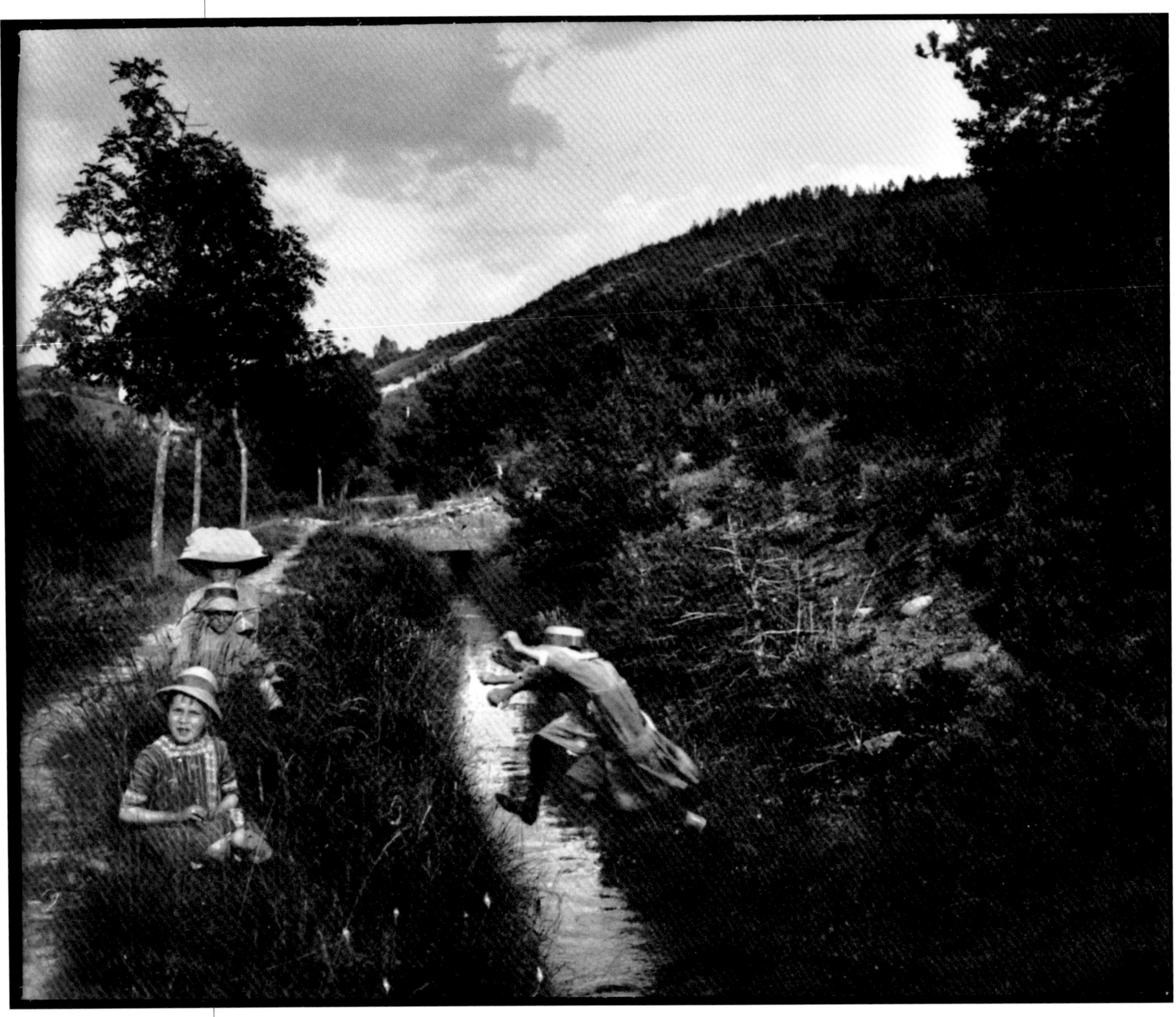

PHOT. 48
02/08/1916

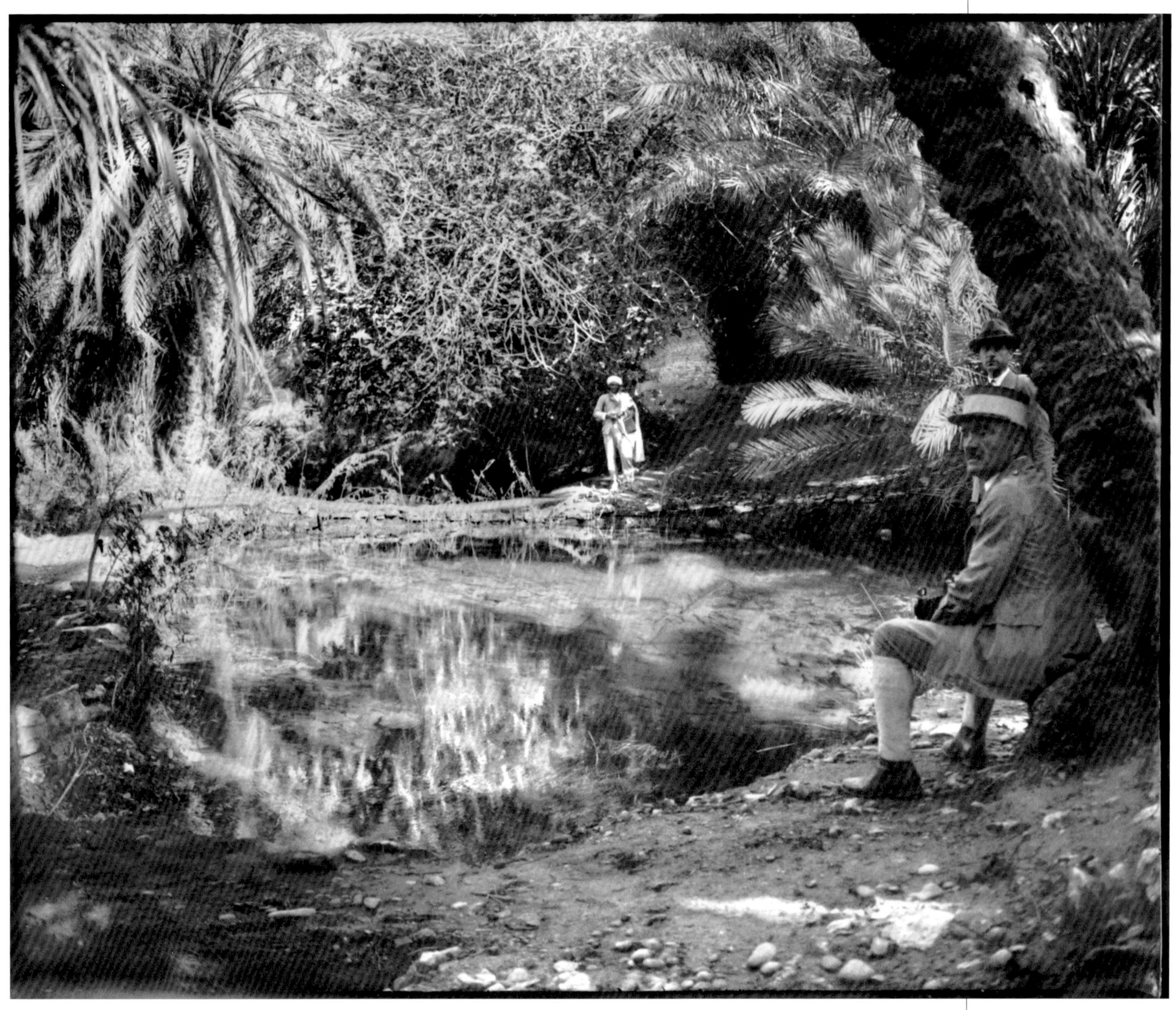

04/1932
Fountain of Meshi

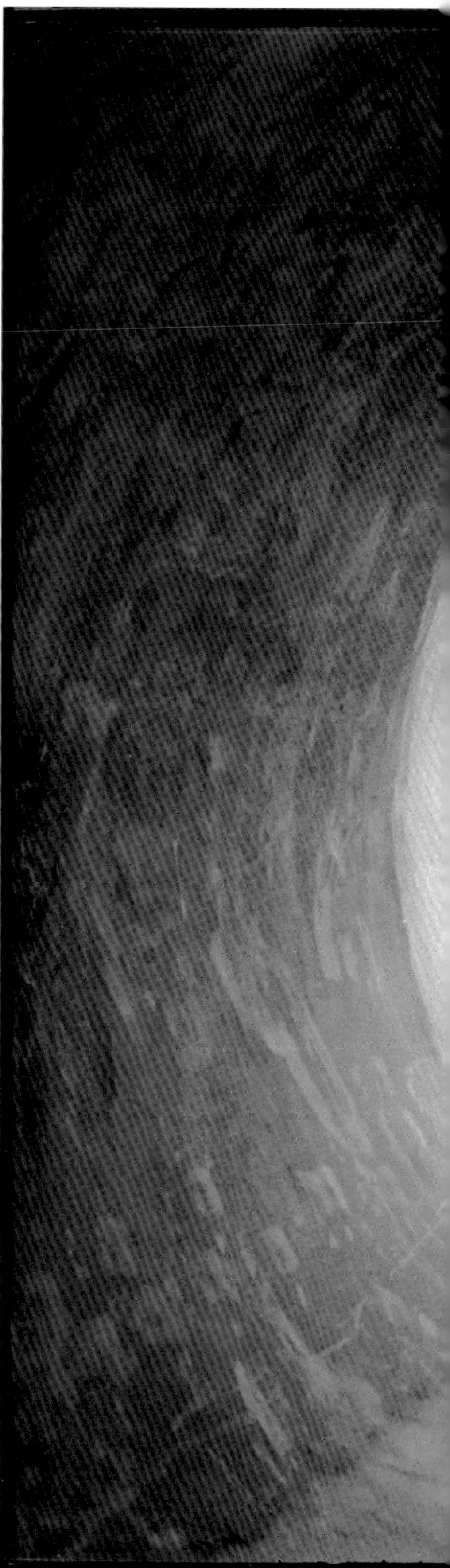

25/07/1919
In the chamber of a mine

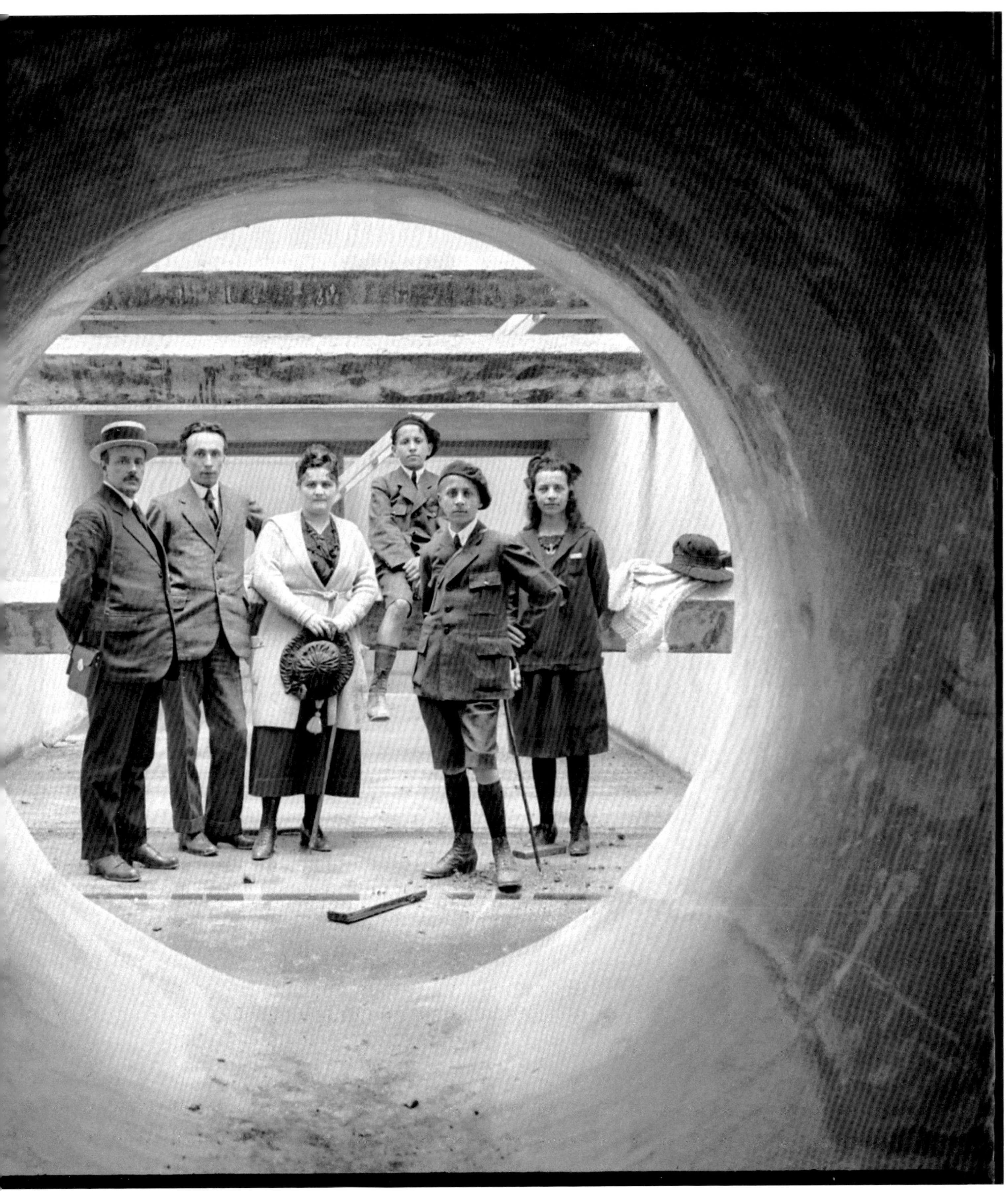

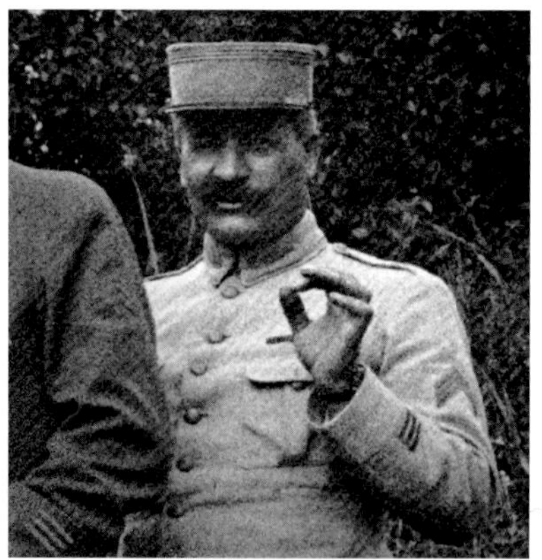

The first Spanish edition of Tangier archive finished printing at the workshops of Industrias Gráficas Castuera in Pamplona, on June 28th 2014, coinciding with the centenary of the murder of Archduke Franz Ferdinand of Austria in Sarajevo.

Givord commanding the (photographic) shot.
FOT. 150: 8/8/-17 (08/08/1917, detail.)